Artificial Intelligence for
Autonomous Networks

Chapman & Hall/CRC
Artificial Intelligence and Robotics Series

Series Editor
Roman Yampolskiy

Contemporary Artificial Intelligence
Richard E. Neapolitan

The Virtual Mind
Designing the Logic to Approximate Human Thinking
Niklas Hageback

Intelligent Autonomy of UAVs
Advanced Missions and Future Use
Yasmina Bestaoui Sebbane

Artificial Intelligence
With an Introduction to Machine Learning, Second Edition
Richard E. Neapolitan, Xia Jiang

Artificial Intelligence and the Two Singularities
Calum Chace

Behavior Trees in Robotics and Artificial Intelligence
An Introduction
Michele Collendanchise, Petter Ögren

Artificial Intelligence Safety and Security
Roman V. Yampolskiy

Artificial Intelligence for Autonomous Networks
Mazin Gilbert

For more information about this series please visit:
https://www.crcpress.com/Chapman--HallCRC-Artificial-Intelligence-and-Robotics-Series/book-series/ARTILRO

Artificial Intelligence for Autonomous Networks

Edited by
Mazin Gilbert

CRC Press
Taylor & Francis Group
Boca Raton London New York

CRC Press is an imprint of the
Taylor & Francis Group, an **informa** business

A CHAPMAN & HALL BOOK

CRC Press
Taylor & Francis Group
6000 Broken Sound Parkway NW, Suite 300
Boca Raton, FL 33487-2742

First issued in paperback 2020

© 2019 by Taylor & Francis Group, LLC
CRC Press is an imprint of Taylor & Francis Group, an Informa business

No claim to original U.S. Government works

ISBN 13: 978-0-367-57096-5 (pbk)
ISBN 13: 978-0-8153-5531-1 (hbk)

Visit the Taylor & Francis Web site at
http://www.taylorandfrancis.com

and the CRC Press Web site at
http://www.crcpress.com

Contents

Preface

Last Monday morning, Lucy, my virtual assistant, woke me up.

While Lucy was monitoring my blood pressure and heartbeat in my sleep, she detected abnormality and transmitted that information to my doctor. Lucy then went on to summarize my calendar for the day, got my coffee ready, and charged my autonomous car. Before leaving the house, I told Lucy to watch over my elderly mom and notify me when she had taken her medicine. While in the car, I received a text message from my boss and decided to hold a holographic meeting with him to discuss the matter. I arrived at work and went straight to my office, and in the meantime, my car drove itself to the repair shop for its annual check-up. During lunch, Lucy whispered in my ear to let me know that my mom took her medicine and that she made an appointment with my doctor per his request.

Perhaps you have already guessed that this scenario is not real, but communication has been progressing so rapidly over the past two decades that this amazing experience is becoming more tangible. Underlying this scenario is a global communication network that is able to connect people, robots, devices, and sensors in real time. This network may be one of the most complex systems on the face of our planet and a monumental breakthrough in the history of humanity. It has been exploding since the advent of smart phones, carrying text, voice, video, and images, and soon fully 360 videos and holograms.

The network continues to undergo a massive transformation from hardware to software and from being reactive to being proactive. In its first generation, also known as *legacy*, the global communication network was monolithic and hardware/vendor-centric. Today, the network is shifting to a second generation, a shift towards a software-centric network, in which service functions are virtualized and run on commodity cloud hardware. Over the next decade, the industry will be launching a third generation of this network transformation, the *autonomous network*. The autonomous network is powered by data and adopts artificial intelligence (AI). AI eats the network; in fact, it is an emerging reality that brings significant opportunities and challenges ranging from algorithms and standardization to real-time implementation and scale. Autonomous networks demonstrate a high degree of intelligence and support the growing demands of 5G, Internet of Things (IoT), virtual reality, and more. Those networks are self-healing and are capable of learning quickly and defending themselves against all forms of cyber attacks. An autonomous network is a living thing that you can talk to and interact with.

This book brings this autonomous network to reality by juxtaposing two unique technologies and communities: Networking and AI. The first five chapters (Chapters 1 through 5) review the technologies behind AI and software-defined network/network function virtualization (SDN/NFV), highlighting the exciting opportunities to integrate those two worlds into enabling secure autonomous networks. The next three chapters (Chapters 6 through 8) will review the software side of the autonomous networks, including the role of public cloud and open source, trends in containers and micro-services, and evolving software and hardware platforms for supporting distributed and multi-tenant AI platforms for autonomous networks. The following six chapters (Chapters 9 through 14) will dive into the application space and benefits of the autonomous network for transforming network operation, cyber security, enterprise services, 5G and IoT, infrastructure monitoring and traffic optimization, and customer experience and care. Finally, Chapter 15 will outline new and exciting AI frontiers for autonomous networks.

I am sincerely thankful to the 31 incredible authors from 8 leading technology companies for sharing their insights and expertise in this book. In particular, I would like to acknowledge the contributions of *Michael Lanzetta, Brian Freeman, Paul Bartoli, Wiley Wilkins, Matt Dugan, Stephen Terrill, Mattias Lidström, David Ward, Chris Metz, Eyal Felstaine, Ofer Hermoni, Rajesh Gadiyar, Ananth Sankaranarayanan, Tong Zhang, Jen Yates, Zihui Ge, Pat Velardo, Brian Rexroad, Anestis Karasaridis, Sandeep Gupta, Kathleen Meier-Hellstern, Michael Satterlee, Rittwik Jana, Mark Austin, Wenjie Zhao, Laurie Bigler, Vijay Gopalakrishnan, Jason Hunt, Sunil Dube, Chris Rice,* and *Anit Lohtia.*

I would also like to acknowledge the contributions of Natalie Gilbert, Swati Sharma, Randi Cohen, and Umesh Desai in the editing of the book. Royalties of this book will be for the Black Girls Code organization.

About the Editor

Dr. Mazin Gilbert is the vice president of Advanced Technology and Systems at AT&T Labs. In this role, Mazin oversees advancements in networking and access systems, machine learning and artificial intelligence, information systems and visualization, algorithms and optimization, and scalable, reliable software platforms.

Mazin earned a bachelor's degree and a doctoral degree, with first-class honors, in electrical engineering from the University of Liverpool, Liverpool, England. He also earned an MBA for Executives from the Wharton Business School of the University of Pennsylvania, Philadelphia, Pennsylvania. He holds 175 U.S. patents in human–machine communication and multimedia processing and has published over 100 technical papers. He is the author of the book titled *Artificial Neural Networks for Speech Analysis/Synthesis*.

Mazin is the technical chair for the Linux Foundation Open Network Automation Platform (ONAP), where his organization is actively contributing code and leading multiple Technical Steering Committee projects. He is also the board chair for the Linux Foundation Deep Learning Umbrella. Mazin and his team are co-founders of the open-source projects on Acumos Deep Learning and Akraino EdgeStack that were recently announced by the Linux Foundation. They are also contributors to OpenStack, Open Network Function Virtualization (OPNFV), and OpenDaylight (ODL), among others.

With more than three decades of experience under his belt, Mazin has worked in the industry at AT&T Labs and previously at Bell Labs, BBC, and British Telecom. He has also worked in academia at Rutgers University, New Jersey, Princeton University, Princeton, New Jersey, and University of Liverpool. Mazin is an IEEE Fellow and a winner of the AT&T Science and Technology Award.

Outside of his technology career, Mazin is an entrepreneur owning six limited liability companies specializing in commercial and residential real estate and the dental industry. He also serves on a number of industrial boards, including the International Computer Science Institute. In his free time, Mazin loves to spend time with his daughters and is an avid runner.

Contributors

Mark Austin
AT&T

Paul Bartoli
AT&T

Laurie Bigler
AT&T

Sunil Dube
IBM

Matt Dugan
AT&T

Eyal Felstaine
Amdocs

Brian Freeman
AT&T

Rajesh Gadiyar
Intel Corp.

Zihui Ge
AT&T

Mazin Gilbert
AT&T

Vijay Gopalakrishnan
AT&T

Sandeep Gupta
AT&T

Ofer Hermoni
Amdocs

Jason Hunt
IBM

Rittwik Jana
AT&T

Anestis Karasaridis
AT&T

Michael Lanzetta
Microsoft

Mattias Lidström
Ericsson

Anit Lohtia
Tech Mahindra

Kathleen Meier-Hellstern
AT&T

Chris Metz
Cisco Systems

Brian Rexroad
AT&T

Chris Rice
AT&T

Ananth Sankaranarayanan
Intel Corp.

Michael Satterlee
AT&T

Stephen Terrill
Ericsson

Pat Velardo
AT&T

David Ward
Cisco Systems

Wiley Wilkins
AT&T

Jennifer Yates
AT&T

Tong Zhang
Intel Corp.

Wenjie Zhao
AT&T

CHAPTER 1

The Role of Artificial Intelligence for Network Automation and Security

Mazin Gilbert

CONTENTS

1.1 INTRODUCTION

This chapter is an introduction to the technologies, opportunities, and challenges of the autonomous network—a product of integrating artificial intelligence (AI) with software-defined network (SDN). It provides an overview of the importance of automation for driving personalization, intelligence, and elasticity in the network. These characteristics drive operational efficiency, improved security, and enable scalability of a new spectrum of ultra-low latency services for supporting Internet of Things (IoT), autonomous cars, virtual reality (VR), and augmented reality (AR).

Section 1.2 presents an overview of the network transformation from proprietary vendor-locked networks to open SDNs running in the cloud, and soon, to autonomous networks adopting AI. Section 1.3 introduces the role of AI for driving an elastic, self-healing, and secure network. Section 1.4 explains the importance of data that fuels the autonomous network. Section 1.5 describes a new world of applications that will be enabled by the autonomous network.

1.2 THREE GENERATIONS OF NETWORK TRANSFORMATION

1.2.1 Back to Basics—The Communication Network

Although early evidence of communication was observed in Africa, the Americas, and China through the use of smoke signals and drums, the real breakthrough happened in the nineteenth century through the invention of the electric telegraph by Francis Ronalds [1]. The telegraph was the first *communication network* of its kind that enabled short-distance transmission of signals. In 1837, Samuel Morse, along with his assistant Alfred Vail [2], invented the Morse code for transmission of information across an electric telegraph. The telegraph used a transmitter, in the form of a sending device or encoder, which enabled sending a series of dots and dashes to represent letters and characters. At the receiving end, a decoder was used to receive the information that was then interpreted by an operator.

A communication network is essentially an interconnected system that facilitates the exchange of information. Behind this communication network, there are several basic technology components. An information source generates a signal, or message, that is then sent to a transmitter. This signal can be video, voice, or text, and is generated through devices, such as a camera, telephone, or keyboard. A transmitter processes this signal by performing amplification and modulation,[1] and then generates an output that is suitable

---

[1] Modulation is the process of converting the signal from a low-frequency to high-frequency range to enable transmissions of multiple signals over small antennas.

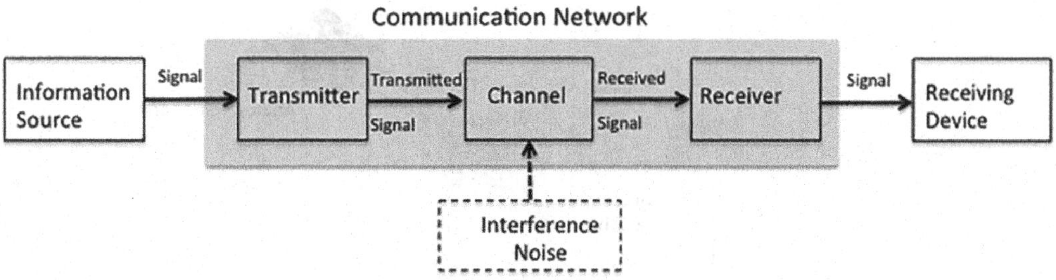

Communication Network

FIGURE 1.1 Basic communication network. (From Shannon, C.E., *A Mathematical Theory of Communication*, Bell Systems Technical Journal, 1948.)

for transmission. The signal in early communication networks is transmitted in an analogue form. Thanks to Claude Shannon [3] and his theory of information, most signals today are converted into a digital form—binary digits of ones and zeros. The encoded signal can be transmitted either through a wireline channel, such as cable wires or fiber optics, or a wireless channel, such as Wi-Fi, BlueTooth, 4GLTE, or 5G. Wireless channels involve transmitting electromagnetic waves from one antenna to another (Figure 1.1).

Maintaining a high-quality signal through the transmission channel is vital for effective communication. Quality is normally impacted through interference or noise. Noise can be environmental, industrial, or electronic and attributed to digitization or circuitry. Proper encoding of the signal and selection of the channel can help to maximize the signal-to-noise ratio as was shown by Shannon [3]. At the receiving end, the signal is demodulated and converted into a form that is suitable for the receiving device, which may be a speaker or a phone.

Modern communication networks are based on the invention of the telephone in 1876 by Alexander Graham Bell and Thomas Watson [4]. A telephone is used at the transmitter and receiver ends, with a centralized switchboard connected to each telephone. This invention gave birth to the Public Switch Telephone Network (PSTN) [5].

1.2.2 From Legacy to New

The telecommunication network, as envisioned by Alexander Bell, was essentially a form of a telegraph with voice on both ends. The network included transmitting electrical currents over electric wires duplicating sound waves. The invention of circuit switching was an improvement to Bell's invention, allowing voice in analogue form to travel over longer distances. The circuit-switching network (Figure 1.2) includes switching nodes that facilitate the transmission of voice from the sender to the receiver. Additional switching nodes are typically developed to improve reliability of the network.

Although circuit-switching networks were suitable for voice communication, they presented several challenges. The first is inefficiency in the system for voice transmission. A voice call requires a dedicated channel capacity for the entire call. The capacity is wasted even when not in use. Establishing a call through the switching nodes also required long delays [6].

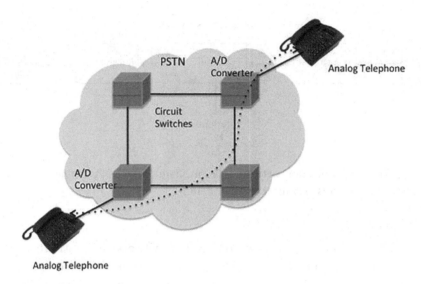

FIGURE 1.2   PSTN with circuit switches.

In the early 1970s, the PSTN began to transform toward packet-switched networks. Typically, messages are divided into a series of smaller packets plus control information, and then routed to its desired destination. In this design, packets can be queued and transmitted as fast as possible based on priorities. Node-to-node connections can be dynamically shared, hence allowing for data to be transmitted even during heavy traffic.

Managing, monitoring, and operating a communication network is a very complex and expensive undertaking. Network functions, such as routers, switches, and firewalls, include both specialized hardware and software that are vulnerable to failures and security attacks. Changes or replacements of this equipment require manual work in specified locations. Nevertheless, with the linear and predictable growth in traffic up to the mid-2000s, operators were complacent in operating and maintaining these hardware-centric networks.

In 2007, the communication network experienced a big bang with the birth of the iPhone and smart devices. Suddenly, traffic started to shift from essentially voice and some data, to mostly video data. Between 2007 and 2016, the AT&T network experienced 250,000% increase in traffic. This exponential increase in the demand is expected to continue that way for the next 10 years, imposing a significant burden on communication networks and requiring substantial investments in capital.

The Internet Protocol (IP)-based PSTN with packet processing and with "legacy" hardware-centric network equipment can no longer support the exponential growth in traffic. With market pressure to provide unlimited plans to consumers, it has become clear that the legacy approach is not sustainable, and operators need to employ new generations of technologies that provide flexibility, elasticity, and automation when managing network functions. Moving to a SDN and network function virtualization (NFV) is necessary to manage the rising operation costs and support the exponential traffic growth [7].

1.2.3 Software Eats the World

In 2011, Marc Andreessen wrote his famous "Why Software Is Eating the World" essay in *The Wall Street Journal*. Software and virtualization may not be new to the web companies, including Amazon, Google, and Microsoft, but it is a new way of thinking for networking and communication companies. Since the article was published, operators have been reimagining their network as a SDN to better manage the increase of their operational and services cost.

The key premise behind SDN is to separate the control, or management, plane of the network, which makes decisions on how packets flow, from the data, or forwarding plane, which move the packets from one node to the other. This design enables programming of data planes, virtualization of network functions, and leveraging commodity off-the-shelf servers. It also enables decoupling of the hardware switches from the software controllers through a southbound interface, or a protocol, such as OpenFlow [8].

As opposed to traditional legacy networks, which use specialized vendor-centric equipment such as firewalls and routers, SDNs allow applications to interface with the controller through a northbound protocol (Figure 1.3). In this design, an operator can integrate different network functions and employ different policies that may involve prioritizing, deprioritizing, or blocking specific packets flowing through certain switches. It also provides the operator the flexibility to run network workloads on a cloud computing multitenant architecture. This results in having more flexibility and elasticity to changing workloads through software while using less expensive commodity switches [7].

1.2.4 Intelligence Sits in the Cloud

Cloud computing is one of the most remarkable breakthroughs of the twenty-first century. The basic concept is to be able to run workloads and access and store data over the Internet instead of a local computer. The key advantage is gaining agility by being able to

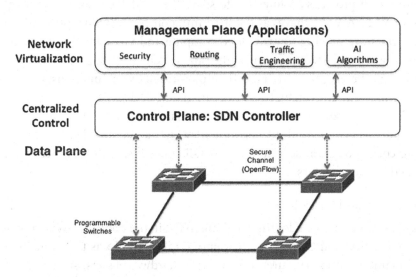

FIGURE 1.3 Basic SDN architecture.

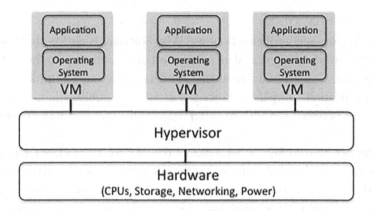

FIGURE 1.4   Cloud model.

get on-demand access to compute, storage, and networking to workloads without making major capital investments. Public clouds, such as Amazon and Microsoft, provide a variety of different compute resources [9].

Public clouds typically offer three types of cloud businesses. Software-as-a-Service (SaaS), where a business subscribes to an application over the Internet. Platform-as-a-Service (PaaS), where a business develops its own custom applications that are shared. Infrastructure-as-a-Service (IaaS), where businesses "rent out" compute and storage on a pay-per-use model. Netflix, for example, provides services by renting IaaS from Amazon.

Virtualization is the underpinning behind the majority of high-performance clouds. It allows decoupling of the physical hardware from the compute operating system. In another word, it hides the compute resources from their users. Hence, a single physical resource, such as a server, can appear to function as multiple virtual resources. A hypervisor is the software layer that sits between the physical hardware and the operating system (Figure 1.4). It provides an interface to share the available resources through virtual machines, or VMs. A VM behaves as if it is running on an individual physical machine.

All businesses are moving toward cloud compute and virtualization to reduce operational and capital costs, while enjoying agility and elasticity for compute and storage. This transformation is helping them to move their physical network functions, such as routers, switches, and firewalls, into virtual network functions (VNFs). VNFs run on VMs and can, in theory, be managed and orchestrated with zero touch in a SDN. Those VNFs, which represent the "intelligence" behind the network, may be chained together to form a complete networking communication service. More details on VMs, VNFs, and containerization are presented in later chapters.

1.2.5 The CapEx and OpEx Story

Service providers are rapidly adopting SDN and NFV in the hope of lowering their Capital Expenditure (CapEx) and Operational Expense (OpEx). CapEx is the funds used to buy, build, and maintain infrastructure, software, and hardware assets, such as creating data infrastructure, building and designing new services, and upgrading IT systems. OpEx is the funds used to run the day-to-day business functions, such as research and development, software changes, and equipment repairs. CapEx and OpEx have different tax implications. OpEx is tax deductible in the year of service, while CapEx must be depreciated over the lifetime of the investment.

SDN along with virtualization of network functions promise to be game changers to lowering both OpEx and CapEx. They have the potential to lowering the cost of compute and servers, reducing service failures and data centers' operational costs, improving efficiency through automation, and expediting service deployments. This is a very similar model to the web companies who develop their applications, for example, search and text processing, as software running on commodity cloud hardware. With this model, web companies are able to scale up and down per demand of their workloads.

From an operator perspective, SDN can provide reduced CapEx. It is a departure from vendor proprietary equipment, such as switches and routers, to all software that runs on a cloud environment. Most large operators are designing their cloud environment to support network workloads. This business model will change as public clouds start supporting networking workloads. Operators will then adopt a hybrid cloud strategy where the majority of their network functions run on their private cloud, while leveraging public clouds for IT workloads, traffic spillover, and geo redundancy. This flexibility provides operators leverage when negotiating purchasing terms with networking and compute vendors.

Another aspect of the saving from SDN is operational cost. SDN enables operators to automate network management functions and to discover and repair network faults more quickly. A recent study by EMA research shows that the admin-to-virtualization ratio is 1:77, that is, each person is able to manage around 77 VMs [10], as opposed to 1:65 for managing physical assets. Virtualization through SDN, automation of service design, orchestration, and life-cycle management of VNFs provide attractive business models for operators [11].

1.2.6 Are We Secure Yet?

Moving to a software-centric network presents the possibility of new security challenges that are not as evident in typical legacy networks. One example of a challenge is the potential vulnerability that may be attributed to the communication protocol between the control plane and the data, or forwarding, plane. Recall that the data plane is where the data, such as packets, is forwarded through the network elements. The control plane is the logic that determines how and where the data are sent in the data plane. As we outlined earlier, this communication protocol may be designed in SDN through OpenFlow [8]. OpenFlow is a perfect target for attackers to saturate the communication channel leading to Denial of Service (DoS) attacks and failure of the SDN controller. Another challenge is that given the centralized design of the controller in SDN, the result can be catastrophic, and it is imperative to have a secure and robust centralized orchestration. A range of solutions has been proposed, including having a distributed control plane but with a logically centralized controller [12], and introducing a controller hierarchy [13].

Despite these challenges, SDN and automation can result in an improved security by offering virtual networks full isolation from one another. This is also known as network slicing where multiple virtual networks can run on a shared physical network infrastructure. Different users, or tenants, can multiplex over a single physical infrastructure of compute and storage, providing agility, flexibility, and added security.

The design of OpenFlow in SDN also provides a centralized ability to filter packets as they enter the network, effectively acting as a firewall at the edge. Suspicious transactions can be redirected to higher-level security controls. Identifying suspicious packets and vulnerabilities in SDN are essential for developing an autonomous network. The next sections will describe how patterns of potential attacks can be learned and detected through machine learning (ML), and how security systems can benefit from the added sophistication of AI systems that drive scalable zero-touch solutions.

1.3 FROM AUTOMATION TO ARTIFICIAL INTELLIGENCE

1.3.1 Framework for Artificial Intelligence

Have you ever imagined a world where patients are treated before experiencing symptoms of a disease or illness? A world when your car experiences failures, it drives itself back and forth to the repair shop? A world where your shopping and meals are completed and prepared by your home robot? In that world, communication is prevalent, and experiences are available where you need them at anytime and anywhere. No more cyber security threats or spinning wheel when you download or watch content. Your smallest device, like a showerhead or a bookmark, has the intelligence of your smart phone today. This is the world that is envisioned with ML and AI, driving autonomous networks, autonomous cars, autonomous medicine, and autonomous robotics.

Let's start with basic definitions. We define ML as a computer program (or software agent) that can learn from data to predict a future state or condition. Traditionally, ML, similar to natural language processing (NLP), is considered a subfield of AI. We define an AI system as a more advanced form of a ML system that is able to act and to continuously optimize its actions over time and context. One analogy to realizing the relationship between ML and AI is the game of chess. ML is equivalent to predicting the next best move given all historical moves. This is an instant decision. AI is equivalent to formulating a strategy, or a process, to win the game. This typically involves optimizing the sequence of next best steps. The strategy is dynamic and updates on every move.

Figure 1.5 shows a framework for AI with a 2 × 2 grid. The upper side of the grid includes AI systems that are hardwired rule-based. Assisted Intelligence is one type of these systems that involve software programs in the form of expert systems that provide automation support to humans. One example is workflow engines used in contact centers to support live agents. Automation using rule-based systems may involve bots that conduct routine or non-routine simple tasks that may not involve an advanced level of intelligence or "thinking." Adaptive ML extends AI into a new dimension by fueling these systems with data. Augmented intelligence includes AI systems that aid humans by processing massive amounts of data. This has significant opportunities in the health-care industry, where machine learners can be used to provide doctors with recommendations on patient diagnosis. Autonomous intelligence is a form of fully autonomous systems that adapt, act, and

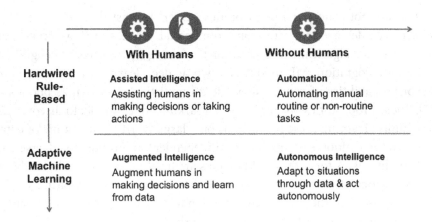

FIGURE 1.5   Framework for AI systems. (From www.pwc.com/ai.)

learn autonomously. Those systems are a subject of significant research (See Chapter 2), as they are critical in areas such as autonomous networks and autonomous cars, among others. Besides the AI 2 × 2 grid, researchers often discuss the field of artificial generalized intelligence. This includes autonomous intelligence systems that can operate and generalize across tasks and problems. Although such systems are in their infancy, they will continue to mature and be widespread over the next 10–20 years.

1.3.2   Artificial Intelligence Revisited

The foundation behind ML and AI was created over many decades by numerous pioneers including Alan Turing, Claude Shannon, Arthur Samuel, and Frank Rosenblatt, among others. Some may argue that the defining moment was inspired in 1950 by Alan Turing and his "Turing Test" [14]. The test computed the length of time or the number of interactions a machine can fool a human in believing it is a human. While at Bell Labs, Claude Shannon advanced the field of AI by creating a memory mouse, named "Theseus," for traversing a maze [3]. The mouse was able to learn, without supervision, the optimal path from the source to the destination. Shannon, intrigued by the experiment, started to establish a broader research effort in AI. In 1956, Shannon and his colleagues Minsky, Rochester, and McCarthy organized the first AI summer workshop at Dartmouth. The workshop made a fundamental breakthrough in the field of AI and, according to the authors, attempted to "make machines use language, form abstractions and concepts, solve kinds of problems now reserved for humans" [15].

Other pioneers in the area of AI included Arthur Samuel from IBM who wrote a program for the game of checkers that developed winning strategies and moves. Frank Rosenblatt, another AI pioneer, developed much of the foundational algorithms behind neural networks [16]—a form of ML that attempts to simulate the operation of the human brain. The theory and the practical experiments developed by these pioneers and many others have led to new scientific fields such as deep learning, which is making its way into smart automation for industrial applications and services.

ML and AI are not conceptual or theoretical. Over the past three decades, ML technologies have been deployed for numerous commercial services, such as Apple's Siri and Amazon's Alexa. ML algorithms are used for face recognition, speech recognition, and NLP. In speech recognition, ML models, known as deep learners, are used to estimate the posterior probabilities of context-dependent linguistic units, such as phonemes and words [17]. Those probabilities are applied in a Markov hidden model to discover the best sequence of units. Training these ML models on a large variety and volume of data helps to make speech recognition systems speaker independent and robust to adverse environments and conditions. A form of ML, known as artificial neural network, has been used to estimate the articulatory parameters of a vocal tract model for generating synthesized speech [18]. This has been the basis behind modern text-to-speech systems. Other types of ML models, known as convolutional neural networks [19], have been used to spot objects (e.g., characters, cars, dress, shoes) in an image-enabling businesses to perform targeted advertising. ML has also been used to predict network failures. This proactive action can result in increased cost saving and improved customer experience [20]. These successful demonstrations of ML applications, along with the advances in compute and the availability of massive data, continue to raise significant interest by companies looking to develop smarter automated systems.

1.3.3 The Perfect Marriage Between Software-Defined Network and Artificial Intelligence

While SDN is about virtualizing the network by having network functions run as software on commodity cloud infrastructure, ML-based AI, on the other hand, is about collecting and analyzing data for improving automation and extracting intelligence and information. The perfect marriage between SDN and AI results in an *autonomous network*. This type of a network is resilient, self-healing, and self-learning. It can collect and analyse data, and take actions to improve its state. As will be evident in future chapters, actions can range from optimizing traffic flow and identifying early patterns of cybersecurity to predicting failures of physical or VNFs and moving traffic accordingly.

Although there are numerous publications on the use of ML and AI technologies for multimodal and multimedia applications [21], there is far less research being done on the application of ML and AI to SDN. Some of the key opportunities that we have identified for using AI include:

1. Self-optimizing networks
2. Cybersecurity and threat analytics
3. Fault management
4. Customer experience improvement
5. Traffic optimization

AI drives an autonomous network by enabling improved stability, security, scalability, and performance (also known as S3P). For example, AI can be applied for identifying patterns of security threats or detecting performance degradations of VNFs. Memory and CPU signals can be collected from VMs supporting a virtual firewall. A set of machine learners can then be trained to predict the health of this firewall over a set period of time. Detected failures can be addressed by either automatically rebooting the firewall, migrating traffic to another firewall, or issuing a ticket for manual intervention.

The same concept of ML can be applied for interpretation of trigger events or signatures when dealing with control loop systems. A deep learner can be trained to map analytics signals and context into a predefined set of policies or actions. At runtime, the learner can select the most likely configuration. The learner can dynamically update its model based on positive and negative reinforcements. The back-propagation algorithm can be used to update the *a posteriori* probabilities to best reflect the correct action or policy [22]. For example, if the learner predicted a no-action policy, and an action was necessary, then the learner will negatively emphasize a "no action" class and positively emphasize the correct action.

The pitfall with deep learning is that one is making an instant decision in time and not optimizing a sequence of decisions toward a common goal. This is fine when recognizing an object in an image, but it presents a serious issue when needing to recommend a set of actions on how best to migrate traffic from one network node to another, for example. Several promising techniques have shown superior performance when integrated with deep learning. Those include dynamic programming, a form of Hidden Markov model, and reinforcement learning [21] (more details in Chapter 2). DeepMind's AlphaGo applied deep learning and reinforcement learning to defeat the world's best Go player [23].

1.3.4 Journey Toward a Software-Defined Autonomous Network

An intelligent service is one that is self-aware, that is, it collects information on its resources (users, devices, networks, and applications) to deliver the best service on the environment in which it operates. It then makes decisions based on this information and its domain knowledge to personalize the service for the users consuming it. An intelligent service receives feedback on its performance and learns. There are primarily three attributes that characterize an intelligent service, known as personalized, adaptive, and dynamic (PAD). A predictive personalized service is one that anticipates a user's need, proactively takes intelligent actions, and recommends valuable and timely personalized information. An adaptive service learns from its past actions of all users and adjusts its behavior to provide superior quality of service. A service that is dynamic is one that is robust and can self-repair or self-organize to avoid service interruptions.

Attaining an autonomous network with PAD characteristics is possible through the introduction of closed-loop systems (Figure 1.6). The basic concept is to compute an error signal between a target state and actual measurements computed from sensors. A feedback control loop is then applied to optimize the system by minimizing the measured error rate. One example is a home thermostat that is continuously controlling the heating/cooling system to maintain a desired room temperature. The basic components of such a system, as shown in Figure 1.6, includes data collection for measuring the current temperature, data analytics to compute the variation between the desired and actual readings, policy rules for recommending the next best action, and a controller for performing the action. The action

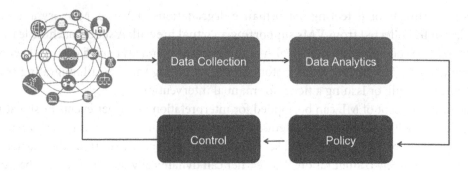

FIGURE 1.6 Basic concept of a closed-loop system.

may include turning the heating on/off, cooling on/off, or doing nothing. Network-based closed loop control systems, in general, involve backend integrations to other Operations Support Systems (OSS) and Business Support Systems (BSS) systems, such as logging, billing, and ticketing.

In autonomous networks, control-loop systems play a vital role in delivering operational cost savings. Control-loop automation can be categorized into open-loop and closed-loop systems. Open-loop systems capture telemetry and diagnostics information from the underlying cloud infrastructure (e.g., syslog-, fault-, and network-performance management events) perform a set of analytics and provide reporting, ticketing, or alarms to the operations team. Closed-loop systems continuously monitor the system for fault and S3P and compute a set of signatures based on the detected anomalous condition. A policy engine then interprets these signatures and appropriate corrective actions are recommended and performed. Once the system has been repaired, a monitoring application checks the status of the system to maintain a desired target state. The goal is to attain zero downtime or minimal interruptions.

1.3.5 Principles of Zero and One

In today's network, every new deployed service requires new software development, testing, and operational support. Deployments and operation are largely human intensive, which create challenges during service failures or when scaling up the number of services. It is every operator's vision to design and deploy a service only *once*, and hope to incur a *zero* operational cost over the lifetime of the service. These principles of one and zero are key characteristics of an autonomous network.

Let's first review the service design. A service is a composition of multiple network functions that are chained together, just like Legos. It is not unusual for these network functions to be developed by multiple vendors. To attain the "principle of one" in SDN, management and orchestration of network functions are designed to be model-driven [24]. The model may include the compute, connectivity, and feature functions that can be composed and operationalized in a cloud environment. In another word, the model is essentially a management recipe that includes the parameters, policies, and processes of a network function. Designing a service includes developing such a model, which is used for instantiation and deployment of the service. This is similar to 3D printing, where a model is developed for an object that is then used to create the actual product. Model-based design is a powerful characteristic in SDN.

Driving zero touch, on the other hand, is where AI becomes central. Most operational costs in support of services are attributed to (a) software upgrades or maintenance, (b) failure detection and recovery, and (c) instantiation, orchestration, and deployment of network functions. AI can drive change management automation for software upgrade and maintenance. Scheduling when to upgrade, what to upgrade, what the dependencies are, how to minimize service impact, what backup policies to revert to in case of failure, and how to monitor the upgrade upon completion are functions that can be executed by an AI system. This is not just a scheduling and optimization problem but also a learning problem where data from past failures and successes aid to improve future outcomes.

Fault and performance managements are also ideal candidates for AI to attain zero-touch solutions. As outlined in the previous section, closed-loop automation is a template AI system that can be deployed for monitoring virtual and physical network functions, VMs, and infrastructure elements, as well as the functional components for the management and orchestration platform. Adopting closed-loop automation systems when deploying SDN can result in the "principle of zero."

1.4 AUTONOMOUS NETWORKS RUN ON DATA

1.4.1 Data Is the New Currency

Over the past decade, data has been growing exponentially. Recent statistics by Inside Big Data show that the size of the digital universe is doubling every two years [25]. While human-to-machine data is growing at 10x faster than business data, machine-to-machine data is growing faster at 50x. It is said that companies who control massive amounts of data will be the new leaders in the AI world. Indeed, data is the new currency, and the ability to collect, manage, move, store, and process data efficiently and at scale are major challenges for building a reliable autonomous network that exhibits the principles of zero and one.

Autonomous networks need to be designed to operate with big data. Beyond considering only the size of the data, as the defining characteristic for big data, Doug Laney from Gartner [26] has offered some further attributes of big data by introducing the "3Vs" of volume, variety, and velocity. Since then, others (Livi13 [27], Data14 [28], Wikibig [29]) have extended the 3Vs to 5Vs or 7Vs to include other characteristics such as variability, validity/veracity, visibility/visualization, and value. These attributes are essential ingredients for developing a high-precision AI system, as will be described in later chapters.

For autonomous networks, big data can originate from applications running on the device, customer edge such as a set-up box, network edge such as data centers, or more centralized private and third-party clouds. No matter where the data originates, maintaining high-quality data is a challenge. Quality attributes include availability, usability, reliability, relevance, and presentation [7]. Another challenge is data management. There are a variety of data management and policy issues that must be determined for a big data system, such as what type of data is collected, how long data is retained, whether data is summarized or anonymized, and how data is processed and accessed in batch versus real time. Moving data across sites is very expensive. Hence, most modern systems tend to bring analytics and ML to the data, as opposed to the other way around. Data is typically preprocessed to enable parallel processing. The Hadoop open source ecosystem has emerged as having leading capabilities for processing and ingesting big data [30].

Despite all the challenges in handling, managing, and processing data, it is essential to care and feed data when developing an autonomous network. Data is vital for addressing fault and performance management, cybersecurity, managing and optimizing data traffic flow, and predicting locations for optimally placing edge clouds, micro and macro cells. Data is as important as currency in the new digital world. Just like money is tracked and carefully handled, data needs to be treated in the same way. Most companies today introduce data governance to set policies on how best to manage, store, process, and secure data to reduce cost of operation, fuel innovation in ML and AI, and stay compliant to data privacy rules.

Data is the fuel behind ML models and the reason for their existence today. The more diverse are the attributes of the training data, the more accurate machine learners become. On the other hand, bad and biased data can lead to inaccurate learners. This is referred as algorithmic bias [31]. High-quality unbiased data is important for building AI systems in SDN. Several chapters in this book are dedicated to data quality and integrity.

1.4.2 Microservices Are Data Powered

One key obstacle to massive adoption of data-powered AI solutions is the high barrier to entry in deploying the technology. AI models are typically built with massive amounts of data, require extensive compute infrastructure, and are trained by experts who have graduate level degrees in the science field. The time cycle from creating models to deploying services with AI is also lengthy and expensive. As an example, researchers in speech and video technologies can spend months building and tuning ML models for recognizing speech, or detecting faces. One in a hundred of these models may end up being deployed and used in any commercial service. There is also little reusability among these models, which makes progress in AI very slow.

Helping to drive reusability in AI and to lower the barrier to entry are great goals that the community has been thriving for years. One key breakthrough is the advent of microservices. A microservice, an evolution of a service-oriented architecture, is a software architectural style in which large applications are composed from small, loosely coupled services with independent life cycles. This term has been popularized by thought leaders such as Martin Fowler [32] who have suggested that the goal of such a service design is to build systems using a collection of smaller common core components that have strong public APIs. This results in several benefits, including (a) ease of deployment of new capabilities, (b) ease of maintenance and upgrades, (c) ease of decommissioning, and (d) being agnostic to the programming languages used. A deeper dive into microservices will be presented in Chapter 7.

Containers are used to build microservices. They help to isolate, transport, and run software on physical and VMs. Containers are different from VMs in that applications running on containers can share the same operating system. Microservices typically deploy faster on containers than VMs. This can be an advantage when needing horizontal scaling. A popular use of containers is through Docker [33]. Docker is an open source project that aims to automate the deployment of applications inside portable containers independent of the hardware or the operating system used. Managing a group of Docker containers requires new technologies and tools. The most popular one being Kubernetes [34], which is an open source project for automating deployment, scaling, and management of containerized applications. Kubernetes, along with other technologies, as will be described in later chapters, are critical for driving services to become cloud native: resiliency, scalability, self-healing.

Although microservices leveraging Docker containers have become very popular, the use of data-powered microservices for AI are not as widely known. This is partially due to the skill gap among the architects who provide the design and requirements, the data scientists who build models, and the software developers who develop and deploy end services. A number of activities have been recently announced by the Linux Foundation to address this gap. One being Project Acumos [35], where the goal is to enable an AI-centric marketplace for microservices, and to streamline the development process from model creation to microservices deployment on a hybrid cloud.

1.4.3 Compute Follows You

Over the past decade, there has been a focused effort to centralize compute and storage, and to develop virtualization infrastructure that meets varying types of workloads. This vision has helped companies like Google, Amazon, and Microsoft to build massive centralized public cloud infrastructures and make those available for a third party to use. Virtualization through public clouds has accelerated growth of many new industries and start-ups, improved operational efficiency, and reduced the total cost of ownership by improving the return on the invested capital. Adopting virtualization also implies that your applications may run thousands of miles away, impacting performance and experience in many cases.

With the advent of new experiences through autonomous cars, drones, and virtual reality, the data is now being generated at the user end of the network, the "edge" [36]. Applications, on the other hand, are demanding real-time communication, creating the need for efficient processing of dynamic data at the customer and network edges. Those applications desire the compute to follow the devices, and not the other way around. This is different than traditional Content Delivery Network (CDN), such as videos and web pages that store relevant and localized caches closer to the end user.

Edge compute is the placement of compute, storage, power, and networking near the application or device (Figure 1.7). This may be at the customer "edge," such as homes, smart cities, small enterprises, or at the network "edge" in regional, national, or local data centers. Edge computing provides significant benefits, including (a) reducing backhaul traffic, (b) maintaining superior quality of service, (c) reducing cost of moving data, and (d) improving latency and performance. Cloud resources can now be distributed optimally depending on user requirements.

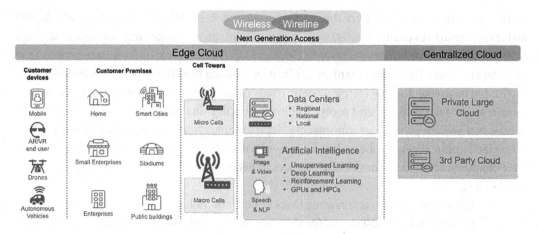

FIGURE 1.7   Edge and centralized clouds.

Over the past year or so, there has been a trend to building cloud compute at the customer "edge" in the form of "white boxes." A white box is essentially a non-branded hardware device [37]. It supports disaggregation or decoupling of hardware and software through open non-proprietary interfaces. Network services, such as routers and firewalls, can be automatically instantiated and orchestrated locally or remotely. The hardware becomes essentially a computer white box that can run on-demand network and application functions. Consider dropping these boxes that act as "baby clouds" into a manufacturing line to help drive a variety of workloads, such as inspection and monitoring.

Moving the cloud infrastructure to the edge provides new opportunities for offloading the processing from the device and making the intelligence reside at the edge. This fundamentally changes the device ecosystem and enables development of very low cost and smart IoT devices. Moving that intelligence to the edge requires distributing AI technologies across edge nodes and running them on GPUs and/or Higher Performance Compute servers. ML workloads, such as deep learning, unsupervised learning, or reinforcement learning will then move from centralized cloud infrastructure to distributed edge nodes. This paradigm shift, along with the advent of 5G and next generation access, will result in new experiences that will fundamentally transform businesses, and even society. More details on edge compute are presented in Chapter 12.

1.4.4 Closing the Artificial Intelligence Loops

Capturing data at the edge of the network provides new opportunities to perform both primitive and complex data processing ranging from data aggregation to advanced ML and predictive analytics. For example, by collecting performance and application data from VMs supporting virtual firewalls and routers, we can run advanced analytics at the edge to perform closed-loop automation. This may involve automatic identification and remediation of cyberattacks, followed by shifting traffic to new VMs, deactivating IP addresses, or rebooting VMs.

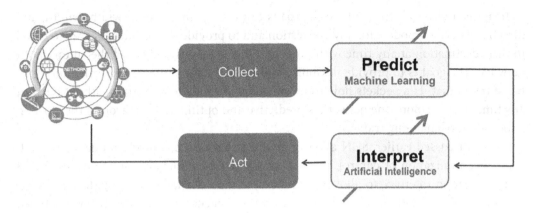

FIGURE 1.8   Closing the loop with AI.

Performing those tasks in semi-real time at the edge is manually intensive and virtually impossible to scale when you are dealing with 10,000+ edge nodes. This is where AI plays a significant role in closing the loop. Rather than performing reactive analytics, which is typically employed in unsupervised learning models, ML helps to predict anomalies or events well in advance, based on time-varying signals. Similarly, instead of applying hard-wired policies, or rules, to guide the system on what best next action to take, AI can make a smarter recommendation based on data, context, previous patterns, and outcomes. Moreover, as the system continues to iterate and more data is collected, ML and AI can learn from successes and failures, and adjust their models accordingly to minimize errors. ML and AI help to transform the system from being static to being dynamic and from being reactive to being proactive. This is depicted in Figure 1.8.

Closing the loop with AI involves collecting data, predicting an anomaly, interpreting the outcome, making a decision, and then taking a corrective action. Closed-loop automation can be considered as a fundamental microcapability for attaining an autonomous network and for developing zero-touch services and applications.

1.5 IT IS A WHOLE NEW WORLD

The marriage between SDN and AI gives rise to new services that can make society efficient, innovative, and safer. This section will review a glimpse of the future.

1.5.1 Operating a Virtual City

How often do we experience traffic congestion? The rise in the population along with the growth in businesses will continue to strain our transportation systems and put challenges on our physical world. A similar picture applies to the network. The exponential rise in data and smart devices will continue to create network traffic congestions and cause delay when uploading and downloading data. Although adding additional spectrum and cell sites adds new network capacity, the linear growth falls short from supporting the exponential increase in data.

Imagine a physical world where the roads can change instantly in width, length, and direction to accommodate for any congestion and to provide a guarantee for cars to travel to their destination at any time with no delay. This is the vision behind the autonomous network. The goal is to provide flexibility and elasticity for traffic engineering and optimization so that data packets flow from one network node to the other without delay at any time. Furthermore, the network is predictive and optimizes itself around the clock in anticipation of changing traffic.

As we discussed earlier, SDN allows the separation of the control and data planes. It enables centralization of control. Protocols such as OpenFlow are sometimes used as a communication interface to allow direct manipulation of the networking devices in the data plane (Figure 1.4). Traffic flow involves routing packets that arrive at a switch based on instructions stored in flow tables. Intelligence in SDN resides in the management plane that includes applications such as routers and load balancers that interact with the network model in the control plane. One leading example of a management platform is the Linux Foundation Open Network Automation Platform (ONAP) [38].

Introducing AI into this ecosystem to enable dynamic traffic optimization and improved security of network traffic is fertile ground. One example is the work by Stampa et al. [39] on the use of deep-reinforcement learning for SDN routing optimization. The machine learner is trained to provide dynamic routing configurations in order to minimize network delay. Different reward functions are applied with associated target policies. This research was an extension to an earlier study by Boyan and Littman [40] who applied Q-learning for discovering optimal routing policies that optimize the number of "hops" a packet will take to avoid congestion.

1.5.2 From Internet of Things to Internet of Everything

IoT is a concept of having any device, from cell phones and cars to fridges and washing machines, connected to the Internet. The autonomous network promises to revolutionize the IoT space by enabling any device to be highly "intelligent" by being connected securely to the "edge" of the network. An example is IoT for smart cities [41]. Street IoT sensors provide information on empty parking spots. The information is then used by autonomous cars to identify the nearest and best parking locations. A similar trend is applied to businesses, where IoT sensors in agricultural farms collect data on temperature, rainfall amount, and humidity. This information is then used to determine time and amount of water to spray.

Many analysts have provided data on the size of the IoT market. One study by IHS Markit [42] expects the number of IoT devices to grow from 27 billion in 2017 to 125 billion in 2030. For these devices to access the network securely and perform closed-loop-type automation tasks (i.e., collect data, analyse, predict, apply logic, and act) poses an incredible challenge to the autonomous network. Just the sheer size of the data that will be generated from this IoT ecosystem is a major undertaking to manage and process. Successful data supply chain of this ecosystem will surely result in smarter AI systems.

Over the next decade, the advent of the autonomous network and the expansion of IoT will give rise to the next big thing—the Internet of Everything (IoE). The IoE is a concept where any device can interact with any device without going directly to the Internet. Imagine your Heating Ventilating and Air Conditioning (HVAC) sensors interacting with your car sensors so that your house temperature gets adjusted when you are within five miles of your house. Having 125 billion devices interconnecting with each other is a phenomenal paradigm shift in our society and gives rise to enormous number of innovative services that employ AI at the "edge" of the customer or network.

1.5.3 Your Service in a Heartbeat

The evolution of the network access to 5G, the move of cloud applications to the edge, and the shift from a SDN to an autonomous network are key drivers for enabling ultra-low latency services. These services can run with sub 20-millisecond round-trip network latency if operating at the network "edge," and sub 5-millisecond round-trip latency if operating at the customer "edge." The only remaining challenge becomes the compute time and not the network latency.

Computing power to support the advent of AI and IoT is progressing rapidly. Modern GPUs, which were originally developed for gaming applications, are capable today to perform high-performance parallel processing for ML training algorithms. GPUs are multi-threaded and enable execution of in-memory tasks in parallel. This provides the speed and efficiency to process massive amounts of data for learning and adaptation of AI systems.

The rapid acceleration of compute and networking will enable large-scale AR and VR applications, as well as mission-critical services, such as autonomous drones and autonomous cars. AR overlays virtual 3D graphics into our real world, while VR immerses us in a synthetic world with a 360-degree experience. Both VR and AR enable us to change businesses and societies by transforming their physical world into a realistic virtual world. This has the potential to revolutionize employee training, conferencing, product and service repairs, and patient diagnostics.

The key requirements for low-latency applications, such as AR and VR, are maintaining a uniform experience without lag, stutter, and stall. Sub 15-millisecond latency is needed for motion-to-photon time to avoid discomfort [43] and to sustain an immersive experience. Furthermore, being untethered and mobile will drive massive adoption of these technologies. Just imagine experiencing a 360-view live sports game at any angle you turn to and anywhere in the world. Every person sees a different view and receives a different experience. This is where 5G and edge cloud become critical technologies for attaining this level of low-latency wireless connectivity. Along with AI and the autonomous network, we are able to capture the large amount of data and provide personalized services on-demand, such as summaries of events, replays, and predictions of next moves, among others.

1.5.4 Flying Cell on Wings to the Rescue

In Hurricane Maria, one of the major natural disasters of 2017 that struck Puerto Rico, AT&T had flying Cell On Wing (COW) drones providing service [44]. The flying COWs hovered around 200 feet above the ground to provide LTE to about a 40 square mile area.

Having wireless connectivity in remote areas, natural disasters, and traffic congestions is vital to save lives and help first responders. SDN and AI, working together, can drive a world where wireless connectivity is there wherever and whatever needed.

Having connectivity and sufficient bandwidths, as needed, is not a trivial problem. The first challenge is detecting when and where connectivity or more bandwidths are needed. In the case of a natural disaster, it is straightforward to realize when the need may arise and the location. However, in a normal day-to-day event, such as traffic congestion, failing cell sites, and major sports events, realizing where there's need is not a trivial exercise. In an autonomous network, data is collected constantly from all micro and macro cells, and failures are detected in near real time. In some cases, machine learners predict these failures and congestions before they occur. In the very near distant future, we will be able to see drones flying autonomously to optimal locations wherever and whenever connectivity and more bandwidth are needed. This is a form of closed-loop automation where the action is a flying COW that is optimally placed on a temporary basis to improve coverage until normal behaviors are resumed.

Improving connectivity and increasing capacity are a few of the benefits of the autonomous network of the future. Other benefits include detecting and repairing physical failures whether in cell sites, street poles, or utility fixtures. Operators today lease or own millions of street poles that they use for extending wires or placing equipment such as small cells. Some of these are in very remote locations, while others are in heavily congested cities. Simple maintenance or repair of this equipment is a major undertaking and a safety hazard to the workers. This is another great opportunity for AI to employ machine vision technologies to detect and perform maintenance autonomously.

In a recent study by AT&T [45], drones were equipped with video analytics capabilities, and deep learning models were trained to detect hundreds of different types of objects in a small cell, such as jumper support and ground bar (Figure 1.9). The video analytics algorithms were also able to identify tens of different types of repair categorizes, such as dirt and rust. Technicians are sent to the scene only when a remote repair cannot be performed or a drone robot cannot fix the problem. This shift toward adopting mobile drones and AI algorithms to aid engineering and infrastructure will have a tremendous impact on lowering the cost of repair and improving quality of life for technicians and engineers.

FIGURE 1.9 Videos captured by drones.

1.5.5 How May I Serve You?

One of the early successful applications of ML and AI technologies was customer care interactive voice response (IVR). Nearly two decades ago, companies started introducing voice recognition as an alternative to touch-tone response. The goal then was to provide a natural interface for understanding the customers' inquires and route customers correctly to the appropriate agent. Incorrect routing has been proven to reduce a customer's satisfaction score and to increase a company's cost of care. Today, customers call and interact with contact centers through voice or chat-based bots and get many of their billing, sales, and repair needs completed without having to interact with a human agent.

As we move toward SDN and cloud technologies with white boxes, customer care will also shift from being reactive to proactive. In a recent study completed for video service broadband [46], an ML algorithm was used to predict which set-top boxes would experience future quality issues. Poor experiences were highly correlated with customers being dissatisfied with their service and calling their contact centers for repair. Once a set-up box with poor performance was identified, it was then scheduled for a reboot during off-peak time. The algorithm was shown to detect 25% of multiple repair attempts with a resulting annual saving of $1Mil for 400K customers. Most importantly, ML was shown to improve customers' net promoter scores and their retention to remain loyal customers. Studies have also shown that such ML algorithms are perceived to be less biased than human agents [47].

As society moves to digital transformation, accepting the AI revolution, robotics technologies will begin to play a bigger role in our lives. China is leading the pack in this space, making conversational robots available to care for its large, and growing, elderly population [48]. These robots have AI algorithms that collect data and learn to adapt to the owner's habitat and preferences. They ensure that the elderly people receive medicine and eat their meals. The robots send out warning signals if they see unusual events, such as an elderly person falling or not breathing well. Widespread use of these intelligent robots in the Western world will happen over the next decade as autonomous networks mature with 5G and edge cloud technologies.

Massive adoption of cost-effective and intelligent devices, sensors, and robotics will only happen when autonomous networks become widely deployed. Chapter 2 will review the algorithms and technologies behind AI. AI systems can be rule based, data driven, or a mix of both. Those systems can be supervised, unsupervised, or semi-supervised. The chapter highlights those differences and reviews the relevant AI algorithms from traditional ones such as regressions and clustering to modern ML techniques such as NLP, deep learning, convolutional networks, reinforcement learning, and more. The chapter also describes some of the successful applications of AI in areas of speech recognition, language translation, video processing, and facial and object recognition.

REFERENCES

1. Ronalds, B. F. *Sir Francis Ronalds: Father of the Electric Telegraph*, London, UK: Imperial College Press, 2016.
2. Morse, S. F. B. Papers at the Library of Congress, invention of the telegraph, https://www.loc.gov/collections/samuel-morse-papers/articles-and-essays/invention-of-the-telegraph/, 1793–1919.

3. Shannon, C. E. *A Mathematical Theory of Communication*, Bell Systems Technical Journal, 1948.
4. Bell, A. G. and Watson, T. 140 years of "call history"—The celebration of the first phone call, http://about.att.com/newsroom/140_year_anniversary_of_first_phone_call.html, 1876.
5. Boettinger, H. M. *Telephone Book: Bell, Watson, Vail and American Life, 1876–1976*, Croton-on-Hudson, NY: Riverwood, 1977.
6. Chapuis, R. J. *100 Years of Telephone Switching (1878–1978)*, Elsevier Science, 1982.
7. Donovan, J. and Prabhu, K. *Building the Network of the Future*, Boca Raton, FL: CRC Press, A Chapman & Hall Book, 2017.
8. OpenFlow-enabled SDN and Network Functions Virtualization, http://www.opennetworking.org/images/stories/downloads/sdn-resources/solution-briefs/sb-sdn-nvf-solution.pdf, 2014.
9. Cloud computing tutorial, https://www.tutorialspoint.com/cloud_computing/cloud_computing_tutorial.pdf, 2017.
10. EMA IT Management Research. Reducing operational expense (OpEx) with virtualization and virtual systems management, 2009.
11. Ashton, Metzler & Associates. The business case for deploying SDN in enterprise networks, 2015.
12. Dixit, A. et al. Towards an elastic distributed SDN controller, *ACM SignComm Computer Communication Review*, 43(4), 7–12, 2013.
13. Yeganeh, S. and Ganjali, G. Kandoo: A framework for efficient and scalable offloading of control applications, In *HotSDN '12 Proceedings of the First Workshop on Hot Topics in Software Defined Networks*, pp. 19–24. New York: ACM, 2012.
14. Turing, A. M. Computing machinery and intelligence, *Mind*, 49, 433–460, 1950.
15. Shannon, C., Minsky, M., Rochester, N., and McCarthy, J. Dartmouth summer research project on artificial intelligence, 1956.
16. Minsky, M. and Papert, S. *Perceptrons: An Introduction to Computational Geometry*, Cambridge, MA: MIT Press, 1969.
17. Deng, L. et al. Recent advances in deep learning for speech recognition at Microsoft, *IEEE International Conference on Acoustics, Speech and Signal Processing (ICASSP)*, 2013.
18. Rahim, M. *Artificial Neural Network for Speech Analysis/Synthesis*, London, UK: Chapman & Hall, 1991.
19. Lecun, Y., Bengio, Y., and Haffner, P. Gradient based learning applied to document recognition, *Proceedings of the IEEE*, 86(11), 2278–2324, 1998.
20. Gilbert, M., Jana, R., Noel, E., and Gopalakrishnan, V. Control loop automation management platform, *Signal and Information Processing (GlobalSIP), 2016 IEEE Global Conference on*, 2016.
21. Mitchell, T. *Machine Learning*, McGraw-Hill Series in Computer Science, 1997.
22. Rumelhart, D. E., Hinton, G. E., and Williams, R. J. *Learning Internal Representations by Error Propagation*, Cambridge, MA: MIT Press, 1986.
23. AlphaGo. DeepMind Technologies Limited. https://deepmind.com/research/alphago/, 2017.
24. ECOMP (Enhanced Control, Orchestration, Management & Policy) Architecture White Paper, https://www.google.com/#q=ecomp+white+paper, 2016.
25. InsideBigData, https://insidebigdata.com/2017/02/16/the-exponential-growth-of-data/, 2017.
26. Laney, D. 3D data management: controlling data volume, velocity and variety, META Group, 2001.
27. Livi13. "The 7 V's of Big Data", Livingstone Advisory, https://livingstoneadvisory.com/2013/06/big-data-or-black-hole/
28. Data14. Understanding Big Data: The Seven V's, May 22, 2014, http://dataconomy.com/seven-vs-big-data/
29. WikiBig. "Big Data", https://en.wikipedia.org/wiki/Big_data

30. Apache Hadoop turns 10: The Rise and Glory of Hadoop, https://www.dezyre.com/article/apache-Hadoop-turns-10-the-rise-and-glory-of-Hadoop/211, February 2016.
31. Cobonchi, F. Algorithmic bias, francescobonchi.com/tutorial-algorithmic-bias.pdf, 2016.
32. Lewis, J. and Fowler, M. Microservices, http://www.martinfowler.com/articles/microservices.html, 2014.
33. Tutorial on docker containers, https://www.tutorialspoint.com/docker/docker_tutorial.pdf
34. Tutorial on Kubernetes, https://www.tutorialspoint.com/kubernetes/kubernetes_pdf_version.htm
35. Project Acumos, www.acumos.com, Linux Foundation, 2017.
36. AT&T Edge cloud, https://about.att.com/content/dam/innovationdocs/Edge_Compute_White_Paper%20FINAL2.pdf, 2017.
37. AT&T white boxes white paper, http://about.att.com/innovationblog/scaling_white_box
38. Open network automation platform, www.onap.corg, 2017.
39. Stampa, G. et al. A deep reinforcement learning approach for software defined networking routing optimization, 2017.
40. Boyan, J. and Littman, M. Packet routing in dynamically changing networks: A reinforcement learning approach. In *Advances in Neural Information Processing Systems*, 1994.
41. AT&T smart cities, https://www.business.att.com/solutions/Family/internet-of-things/smart-cities/
42. IHS Markit. Number of Connected IoT Devices Will Surge to 125 Billion by 2030, https://technology.ihs.com/596542/number-of-connected-iot-devices-will-surge-to-125-billion-by-2030-ihs-markit-says
43. AR and VR - Pushing connectivity limit, https://www.qualcomm.com/media/.../files/vr-and-ar-pushing-connectivity-limits.pdf
44. AT&T flying COW, http://about.att.com/inside_connections_blog/flying_cow_puertori
45. Video analytics with drones, http://about.att.com/innovationblog/drones_new_heights
46. Flynn, C. Customer video service with early problem detection, *JSM*, 2016.
47. Artificial intelligence and robots key in enhancing customer service, http://www.information-age.com/artificial-intelligence-robots-key-enhancing-customer-service-123468933/
48. Machines with Brains. Inside China's experiment to find friends for 230 million old people, https://qz.com/se/machines-with-brains/1016249/china-is-developing-care-robots-to-provide-companionship-to-elderly-nursing-home-residents/, 2017.

CHAPTER 2

Machine Learning, Deep Learning, and Artificial Intelligence

Michael Lanzetta

CONTENTS

2.1 INTRODUCTION

Artificial intelligence (AI) is a field where one size definitely *does not* fit all, and an understanding of the different types of machine learning (ML) available to us is key to building successful solutions for autonomous networks. AI systems can be rule based, data driven, or a mix of both. These systems can be supervised, unsupervised, or semi-supervised. In this chapter, we discuss differences such as these and their effects on the solutions we create. We review the relevant AI algorithms from traditional ones, such as regressions and clustering, to modern ML techniques, such as natural language processing, deep learning (DL), convolutional networks, and reinforcement learning. We will also describe successful applications of AI in areas of speech recognition, language translation, video processing, and facial and object recognition.

Section 2.2 provides historical perspective on the evolution of machine intelligence and the innovative researchers involved, from early "perceptrons" through expert systems, optimization, and forecasting, down to modern DL. Section 2.3 gives an overview of the different types of traditional ML problems (e.g., detecting anomalies, classifying spam, predicting device failures) and how they're solved. Section 2.4 walks through the reasons behind and the possibilities of the DL revolution with details on where the hype is warranted and where it might be a bit too breathless. We end Chapter 2 with a discussion on the current breakthroughs of AI and what the future holds, both its challenges and its opportunities.

2.2 ARTIFICIAL INTELLIGENCE—AN ABBREVIATED HISTORY

What is AI? According to one of the luminaries of the field, "as soon as it works, no one calls it AI anymore [1]." The definition of what qualifies a system as AI has changed over time, but with the recent resurgence in ML, people typically use AI to refer to a solution that uses ML and "closes the loop" by taking actions, and potentially learning. You can distinguish further between the AI above and the artificial general intelligence (AGI) of fictional machines like HAL9000 or the Terminator.

In this book, we'll concentrate on ML and AI models that help autonomous networks function, and AI systems that stitch together models into cohesive systems for fault prevention, intrusion detection, and self-reparation. In order to understand these systems, we will examine the history of ML and AI, and look at the various types of ML and how they are used.

2.2.1 Early Machine Learning

Machine learning has been around for decades. Some might even say centuries if you include statistical methods like Bayes' Theorem. For our purposes, we'll start in the 1950s when Marvin Minsky and Dean Edmonds built the first neural network machine (the Stochastic Neural Analog Reinforcement Calculator [SNARC] [2]) and later Frank Rosenblatt created the Perceptron [3]. Alan Turing had written a seminal paper [4] in 1950 that introduced the world to the "Turing Test," and with that measure of intelligence in the mind of the public and the fresh success of SNARC and the Perceptron on real problems, a "golden age" of AI bloomed with excitement and research money flowing in abundance.

During this golden age, advancements in AI methods led to the development of many "problem solvers" like Herbert Gelertner's "Geometry Theorem Prover" and Newell's "General Solver [5]." These devoted themselves to trying to solve problems in what they considered a "human" fashion, by *searching* over the space of possible options at each step, backtracking, and considering new ones (think of us solving a maze). Others devoted research to solving the problem of understanding and communicating in natural language like Weizenbaum's ELIZA, which could hold simple therapist conversations. These and other advancements led Minsky to predict in 1970 that "In from three to eight years we will have a machine with the general intelligence of an average human being [6]." The advancements led Defense Advance Research Projects Agency (DARPA) among others, both governmental and corporate, to invest huge sums in AI research, with both Minsky and John McCarthy forming influential labs at MIT and Stanford.

Yet even as Minsky predicted "average human being" machine intelligence appearing in the near future, the first "AI Ice Age" was already beginning. Minsky himself published a critique [7] on the capabilities of Perceptrons (neural networks) that shut down all research into them for years, with research funds drying up as researchers realized the computation limitations and combinatorial explosion of the problems they were trying to solve. Computer scientists adopted the easily used and predictable components like search methods, which then ceased to be considered "AI," and AI research itself stalled.

2.2.2 Expert Systems and the Fight against Probability

During the mid-1970s, the first AI Ice Age finally started to thaw with the advent of "Expert Systems." These were knowledge-based systems that encoded both domain expertise and business processes to allow machines to both make and guide decisions in the workplace. These rule-based decision-support systems differed from the previous generation of AI systems in two key ways: first, they were encoded explicitly with detailed knowledge of the domain in which they worked instead of trying to learn it from basic principles, and second, they were scoped in their predictive abilities to a single problem instead of trying to be a generalized model capable of learning "probabilistic reasoning" across any domain.

This second "golden age" saw the development of incredibly skilled chess-playing programs combining the search methods from the first golden age and the domain knowledge of thousands of recorded games from chess masters [8]. In a similar fashion, search was combined with corpora of knowledge in other domains like medicine, and even areas as mundane but impactful as computer configuration (e.g., XCON). Once again, the promise brought money flooding in and a new wave of grandiose predictions. Once again, those predictions failed to materialize, and the second AI bubble burst, leading to another AI Ice Age at the end of the 1980s.

2.2.3 Predicting the Future, Optimizing the Present

During this new AI Ice Age in the late 1980s and early 1990s, techniques that were in the same family as AI but had dodged its stigma took business by storm. Optimization and other techniques from the operations research community started advancing beyond their original industries. Forecasting methods started being deployed more widely and used to solve problems beyond finance. General optimization methods and genetic algorithms swept across industries, leading to advances in circuit design, biotechnology, and many other domains where the search spaces of possible answers felt insurmountable.

2.2.4 Current Machine Learning and Taking It Deeper

With the rise of the internet and e-commerce in the late 1990s and 2000s, vast amounts of business data were accumulated and the "big data" revolution began. Massive amounts of log data were generated by commodity server and cloud service deployments. Large online advertising platforms evolved. All of these system owners needed methods to understand what was happening and how they could effectively leverage the information they had gathered. Traditional ML techniques started coming back into prominence, and a new ML boom began. Suddenly statisticians, who went from regressing over data to constructing complex predictive models, were rebranded as "data scientists," and those who could cope with data at scale started earning their weight in gold [9]. As we entered 2010, systems like SparkML [10], H2O [11], and others evolved to perform ML at scale, and more advanced ML methods like Support Vector Machines and Boosted Decision Trees soon dominated the landscape.

Meanwhile, a small group of people in Canada had refused to abandon the promise of neural networks, and they were about to explode onto the scene. Geoffrey Hinton and his student Alex Krizhevsky invented AlexNet [12], handily beating the best solutions to the ImageNet image recognition challenge in 2012 and launching DL onto the stage. These deep neural networks built on the previous work of Hinton et al. (back-propagation [13]) and Fukushima (convolutional neural networks), and their work was enhanced and extended by Yann LeCun [14] and Yoshua Bengio (among many others) with more hidden layers and specialized neurons. Since then, deep networks have expanded in size and capabilities, beating grand masters at Go (a problem we thought was decades from a solution) and detecting skin cancers and pneumonia better than human experts. Traditional ML still has a place, but DL models based on multilayer neural networks (Figure 2.1) are bound to expand their reach, and we're still early in their revolution.

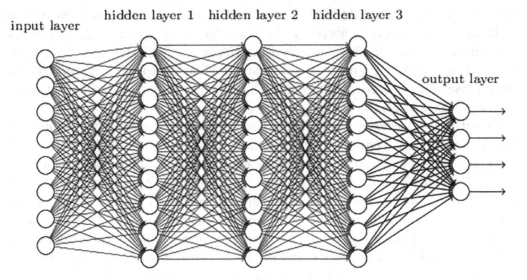

FIGURE 2.1 Multilayer neural network.

2.3 FLAVORS OF MACHINE LEARNING

A brief history of ML is helpful but gives us little insight into how ML operates in the wild. In this section, we'll cover the different "flavors" of ML and where they apply, as well as what's required in order to make use of them. One dirty secret among most ML practitioners is that 80% of our time is spent dealing with data—finding it, cleaning it, and figuring out what it means. "Garbage in, garbage out" is very relevant in the ML realm, so our first few sections will focus on data. We'll then walk through how we use that data from "supervised" problems where we know what we're looking for, to "unsupervised" problems where we're trying to discover structure from the data we have. We'll then close with a look at systems that teach themselves.

2.3.1 Learning from Data: Features, Labels, and Solving the Right Problems

Machine learning is, at its core, defined by the data that goes into it. In order to learn from data, the systems need to be provided with it, and in a format they can understand. Most ML systems don't deal with raw data; it needs to be turned into "features" (typically numbers) by a process called "featurization," transforming incoming data into a format the system can use and extracting the relevant details from the irrelevant. If you know what you're looking for in the data, your data may also have "labels," which can either be numeric (in which case you have a *regression problem*) or categorical (in which case you have a *classification problem*). Think of a case like image recognition; your "features" would be the pixels of the image and your "labels" would be the main object in the image (e.g., "cat") from a fixed set of "classes" like "cat," "dog," "boat," etc.

Given that ML models are trained on numbers, one of the first problems we run into as data scientists is converting our non-numeric data into numbers that operate as features for training. There are many methods to do so, depending on the type of data we're dealing with. For "categorical" data (think of discrete categories like colors or types of flowers), we could just encode them as numbers (e.g., "red" = 0, "green" = 1, "pink" = 2, ...), but this can confuse the model, leading it to believe incorrectly that "red" and "green" are closer than "red" and "pink." We'll often use a method called "one-hot encoding" to combat this, which converts the categorical feature into a binary vector with only one bit "hot" (e.g., "red" = [1, 0, 0]) ensuring each category is independent.

For text data, we'll often use methods from natural language processing (NLP). These can involve "stopwording," a process to remove irrelevant words like "of," "and," and "the"; and "stemming" or "lemmatization," both of which are meant to turn similar words with common roots into the same word ("learn," "learns," and "learning" all get converted to "learn" for instance). This allows us to remove nonpredictive words, and to collapse words that are semantically similar. We then might decide we only want the top 10,000 most common words in our vocabulary, so we convert each document into a 10,000-element vector of word counts. This would potentially turn a large document into a dense 10,000-length vector of numbers, or a small document like a tweet into a very sparse vector. We also often consider "hashing," which allows us to use the full vocabulary but still constrain the number of features, by putting each word into a "hash bucket" that might collide with other words [15].

Featurization sometimes employs a technique known as Term Frequency/Inverse Document Frequency (TF/IDF) [16], which weights words that are uncommon overall but common in a given document more heavily (for instance, "machine" and "learning" appear more in this book than in all books generally). We can also use "word embeddings [17]," or simple neural networks that learn vectors for each word such that contextually similar words are "close" to each other. These can learn some fairly deep semantics, even allowing you to "do math" on the learned vectors in interesting ways. Consider the famous example in the field: if you add the vectors "King" – "Man" + "Woman," the closest vector result will be "Queen." Word2Vec became famous in this space, later becoming somewhat infamous as people realized it was not only encoding similarity but also algorithmic bias (sexism and racism) in the underlying data [18].

A key part of featurization is "feature engineering," where you reduce your data to only those components that are relevant to the problem at hand. An example may help. Consider a networking case where you're attempting to detect anomalies. Your initial data may be the timestamp and size of every incoming and outgoing packet on every switch. This is a huge amount of data, most of which is likely irrelevant. You may choose to do feature engineering by aggregating the number of requests in a given time window with the average and maximum request sizes. You might also choose to do this at multiple levels of aggregation. For instance, 1 millisecond periods for the last 30 milliseconds, then 5 milliseconds periods for 30 milliseconds, etc. If you have existing, known anomalies, you can then generate a "labeled data set" and start training a model.

Training (or "fitting") a model is the process of taking an existing ML algorithm and using data to teach it to solve a given problem. To do so in a supervised learning problem (where we have data and labels we're trying to predict), we typically divide our data into different sets—the "training set" is data we show the model in order to train it, and the "validation set" is used to test our trained model and see how well it does on data it has not yet seen. Often a third "test" or "holdout" set is used to allow us to compare multiple models against each other on data that none of them has encountered. As data scientists, our job is to determine how we divide our data into those sets, trading off the size of data we have to train against versus the ability to test our final model candidates' performance. If we do our jobs well, we end up with models that "generalize" and can work well in production systems on new data. If we do our jobs poorly, we could end up "overfitting" and our model learns to perform well on the training data but performs poorly on the test data. Evaluating the model throughout training on the validation data helps to minimize overfitting.

It is the need for training data, in part, that drove the "big data" revolution. As companies sought to glean intelligence from their data, they started instrumenting and logging everything to the point where modern tech giants like Microsoft [19] and Google [20] have exabytes of data used for training models.

2.3.2 Data Quality: Big Data Is (Often) Not Enough

Data is not enough to drive a quality model. ML, even more than other areas of software, is vulnerable to the "garbage in, garbage out" curse. Gathering petabytes of the wrong data is useless, and even with valid data there are often issues that must be addressed before you can make use of it in model building. An exhaustive list of all data quality issues is beyond the scope of this section, but we'll discuss a few in detail to give you a sense of the techniques available and the types of problems ML practitioners encounter.

Often in ML problems we run into situations where we're trying to categorize incoming data into one of two or more classes, and one class may be far more prevalent than the others. Consider spam detection where spam emails are far more common than non-spam, or breach detection where most network traffic is not a breach. In "unbalanced" or "skewed" cases like this, you might need to throw away data in the majority class to create greater balance, or use artificial means to expand the minority classes by either duplicating data in those classes or using data-generation techniques like Synthetic Minority Over-Sampling Technique (SMOTE) [21]. The same phenomenon can occur with features as well. Think of a medical scenario where blood type is a feature; AB- patients will be incredibly rare, which can (among other things) cause ML models to ignore that feature, even if it winds up being highly predictive. Similar data augmentation techniques can help solve these issues as well.

Another frequent issue in ML is the "curse of dimensionality," which is actually a family of problems that occur when the number of features in your data grows beyond a handful into the realm of hundreds, thousands, or even hundreds of thousands, potentially dwarfing your number of samples. When you're trying to train a model with that many features, you may not have enough data to teach your model—consider trying to learn a model to draw a squiggly line from just two or three points. ML practitioners deal with these issues by reducing the number of features and/or adding more data. We'll often examine our features and do "significance testing" to determine which features have the most predictive power for our models and throw out the others. We can also use techniques like principal component analysis (PCA) [22] to transform the original features into a new composite feature space to enable us to cherry-pick the most predictive constructed features from this new space. PCA is powerful in situations where the input features are large and sparse, such as in image processing. It can consolidate those features into far fewer cleanly separated composite features, making the model's training much easier.

Often with new systems you'll run into the opposite problem—the cold start. How can you bootstrap a ML system when you have no existing data? Most times, the best answer is to start collecting data first and build the ML components later. However, if you're working on a new system in a known domain, you can use methods of simulation and data augmentation to help bootstrap your model. For example, when building out a new network, you may have insights into what traffic you expect based on your domain knowledge of networking, and you can use this to build a simulation and use that generated data to create your initial model. As you gather data, you can tune your simulation to better model your network and use augmentation techniques to extend your data set. This feedback loop can be quite effective.

These are just a few of the problems you can encounter with data, and knowing how to choose or build the correct features and select the most appropriate model is as much art as science. It comes with experience, domain expertise, and experimentation. New techniques like auto-ML [23] and new tools like PROSE [24] can help alleviate some of the burden, but with any ML project, we still expect to spend most of our development time processing, cleaning, and experimenting with data.

2.3.3 Anomalies and Clusters

We commonly break ML down into two main types: supervised learning where we know what we're looking for and have knowledge of the target labels, and unsupervised learning where we are trying to learn classes or inferences without target labels. This section is devoted to unsupervised learning techniques.

Sometimes we wind up with data sets where we believe there may be some underlying structure, but we aren't sure and need to find out. Clustering can help us discover this structure by grouping similar items together in various ways. We can then examine the features of items in the same cluster to determine what characteristics make items similar and whether we think those have genuine real-world meaning or are just an artifact of the data set we've gathered. Clustering comes in several different forms, but the common method is grouping items based on computing the distance between their features. This means that all of our data must be turned into a numeric form where that distance measure has some meaning, using various means like one-hot vectors or embeddings as described earlier. One example is k-means clustering [25] where "k" different clusters are computed based on the most predictive centroids of the data set given the distance measure you're using.

Clustering can also be used to detect data points that seem abnormal—anomalies or outliers. Once we have clustered our data and know what it looks like, points that are too far from any given cluster can be considered anomalous. This is just one technique in a family of methods for anomaly detection, which is useful in a wide variety of fields but can be pivotal in the networking space to discover failures, for example. Since this is an unsupervised method, we don't know *a priori* what an anomaly looks like, and we rely on our models, experimentation, and domain expertise to choose the right threshold (e.g., what is "too far" from a cluster). Instead of clustering, we might use methods from time-series forecasting to determine, for instance, if the traffic pattern looks right for this time of day/week/month. We could do this by using a seasonally adjusted moving average or potentially Auto-Regressive Integrated Moving Average (ARIMA) methods [26] and then comparing our actual data against the results of our forecasting. Often in production systems these may be combined with other models (some even supervised if we have labeled data) to give a better answer. In networking, as will be seen in the next chapter, several signals will move in the same direction at the same (or similar) times and can be indicative of cascade failures or other correlated issues. Looking for correlation among multiple input signals can help you identify emerging and chronic issues, and tracking these over time can lead you to labeled data set creation allowing for supervised models to be trained.

2.3.4 Learning under Supervision

Supervised learning is by far the most common form of ML. When you know what you're trying to predict and have existing examples and known target labels, then you have a supervised learning problem. Consider the example from the previous section of detecting anomalies in networks: one typical way that people try to solve this problem is to find previous network anomalies, label them as such, and then train a model to classify incoming data. Note that this differs from the unsupervised method in that you need labeled data, but it can perform better in some cases and can potentially give you targeted answers as to what type of network issue you might be seeing. One flaw with this, however, is that it can only predict issues that it has seen or are similar to ones it has seen. This is why it may not work well for problems like breach detection where the bad actors constantly change tactics. In cases like that, we might consider combining our supervised model with an unsupervised method, which could potentially be stronger than either individually. This technique of *semi-supervised* learning uses the unlabeled data to better understand the labeled data's distribution, enabling the model to generalize better as new data is encountered.

Supervised methods typically break down into two types: classification models that try to predict the class of an item, such as "it's a cat" (for a *multi-class* model) or "yes, this is an issue" (for a *binary* model), and regression models that give a numeric prediction like "we expect 300 m rps." These models range in complexity from simple line-fitting (linear and logistic regression) to complex Decision Tree families. Much of the work in ML during the period before DL burst onto the scene was devoted to creating more complex and high-performing models. A robust discussion of ML models is beyond the scope of this chapter (and most books), but there exist few techniques that are still widely used and capable in certain domains of competing or beating DL models, often at a fraction of the cost in training and scoring time, like the Boosted Decision Trees described at the end of this section.

Machine learning researchers know that while a model they train may perform well on some examples, it can do poorly on many others. Often, attempting to train a model to do well on all examples would result in lower aggregate performance. This problem led them to realize they could segment their data and train different models targeted at particular subsets of the data, *ensembling* (or combining) them together to produce a final result far better than the result of any of the individual models. This *weighted ensemble* model-of-models method came to dominate Kaggle (https://www.kaggle.com/) and other public ML competitions and produce robust models in production; it can even allow existing models to adapt to new data without forcing people to discard all of their existing work by just ensembling in a new submodel targeted at the new data segment.

Eventually, researchers realized they could more effectively target weaknesses in their existing ensemble by watching the error gradients (error gradients are discussed later in the "Deep Learning" section). This signal allowed them to build a new model targeting the weak points, add that new model to the ensemble, and iterate. After a few iterations, this *gradient boosting* process resulted in a model with higher performance than a similar-sized ensemble, and *much* higher performance than any single model. These gradient boosted trees are state-of-the-art for non-DL techniques now, but there's no reason to think we won't see advances beyond them in the future, especially as the field of auto-ML advances (see Section 2.5.5).

2.3.5 Learning to Learn

2.3.5.1 Retraining and Dynamic Learning

Once you deploy a supervised learning system into production, how do you ensure it continues to perform? We'll go into more detail on the end-to-end process in Section 2.5.1; the primary mechanism is the capture of new labeled data and the regular retraining of the model. Most ML models improve their performance as they are exposed to new data from which they learn, and this process can repeat over time, resulting in gradual improvements. Taking this iterative process to the extreme, we wind up with a process called *online learning* where models are structured in such a way that they retrain continuously, updating their best estimates at each exposure. We can use real-time signals from users and systems to tune these models (e.g., did the user click on the ad? What was the actual latency of the request?). *Vowpal Wabbit* is one example of such a system, open sourced by Yahoo and currently maintained by Microsoft, but there are many others. These systems lend themselves well to unsupervised learning problems in the wild, but can often learn biased models and are vulnerable to gaming and bad actors.

2.3.5.2 Reinforcement Learning

Although unsupervised and supervised models are incredibly useful, neither of them falls into the conventional definition of "intelligence." Where are the chess players? Where is the self-driving car? How do we teach machines to teach themselves? This is the field of reinforcement learning (RL) or ML methods where the resulting models become better through positive and negative reinforcement. A full discussion of RL is beyond the scope of this chapter [27], but an understanding of the basics is important and will help you understand how DL is impacting this area as well.

Reinforcement learning systems work through the definition of a concept called a *Q-function*, which is a convenient mathematical representation of the expected reward for a given action. For instance, if I were to take your queen on this current move, what's the likelihood that I would go on to win the game? My Q-function would give me its prediction, and that would influence my behavior. As I continue to play multiple games, I keep teaching my Q-function to produce better reward estimates, leading me to play better games. This same technique scales far beyond chess, and as we'll see with deep reinforcement learning (deep RL) [28], it can be used to tackle games as challenging as Go and problems as complex as self-driving cars.

2.4 DEEP LEARNING—THE PROMISE BEHIND THE HYPE

2.4.1 What Is Deep Learning and Where Did It Come From?

I've briefly mentioned DL in previous sections of this chapter, but I haven't gone into details as to what it is, how it works, and why it has suddenly come to such prominence. That changes now. As mentioned in the history section, neural networks had been all but abandoned by most in the ML field except for a few isolated teams convinced their previously shown promise could be realized with sufficient time and effort. Their dedication paid off earlier this decade as a confluence of techniques were all brought to bear. "Backpropagation," "stochastic gradient descent," and "nonlinear activation functions" all combined to allow training of deeper networks with fewer resources that could learn ever more complicated nonlinear functions. In the following section, I'll give you a bit of background on each of those, the new types of networks they enable, and the problems they can (and can't) solve. Bear with me as I get a bit "math-y," but I'll try and keep it to a minimum.

2.4.1.1 Back-Propagation

Back-propagation [29], introduced by Rumelhart, Hinton, and Williams in 1986, is the technique that allows neural networks to learn from every prediction. We are creating these complex networks, which model large nonlinear functions, but if we ensure that they are *differentiable*, then back-propagation can work. Differentiable functions mean that we can differentiate these functions and get a new function that allows us to compute the rate of change in the original function (think of "location" as the original function, and "velocity" as the differentiated function [or rate of change in location]). We *forward-propagate* the signal from our current input value until we reach the end of the network, and then we compare against our expected value or "label." Once we have those differences at the last layer, we can *back-propagate* those differences through the network, with fractional differences (the partial derivatives of the error with respect to each weight) adjusting the network weights and biases, gradually pushing the network in the right direction (Figure 2.2).

2.4.1.2 Optimization Functions and Stochastic Gradient Descent

One of the biggest problems with optimizing networks using back-propagation was the actual optimization process. General optimization uses a technique called "gradient descent" (GD), which looks at the error in the current result versus the error in previous results and pushes the function "downhill" (i.e., in the direction of descending gradient). With deep networks containing potentially hundreds of millions of weights and biases and tens of millions of input data points, it's impossible to process the entire input and update all of the weights in a single gradient step. Stochastic gradient descent (SGD) simply solves

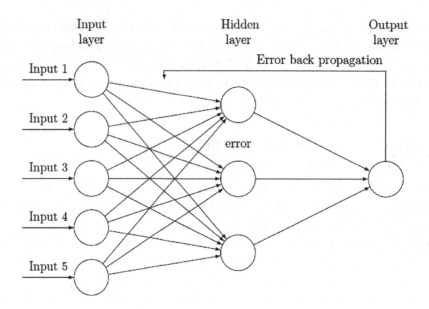

FIGURE 2.2 Back-propagation.

this problem: it pulls a single sample from the input, runs the network, and adjusts the gradient based on the error in that single sample.

Training once on the entire input set is known as an *epoch*, so GD works by running through an entire epoch before updating the weights, doing so for multiple epochs until we reach our predefined error threshold for stopping or realize we've reached our limit (the network is not getting any better or we've run out of time). Stochastic gradient descent runs through multiple epochs in the same fashion but updates the weights after every single example from the input, possibly shuffling the input set in between epochs—think of GD as walking straight downhill to the bottom, where SGD stumbles about, but gradually heads downhill in the same direction.

Since SGD, we've invented many new optimization functions that improve upon it (converging faster). I won't go into sufficient detail for you to implement any of these, since they are already implemented in most toolkits, but hope to explain them in enough detail that you can make the right choices. The simplest is *SGD with momentum*. This is a shuffling downhill walk, but as you walk in the same direction you stumble faster. Mini-batch gradient descent (MBGD) [30] is like SGD, but in this case, you process multiple examples at a time. This makes it more likely you'll stumble a bit less randomly at the expense of more of your GPU's memory and can be combined with momentum for further gains. Adaptive gradient descent (AdaGrad) [31] stumbles more aggressively downhill in directions that seem promising because they are more stable, for each example from the input or mini-batch. Root mean square propagation (RMSProp) [32] is like AdaGrad, but it uses a decaying moving average to work across multiple recent gradients. Adaptive Moment Estimation (ADAM) [33] is the current favorite and attempts to combine the benefits of AdaGrad and RMSProp.

2.4.1.3 Sigmoid, Rectified Linear Unit, and Beyond

I mentioned earlier that deep networks model large, nonlinear formulae. This differs from early neural network efforts that modeled simple linear equations by adding *nonlinear activation functions* between layers. Deep networks accomplish this by adding an "activation function" after a neuron, controlling whether its signal propagates down the network and allowing it to turn off for some inputs. If that activation function is nonlinear, the network can learn to control neurons in incredibly complex ways.

During the early days of DL, we used simple nonlinearities like Tanh and Sigmoid that we were already familiar with from other applications. These worked well (and are sometimes still used), but they are computationally expensive and can significantly increase training and evaluation times in large networks. We found that in many cases, a simple nonlinearity letting through positive values and suppressing negative values worked quite well. This rectified linear unit (ReLU) [34] is a simple piecewise-linear function that leaves positives alone and sets negatives to zero and is one of the most common activation functions in practice.

Several recent modifications to ReLU have been proposed in the past few years in attempts to improve accuracy and generalizability of networks while keeping ReLUs performance characteristics. Leaky ReLU [35] modifies ReLU by allowing a small constant amount of negative signal through, while parameterized ReLU [35] turns that constant into another network parameter that is learned during training, which increases the training time and size of the network without impacting the evaluation burden. Activation functions continue to be an active area of research, so I have no recommendation here since it would likely be out of date by the time this is published.

2.4.2 Whole New Types of Networks

Deep neural networks have evolved from their basic neural network roots, going from simple *dense networks* to networks with their own custom neuron types and complicated topologies that are tuned for helping them solve particular tasks. In this section, we'll discuss the primary two flavors of networks in use today: convolutional neural networks (CNNs) and recurrent neural networks (RNNs) as well as their dense network ancestor.

2.4.2.1 Dense Networks

Deep networks evolved from simpler neural networks, and often for straightforward classification problems we can still train simple dense networks of fully connected layers with nonlinear activation functions and get fantastic results. For instance, the network in Figure 2.3 is a simple dense network that predicts whether a transaction is fraudulent.

2.4.2.2 CNNs

Convolutional neural networks [36] are neural networks with specialized *convolutional* neurons. These are fantastically effective at processing image data because these convolutions are able to learn to pull out predictive features from local structure. Convolutions are small matrices that *stride* across the input matrix (e.g., the pixels in an image) and *convolve*

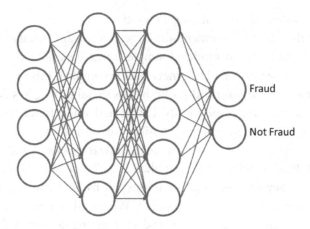

FIGURE 2.3   Dense fraud prediction network.

with them to produce new outputs, which are then *pooled* in a subsequent layer to focus in, increasing the *receptive field* of subsequent layers. Stacking these layers allows subsequent convolutions to learn even higher-level features so that at the beginning, the network may be learning things like "this is an edge," but in the final convolution layer it might be learning "this is a dog's ear."

Typically, these CNNs are used on image data, and the explosion of DL onto the scene was actually due to a CNN called AlexNet [12] (named after its creator Alex Krizhevsky, in partnership with his adviser G. Hinton and I. Sutskever), which dominated the ImageNet challenge for image recognition (e.g., "this is a picture of a cat") in 2012. Since then, CNNs have gone on to dominate the ImageNet challenge in various forms but have also expanded beyond images to many other forms of data with local structure. They were used for image and video generation, and with "one-dimensional convolutions" they have even replaced more complicated network structures. Understanding CNNs is core to understanding DL, and they are likely to be core to DL solutions for years to come.

2.4.2.3 Recurrent Neural Networks, Long Short-Term Memory Networks, Gated Recurrent Units

Not all data has local structure. Speech, text, and other sequential data often have a combination of local structure and long-term trend or structural features, which need to be captured in order to produce an effective prediction. Recurrent neural networks [37] (RNNs) are one solution to this problem, with internal *recurrence* allowing previous network values to feed into current results and letting the network learn long-term structure. These RNNs showed promising results on sequential data (language translation, etc.), but they were prone to issues, which often caused network training to fail. Because they had to back-propagate gradients across both space and time (previous values) by unrolling the network, the resulting gradients were prone to degenerating, either exploding or vanishing and causing the network to fail to converge.

Researchers developed a few different techniques to combat this problem, with two currently dominating the scene. Long short-term memory (LSTM) networks exchange the

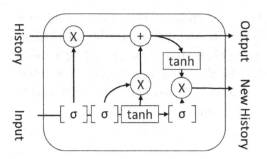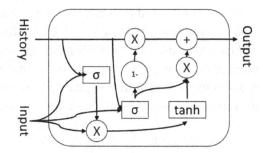

FIGURE 2.4   LSTMs versus GRUs.

basic recurrent cell for a more complicated cell that learns to forget using a *forget gate* (Figure 2.4). Gated recurrent units (GRUs) [37] are an alternate recurrent cell replacement with a simpler structure that trains faster but has less expressive value (Figure 2.4). The field is still debating which is more effective in practice, but both seem effective in combating the vanishing/exploding gradient problems.

2.4.2.4 Attention Networks

Researchers realized when focusing on various RNN models for machine translation, for instance, that the network was learning to encode the entire context of a sentence into the outputs at the last hidden layer. They would run a sentence through the network, and when it hit the end-of-sentence token, at that point it had to use the information it had learned to produce a full translation based on just the information in that last output layer. What if the network was allowed to look at previous inputs when it made its decision about each word in the translation? What if we let it learn how to *pay attention* to various parts of the input for each part of its output? Attention mechanisms [38] modify existing networks by adding some form of memory of previous inputs, similar to LSTM but more explicit. These modified networks costs more in RAM, as you may need to store attention values for each input/output token combination, but they can be dramatically more accurate than their LSTM-style counterparts for some problems. Attention mechanisms are an active area of research, and there is no current "best practice" in this space, so discussion of any mechanism in detail is premature.

2.4.2.5 Mixed Models and Generative Adversarial Networks

Some tasks have both local structure and a requirement for long-term focus—consider video processing, image captioning [39], or correlating incoming time-series signals. We can often produce mixed models (CNNs + LSTMs, for instance) that produce far better results than either could produce alone.

We've also found that models can be trained together in an adversarial fashion to generate new data that mimics real-world inputs in a process called generative adversarial networks (GANs) [40]. These GANs combine a generator network that can generate new fake inputs and a discriminator network that can tell fake data from real data. We train these together until the discriminator is totally confused, and at that point we determine that the generator has learned to create fake input that looks real enough to fool the discriminator (and in some cases the human eye). Currently, GANs are useful for generating fake images and have been used for enhancing existing images to higher resolutions, resulting in much more realistic outputs than current methods like bicubic sampling, but they hold most promise in the area of training data generation for domains where gathering training data is expensive or otherwise difficult (e.g., some medical data).

2.4.3 What Can Deep Learning Do?

2.4.3.1 Images

Convolutional neural networks and image recognition gave DL recognition onto the world stage. Although we started with simplified image recognition (e.g., "this is a cat"), but as DL methods evolved, we've been able to model much more complex objects and actions. Object detection models are capable of not only telling you that "this is a cat," but also *where* that cat is in the image by identifying a bounding box containing the object. The models typically do this through a mechanism called *regions of interest* where several regions are proposed for each label and the resulting prediction gives probabilities based on label/region combinations (Figure 2.5).

We've gone beyond even those models recently with *semantic* and *instance segmentation* [41]. These models generate predictions on a pixel-by-pixel basis telling you exactly what class each pixel in the image belongs to. Semantic segmentation gives you the class but can't differentiate between different *instances* of that class—for instance, a pair of cats would just be a single "cat" blob. Instance segmentation takes this one step and is capable of telling each instance of sheep apart from the others (Figure 2.6). These are both very active areas of research, and we expect the performance of these models to dramatically increase over the next few years as new labeled data sets are produced in this area. These methods are being deployed currently in "smart city" scenarios for car and pedestrian counting,

FIGURE 2.5 Recognition versus object detection label; which one is recognition versus detection.

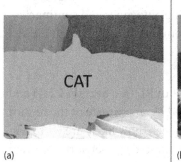 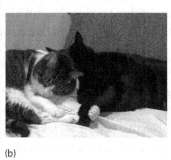 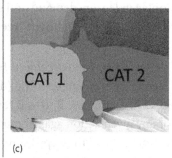

(a)   (b)   (c)

FIGURE 2.6 Semantic versus instance segmentation: (a) semantic segmentation, (b) original image, and (c) instance segmentation.

allowing better traffic estimation and could allow smart networks to become more adaptive to human traffic patterns.

2.4.3.2 Sequential (Text, Speech)

Recurrent neural network methods like LSTM and GRU came to prominence in the areas of machine translation and speech-to-text processing. These efforts continue with attention networks, and as larger and more robust data sets surface in these domains, we expect results to only improve. We've found in practice that once we train networks to translate between two languages, we can use that network to bootstrap training for additional languages, and the resulting network can often do a better job of translating both languages. This form of *transfer learning* [42] is common across DL, but in machine translation it is proving remarkably resilient, enabling new translation networks to be trained from very few examples.

These attention and recurrent networks are also making progress in processing large-scale text data, with some networks being trained to produce summary text from large corpora, others learning to predict sentiment, and still more learning more robust *embedding* of meaning and context that can be used to drive other predictive models. These models will revolutionize contact and call centers as context is pulled from previous call logs and manuals, made searchable, and incoming calls are parsed and turned into intelligent queries. This is an active area of research, and one area in which we as an industry need to guard against built-in bias in our training data, as we've seen word embeddings learned from existing text corpora like newspapers displaying sexist and racist biases [18].

2.4.3.3 Mixed (Video)

Video data combines the local structure of images with a long-term sequential nature. Currently, most video processing models typically use keyframing techniques to process single images with CNN models trained on image data, but the industry has been actively researching methods to use sequential models like RNNs and attention mechanisms to learn long-term structure from video streams. We've seen exciting research in video summarization and even video generation, and as video data sets become more readily available, we expect this field to become increasingly active. These techniques may revolutionize video-on-demand and streaming services by providing autogenerated summarization, intelligent "highlight" reels, and even improved data compression models [43].

2.4.3.4 Deep Reinforcement Learning

Deep reinforcement learning (deep RL) [44] takes the concept of RL (see Section 2.3.4) and uses DL to improve it. If you remember, the Q-function is used as an estimate of the reward for any given action against our objective (e.g., if we take the queen, how likely are we to win the match?). With deep RL, we replace a simple Q-function with a deep network, allowing our Q-function to learn much more complex strategies for rewards. In the case of AlphaGo, Google used a complex Q-function with a 51-layer CNN encoding various domain-specific knowledge of the board, and over the course of thousands of training matches, this Q-function learned a representation complex enough to allow it to defeat the Go grandmaster. These deep RL techniques are incredibly robust areas of research right now, and self-learning systems based on deep RL are bound to make huge impacts in every area of automation.

2.4.3.5 Generative

I've previously mentioned GANs, but those are just one family of generative networks that exist. These networks can be trained to generate output in a variety of modalities, from neural-style transfer using simple CNN mixing to text generation using LSTMs and modern systems like LyreBird [45], Google's WaveNet [46], and Baidu's Deep Voice [47] who are using generative models to create speech in a variety of styles. As these models mature, we will need to develop methods to ensure that they are used for good (better accessibility for the blind, for instance) rather than evil (an existential assault on truth, as real-sounding fraudulent "recordings" can be generated by anyone with a GPU).

2.5 THE PRESENT AND FUTURE OF ARTIFICIAL INTELLIGENCE

2.5.1 Artificial Intelligence in the Wild

Machine learning doesn't live in a vacuum. In the real world, ML needs to be incorporated into existing systems and deployed into production, and then used by people either directly or indirectly in order to provide value. With the incredible explosion of research in DL, we've seen a growing gap between the published results in academic sites like arXiv.org and actual production-deployed models. This is due in part to the fantastic rate of change, and in part to a gap in tooling between model construction and model productionalization, which we expect to close rapidly leading to even faster *use* of our progress in AI in real-world scenarios.

This naturally leads to the question, What does it take to put a model into production? There are several aspects between modeling and experimentation and having a robust production deployment. First, the majority of any ML project is in data preparation, so building a robust data pipeline is key. This encompasses not just data acquisition but cleansing (and testing/regression of your cleansing process, as well as recleansing as it changes). It also accounts for data provenance—where did your data come from? This is increasingly important as General Data Protection Regulation (GDPR) [48] and other privacy laws roll out.

Next, the model itself needs to evolve. We'll need versioning, and we need to know what data that version was trained on and how it performed in test. We'll need the ability to "flight" new models—A/B testing to determine how well they do on real data, and staged rollouts to ensure they perform well as they come under load. We need robust monitoring for speed and accuracy, with an accuracy measure appropriate to the system (e.g., cancer prediction doesn't value false-positives and false-negatives the same). Models also "expire"—as new data comes in and the system evolves, previously labeled data may become less accurate and model predictions may start failing. This failure highlights the need for tracking accuracy over time, evaluation of missed predictions, and a robust mechanism for retraining and re-deploying your models.

Finally, we need to consider the deployment itself—are we dockerizing [49] the model and deploying containers (self-contained application+OS instances) into the cloud? Are we running on GPU or CPU, or do we have custom hardware Application-Specific Integrated Circuits (ASICs) or Field-Programmable Gate Arrays (FPGAs)? Are we deploying on devices? If so, how do we ensure we can push updates or support old versions? Does it make sense to have hierarchical models, for example, where a simpler potentially compressed model runs on an IoT device and determines whether to send batches of data to a more complex cloud-based model for more detailed analysis?

These productionalization scenarios are more complex than traditional software systems but share a lot of the common cross-cutting concerns (logging, monitoring, fault-detection and recovery, Continuous Integration/Continuous Delivery [CI/CD]), so your existing insights will serve you well here. Where your instincts break are where your determinism assumptions fail. Remember that ML systems are probabilistic, so some percentage of misprediction and failure is inevitable, 100% accuracy in training is a bug (overfitting) and is impossible in the real world. Tools like Microsoft's Azure Machine Learning Workbench [50], the recently announced Linux Foundation open source Acumos project, and Pachyderm [51] have evolved to meet some of these needs, and we expect more tools to surface and these tools to continue evolving.

2.5.2 Understanding, Speaking, and Translating

As we've seen earlier, existing DL models have already made incredible strides in the areas of translation, speech-to-text, and text-to-speech systems. We expect this progress to continue over the next decade and, with model compression and quantization, to be deployed on more places (the Babelfish from *Hitchhiker's Guide to the Galaxy* is almost here). Additionally, we see advances in contextual inference and understanding becoming increasingly important as new data sets and corpora are made available (through Kaggle competitions and other means). This will lead to improvements to sentiment analysis at first, but will then branch out into document summarization and even automining of data warehouses by intelligent agents. Sentiment analysis is key to customer churn and customer service scenarios—in churn we can tell when customers are angry and likely to leave, and during an automated customer service session, sensing customer frustration and directing them to a human agent can save their business.

2.5.3 Reasoning about Pictures and Video

Image processing was one of the first domains revolutionized by DL models, and at this point, basic recognition is almost considered a solved problem. Researchers are moving on to the more complicated tasks of instance segmentation, video processing, and semantic extraction. Combining these techniques with the earlier speech processing techniques will allow for complete video processing solutions (like Microsoft's Video Indexer [52]) to continue improving, introducing not just object and person detection and identification throughout the video, but multilingual autocaptioning, autosummarization, and robust metadata tagging.

We can then look at the future of generative models in this space—we'll see generative models first take root in "playground" apps ("make me a funny image based on X"), but then extend to applications for creatives ("fix the eyes to look more like Y"). Eventually, they'll extend to full-on generation of images and video based on mere descriptions, or large visually compelling modifications of existing work. This will pose serious questions around fair use, ownership, and copyright that will need to be resolved.

Generative models will also be used to autogenerate training data in scenarios where it is difficult or questionable to gather (as mentioned earlier), and this coupled with the increasing computational power of cloud-based GPUs and custom ASICs will result in significant advances in model performance in medical diagnostics, drug discovery, autonomous networks, and security.

2.5.4 Adversaries of the Future

Generative models hold other promises in store as well, particularly when we consider their use in adversarial situations. What happens to our social networks when #FakeNews stories that are autogenerated by deep models are indistinguishable (or better) than those generated by paid bad actors? How does this impact our political systems?

Once generative models can, with just a small amount of voice or image data, produce realistic-sounding or looking fake audio or video recordings of anyone, what does that do to the evidentiary process? How do we litigate bad behavior in the public square when we have no way of verifying whether it actually occurred based on recorded evidence? We've already seen models capable of removing watermarks from images, so tagging video streams with watermarks would be a trivial postgenerative process. We'll need to evolve ways of identifying fraudulent material in the face of these threats, and researchers are actively looking into methods to detect the outputs of generative models.

Current deep models are also prone to mislabeling in the face of adversarial examples, because they're navigating such a complex search space in order to produce their predictions. We've seen examples of this in image detection models where a small amount of "smart noise" can cause a model to misidentify a gibbon as an ostrich, and more significant examples where a self-driving vision model misidentified a stop sign due to some noise (special tape) applied to the sign. We can expect to see an arms race here between fraudsters and hackers and the companies, governments, and researchers generating models.

Privacy can also be an issue with deep models, as they encode a large amount of information in their parameters. We've seen example of DL models generated for face detection being able to actually reproduce training images from the trained model using a process called deconvolution [53]. With laws like GDPR, this leads us to a discussion of data privacy in the face of deep models—if someone wants their information removed, do we need to discard all models trained using it? Is there a way to protect us from having to do so? These are areas of active research, with chained models looking like they might provide a solution.

2.5.5 Machines Learning to Make Learning Machines

What happens when we turn ML techniques on themselves? How can we teach machines to learn more effectively? This area of research known by names such as meta-learning and auto-ML is a burgeoning area of research right now. Some of the most painful parts of DL research at the moment is *hyperparameter tuning* and *model selection*. Since it sometimes takes days or weeks to train a model, picking the right model structure, optimization techniques, learning rates, and other hyperparameters can make the difference between success and failure. We've been busy designing systems that will automatically go through this process, navigating the hyperparameter search space, and, in some cases, designing whole new model topologies based on a form of meta-learning (or *learning about learning*).

As GPUs become more prevalent, compute power on the whole increases, and more labeled data sets arise, this form of meta-learning will increase. Currently, the big players are sharing their findings (new neuron types, etc.), but we expect that to become rarer as new neuronal structures become valuable Intellectual Property (IP). It also won't be long before the structures of new neurons and networks become more complicated than researchers can easily understand, and the machines start superseding our knowledge in even the ML space. Traceability, understandability, and debuggability become key in these scenarios, as we're forced to trust systems that even their creators don't necessarily understand.

2.5.6 Artificial Intelligence's Industrial Revolution

The AI revolution will help to drive a network that is self-healing, self-securing, and adaptive to changing needs. With the revolution in AI systems, networks can detect early patterns of cyberattacks, automatically deploy resources where needed as traffic patterns change and evolve, and improve automated routing around network failures and other issues. The rest of this book will discuss these scenarios in more detail, giving you a sense for what can be accomplished once AI becomes a pervasive part of the network.

REFERENCES

1. John McCarthy (attributed in Vardi in 2012).
2. Russell, S., Norvig, P., History of artificial intelligence, in *Artificial Intelligence: A Modern Approach* (Prentice Hall, Upper Saddle River, NJ), p. 16.
3. Rosenblatt, F., *Principles of Neurodynamics: Perceptrons and the Theory of Brain Mechanisms* (Spartan, Washington, DC, 1962).
4. Turing, A., Computing machinery and intelligence, *Mind*, 49, 433–460 (1950).

5. Russell, S., Norvig, P., History of artificial intelligence, in *Artificial Intelligence: A Modern Approach* (Prentice Hall, Upper Saddle River, NJ), p. 18.

6. Minsky, M., Darrach, B., Life (1970).

7. Minsky, M., Papert, S., *Perceptrons* (MIT Press, Oxford, UK, 1969).

8. Larson, E., Computer chess gets good, in *A Brief History of Computer Chess* (https://thebest-schools.org/magazine/brief-history-of-computer-chess/)

9. E.g. quote from Google's Chief Economist Hal Varian: "sexy job in the 2010s is to be a statistician" (https://www.youtube.com/watch?v=D4FQsYTbLoI)

10. https://spark.apache.org/docs/latest/ml-guide.html

11. https://www.h2o.ai/

12. Krizhevsky, A., Sutskever, I., Hinton, G., ImageNet classification with deep convolutional neural networks, *Neural Information Processing Systems*, 1, 1097–1105 (2012).

13. Rumelhart, D. E., Hinton, G. E., Williams, R. J., Learning internal representations by error propagation, in *Parallel Distributed Processing: Explorations in the Microstructure of Cognition. Volume 1: Foundations* (MIT Press, Cambridge, MA), pp. 318–362.

14. LeCun, Y., Gradient-based learning applied to document recognition, *Proceedings of the IEEE*, 86, 2278–2324 (1998).

15. http://scikit-learn.org/stable/modules/feature_extraction.html#vectorizing-a-large-text-corpus-with-the-hashing-trick

16. https://spark.apache.org/docs/latest/ml-features.html#tf-idf

17. Mikolov, T., Sutskever, I., Chen, K. et al., Distributed representation of words and phrases and their compositionality, in *Neural Information Processing Systems* (2013).

18. Bolukbasi, T., Chang, K., Zou, J., Man is to computer programmer as woman is to homemaker? Debiasing word embeddings (https://arxiv.org/abs/1607.06520)

19. https://www.datanami.com/2015/04/29/microsoft-scales-data-lake-into-exabyte-territory/

20. https://www.cirrusinsight.com/blog/much-data-google-store

21. http://contrib.scikit-learn.org/imbalanced-learn/stable/over_sampling.html#smote-adasyn

22. http://scikit-learn.org/stable/modules/decomposition.html#pca

23. https://github.com/automl/auto-sklearn

24. https://microsoft.github.io/prose/

25. http://scikit-learn.org/stable/modules/clustering.html#k-means

26. Brockwell, P. J., Davis, R. A., *Introduction to Time Series and Forecasting* (Springer, New York, 1996), Sections 3.3 and 8.3.

27. Sutton, R., Barto, A., *Reinforcement Learning: An Introduction* (Fairview, 1998).

28. https://www.youtube.com/watch?v=PtAIh9KSnjo

29. Rumelhart, D. E., Hinton, G. E., Williams, R. J., Learning internal representations by error propagation, in *Parallel Distributed Processing: Explorations in the Microstructure of Cognition. Volume 1: Foundations* (MIT Press, Cambridge, MA), pp. 318–362.

30. Li, M., Zhang, T., Chen, Y., Efficient mini-batch training for stochastic optimization (https://www.cs.cmu.edu/~muli/file/minibatch_sgd.pdf)

31. Duchi, J., Hazan, E., Singer, Y., Adaptive subgradient methods for online learning and stochastic optimization, *JMLR*, 12, 2121–2159 (2011) (http://jmlr.org/papers/volume12/duchi11a/duchi11a.pdf)

32. Introduced by G. Hinton during a lecture: https://www.youtube.com/watch?v=defQQqkXEfE

33. Kingma, D., Ba, J., ADAM: A method for stochastic optimization, in *ICLR* (2015) (https://arxiv.org/pdf/1412.6980.pdf)

34. Nair, V., Hinton, G., Rectified linear units improve restricted Boltzmann machines (http://www.cs.toronto.edu/~fritz/absps/reluICML.pdf)

35. Maas, A., Hannun, A., Ng, A., Rectifier nonlinearities improve neural network acoustic models, in ICML (2013) (http://web.stanford.edu/~awni/papers/relu_hybrid_icml2013_final.pdf)

36. Goodfellow, I., Bengio, Y., Courville, A., *Deep Learning*, Ch. 9 (MIT Press, Cambridge, MA, 2016).
37. Goodfellow, I., Bengio, Y., Courville, A., *Deep Learning*, Ch. 10 (MIT Press, Cambridge, MA, 2016).
38. Vaswani, A., Shazeer, N., Parmar, N. et al., Attention is all you need, in *Neural Information Processing Systems* (2017) (https://arxiv.org/abs/1706.03762)
39. Soh, M., Learning CNN-LSTM architectures for image caption generation (https://cs224d.stanford.edu/reports/msoh.pdf)
40. Goodfellow, I., Pouget-Abadie, J., Mirza, M. et al., Generative adversarial networks (https://arxiv.org/abs/1406.2661)
41. E.g. in https://arxiv.org/abs/1703.06870 "Mask R-CNN."
42. Goodfellow, I., Bengio, Y., Courville, A., *Deep Learning*, Ch. 1 (MIT Press, Cambridge, MA, 2016).
43. Hu, F., Pu, C., Gao, H. et al., An image compression and encryption scheme based on deep learning (https://arxiv.org/ftp/arxiv/papers/1608/1608.05001.pdf)
44. Li, Y., Deep reinforcement learning: An overview (https://arxiv.org/abs/1701.07274)
45. https://lyrebird.ai/
46. Van den Oord, A., Dieleman, S., Zen, H. et al., WaveNet: A generative model for raw audio (https://regmedia.co.uk/2016/09/09/wavenet.pdf)
47. http://research.baidu.com/deep-voice-2-multi-speaker-neural-text-speech/
48. https://www.eugdpr.org/
49. https://www.docker.com/
50. https://azure.microsoft.com/en-us/services/machine-learning-services/
51. http://www.pachyderm.io/
52. https://azure.microsoft.com/en-us/services/cognitive-services/video-indexer/
53. http://www.matthewzeiler.com/wp-content/uploads/2017/07/iccv2011.pdf

CHAPTER 3

The Shift to a Software-Defined Network

Brian Freeman and Paul Bartoli

CONTENTS

3.1 INTRODUCTION

"Mr. Watson, come here, I want to see you" was the first phrase that formed the foundation of the network 140 years ago. Since then, the network and its traffic have been growing at an exponential rate across national, regional, and edge data centers, and from wireline to wireless. In recent years, in order to deal with these massive changes, the industry has moved quickly to embrace network function virtualization (NFV) and software-defined networking (SDN). These two efforts combine to create a new environment for deploying and scaling services. Control and management of this environment requires new software ecosystems for service creation, orchestration, and marshalling of resources and services, configuration, and full life-cycle management. This chapter explains how the worlds of cloud technology, NFV, and SDN combined to create this new networking environment and goes on to discuss one of the next major areas of innovation and disruption: network artificial intelligence (AI), the application of AI to this ecosystem to, for example, achieve new, higher levels of management, monitoring, recovery, and predictive closed-loop control. This chapter discusses how the NFV and SDN ecosystems provide the means to enable network AI and describes an overall architecture.

3.2 HISTORY OF SOFTWARE-DEFINED NETWORKING

Software-defined networking has been in use for decades in telecommunications. In fact, it was one of the first commercial applications of computing [1]. It is interesting to see the similarities in problems and solutions that have occurred over time as networking evolved from session-oriented time division multiplexing (TDM) switching, to packet switching and to today's virtualized networking.

Early telecommunications networks started from mechanical switching systems with plug boards and human operators setting up and tearing down calls. As the networks grew in complexity and scale, a means to automate the task of making phone calls using early electromechanical machine/computers were designed and deployed to replace

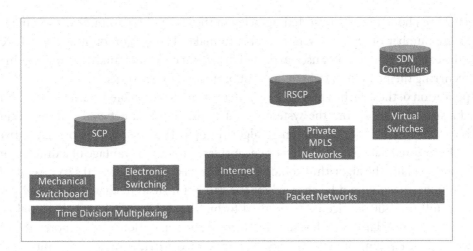

FIGURE 3.1   Evolution of telecommunications networks.

switchboard operators [2]. When electronic switching became possible through modern electronics like the transistor, the concept of stored program control was applied to network design. A computer program would collect various events, do simplified analysis, and trigger actions. The simple functional control loops would be the basis for advanced AI in communications networks, but let's start from the basics of what problems were being solved (Figure 3.1).

3.2.1 The First Software-Defined Networks—Separating the Signaling and Bearer Plane

Early telecommunications network had a simple task—analyze the request for a phone call and create a path through the network to connect calling party A with called party B. A simple task when there are simple connection options, but as the network grew bigger and bigger, it became difficult to find the "optimal" communication path through the network. It also became more complicated when the question included who should pay for the call, the calling party (normal) or the called party (collect calls).

As computers grew in power, it also occurred to engineers that more powerful services could be created if we separated the signaling path from the bearer path. This was the basis of signaling system number 6 standardization as the introduction of common channel signaling, which was eventually replaced with signaling system number 7 (SS7) [3]. The signaling between computers could be on a preexisting shared channel that would not need to be setup and torn down for each call. The separation of control and bearer planes enabled an awesome array of features defined only in software as a set of decisions.

A decision on the route could be done either by peer-to-peer communication or by a centralized algorithm based on the dialed digits. Additional data could be applied to the decision of the path and even the destination could be changed during the processing. Basically, as computers became fast enough to do additional analysis before the caller expected the phone to ring (post dialing delay in those days was around two seconds), an increasing number of features were available to make the decision on how and where to route the call. This trade-off of user-expected delay and computer analysis time is going to be a recurring theme even in today's Internet protocol (IP) networks.

Application of these techniques led to a better way to do automated collect calls. A caller dialed a special number and the system would translate it to a network routing number (NRN) and connect the call based on an algorithm [4]. This was the first overlay network where the original data was rewritten or encapsulated to take advantage of a different network routing plan. The algorithm could even decide based on the special service code that the calling party would not be charged for the call but instead to charge the called party. This was toll free 800 service in its original form. The technology led to the "intelligent network" (IN) standards that leveraged control plane separation to add more advanced services, enable equipment inter-operability and service provider inter-operability.

The centralized algorithm in the control plane included not only the basics to connect the calling and called parties and record information for billing but complex functions that could be put together in call processing decision trees. For example, the centralized algorithms could look at the calling parties phone number (Automatic Number Identification [ANI]) and make decisions on the area code (three digits) or NPA-NXX (six digits) to distribute calls to the closest call center. The algorithm could distribute calls in the morning to the East Coast of the US and in the evening to the West Coast of the US.

When AT&T added equipment in the central offices to play announcements and collect digits from the caller, the algorithm could add even more input into the decision on the destination. This also gave rise to the first TDM-based SDN, where private dialing plans were created for a corporate customer to be able to use custom dialing plans nationwide without a dedicated network [5]. This was virtualization of the TDM network—create a second private network as an overlay on the national public network. The combination of the algorithms, equipment for announcements, and digit collection and mapping of dialed numbers into NRNs was the first software-defined overlay network—in session-oriented phone calls.

The circuit-switched networks also went through a transformation from monolithic switching equipment that was contained in a mobile switching center (MSC in mobile networks) or a local exchange (in fixed networks) that took the separation of the control plane and user plane one step further. In this transformation, the signaling and service logic was separated from the switching equipment to make two specialized nodes—a server and a switch that could be physically separated and allowed the centralization of the server and its algorithms while retaining optimal placement of the switching equipment. The protocol to connect that was a joint effort between the Internet Engineering Task Force (IETF) and ITU-T SG-16 and was documented in the specification H.248 [6].

The real-time implementation of these algorithms was in Network Control Points or Signaling Control Points. These "controllers" would use the SS7 network to receive requests, provide instructions to switches, and enhance the data via the announcement and digit collection platforms. They managed the state of the custom private network and embodied centralized function for the customer. The controllers had supporting operation support systems (OSSs) that would allow the customer to change their private network in near real time—changing the preferred routes, adding additional dialing options, etc. It was a truly customer programmable environment even if the programming was typically through a Graphical User Interface (GUI) on an OSS rather than writing C or C++ code.

3.2.2 Network Management

As these large SDNs emerged, another set of problems occurred. Bursting of traffic could be observed as things in the real world caused mass calling. Networks had already seen congestion situations when natural disasters occurred like floods, tornadoes, or hurricanes and needed a mechanism to throttle traffic. The basic idea was to identify "likely to fail" calls and block them at the source so they did not consume the scarce resources at the impacted area. So, network management controls came into effect—an action that could be applied to stop traffic coming to a disaster area and only permit calls outbound from that area. This gave a priority to phones that were working and were being used to make outgoing calls from an affected area and blocked calls in to areas that might not even have phones still connected to the network.

With the advance of SDN, even more need for network management occurred. When a snowstorm hits, travel agencies are bombarded by their customers trying to replan their flights and travel arrangements. With only a set number of agents and or connections at a data center, the network needed to throttle calls to prevent high demand from one customer from blocking other customers' traffic.

The detection of these conditions (focused destination overloads) required gathering telemetry on ineffective attempts, calculating the source switches, and then putting time-based gating mechanisms on the source switched. The system that did this calculation and determined based on the telemetry what level of control (call gapping) and where to place the control was the Network Management Operations System (NEMOS) [7]. This was a case of an external network management algorithm using telemetry from the network (performance reports) to control a SDN. It could be argued that these were the first applications of rudimentary AI to telecommunications, albeit they were hard-coded algorithms.

As the private networks became larger, there was also the need to address fraud. The Call Detail Records made when every call was completed could be analyzed, summarized, and pattern matched to determine that the pattern of calls was likely fraud and then to call actions in the SDN to reduce fraud [8]. The end-to-end system of both the software-defined private overlay network and the analysis and control elements that comprise the network management systems in total make up the necessary parts of a SDN. In today's terms, this is ancient technology, but it was the groundwork for what would be needed for future networks like the public Internet.

3.2.3 The Public Internet and Growth of Virtual Private Internet Protocol Networks

When IP emerged as the winning protocol in packet networks, a similar set of drivers for its evolution occurred. It was initially purposefully designed in a distributed manner with no centralized control, and initially there was no separation of control and forwarding planes. Individual switches and routers made simple decisions—see a packet, look up destination, and forward the packet to the link toward the destination. Path was determined based on a local decision of link state and least cost path as viewed by the current point in the path. The only centralized decisions or algorithm might be the Domain Name System (DNS) service that translated the user-friendly destination name www.att.com into an IP address 12.1.2.3. This translation could vary by source but generally because of its caching and technical aspects really wasn't the fine-grained control needed.

Separation of the control plane from the user plane (a.k.a., bearer plane) started to occur with various link state and routing protocols like Border Gateway Protocol (BGP) to allow the decisions of where to route the packets to be more dynamic, but it still didn't provide any direct corollary to the private networks that were possible with TDM SDN. However, with a separation of control plane and signaling plane, the next step toward network virtualization was possible.

Multi-protocol label switching (MPLS), enabled by BGP signaling, allowed network operators to create customer specific routing tables so that only their end points were in the routing table. These routing tables created virtual private network (VPN) where overlapping private address space (10.1.2.3) could be used in multiple networks simultaneously just like in TDM where extension 10123 could be used in multiple private dialing plans. This virtualized private network was an entirely SDN in IP, a private Internet of destinations that were part of the same company and did not risk interaction with the public Internet. This private Internet was an overlay with layer 2 separation that AT&T markets as AT&T Virtual Private Network (AVPN); other IP service providers have similar offers. This private IP SDN was similar to the TDM SDN in that it is an overlay, but it's all connection-less IP packets instead of connection-oriented phone calls.

3.2.4 Virtualization of Internet Protocol Networks before Cloud

As MPLS grew, it also became feasible to change those routing tables in unique ways to bridge private networks. The Integrated Route Services Control Point (IRSCP), like Network Control Points (NCP), were invented to be able to manipulate the MPLS routing table in real time based on customer and network policies. The IRSCP was used for private interdomain routing updates that would not be vulnerable to the Internet routing security issues and again empower customers to control how they wanted their virtual overlay networks to operate.

It was about this time that BGP flowspec was also invented that permit the controller to communicate the desired flow processing via BGP messages to the routers. The flowspec could define the desired routing in an N-tuple match of the data in the header of the IP packet like the source IP address, the destination IP address, the address family (Internet or private VPN), or the transport protocol so that routers could implement not only custom routing tables but advanced routing decisions based on the N-tuple matches effectively providing the ability to carve out "flows" of packets that met the same criteria. The flows could be separately routed so that things like "distributed denial-of-service (DDOS) scrubbers" could be service chained into the network for only the "likely to be bad" traffic. Again, an example of a private overlay on a public network.

All of this IP networking was being used for users to access servers and server applications. Tremendous growth in server technology and the economies of scale with large server farms led to the first private clouds like Google, eBay, and Amazon. These clouds needed to deal with network problems inside their server farms where a virtual machine could be created on one physical server and later moved to another physical server based on a growth in load or maintenance on the physical server, without impacting the external networks. They needed an overlay technology so that the application would be shielded from the movement of the virtual machine. Various tunnel overlay protocols were developed and are still used with Virtual Extended Local Area Network (VXLAN) perhaps being the most popular, but they all had the need for management of the assignments and updating as changes occurred.

3.2.5 Today's Software-Defined Networking

It was about this time, around 2009, that academia was proposing a new paradigm for the separation of the control logic and the forwarding plane in the routers and proposing a new protocol called OpenFlow [9]. The basic concept was to have a controller push data (or reply to a query when a new flow appeared at a switch) with decision table data that the switches would use for packet forwarding. The tables had a relatively small set of functions and decisions but could be tailored for a customer based on an N-tuple set of attributes (in principle similar to flowspec already mentioned). A key aspect was that the packet forwarding was flow based so that it could set the behavior at the start of a flow and then keep the same packet processing decisions for the duration of the flow. In this sense, it was very similar to the old TDM and H.248 flows in the evolution of the circuit-switched networks. Importantly though, it was still dealing with packets so all the advantages of a packet network with respect to forwarding decisions could still be applied. What perhaps also distinguished the modern SDN flow controller was that it would rewrite the packet headers so that the packet could not only be encapsulated but also could replace packet header information changing the processing that subsequence steps in the routing algorithm would take. The ability to actually define new routing protocols in a running network is a next generation of SDN.

Software-defined network in an OpenFlow network is very powerful and some very large cloud data centers use it at scale but for the general Wide Area Network (WAN) problem the complexity has limited its application to mainly the local cloud environment.

It's the combination of WAN and LAN networking that is really needed to meet the needs of corporate private networking (Figure 3.2).

3.2.6 Applications of Internet Protocol Software-Defined Networking

With the previous background on SDN, let's talk about some of the applications (Figure 3.3).

3.2.6.1 Path Optimization

Path optimization is based on combining the topology of the links in the network with telemetry from the network on the traffic flow through the current paths, the link capacity, and the link occupancy to calculate a cost/optimization function for the network. With a cost/optimization function like overall link utilization, an algorithm can calculate if different paths through the network would result in improved utilization or better resiliency under failure. Today SDN controllers can be part of a closed-loop system that receives

Feature	Stored Program Control	MPLS VPNs & Flowspec	OpenFlow
Control Bearer Separation	CCIS6 SS7	BGP	OpenFlow
Overlay	Networking Routing Numbers	Route Distinguisher Route Target	Packet Header Rewrite
Customer Specific Logic	SCP	IRSCP	SDN Controller
Stream Type	Connection Oriented	Connection-less	Connection-less Flows

FIGURE 3.2   Comparison of software-defined networking attributes.

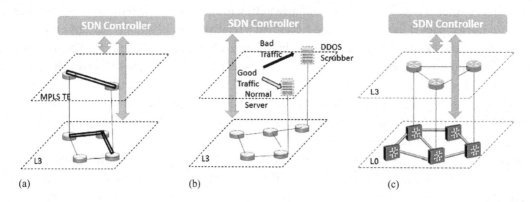

(a)   (b)   (c)

FIGURE 3.3   Applications of IP SDN: (a) path optimization, (b) destination rewriting, and (c) multi-layer SDN.

this telemetry through BGP-Link State (BGP-LS) and Path Computation Element Protocol (PCEP) data, apply analytics and then change the Multi-Protocol Label Switching – Traffic Engineering (MPLS-TE) overlay tunnels on the backbone to increase path optimization. The combination of telemetry, analytics, Application Program Interfaces (APIs), and a more complete view of the network from the centralized control point are the enablers for this type of optimization loop.

3.2.6.2 Destination Rewriting

We have already briefly mentioned using SDN controllers to setup N-tuple match criteria for routing flows. An application of this type of control when combined with telemetry and algorithms would be a DDOS scrubbing application. Telemetry on network traffic and server statistics can be used to identify that a set of flows matching a criterion (a large number of flows from this network or coming over these peering links) is DDOS traffic. The algorithm can determine that a flow rule of this N-tuple match could be applied at the controller so that these flows would not go to the original destination IP but instead be routed to a scrubber complex where bad traffic would be removed and only the valid traffic would be forwarded to the original destination. The controller capability to both classify the flow and take an action on those flows different from normal flows is useless without the algorithms to determine what to do.

3.2.6.3 Multilayer Software-Defined Networking

Software-defined network is not only a Layer 2/Layer 3 phenomenon. Optical networks also have software control capability. One of the most exciting is the OpenROADM project where interoperable components can be configured via industry standard APIs [10]. This capability enables the addition of new high bandwidth circuits to the network in near real time (single-digit minutes). We have recently combined this capability with the L3 SDN to enable exciting new capabilities for L3 networks. Under load or failure, a Layer 3 controller can determine that there are no more options for path optimization and instead of giving up it can ask a Layer 0 controller if there are resources that would allow a new circuit between two end points. For example, if there is congestion between New York and Los Angeles, the Layer 3 network can reroute traffic engineering tunnels but still have high packet loss. The Layer 3 controller can ask the Layer 0 controller if an additional wavelength from NY to LA is possible for the next eight hours. If so, the Layer 0 controller can set up that circuit and tell the Layer 3 controller when it is done. The Layer 3 control can then use its software-defined APIs to attach that circuit to the Layer 3 routers network interfaces, turning the circuit into an IP link. Finally, the Layer 3 controller can put new MPSL-TE tunnels over that link. Each time traffic optimization algorithms are fired to select the right path in Layer 0, the right route for Layer 3 links and the right MPLS tunnel paths and weights in the tunnel overlay network.

3.3 THE PATH TO NETWORK FUNCTION VIRTUALIZATION

As mentioned in the previous section, at about the same time as cloud technology was being adopted and network virtualization was being pursued, the networking industry was working on the SDN architecture that brought a new approach to control-plane and user-plane network architectures. This section discusses how cloud technology and NFV together enabled a revolutionary approach to networking.

3.3.1 Data Center Evolution to Cloud Technology

Early cloud technology and its application to data centers was driven by the need to run and manage traditional data centers in more cost-efficient ways. This included using hardware as efficiently as possible as well as minimizing the life cycle costs of managing and maintaining the hardware and software. Cloud technology provides the ability to create and manage application workloads and deploy them to servers in data centers under program control. Using these capabilities, an enterprise can create and implement strategies for disaster recovery (DR), for example, by using cloud capabilities to instantiate application workloads consistent with their DR strategies, such as redundancy (geographical or otherwise). Cloud technologies can be used to achieve required availability and resiliency but enable users to realize the necessary geo-redundancy, distribution, and connectivity [11].

Server hardware can be used in more optimal ways by creating application workloads that require a mix of CPU, memory, storage, and connectivity to make more efficient use of server resources. In addition, cloud technology provides the ability to manage workloads to provide the capability to:

- Dynamically adjust the resources provided to an application (e.g., CPU, storage, memory)

- Instantiate (spin up) additional instances of the same application in the same data center

- Spin up additional instances of the same application in data centers in other geographical locations

3.3.2 Movement to White Box Hardware

As mentioned previously, one of the main drivers of cloud technology was to meet the need to manage data centers in more cost-efficient ways. In addition to cloud software and its ability to perform the functions cited earlier under program control, another significant cost component, the cost of the hardware itself, needed to be addressed. This was dealt with by the industry coalescing around standard hardware configurations for servers called White Box hardware. White Box hardware tended to be x86 technology in a variety of standard configurations. Now these standard servers could be bought in large quantities allowing economies of scale to be realized [12].

3.3.3 Early Application Adoption/Movement to Cloud Technology

The initial movement to cloud technology was done by enterprises that wanted to improve data center economics and flexibility. Among the first applications to move to the cloud were a wide variety of corporate applications such as finance, human resources, payroll, real estate, marketing, and sales. These applications benefitted from the ability to create workloads that optimized use of server hardware and the ability to dynamically allocate resources (CPU, memory, storage), provide geo diversity, DR arrangements, and application scaling. This was done while introducing higher levels of automation, thus reducing operating costs by reducing manual operations.

3.3.4 Network Virtualization

In parallel with the work being done on SDN and at around the same time as cloud technologies were emerging, the networking industry had come to the realization that traffic was growing at a rate that could not be supported in a cost-efficient way by continuing to invest in more traditional physical network elements (NEs) as had been done in the past; the network traffic was simply growing faster than network providers could keep pace with traditional network equipment buildouts. Traffic growth was faster than revenue growth, and continued purchases of NEs could not be financially sustained in an environment of stiff competition and margin pressures.

In order to address these issues and provide a financially viable way forward, the networking industry was investigating the feasibility of transforming NEs, built with specialized hardware and software, to applications that could run on standard hardware (White Boxes). The idea was that if NE functions could be transformed into software applications that can run on standard hardware, then that would change the economic equation for the better. Applications providing network functions that can run on standard White Box hardware can capitalize on the lower cost of hardware compared to specialized hardware previously used in traditional NEs.

The transformation of traditional NEs (specialized hardware and software) into applications that can run on standard hardware (e.g., x86 servers) did, indeed, prove to be technically feasible. Service providers enthusiastically pursued this technology pivot in order to change the economics of networking. At this point, there was a strong consensus among providers that the cost curve could be bent in favor of better economics.

3.3.4.1 Virtualization of Network Functions

Network function virtualization started with smaller NEs and edge devices (e.g., firewalls and switches) for performance reasons, and then, as performance of virtual NE software improved, it moved to larger capacity elements like provider edge routers and DNSs.

3.3.4.2 Movement to White-Box Hardware

The movement to standard hardware was a major theme of network virtualization. Standard hardware was lower cost and could be deployed, scaled, and managed on a more cost-efficient basis than the specialized hardware that had been heretofore used in traditional NEs. Data center operations personnel were experienced with deploying and managing, for example, performing break-fix operations on standard server hardware.

3.3.5 The Convergence of Cloud Technology and Network Function Virtualization

As discussed previously, in the early stages of network virtualization, there were two prominent themes being pursued: cloud technology to more efficiently define, deploy, and manage application workloads to data centers under program control, leveraging the dynamic capabilities that technology provides, and network virtualization—the transformation of specialized networking hardware and software into applications that run on standard hardware servers.

These two initiatives set the stage for one of the most dramatic technical paradigm shifts in networking to come along in decades.

3.3.5.1 A Confluence of Technologies

As cloud technology and network virtualization were progressing, it was realized that if the emerging virtual network functions (vNFs) (NEs refactored into software applications) were run as applications in cloud data centers, then all of the dynamic control provided by cloud could be used in building large-scale provider network infrastructures and services.

And this could be accomplished with minimal manual intervention. This confluence of cloud and network virtualization led to the current industry direction of shifting their networks from traditional to vNFs running in cloud data centers.

3.3.5.2 Dynamic Control Brought to Networking Functions

With the convergence of cloud and NFV, network and service providers now had the ability to deploy ("spin up") NEs—vNFs (applications)—in data centers, assign resources to those NEs (CPUs, memory, storage), and manage those vNFs. All of these functions can now be done dynamically and under program control.

This powerful flexibility has profound implications on how providers deploy and manage their networks and services. A wide range of situations can be addressed in new ways exploiting cloud and vNFs. For example:

3.3.5.2.1 Instantiation and Management

- Control of resources—Resources like vNFs can be deployed to data centers (instantiated) to create network infrastructures. vNFs can be assigned CPU, memory, and storage consistent with their requirements and the requirements of the network and services they need to support.

- Network and service configuration—vNFs can be configured for a particular infrastructure or service capability.

- vNFs, networks, and services can be monitored and managed, all in a dynamic fashion with minimal manual intervention. For example, under conditions of high network traffic loads, providers can spin up additional NEs (e.g., vNFs such as routers) in the affected data center or in other data centers in different geographic locations, depending on the type of problem and the desired method(s) of handing the situation.

- DR can be performed in new ways, for example, spinning up vNFs in disaster-free data centers and locations under program control.

- With the vNFs running on standard hardware, servers can be deployed to data centers in pods consisting of many servers. When the number of working servers decreases to a predetermined level, the entire pod can be refreshed with new servers of the same or newer generation. This transforms server maintenance from an on-demand, event-driven process (alarms trigger the dispatch of personnel) to a regularly scheduled hardware refresh. This results in fewer personnel dispatches and presumably lowers hardware maintenance costs.

3.3.5.3 The Management Ecosystem: Service Creation, Instantiation and Orchestration, Monitoring and Management

As this virtual networking landscape began to take shape, it was realized that along with this new, highly dynamic virtual networking environment, a new approach to network management, in the broadest sense, was needed to address service definition, instantiation, and management in a world where vNFs can be spun up, deleted, or moved dynamically and where resources for these elements can be allocated and modified under program control—all in near real time. This new management ecosystem needed to be as agile as the networking environment it was to manage. AT&T's response to this challenge was the creation of the Enhanced Control, Orchestration, Management and Policy (ECOMP) platform [13]. Subsequent to the creation and deployment of ECOMP, AT&T later open sourced the ECOMP platform code. The open-sourced code is called Open Networking Automation Platform (ONAP) and is managed under the auspices of the Linux Foundation [14]. This was done to advance the industry's move to a standard platform for the management of the new virtual networking infrastructures that providers were pursuing worldwide.

3.3.5.4 The Open Networking Automation Platform Architecture

The current version of ONAP (Amsterdam release) inherits most of its capabilities from the contributed ECOMP code and the Open-O initiative. This platform code base will evolve over time as more and more industry participants contribute code to advance the platform. The following sections describe the ONAP architecture.

3.3.5.4.1 Two Key Frameworks: Design Time and Execution Time   There are two fundamental and complementary dimensions, or frameworks, in the ONAP platform dealing with design time (e.g., network and service design) and execution time aspects (marshalling of required resources, network and service configuration, monitoring and management) (Figure 3.4).

3.3.5.4.2 Design Time Framework—Service Design and Creation   A key early strategic driver for ECOMP, and subsequently ONAP, was efficient use of capital and achieving more agility in service creation and instantiation. The architecture addressed this requirement by incorporating model-driven concepts wherever practical. The execution time framework is

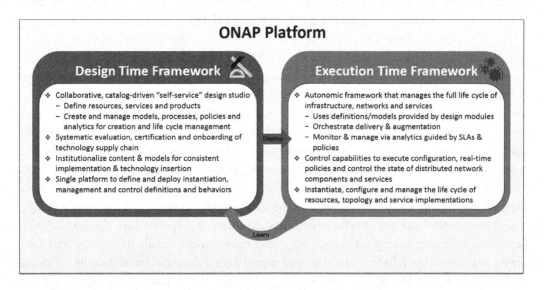

FIGURE 3.4   ONAP platform consists of design-time and execution-time frameworks.

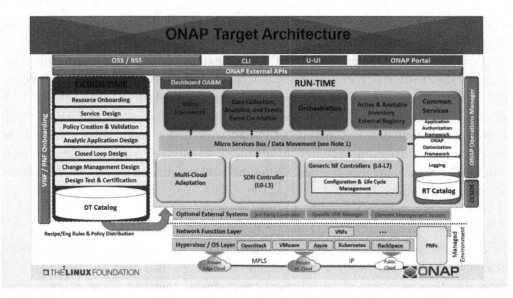

FIGURE 3.5   ONAP target architecture.

model driven. This means that the behavior of the execution time platform is determined by metadata supplied to it rather than by writing or modifying software through traditional software development processes and cycles. This allows one to change the behavior of the system by changing the metadata supplied, rather than by writing code to specify the systems behavior. The service design and creation platform (SDC), shown in Figure 3.5, provides users a design studio paradigm for manipulating vNFs to define infrastructures and services. The SDC generates required metadata to define the behavior required of the execution time framework to instantiate, configure, and manage services based on customer requests (or internally generated events such as alarms).

The SDC provides users the ability to on-board vNFs (i.e., ingest their metadata descriptions so they can be used in designing services) and manipulate those vNFs to create services. Once defined, the SDC platform auto generates the metadata descriptions of the defined service. This metadata, along with customer requests for service, are then used by the execution platform to instantiate an instance of that services, configure it for use, and perform the monitoring and management of that service. At service design time, the SDC platform is also used to define how the service is to be managed. For example, users can define the data to be collected, analyzed, and acted upon to manage the network or service.

Using a simple IP MPLS VPN example, once the vNFs have been on-boarded, SDC users can define the service by organizing the vNFs into the desired service using a design studio metaphor. Once the service is designed, the user can specify how the service is to be managed. In this example, the user (e.g., operations) could decide to manage based on site-to-site throughput. In this case, the user would define the data that should be collected to calculate site-site throughput, the analytics required to calculate throughput, and the actions to be taken should the throughput fall out of defined thresholds. The SDC platform will then generate the metadata needed to enable the execution platform to perform these management functions.

The model-driven nature of ONAP addresses the strategic goal of efficient use of capital and service creation agility by minimizing the dependence on traditional software development process and timelines for service design and creation. This approach also enables services to be defined/created faster than traditional development processes. This allows for more efficient use of capital in the creation and modification of services over traditional development methods.

3.3.5.4.3 Execution Time Framework   The ONAP execution time framework is responsible for processing requests for service as well as responding to events generated internal to the environment that require actions to be taken. The following sections describe the capabilities of the execution framework.

3.3.5.4.3.1 *Orchestration and Control*   Orchestration is responsible for marshalling resources such as vNFs in the appropriate data centers to meet a particular request. In the MPLS example cited earlier, this could be deploying the appropriate provider edge routers to the right centers to meet a customer request for service. For example, this could be done based on geographical location of customer sites. Orchestration does this by interaction with cloud environments to request the spin up of the particular resources (e.g., provider edge router [vNF] in the data center). Once the appropriate resources are made available, control passes to the controller domain. The controllers are responsible for the configuration of the vNFs (e.g., to meet a request for service, or in response to an event from the environment). It should be noted that orchestration deals with marshalling the appropriate resources; it is not service aware. For example, it does not know how to configure a NE for a particular service. Configuration is the responsibility of the controllers. In addition, when orchestration completes a unit of work, it is no longer in the control flow. Controllers, on the other hand, retain the state of the environment they are controlling.

3.3.5.4.3.2 *Active and Available Inventory*   As mentioned throughout, virtual network infrastructures are dynamic, where resources like vNFs can be spun up, deleted, and moved under program control in near real time. In order for ONAP to manage this successfully, there needs to be a source of inventory information that is up to date on the same time horizons that the dynamic changes can be made. In ONAP, A&AI provides this capability.

3.3.5.4.3.3 *Data Collection, Analytics, and Events*   The data collection, analytics, and events (DCAE) component of ONAP is the ecosystem that enables data collection and analytics on that data as well as the storage and distribution of that data to other platform components. DCAE was designed to be a highly distributable platform. That was done for two primary reasons: to better support the low latency of certain management functions by placing the data collection and analytics close to the managed elements, and to allow for the processing of data close to the managed environment so that data needing to be sent upstream can be of higher quality (processed near the sources) and lower volume. In this way, management data that needs to be sent to upstream systems can be more manageable.

Thus, the degree to which DCAE instances are distributed is generally up to the provider based on requirements, such as management response time, performance, and data volumes.

3.3.5.4.3.4 Policy ONAP provides the ability to define policies—actions—that can be invoked based on the result of receiving events of a certain type (signatures). These signatures can be the result of analytics performed on (network) data collected by DCAE. The ability to perform data collection and analytics and determine actions to be taken (policies) based on the results of those analytics is a *design pattern* that represents a fundamental capability of ONAP. As mentioned earlier, the data collection, analytics, and policies are defined at design time using the SDC platform. Different instances of this design pattern, driven by different types of metadata—network, cloud or service—can be used repeatedly so that whether one is managing the network, cloud environment, or a service, instances of the same design pattern can be used.

3.3.5.4.3.5 Open and Closed Control Loops In ONAP, a control loop is a design pattern that represents a process flow where data is collected from the networking environment (e.g., vNFs, PNFs, cloud environment), analyzed, and actions (as defined by policies) are determined, based on the results of the analytics (signatures). In addition to the actions to be taken, policies also define the actors responsible for taking particular actions. Typically, an actor can be a service orchestrator, a controller, or vNF, depending on the scope of the problem and action required to remediate. Control loops (i.e., the data to be collected, the analytics to be performed, and the actions to be taken) are defined at design time in SDC.

Control loops can be open or closed. An *open loop* is a control loop where the action(s) to be taken is performed through manual processes. For example, a service provider may decide that operations personnel are the appropriate actors to take a particular action. Open loops may also be used in order to validate the actions defined by policies.

A closed loop is a control loop where the actions to be taken are performed in an automated fashion under software control. Closed-loop control can be used to provide high degrees of automation in support of Operational Expense (OpEx) reduction by eliminating manual processes in managing various aspects of the network (e.g., fault and performance management). In addition, closed-loop automation can analyze and take actions on timescales ranging from submilliseconds to milliseconds to seconds, minutes, or longer.

The timescale of a control loop depends on the actors needed to remediate the problem. Control loops can be nested from the shortest timescales to the longest. In general, if the appropriate actor for a particular remediation is the vNF, these actions can be taken on the shortest timescales. Control loops of this type are the "tightest" control loops. The next type of control loop in the nesting are control loops where the appropriate actor in the loop is a controller (e.g., a controller may need to interact with one or more vNFs to remediate a problem). The next in the nest are control loops where the appropriate actor is a service orchestrator. An example of this loop is a situation where the remedial action is to instantiate a vNF in another data center. In this case, orchestration is required much

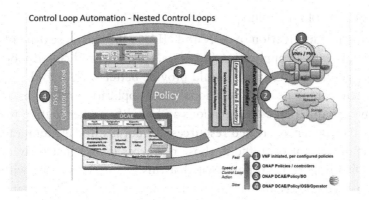

FIGURE 3.6   Control-loop automation—nested control loops.

like when the vNF was initially instantiated. Finally, the outer most nest is when the appropriate actor is an application or system outside ONAP and the network environment, such as an OSS. Control loops of this type typically operate on the longest timescales (Figure 3.6).

In closed-loop automation, particularly, the loops operating on the shortest timescales are proving to be critical to supporting the management functions on the timescales required in managing aspects of 5G networks, for example in supporting applications such as AR/VR or self-driving cars, where low-latency network connections need to be maintained.

3.4 PUTTING IT ALL TOGETHER

Software-defined networking and NFV together address the challenges of rapidly increasing traffic, services on demand, and closed-loop management and control. Independently, they are powerful tools but taken together the ability to create new resources in the cloud-based network and flow traffic to those resources just as dynamically is a powerful combination.

3.4.1 Creation of New Bumps in the Wire

Let us examine the possibility of adding new functions into a dynamic SDN/NFV environment. One way to deal with DDOS attacks is to route the suspect traffic to a scrubber application located in a convenient data center. This adds delay and adds to overall network utilization since the traffic has to be diverted from the shortest path. In an SDN/NFV world, the intelligent network can decide to create a new NFV-based scrubber in the same cloud as the virtual router, stitch, or service chain the scrubber into the local path of packets. This costs no additional WAN resources and minimizes the latency impact to the bare minimum for the traffic scrubbing. After the DDOS subsides, the "bump in the wire" can be removed. This approach of service chaining functions into the path can be done even for more beneficial features like encryption applications, web acceleration, and firewalls.

3.4.2 Elastic Scaling of End Points

Another interesting application of SDN and NFV is the elastic scaling of end points. As traffic through or to an application increases, telemetry and closed-loop control can determine that additional resources would provide better service to the customer. The SDN/NFV system can orchestrate additional NFV application resources at the current cloud location or in different cloud locations and modify packet routing to move traffic appropriately to those newly created resources. It's not just the creation of the resource (NFV) but the movement of traffic to those resources (SDN) that truly unleashes the potential. It's also important to point out that this is not just scaling within one data center but across data centers. This can enable unique solutions like private cloud-based NFVs, using public cloud resources for surge traffic, changing the cost model since the service provider doesn't have to deploy burst traffic resources on their private edge clouds for all scenarios. This type of hybrid cloud scaling is a direct improvement in the bottom line.

3.4.3 Moving Services Across Locations

Like the elastic scaling example, moving services across locations is a different way to handle optimization of traffic. Virtual functions can be moved even if the traffic is in overload. Customers move, add offices, change work habits, and even have to deal with snowstorms where their staff can't get into the office. In the old world of physical network functions, latency, and congestion could result from these changing traffic patterns that were not practical to solve. With virtual functions, the vNF can be moved to an optimal data center for the current traffic either semi-permanently or temporarily. Again, it's the combination of the ability to create the virtual function in a new data center and route traffic to it, no matter where it is moved to, that makes the network more flexible.

3.5 SUPPORT FOR NETWORK ARTIFICIAL INTELLIGENCE

Just as with SDN, cloud, NFV, ECOMP, and ONAP ushered in new technologies and approaches to networking and services. The industry is on another cusp of technological change—AI and machine learning (ML). This section discusses how these technologies can be used in ecosystems like ONAP to provide the next level in closed-loop autonomous control and management of networks and services.

3.5.1 Telemetry

The application of AI/ML to management ecosystems like ONAP begins with the data collected from the networking environments on which advanced analytics are performed, and results are used to make policy decisions. So having the correct and highest quality data is essential. There are opportunities for AI in cleansing network data so it can more easily be used by other AI and analytic applications with the goal of improving the quality of analytics and decisions made using the results of analytics.

3.5.2 Knobs

Once the network data is cleansed and aggregated as discussed earlier, the next important phase is to apply AI to improve the policies that are used to manage the network. Policies are the rules that define what actions should be taken based on signatures, or the results of analytics performed on the network data. The rules that determine the actions to be taken upon receipt of certain signatures can be improved by using AI techniques [15]. AI can determine if the actions being taken, based on policies, are effective and whether they can be improved upon so that, for example, the new actions can fix a problem faster, enhance network performance in certain situations, or perhaps be used to define better ways of recovering from vNF failures of particular types.

3.5.3 Open Loops and Closed Loops

Artificial intelligence and ML can be used to improve and enhance closed-loop control. As discussed earlier, closed-loop control consists of data collection, analytics, and actions that are based on the results of the analytics. All of the components of the closed loop can be improved and enhanced through AI and ML to improve the speed, accuracy, and ultimately the effectiveness (value) of closed-loop control. In particular, predicting events and failures earlier as well as determining more effective remedial actions.

This in turn will positively affect network provider economics, OpEx, and network quality—a competitive differentiator.

3.5.3.1 Smart Tickets

Use of AI/ML will enable higher quality "smart" trouble tickets by incorporating relevant information in the trouble ticket (e.g., results of testing performed) and eliminating extraneous or non-root cause information. The AI natural language processing can help interpret and process notes, where used, to maximize automation of the closed loop.

3.5.3.2 Avoiding the Need for Tickets

As the quality of closed-loop control and the policy decisions it enables improves through the application of AI/ML, it should be possible to avoid the need for trouble tickets.

3.6 SUMMARY

As you can see, there are many controls that a modern Software Defined Network makes available to service providers. Using those controls manually has some value for resolving problems faster, but the real advantage comes from automation, where, for example, the aspirational goal would be to drastically reduce, if not eliminate, trouble tickets, resulting in operational efficiencies. Subsequent chapters like Chapter 9 on Artificial Intelligence for Network Operation will provide more details on the application of AI to Network Operations. The three areas of Network Provisioning, Network Maintenance, and Network Administration are all rich areas for application of AI. Other chapters in the book will also be applicable, since the actions that AI and Machine Learning algorithms can take are only constrained by how flexible the APIs are in the Software Defined Network and Network Function Virtualization layers.

REFERENCES

1. G. Duhnkrack, *The Electronic Switching System*, Whippany, NJ: Bell Telephone Laboratories, 1960, p. 3.
2. R. Ketchledge, The no. 1 electronic switching system, *IEEE Transactions on Communications*, 13, 38–41, 1965.
3. *ITU-T Recommendation Q.700*, p. 4.
4. C. W. Haas, D. C. Salerno and D. Sheinbein, Stored program controlled network: 800 service using SPC network capability, *Bell System Technical Journal*, 61(7), 1737–1744, 1982.
5. W. G. Bolter, J. W. McConaughey and F. J. Kelsey, *Telecommunications Policy for the 1990s and Beyond*, 296, Armonk, NY: M.E. Sharpe, 1990.
6. *H.248.1: Gateway Control Protocol: Version 3*, Geneva, Switzerland: International Telecommunication Union - Telecommunication, 2016.
7. J. N. Brunken, R. Mager and R. A. Putzke, NEMOS-the network management system for the AT&T long distance network, *IEEE International Conference on Communications*, 3, 1193–1197, 1989.
8. R. A. Becker, C. Volinsky and A. R. Wilks, Fraud detection in telecommunications: History and lessons learned, *Technometrics*, 52(1), 20–33, 2010.
9. N. McKeown et al., OpenFlow: Enabling innovation in campus networks, *ACM Communications Review*, 38(2), 69–74, 2008.
10. Open ROADM home page, AT&T, March 2016 [Online]. Available: http://openroadm.org/home.html.
11. J. Donovan and K. Prabhu, Chapter 5: Architecting the network cloud for high availability, in *Building the Network of the Future*, Boca Raton, FL: CRC Press, 2017.
12. Z. Kerravala, White boxes are now ready for prime time, *Network World*.
13. AT&T, ECOMP (enhanced control, orchestration, management & policy) architecture white paper [Online]. Available: http://about.att.com/content/dam/snrdocs/ecomp.pdf.
14. Linux Foundation, ONAP - Open Network Automation Platform, Linux Foundation [Online]. Available: www.ONAP.org.
15. J. Yates and Z. Ge, Artificial intelligence for network operation, in *Artificial Intelligence for Autonomous Networks*, M. Gilbert (Ed.), New York: CRC Press, 2018.

CHAPTER 4

Blockchain and Cryptography for Secure Information Sharing

Matt Dugan and Wiley Wilkins

CONTENTS

4.1 INTRODUCTION

This chapter introduces the role of information security and consensus mechanisms as they apply for autonomous, artificial intelligence (AI). It provides an overview of different consensus mechanisms and illustrates the need for incorruptible information records corresponding to the AI decision inputs, decision records, and feedback records used to correct and supplement AI decision making. Leveraging Blockchain and cryptographic principles allows AI functions to operate in a distributed network or geographic topology and support combinatorial decision making using information sets (or other AI decision outputs) from distinct information domains.

Section 4.2 presents an overview of Blockchain and cryptographic implications, which are leveraged both in common and by default among leading Blockchain implementations. Section 4.3 introduces consensus algorithms commonly used in Blockchain solutions and discusses the trade-offs therein. Section 4.4 discusses the key reasons to leverage Blockchain features to supplement AI. Section 4.5 looks forward to how distributed ledgers can support distributed AI, closed-loop feedback mechanisms, and introduces a future relevant concept of parliamentary AI for higher order decision making using secure information sharing.

4.2 BLOCKCHAIN OVERVIEW

4.2.1 What Is a Blockchain?

At its core, a Blockchain is a digital ledger. In the same way as a physical ledger [1], a Blockchain is used to record an ordered set of transactions. These transactions may be looked over at any time, and they may be adjusted via new entries to the ledger. However, the ledger entries should not be changed or rewritten—only amended. In this sense, the ledger transactions are considered immutable and the ledger, or chain, is append only.

In a physical ledger, order is enforced in a physical way. Each new entry is added on the next line below the current entry. If a correction is needed, a new line is appended to make the correction. An observer watching a ledger being modified would easily spot fraudulent actions, like skipping an empty line to use it for an entry that came later or going back and changing an entry that is already written. In a digital environment, verification is more difficult. The literal bits of a digital record can be modified by any system or actor with access to the bits. The idea of an observer is more difficult as soon as multiple systems are involved, and exponentially difficult when multiple networks are involved.

In a digital ledger [2], cryptographic principles like hashing, encryption, keys, and signatures are leveraged in order make order verifiable. In the simplest mechanism, each new entry—or block—added to the ledger includes a value corresponding to the previous block. This way, blocks are chained together by each block containing a component of the previous. Corrupting the chain becomes difficult without writing a completely new chain from a given point in the ledger.

Most Blockchain [3] implementations leverage a community of system peers to distribute copies of the ledger among them. Each Blockchain node has a copy of the ledger, receives and validates new entries as they are made, and can propose entries. The risk of having the chain surreptitiously rewritten is mitigated by requiring *consensus* among the nodes to accept new entries. Each node has the ability to spot a rewrite happening and choose to reject it.

With chained blocks, a cryptographic scheme to check for integrity, and a distributed set of system peers to check, validate, and enter transactions, the only item left is a sense of purpose. There are a variety of Blockchain implementations, which can be distilled to a few root categories:

Currencies and asset trading: Including the popular *Bitcoin* [4], these implementations exist to mine, manage, trade, and transfer a digital commodity of some designated worth between the participants.

Identity and attribute verification: Because of the strong verification capabilities, Blockchain implementations like *Sovrin* [5] are used to validate references to identities or attributes of an identity without centrally locating all identities and all attributes to a common entity.

Distributed computation: Including the popular *Ethereum* [6] network, these implementations often have some currency elements, where the currency is used to pay for arbitrary logic execution among the Blockchain peers and return a result back to the submitter.

General purpose/framework: Other Blockchain efforts like the Linux Foundation's *Hyperledger* [7] project seek to create enterprise grade Blockchain implementations, which can be used to solve for arbitrary business needs by creating Blockchain framework enabled applications. The kinds of problems Blockchain can address are more important to these implementations than solving a given instance of a problem.

4.2.2 How Are Cryptographic Principles Used in a Blockchain?

Because of their digital nature, Blockchain implementations require mechanisms to provide assurance of the chain integrity. This problem is not new to Blockchain—one of the first commonly used examples of these techniques is in encrypted and signed emails.

Each participant in the conversation first creates a key pair. These pairs are comprised of both a public key, shared with everyone, and a private key kept by each participant. When an author composes as message, the message is encrypted using the public key of the designated recipient. This ensures that only the recipient can read the message, by decrypting with their own matching private key.

However, when conversations need not be private, such as on a message board, the authors are more concerned with knowing that their thoughts in public view are their own—that they have not been tampered with. To achieve this, each author signs any message they compose. The signature takes into account the content of the message and the sender's certificate and private key. The signature is then included in the message. Anyone reading the message can validate that the message is intact by computing against the content of the message and the signature using the senders published public key. When the computed hash value results match, the authenticity of the message is confirmed.

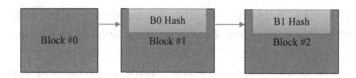

FIGURE 4.1   Simple Blockchain illustration.

Blockchain implementations leverage both of these cryptographic principles. To authenticate to the chain as a member node, the private and public keys are used to confirm a known chain participant's identity. If that identity is recognized as a member of the Blockchain, the participating node is joined, synchronizes their copy of the chain, and can propose new blocks, validate other proposals, and operate on the chain of existing blocks.

As shown in Figure 4.1, when new blocks are created each block carries the hash of the prior block, the signature of the creator, and any other information specific to the purpose of the Blockchain implementation.

Using this technique, where the hash of each subsequent block includes the value of the hash of the prior block, each block is irrevocably chained to the previous.

While the concept described previously is the core technique, some specialized techniques are required in order to achieve distributed scale in validation and multiparty transactions with blocks. The most common method leverages Merkle Trees in order to perform Merkle Proofs. Merkle Proofs [8] were first applied in the Bitcoin Blockchain as a mechanism to include transaction information in the blocks so that the history of transactions could be validated within block headers rather than having to download and reverify the content of each block. In other words, the state of the ledger could be validated while only needing to transfer and store a small amount of data.

When an individual transaction needed to be verified, the proof can be asserted to show the transaction is within a Merkle Tree with its top-level parent (the root node) existing in a block header within the chain. Because Merkle Proofs allow a convenient method of validation for a given attribute, additional Merkle Trees can be used in a Blockchain implementation to provide proofs about the states of other attributes—such as the current owners of Blockchain tracked assets, account balances, or if a particular result of a transaction has created some additional information—or value, which needs to be understood in the ecosystem of chain participants.

4.2.3 Examples of Leading Blockchain Implementations

As described prior, there are several varieties of Blockchain implementations, each targeting a certain primary purpose. The most popular domain by number of implementations is the currency and asset trading domain, popularized by the far-reaching penetration of the Bitcoin economy.

Bitcoin first went online in January 2009 with the first Bitcoins created and an open source client released. Credited to the online pseudonym Satoshi Nakamoto [9], Bitcoin was used primarily by those with a hobbyist interest in cryptography and the concept of combining cryptocurrency, anonymity, and a self-actualized value system independent of any established institutions. During the first two years, the protocol was exercised by a growing number of enthusiasts, leading to the discovery and correction of the first major system vulnerability allowing creation of an unlimited number of Bitcoins. The ecosystem self-corrected, choosing to re-base the ledger from just prior to the point of exploitation with an updated implementation that closed the defect.

Since 2011, hobbyists, enthusiasts, would-be competitors and others have leveraged the open source Bitcoin protocol implementation to create other boutique cryptocurrencies, though none have reached the size and participant scale of Bitcoin. Companies such as Mt. Gox and Coinbase emerged to provide for buying and selling of Bitcoin interests using traditional currencies. The value and demand for Bitcoin, while volatile, has continued to increase.

The next largest Blockchain implementation is called Ethereum, released into public use in 2014. The Ethereum project set out to accomplish very different technological and ecosystem goals. Rather than focus solely on currency, Ethereum created a computation economy facilitated by a Blockchain with a native cryptocurrency supporting the effort-to-value exchange. At the core, the Ethereum Virtual Machine used by Ethereum nodes supports Turing complete languages, meaning it can be used to solve arbitrary computation problems. Ether, the currency used in Ethereum, is used to purchase "gas," which represents the computational expense the Ethereum network incurs to execute application code within the distributed Ethereum Virtual Machine, resulting in block creation. This approach, while more complex than Bitcoin, allows for a general-purpose environment using instances of Ethereum networks and a common, resilient network for computation of arbitrary business methods submitted by the ecosystem of Ethereum users.

With a complex system comes the potential for more elaborate vulnerabilities. In 2016, the Ethereum implementation was updated corresponding to re-basing the ledger three times prior to exploits. Several techniques have been developed to provide greater resiliency and error checking of arbitrary application code, called smart contracts, so that exploit conditions can be detected and resolved. In order to scale the now general purpose Ethereum compute ecosystem, the Ethereum project is moving away from Proof-of-Work consensus to a Proof-of-Stake implementation, described later.

The Sovrin Blockchain implementation discards the notions of a competitive ecosystem and currency altogether. Instead, Sovrin sets out to create a network of individual, human identities with individual ownership but decentralized operation. The goal of the Sovrin identity network is to facilitate verifiable trust between parties, by exercising a Blockchain verification of identity attributes in a secure manner—avoiding leaking of private identity attributes to other parties. Participants in the Sovrin identity network, which can be individuals or organizations, store individual human attributes like age, names, date of birth, and address. The attributes are verified in a privacy preserving way.

The easiest example of a Sovrin identity attribute verification is an assertion. An organization may require patrons to be over 18 years of age. A query to the Sovrin network will validate that "yes" an identity is over 18. The query will not reveal the specific age of the patron. Throughout, the identity owner is in control of the attributes, how and when they are shared, and the provenance thereof.

Finally, the Hyperledger project by the Linux Foundation sets out to create a generalist Blockchain framework for arbitrary needs. Targeted at developers and enterprises, a person or organization could modify, leverage, or host components of the Hyperledger platform to create cryptocurrencies like Bitcoin, ecosystem networks like Ethereum, identity platforms like Sovrin, or solve for other combinations of arbitrary concerns. Hyperledger is best described as a common open source ledger implementation and a number of frameworks, tools, and software libraries to enable custom operations to be encoded on the common ledger instance by a network of peers running purpose specific instances of Hyperledger client tools.

4.2.4 Supporting Secure Information Sharing

The Sovrin Blockchain implementation allows for secure information sharing, where the specific information is descriptive of human individual attributes. Both Ethereum and Hyperledger can support secure information sharing given appropriate application code or custom modifications, respectively. The principle of secure information sharing is much like the private email technique described previously, using the public and private keys of the recipient, and the verified signature of the sender.

Leveraging a Blockchain, blocks can be encoded with private information. The public key of an intended recipient can be used to encode a message including the senders signature. While the encrypted payload could appear in the public ledger and be seen by all members, it could only be read by the designated party. In this way, distributed systems could allow for resilient secure information sharing without the liability of a centralized authority. Using Hyperledger, chain-groups could be used in combination with a conversation negotiated on the primary public chain and carried out in a separate chain exclusive to the conversing party. The conversation chain can be proven to have been negotiated within the public chain by finding the block hash, and its integrity can be checked by asserting the Merkle Proof.

Using these simple methods, many use cases become possible—such as creating applications that alleviate the need to dictate or publicly display guest Wi-Fi passwords to visitors, or the ability to create a message wall resistant to tampering. An application of Blockchain for secure information sharing in a Software-Defined Network could include informing a destination party of a discovered network threat without advance knowledge of how to route the information to the destination node. The recipient would be able to validate the authenticity of the sending agent's message without connectivity (and trust) with the sending agent.

4.3 CONSENSUS

4.3.1 What Is Consensus in a Blockchain?

Because Blockchain implementations leverage a distributed peer group of participants, mechanisms must be used to create trust in the computed results. While the Proof-of-Work method is the most common by far, other methods exist to arrive at a similar conclusion—the results submitted by a given participant node are correct, and the nodes in the participant network accept the results into the ledger.

The problem of consensus is not unique to Blockchain, though Blockchain implementations do require some form of consensus. Any distributed or multi-agent system requires a consensus mechanism in order to realize computed results. In multi-threaded computing, memory is shared from a parent thread to child threads. Because multiple child threads could modify a single shared memory space, a locking mechanism is used. At a given point in time, either no threads are modifying the memory space, or only a single thread is modifying the space. If a concurrent thread seeks to modify the memory, it must wait until the lock is released. This form of consensus provides that a single thread among multiple is responsible for the point-in-time end state of a transaction on a shared memory space.

Similarly, in order for Blockchain networks to proceed with appending new entries to a ledger, the prior result must first be recognized. Within a Blockchain, series of computations, data creation, and data modification can occur as part of a single transaction. Multiple peer participants may be working in parallel, each seeking to propose the next block with their results. As these blocks are proposed, Blockchain implementations execute their active consensus algorithms in order to decide which of these proposed blocks are accepted into the ledger, and in which order. Due to the nature of these distributed participant networks, groups of nodes can "agree" to continue upon different ledger entries. As in the case with Bitcoin and Ethereum, the ledger is considered "forked" from this point of divergent consensus.

4.3.2 Methods and Trade-offs: Proof of Work

With implementations used in Bitcoin, derived currencies, and in Ethereum at the time of this writing, Proof of Work is the most commonly used method of consensus. The basic concept of a Proof-of-Work mechanism is that it is difficult to perform the work but easy to verify that the work has been performed. Much like mining for gems or precious metals, the act of mining the metal is effort intensive, but the act of validating the output metal to exist is trivial by comparison. The term "mining" is used in Blockchain implementations to describe the act of performing the work step.

Proof-of-Work functions can vary in style—some are more demanding of network activity, system processor computations, or system memory allocation. While the Proof-of-Work algorithm used in Bitcoin is very processor computation intensive, the algorithm leveraged in Ethereum is system memory intensive. In each case, the Proof-of-Work algorithm is a fixed, semi-fixed, or variable resource cost function to cause the network node performing the work to have to spend effort to do so. In the case of Bitcoin, the opportunity for potential value in the cryptocurrency has led to a large concentration of specialized computation resources (known as Application Specific Integrated Circuits [ASICs]) owned by organizations. This concentration of power is an attempt to maximize their ability to reach consensus quickly on blocks mined locally.

The trade-off for Proof of Work is that the energy and expense to produce the work is usually material waste—the effort spent to perform the work was not spent on a business, social, or economic need. Instead, the work represents a burden of cost on the party performing the work, in order to earn the privilege of active participation in the Blockchain implementation. While this works well for distributed participant groups with no inherent trust relationship between them, it is a poor choice for organizations that are leveraging an internal Blockchain or collaborating with another organization where a good faith measure is already established, such as a legal agreement or service contract.

4.3.3 Methods and Trade-offs: Proof of Stake

When initially investigating Proof-of-Stake alternatives, the Ethereum project determined it a nontrivial undertaking. While several Proof-of-Stake methods are being leveraged in Blockchain implementations, these Blockchain implementations do not have large ecosystems of participants and have a competitive value exchange that is far below Ethereum or Bitcoin. When traditional Proof-of-Stake methods, including randomization, age-based designation, quantity-based designation, or most others are examined in ecosystems with value exchange systems, they fall victim to vulnerabilities in game theory—some amount of value or external pressure delivered to a holder of stake that incentivizes the holder to relinquish their stake to another actor.

Leaving traditional Proof-of-Stake-algorithms aside, the Ethereum project is preparing a Proof-of-Stake implementation, Casper [10], which utilizes stake in the form of currency escrow along with punishment (loss of escrow stake) and reward (discovery of stakeholder misbehavior) in order to mitigate gaming incentives in the Ethereum network. The Casper method will be leveraged in 1% of block transactions, initially, in order to prove viability.

In environments where incentives, influences, and gaming competition do not exist, or they are controlled via other means, another Proof-of-Stake implementation becomes viable. The Tendermint [11] protocol implements Byzantine Fault Tolerance (BFT) to ensure consistency of new blocks in a Blockchain. Using an algorithm of sequential rotation of peers elected as block proposers along with a time-limited series of pre-commit votes requiring a two-thirds super-majority to ratify blocks between members before an automatic default to a new proposer election. Byzantine Fault Tolerance is not unique to Blockchain implementations and has wide applications within computer science problems. Instead, the advent of Blockchain use has been a benefit to the way of implementing BFT systems—using a Blockchain to support BFT elections is a natural fit.

4.3.4 Methods and Trade-offs: Proof of Authority

Both Proof of Work and Proof of Stake make special considerations to mitigate an inherent lack of good faith in the external influencers and behavior of the participant nodes in the distributed peer network. When this assumption can be discarded, such as within private networks, single-owner networks, or networks that use an alternate mechanism for asserting trust and policy (such as a Software-Defined Network) a consensus optimization can be achieved. Trust asserting networks can leverage Proof of Authority for achieving consensus at orders of magnitude of the scale, which could be otherwise achieved with Proof of Work or the complexity in Proof of Stake.

Proof of Authority consensus relies on designated nodes rather than elected or algorithmically selected peers. These authority nodes propose and validate new blocks in the Blockchain. New authority nodes are confirmed (or excluded) by the set of existing authority nodes. Because no expensive cost function or algorithm to apply economic rewards and punishments is required, the authority nodes can create blocks with a speed equivalent to the time it takes to compute the hash of the block data and synchronize the new block among the network of authority nodes. Node group divergence need not occur in the absence of a business reason to do so.

While not generally suitable for public, distributed networks without strong identity or established good-faith relationships, Proof-of-Authority consensus mechanisms can work in the public domain for some use cases. Time server synchronization, post-facto audit verification proofs for in order events, or keyless signing infrastructures can be created and leveraged publicly or privately with Proof-of-Authority consensus mechanisms. Privately, Proof-of-Authority consensus mechanisms can be used to convert organizational system accesses and information modifications into a sequence of events evidence trail for automating system audits, facilitating threat detection, tracking file synchronization between systems on different networks, or providing a conformed dimension to data patterns existing between systems.

Within a Software-Defined Network, Proof-of-Authority consensus could be leveraged to maintain Border Gateway Protocol (BGP) route lists and assert source verification tagging to track and limit spoofed traffic appearing to come from a source that could not have legitimately supported the routing of the traffic. Audit trails of deployments and changes to network microservices can be tracked and validated, even (and especially) when multiple network operators and instrumentation agents are involved. Authority nodes in a Software-Defined Network could correspond to or be co-deployed with the control plane elements for policy certification and verification needs.

4.3.5 Other Types of Consensus

Not unique to Blockchain implementations, consensus among distributed peer groups about any system state, information, or economic transaction presents a computer science problem. Consensus is applicable to many use cases, from back-office data replication to fast-paced online multiplayer games. Many consensus algorithms exist, and only a subset of them have been applied to a Blockchain implementation at scale.

The Ripple [12] consensus algorithm facilitates a distributed ecosystem of financial record keeping. Ripple assumes the validating nodes do not have an inherent vested interest in confirming fraudulent or incorrect transactions, and uses a many-ledgers approach. In Ripple, a new ledger can be created every few seconds. These ledgers are ordered and represent the sequence of peer-agreed transactions that have occurred, and are committed along with the enumerated ledger containing the transactions. The chain of ledgers together corresponds to the ordered sequence of groups of financial transactions that are considered committed. Transactions not appearing in any of the ledgers were provisional for a moment in time, prior to finalizing the open ledger, but they are ultimately rejected due to lack of consensus support among the validating peer group and do not appear in the finalized ledger appended to the ledger list.

The family of protocols in Paxos [13] facilitates consensus where, contrary to Ripple, the network peers are considered unreliable and may often fail or otherwise be unavailable.

Paxos, first published in the 1980s and 1990s, predates any Blockchain implementation and has instead been used in enterprise data replication. As Paxos attempts to create durability in verifiable replication, it is well suited for situations where data consistency and fault tolerance between volumes, systems, or data warehouse constructs is desired.

In multiplayer gaming, consensus algorithms are applied to rationalize the client side of a player state with other proposed player states in order to decide in-game events where resources are finite. For example, if two players both cross an in-game item, the server must rationalize which player received the item and distribute it to that player. In order to provide the most fluid user experience most of the time, the client will accept a certain degree of movement and player action without server synchronization. In cases of nonuniform network conditions or server congestion, the corrective action of the client to match server state can disturb the player experience.

4.4 SUPPORTING ARTIFICIAL INTELLIGENCE WITH BLOCKCHAIN

4.4.1 Taking Artificial Intelligence to School—Lessons, Notes, and Academic Records

Creation of AI services requires careful attention to the information inputs and cross domain exposure of the AI training inputs and feedback. Cognitive systems unmitigated by instinct, conscience, or subjected to even unintentional systematic confusion are easily corrupted with bias and latent flaws. In order to create autonomous AI subsystems, which can be instrumented in trusted situations, careful attention must be made to the learning materials, the pace of learning, and the quality of feedback and scoring.

Beyond the need to create an AI initially, the ability to tweak and re-create pristine, testable AIs is necessary to achieve scale and domain-specific certification and instrumentation. When AI learning plans are mechanized and automated, the integrity of the learning plans must be protected. Blockchain could be used to encode the learning plan across dimensions of time, knowledge, exposure, and feedback. Encoded to a Blockchain, the learning plan is inherently verifiable in its native state. Adjustments to the learning plan can be appended and the ledger re-based or conditionally reverted based on testing results.

During testing, preproduction, and post-deployment phases, the scores, classifications, recommendations, or other AI actions can be recorded in the native Blockchain associated with the AI over its useful lifetime. Should a fault occur or a study be desired, a snapshot of the ledger state would provide for detailed forensic analysis, replay, and simulation of the AI actions. Conditionally with the implementation of the AI's observance of the time domain, scalar adjustments to the time periods could be used to accelerate or decelerate the periodic frequency of the AI input to action, facilitating rapid retraining and simulation for certification. In other words, an automated process executing the training plan can artificially speed up the passage of time while training an AI and still achieve precise point-in-time feedback that is designed into the training plan.

4.4.2 Reinforcement Learning and Correction

Typically, reinforcement learning techniques leverage a reward system during an observed process. When the observer interprets the new environment state after an AI action to be positive, the learning process is issued a reward. This process usually operates with real information within a localized environment or complete simulation. Rewards can be positive, negative, or simply "less positive" in order to provide the AI subject with learning continuous feedback. Refer to Chapter 2 for more details on Reinforcement Learning.

However, the incentive system must be carefully constructed, the observer vigilant, and the environment representative for the AI actions to converge optimally. Considering a network integrated AI informing firewall functions with poor observer interpretation. When the AI is provided reward incentive for blocking ports undergoing a vulnerability scan, it will continue to do so more often. This action can be manipulated by an attacker uninterested in finding a network vulnerability, when the attacker can simply convince the AI to perform a firewall enabled denial of service by closing service ports—effectively disturbing service continuity for legitimate clients. Rewarding a medical procedure AI on lack of future complications with a given limb will result in a bias toward amputations.

In order to train an AI to act more intelligent in complex situations, new methods have emerged to create an alternate form of a reward and correction system. In using apprenticeship via inverse reinforcement learning (AIRP) [14], the AI reward system is based on how closely it mimics the human impetus. The desired system state is directly observed as a result of the expert human action. By codification of the sequence of inputs and human actions into a Blockchain, the native inefficiencies of human action (such as comprehension time, reaction time, and errors) can be mitigated. Variance in speed to act, responsiveness to decision making, precision of input, and attention to all relevant information inputs all at once can be adjusted offline to reach a theoretical optimum. During playback, the AI can learn to mimic behavior from the "perfect" human.

4.4.3 Communicating Learning

By encoding the training model as well as runtime experiences of the AI within an instance-specific Blockchain, the sequence of events and desired decisions can be integrated into new or existing AI via playback. Leveraging a snapshot of the ledger corresponding to one instance, another instance could be created initially as a clone and begin instance specific divergence according to unique inputs and opportunities for AIRP where appropriate. Reuse of the parent training ledgers presents a licensing and certification opportunity for given specific information domains.

Beyond specific domains with very similar AI instances, leveraging principles of machine transfer learning will allow AIs trained to understand a type of action in a given information domain to create a competency for the same type of action in another information domain. For example, an AI trained to perform a security risk assessment for network authentication events may be portable to an insurance domain to quantify risk as a component of claim adjudication.

Domain adaptation can be accelerated by applying AIRP to the communicated AI instance within the new domain to quickly bring it to an acceptable level of performance. Using the adapted instance in an A/B mechanism allows a fresh instance to be created using AIRP, which can now have a ledger exported and optimized. The new optimized ledger is now representative of a domain-specific training plan.

As an organization builds practicum for AI construction, careful mixing of elements from adjacent domains into ledger plans will allow for best-of-breed AI mutations with high adaptability and lower information sensitivity. These assets can result in new revenue opportunities for organizations that can create them effectively.

4.5 PUTTING BLOCKCHAIN TO WORK

4.5.1 Closing the Loop

Applying Blockchain-backed AI instances within orchestration systems such as Software-Defined Networks allows for native closed-loops of inputs, action, results, and corrections. Within the control plane functions, instances of AI should receive analytics inputs of network behavior. These analytics represent the traffic shape and characteristics of the network usage, segmented by a number of variables including origin, destination, type, throughput, and other details. Refer to Chapter 3 for more details on closed-loop processes.

As the AI emits actions in response to the network, these actions along with the corresponding analytics features are stored into a data structure for a block. The emitted AI actions are received by an observer process, which conditionally emits policy instances in response to AI actions, where applicable. The result of implementation for a given policy, whenever it occurs, is appended to the block structure and the block finalized.

After a policy is issued, the next appearance of the new network environment state can be measured and compared to the prior state for divergence. If divergence is localized to the absence of a threat pattern identified in a previous action, the AI receives a positive reward. If the divergence includes significant changes in the nonthreat portion of the network characteristic, the AI should receive a zero or negative reward.

Where possible, the initial policy action could prompt dynamic network path simulation to create an A/B testing condition. The AI result can be tested and reinforced in the simulated network path prior to certification and application in the network service path.

4.5.2 Distributed Artificial Intelligence with Distributed Ledgers

Within control plane elements of an ecosystem, whether in a Software-Defined Network or other domain, AI instances may be backed by a single common ledger or multiple stand-alone ledgers. For instances where real-time instrumentation is less important than consistency, a common ledger can record the inputs, exposure, and feedback of multiple AI instance identities. Without the need for a centralization function, the distributed ledger consensus mechanism will reconcile the emitted action of all instances and synchronize the best agreed result.

However, in some cases it is more useful to apply an alternate consensus such as Proof of Authority to ensure that rules applied first by any one AI instance are automatically replicated to each instance, ensuring public consistency. Given the appropriate rule of consensus, the authority could be mixed and ledger blocks voted for inclusion for some actions and authority delegated to the observing node for others.

Apart from network instrumentation, consensus mechanisms leveraged across distributed ledgers backing AI instances can ensure multiparty cooperation and mutual benefit from distributed AI instances. Transfer learning [15] can be automated, more mature instances may serve to model behavior for newer instances, and the audit trail for all instance actions among the distributed AI instances is shared and verifiable.

4.5.3 Parliamentary Artificial Intelligence—Consensus, Voting, Rationalization

Organizations vested in AI construction should match business domains to several mature best-of-breed AI implementations through careful training plan mutations, selective domain adaptation, and expert apprenticeship reinforcement. These instances can be orchestrated to commit results to a special ledger, designed for high-level autonomous operation. For example, an e-commerce company may create AI domain implementations for customer preferences, online shopping behaviors, network security, mobile device usage characteristics, and inventory logistics.

Using these domain AIs together presents an opportunity to train an AI to understand high-level business process actions according to company Key Performance Indicator (KPI) measures. If a flood of orders comes in for a legacy product, the parliamentary instance would examine the current ledgers of the online shopping behaviors, network security, usage characteristics, inventory, and preference instances to determine a significant portion of the orders to be fraudulent. An action would be dispatched by the parliamentary instance to place an inventory stay action pending human feedback.

With the consensus of results from multiple instances of domain-specific AIs, the parliamentary AI is able to rationalize the voted actions from each domain into business process patterns. This functionality can provide an organizational or ecosystem fail-safe as well as an information system to monitor the overall organizational health between domains—identifying potential risks or opportunities for optimization across traditional organizational domain boundaries.

In order for otherwise disconnected domains to communicate action and results through to the parliamentary system, secure information sharing should be leveraged to protect the critical higher-order functions and impacts of input data influence or output execution. Each domain AI instance would be provided a unique key resolving for the parliamentary instance. When submitting results, the parliamentary ledger records the payload, and the parliamentary instance is responsible for decrypting and processing the instruction.

Secure information sharing enables organizations distributed across networks, geography, or internal connectivity boundaries to create systems of AI collaboration, maintain auditability and verifiability, and mitigate risk of strategic business information leaking in transit.

4.5.4 Permeation in the Autonomous Network

Parliamentary AI constructs, distributed ledgers, secure information sharing, strong validation, audit-friendly decision path recording, and appropriate choices using Proof-of-Authority consensus enable creation of a learning, evolving autonomous network. Whether faced with traditional security threats, game theory attackers, VNF vendor license auditing, continuously variable business and traffic needs, or selective regional service interruption, the techniques described provide for a network that can self-manage and adjust.

Networks today already include self-healing mechanisms and are built for a certain level of redundancy and the physical layer. However, as the network evolves from a single or dual mode physical layer with common, general purpose traffic characteristics to mixed-domain parallel usage patterns, the capability to define actions in software must be supplemented by software-driven configuration, adjustment, and policy.

Network sessions should reach physical beings to provide experiences that transit between devices, seamlessly. Capacity should move, predictively, with anticipated business needs. The ecosystem of services that individuals and organizations consume should always have network affinity to their customer.

All the while, the autonomous network must remain a safe haven for data, transactions, digital assets, and protect individual propriety. Autonomous networks of the future must incorporate many advanced approaches like those discussed here in order to be self-contained, self-optimizing, and self-guarding. In Chapter 5, autonomous networks are described in detail, as is the need to evolve from purpose-built, specification-designed networks of today to evolving, dynamic networks of the future.

REFERENCES

1. Ledger, in *Ledger and Trial Balance* (http://www.accountingexplanation.com/ledger.htm)
2. UK Government, Sir Walport, M., Distributed Ledger Technology: Beyond block chain (2016) (https://assets.publishing.service.gov.uk/government/uploads/system/uploads/attachment_data/file/492972/gs-16-1-distributed-ledger-technology.pdf)
3. Blockchain (https://en.wikipedia.org/wiki/Blockchain)
4. https://bitcoin.org
5. https://sovrin.org
6. https://www.ethereum.org
7. https://www.hyperledger.org
8. Buterin, V., Merkling in ethereum (https://blog.ethereum.org/2015/11/15/merkling-in-ethereum/)
9. Nakamoto, S., Bitcoin: A peer-to-peer electronic cash system (https://bitcoin.org/bitcoin.pdf)
10. Buterin, V., Understanding serenity, part 2: Casper (https://blog.ethereum.org/2015/12/28/understanding-serenity-part-2-casper/)
11. Buchman, E., Tendermint: Byzantine fault tolerance in the age of blockchains (https://atrium.lib.uoguelph.ca/xmlui/bitstream/handle/10214/9769/Buchman_Ethan_201606_MAsc.pdf)
12. Schwartz, D., N. Youngs and A. Britto, The ripple protocol consensus algorithm (https://ripple.com/files/ripple_consensus_whitepaper.pdf)
13. Turner, B., The Paxos family of consensus protocols (http://www.fractalscape.org/files/paxos-family.pdf)
14. Abbeel, P. and A. Y. Ng, Apprenticeship learning via inverse reinforcement learning (https://ai.stanford.edu/~ang/papers/icml04-apprentice.pdf)
15. Raina, R., A. Y. Ng and D. Koller, Constructing informative priors using transfer learning (http://ai.stanford.edu/~ang/papers/icml06-transferinformativepriors.pdf)

CHAPTER 5

Building the Autonomous Networks of the Future

Stephen Terrill and Mattias Lidström

CONTENTS

5.1 INTRODUCTION

Nils Bohr said, "Prediction is very difficult, especially if it's about the future," and Winston Churchill is known to have stated, "In politics when you are in doubt what to do, do nothing...when you are in doubt what to say, say what you think."

This chapter outlines some of the fundamental technical challenges in today's software-defined networks, which are, at the same time, opportunities to move toward an autonomous network—an autonomous network is a network that is self-contained; it self-manages, self-optimizes, and protects itself from all forms of cyberattacks. An autonomous network reacts to external and internal stimuli in the same way as the human body or an animal does. A good example of this is a self-driving car, which can autonomously navigate to a programmed destination.

Section 5.2 illustrates a vision for the future network, followed by Section 5.3 that captures who/what the uses of the future network are. Section 5.4 describes how we envisage the future network is managed and controlled, followed by Section 5.5 that discusses the challenges. Finally, Section 5.6 in this chapter goes into a few use cases to illustrate the future network.

5.2 THE FUTURE NETWORK

5.2.1 The Future Network Vision

Communications networks were previously single purpose. The equipment in the network was focused on providing a well-functioning single service (e.g., voice services or data services) and tended to consist of physical equipment and have a well-known usage pattern. The services were well specified through standards, they were predictable, and the service definition was built into the equipment. The network equipment was rather isolated from the business support systems, and the operational support systems were just that—support systems to the operation of the network equipment.

This has now changed in a number of fundamental ways. The communication networks are now supporting multiple services [1], and each service has different characteristics and requirements. The usage patterns are no longer predictable and can vary rapidly, for example, due to the introduction of a new consumer device or the success and failure of a popular consumer applications. Physical equipment is becoming virtual and multipurpose, and networks are becoming programmable. The move from physical functions to virtual functions, together with programmable networks, creates the possibility for network functions to be relocated in real time. This in itself enables new optimization possibilities that were previously not possible. Furthermore, the increase in available compute power facilitates that the network functions are not only multipurpose but also become smarter, meaning that they can learn the required task within set parameters. The operational support systems are evolving from supporting the network and equipment to defining and managing the service provided by the network, leveraging the evolving programmability of network equipment. The operational support systems are also evolving to have a tighter coupling to the business support systems to enable the rapid introduction of services and more responsive customer care. With the introduction of

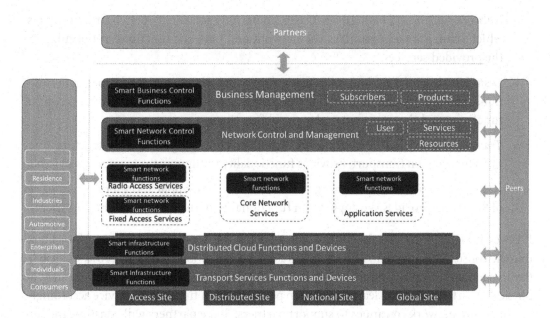

FIGURE 5.1   Future network architecture.

artificial intelligence (AI) and increasing programmability and the need to support radically different use cases, this change is accelerating.

The future network, which is rapidly approaching, will supply multiple services, and each service will have radically differing characteristics and unpredictable usage patterns. The consumers of the provided services will vary, ranging from humans with fixed/mobile devices to non-human devices (e.g., Internet of Things [IoT]/machine-type communication). The non-human devices include items such as surveillance cameras to doorbells and home white goods (e.g., fridge and washing machine), as well as semiautonomous/autonomous vehicles and industrial equipment.

The network equipment and networks functions are resources to support the service delivery. They will be tailored to support either a single service or several services and become *smart network functions* (*SNFs*). Being smart implies self-learning capabilities provided by AI coupled with intent-based policies that capture the constraints. This implies they can learn within their own context how best to perform their allocated task. To illustrate how a network function can become smart, consider how the network functions allocates their available resources. Some user information is best kept in fast memory; however, for other users, it may be best to off-load the subscriber state information toward mass storage. Then learning about changes in user behavior can allow the function to move data from mass storage to fast memory in preparation for user activity.

The future network architecture is illustrated in Figure 5.1. The main layers are described as follows:

- *Business management layer*, containing smart business control functions. The business management layer supports product identification, customer and partner management.

- *Network control and management layer*, containing smart network control functions, which manages and optimizes the network and network functions to optimize for the provided services.

- *Distributed cloud functions and devices layer*, containing smart infrastructure functions, and providing an execution environment for the SNFs, smart business control functions, and the smart network control functions.

- *Transport services functions and devices layer*, also containing smart infrastructure functions focusing on transport, provides functionality to support the transport services.

- *Network functions layer* covering the access, core, and application services, consists of SNFs and provides the application functionality of the network to the end-users.

It is worth highlighting that the distributed cloud and transport layers can be said to extend into the consumer equipment. The smart infrastructure functions primarily provide capabilities to support the execution environment (compute, storage, and networking) and may be physical or virtual. They can learn application patterns and optimize their service accordingly.

The future network continues to support partners. Some partners will consume the services provided by the network to support their business needs, and some partners provide services that are required to execute on the end-to-end service. The different parts are expanded in more details in the following section.

The network functions described as a grouping[1]:

- SNFs to support radio access services

- SNFs to support fixed access services

- SNFs to support core network services

- SNFs to support application services

The SNFs provide the application functionality toward the end-users of the network and execute on a distributed cloud infrastructure consisting of smart infrastructure functions. The exact sites of a distributed cloud are dependent upon the operator's network. However, commonly there will be smaller data centers that could be located in the access network (at the network edge), on the customer premise, through to more global sites hosting large data centers.

The operational support system of the future network is referred to as network control and management. The smart network control functions (of the network control and management layer) fundamentally work with the concepts of users, services, and resources. That is, it manages resources to provide a service (that is defined and managed by the network control and management layer) to the end-users. The resources are the SNFs and the smart infrastructure functions. It is responsible for the complete service and resource life-cycle management, from definition, through to assurance and optimization and retirement. The smart network control functions become the brain of the network, programming the SNFs

---

[1] Note: This grouping is for descriptive purpose only and doesn't imply how the network is organized or deployed.

to provide the necessary services. The smart network control functions, together with the SNFs, learn the common service and usage patterns, hence gaining the understanding of how to both optimize the network as well as learning how to deploy new solutions to support the provided services and to optimize the network [2].

The smart network control functions, and to some extent the SNFs, will be able to anticipate future user needs. This will enable them to allocate the necessary resources in advance, maximizing the users experience at minimal additional cost. The smart network control function is like a puppeteer who pulls the strings of the puppets to create a pleasing experience to the audience, which are the shows' consumers. The smart network control functions have the task to simplify the operational complexity of the network for the service provider.

As the smart network control functions enable the network to become autonomous in providing the network services to the users, the network operator's role will shift from managing the network to managing automation.

The location of the both the SNFs and the smart network control functions will be optimized, balancing the service experience and the operational cost, both of which are dependent upon a number of complex factors. The smart infrastructure functions can support both generic and specialized network functions. Equally, the transport services and functions become smart and can learn. The transport services are considered to be smart infrastructure functions. The way in which infrastructure functions become smart is in learning how to optimize the infrastructure services. One example is responding to providing services and optimizing the use of Input/Output (I/O) functionality or storage functionality based on the application patterns.

Optimizing these networks will balance the tension between providing an optimal end-user experience and the efficient resource and cost utilization (cost is a function of many factors, such as power, transmission, and licensing). As the majority of the SNFs will be virtual functions, they can be placed where it is most cost effective and optimal for the provided service at any given point in time.

The future networks will still require the support of the business process, such as billing, customer, partner, and subscriber relationship management. This is the role of the business management. This, as explained previously, is comprised of smart business control functions that understand the concept of subscribers (those who pay), products, and partners (partners are actors that the operator has a business relationship with and either provide services to the operator or consume services from the operator). It will provide functionality to focus on the subscribers and partners' needs, including the necessary product understanding, as well as efficiently support the business needs, such as charging, billing, and relationship management.

It may be easy to gain the impression that the intelligence is centralized; however, that will be far from the case. The decision-making will be pushed as deep into the network as possible, where higher layers are delegating the decisions as deep as possible (with indicated constraints), while retaining the ability to influence.

It would be easy to state today that the earlier functionality is realized through a microservice architecture; however, the realization technologies will also evolve. Even with new realization technologies, the underlying principle will remain the same though, and that is of reusable components, which will have its capabilities exposed via model-driven interfaces and which can be combined with other the services from other components to create the necessary applications.

As a reader, you may imagine another future network. Even so, you could likely relate your vision to the earlier description. Whatever your vision is, one thing is clear though, and that is that smart is distributed everywhere.

5.2.2 Flexibility—Opportunity and Curse

Traditionally, many of the decisions affecting the architecture of a deployed service provider's network were made during the planning and network design phases based upon a well-understood service definition. Furthermore, the behavior of the network equipment was taken as an input.

This included decisions such as:

- The location of the functionality

- The amount of redundancy to apply, and the redundancy scheme

- Internet protocol (IP) network topology

- The network function topology

- Location of the network functions and network equipment

A great deal of time and consideration was dedicated to making these decisions, and once made and the network deployed, significant effort in time and costs was required to change them. For example, it is not a trivial effort to move a physical node, such as a Mobility Management Entity, Serving GW, or Packet Data Network Gateway (based on the 3GPP standards[2]) with a static network termination point, to another site. There is hardware to relocate, IP networks to redesign, power to establish, and so on. The same applies for simple network expansion. If the network operational staff wanted to change the deployed network (e.g., by relocating functionality or deploying new functions of the same type) the time-scale required was quite long, so in general the operational staff focused on more short-term, less-impacting decisions.

Virtualization and network programmability is changing this. Suddenly it is possible to quickly instantiate new network functions in different locations, to program the IP network to support a new network design and to tailor the network functions to support different needs as the service needs adapt. This allows for virtual networks that are tailored for a specific business purpose to be deployed in parallel (often referred to as network slicing, that is a separate logical network for a specific purpose or set of characteristics). Coupled with the evolving network capabilities, the need for utilizing this new flexibility is also increasing. The nature of the provided services is becoming irregular, and there are continuously new services

---

[2] www.3gpp.org

to manage, some quite short-lived. Overall, virtualization and network programmability results in a huge increase of agility in the network. This is certainly a blessing.

The flip side of the network agility is that many of decisions that were previously made during the planning and network design phases now need to be made during the network operations phase. The time to consider all of the nuances of a decision is reduced, and the required rate at which these decisions need to be made is much higher. Furthermore, the time between upgrades of the network functions is dramatically decreasing from yearly or one-half yearly upgrade plans to Continuous Integration/Continuous Deployment (CI/CD) methodologies leading to and including the DevOps paradigm. This results in an increase in the rate of required decisions and rate of deployment execution expected of the operational staff. To expect this of the network operations staff using the traditional network management methods and technologies, while at the same time, keeping operational costs stable, is nearly impossible. This is the curse.

This curse can be overcome and the complexity managed through a combination of separations of concerns combined with network abstraction and the employment of smart technologies in the form of AI. Artificial intelligence, as a technology, will be crucial for enabling the automation of the required rapid decision-making and predicting future needs (e.g., new services or expansion of resources) that can manifest itself in preapproved actions to be executed on, as well as detecting and predicting failures, hence, ensuring that the network is self-reliable. This will simplify the network operations.

5.2.3 The Road to the Future Network

There are several transformations ongoing when considering how to reach the future network.

- Cloud and network function virtualization.

  - Virtualizing the network (network functions, infrastructure functions, management and control, and business management) enables flexibility in how the network, including the support systems, is deployed and managed. There is economy of scale in the common infrastructure functionality to efficiently support network function virtualization.

- Network function and device evolution.

  - Network functions and devices are being virtualized and evolving to virtual network functions. In doing so, they are becoming more multipurpose and being "programmed" for how to behave. At the same time, they are becoming smart, in that they are being developed with capabilities that enable them to learn how best to do their assigned task.

  - Still, some network functions and devices will, out of necessity, remain physical (e.g., switches, servers, radio base stations). This will still tend to become programmable and smart, and from a network function or device external perspective, they will look a lot like a virtual function, with some more limited capabilities (e.g., not able to scale or relocate).

- Networks are programmable (via software-defined networks).

  - The move toward transport networks becoming programmable, that is, being programmed centrally for the task at hand, has already started and well on the way. The centralization of the control of transport networks provides a more complete overview of the network supporting optimization approaches (allowing a model and policy driven approach to network management) that were previously not possible in a decentralized approach where all decisions were taken locally. Further to this, the programmability of transport networks provides the capability to rapidly reconfigure the network to support a new situation. This is essential in order to support the dynamic allocation of virtual network functions. Network programmability is also referred to as software-defined networks.

- Networks become intelligent.

  - As the network functions and devices evolve to be smart, the networks become intelligent. They become capable of learning and adapting to the current situation based on past experience. They can be influenced by the higher layers (orchestration, policy, analytics, and AI) via programmability.

- Operational support systems generalization.

  - The operational support systems today are dedicated to their domain (e.g., operational support systems for transport, for radio access networks, for cloud infrastructure). The model-driven approach to operational support systems implies that they will become more horizontal in the terms of being more multidomain (the same support system supporting multiple domains), while providing domain-specific support via models for the said domains (radio, transport, core, cloud infrastructure). At the same time, the operational support systems take a greater role in the service definition and become smart.

- From automation to autonomous networks.

  - Automation is ongoing today. The starting point is scripting repetitive tasks, and also via orchestration. In the current techniques, the known knowledge is captured in a predescribed manner. This is insufficient, as it cannot handle situations not included in the known knowledge, and a more autonomic approach is required [3].

  - Automation will, however, move toward autonomics. This will enable networks to handle unknown situations (e.g., situations not previously considered) and still handle them supporting the defined services and within the set boundaries. This will lead to an evolution of closed-loop automation where AI will understand the current and desired network situation and suggest the appropriate actions, and adaptive policy will control the boundary conditions.

In summary, existing functionality in the network will become smart in a stepwise fashion. That is, they will move from being programmed or scripted for following a predescribed routine based on previously known knowledge to being autonomic and learning the best approach within described boundaries (constraints).

5.3 WHO ARE THE FUTURE NETWORK USERS?

The network users of today will continue, then there are future users we can already identify today, and there are other future users we don't yet imagine. Consider any random street of any major city, and there will be people, cars, taxis, buses, trains, traffic lights, shops, doors, bins, air sensors, and all sorts of things. Consider a rural area where farm equipment, such as tractors, harvesters, crop sensors, and agricultural animal tags will be present. Consider an enterprise; there will be computers, cash registers, communication equipment, printers, servers, and so on. Consider any industrial factory or industrial enterprise; there will be production machinery, inventory, produced goods, transport equipment, and so on. Consider a random family home; there will be alarms, lights, heating, entertainment equipment, white goods, garden sensors, controllers, and so on.

These are simple examples of what could be the future network users. The list could go on quite somewhat, as further examples consider hospitals, malls, conference centers, shopping centers, restaurants, sports centers, emergency services, and so on.

The needs of the future users will vary markedly. Understand their needs, providing a suitable commercial proposition to the users, and providing the necessary network support will be required to be done, yet done in a simple way in the face of such remarkable variation.

The following examples will also illustrate that a simple classification of future users as described is not sufficient to understand their needs.

5.3.1 The Private Consumer

The private consumer is typical of many network users today. This can include households with a broadband connection through to mobile broadband users with mobile devices of different types (phones, tablets, computers, watches, or other wearables).

The private consumer is cost conscious and only wishes to pay for the value and usage they receive. This implies a tailoring of the offered services to them addressing the value that they perceive. Aside from increased bandwidth and the expectation of always being connected, the private consumer will also have increased expectations on security. Further, the private consumer will also have other devices behind the network-connected device (increased connected machines, security and surveillance, equipment that may need additional security support due to the device manufacturers cost pressure, and time-to-market leads to that the device may not be inherently secure).

5.3.2 Internet of Things

The IoT typically refers to machines and machine-type communication. This in itself can be varied and range from low-power low-bandwidth devices (e.g., garden water sensor and connected doorbells) to high-bandwidth and high-powered devices, such as surveillance equipment or remotely controlled devices. It covers other varying aspects, such as mobility, rate at which data should be sent, and scheduling of such data. These users will need network predictability and hardened security. Some classes of IoT devices will also benefit from other network support, such as analyzing the data, informing the owner of problems, and device upgrades.

While today a user purchasing an IoT device relies on existing mobile or fixed broadband capabilities, together with the existing service definition, future networks will provide support for tailing the network to the IoT device's needs through autonomous networks. The virtualization capabilities of the network will enable separate logical networks that are specialized to the device's needs, and indeed may come as part of the contract to use the device.

5.3.3 Enterprises

Enterprises are businesses that are small or large and require communication services, such as connectivity, mobility, and person-to-person communication. In addition to an office, they could be specialized businesses: pharmacies, doctors, hospitals, commercial shops. The enterprises' requirements will evolve to require more flexible relationships tailored to their needs and also further network support in terms of specialized applications that can be made available to the enterprises through a single-sign-on and a one-stop shop. Security will also be key as well as securely hosting the enterprises compute infrastructure for the enterprise.

Take as an example a hospital as an enterprise. It may require on-demand interoperability with other hospitals or medical specialists, to both consult on a situation with a patient, perform remote procedures, or to share access to specialized equipment. This will require flexible and dedicated communication solutions that cannot be compromised or become unavailable. It will require the support for privacy and secure communication. Transferring specialized analysis data can require extreme and unpredictable transmission bandwidth. This is not feasible without support from the network to provide prioritization and secure, reliable communication.

5.3.4 Industries

Industries could be considered mining, manufacturing, or infrastructure utilities that provide services, such as electricity, gas, or even transportation. Their individual needs will be radically different and will include extremes in terms of coverage, availability, and bandwidth. For example, mining or manufacturing operations cannot be exposed to network outages, and hence requires high availability, while the reporting usage from meters and device management have completely different requirements. Applying the same availability mechanisms required for mining and manufacturing to meters would be cost prohibitive.

Today, these some of these industries create and operate their own specialized network. This is a means to provide the required availability and security that these industries do not see as available in the typical broadband or mobile broadband networks of today. The future networks, to address the industries, will provide the availability and security required of the industry by providing networks logically isolated from the networks supporting private users and enterprises. Without tailored support for each industry, either the costs for the networks for the IoT consumers, private consumers, or enterprise consumers will not be economic, or the characteristics of the networks for other industries will be compromised.

5.3.5 The Unknown

As previously described, the future network needs to be equipped to handle the future users' needs that we cannot predict today, in terms of handling their characteristics, tailoring the offering, and getting the offerings to them quite rapidly. In short, the future network needs to support both business agility and network agility.

5.4 FUTURE NETWORK OPERATIONS

5.4.1 Paradigm Shift: From Managing the Network to Managing Automation

As described in the previous section, networks used to be centered around one service, and the networks were purposefully built to support this service; the same was true for the management of such networks. All operations and management were focused on providing this one service for the end-user. As networks have evolved, so has the complexity of managing these networks. For every new service that was added, so was an additional management and monitoring function. In time, these have begun to interfere with one another. Furthermore, orchestrating the management of the complete network consisting of many different services and components has become a priority in managing the whole network.

Today we are still managing networks and all functions of the network in detail. That is, the operational staff of a service provider are managing and configuring the network functions, network, and devices directly. If a comparison was drawn between how the operational staff manage the network today to how the climate control was managed in a car, it would be as if the car operator was turning on and off the heating and cooling components in the car instead of setting the desired temperature.

A step in making the network smarter is introducing machine learning and AI in the networks to create smart functions that handle parts of the network. Data-driven functions for networks will improve on existing solutions by utilizing more and more current information than what has been possible before. This will make it possible to continuously train and adapt these functions, allowing a flexibility in network behavior that has not been seen before. It will even be possible to solve problems that were previously not feasible to solve. Machine learning technologies, such as random forest or deep-learning algorithms with neural networks, can utilize much more data and parameters than a human expert can in order to rapidly test and find new solutions. This is applicable both for existing problems and new problems that will arise as the networks become more complex in order to cater for new required capabilities. Each function introduced in the network will operate on a given set of data and solving a specific task.

As automation increases for managing details of the networks, it will become the role of the network manager to manage the goals and targets for the network. Smart functions in the network will self-tune based on a given task for each function. In order to maintain a network where everything is automated, it is important to understand how this will change as the network evolves. As more and more smart functionality is built into the network, configuration parameters are abstracted away from the network management. Each function can be viewed as a service for your network; this service will have a specific role from a management point of view. Examples of such services could be latency optimization, bandwidth utilization, SLA monitoring, usage prediction, or link monitoring. Output from functions like these will provide a current view of the network. By having this real-time view of the network, it will be possible for applications to interact with the smart functions to create predictions and set expectations before execution. In addition to this, each service will operate within a given context; this context is given from a global perspective to avoid local optimization that can affect the network on a larger scale. If we come back to the comparison to the climate control in a car, this is equivalent to setting the desired temperature in the car and allowing the car to work out how to use the heating and cooling components to get to that temperature instead of turning them on and off directly.

When an application wants to execute on the network, certain guarantees can be asked of the network, and smart infrastructure functions will then provide necessary resources for the application to execute. It is also the network's task to make sure that applications are operating within the set parameters previously agreed upon. This behavior is also learned over time and can be an important feedback mechanism for services and crucial for understanding the application interaction impact on network functionality.

Abstraction is also part of the shift from managing networks to managing automation. At different levels in the network application, needs are described in various levels of detail. This can be requirements, such as latency, bandwidth, or other parameters relevant for the service's service level agreement (SLA). The more accurate the description, the more accurately the network will be able to adapt to service and applications. Since the services and applications will be more observable as well, it is possible to learn this behavior and subsequent requirements over time. This will also affect how the networks are built, possible settings or parameters that can be manipulated by the network operator will decrease, or rather these will be abstracted away as well. Since more information is available for the services running on top of the network, it will be easier to tune the network to suit these services. In a similar manner, it will also be possible to learn how settings and parameters work together with a given mix of services that needs to be supported. Once this is known, it will also be a natural next step to abstract the methods for which to tune the network for different services by grouping these features and offering an abstracted view on how to optimize. In a simple example, Service A requires additional resources. In order to increase the resources, parameters X, Y, and Z needs to be altered. The operator will only need to decide to increase resources for A, and the network will work out how to change X, Y, and Z in order to reach these demands. Here it is also possible to monitor services and applications to ensure that they are playing by the rules. Once a service misbehaves, it can be detected and raised to the service provider as a problem. The resolutions will be dependent on the service and type of problem that has arisen.

5.4.2 The User's Perspective

Users today are getting used to being able to access any service from any device at any time. The user perspective is simple: everything should just work all the time. This will also be true for the autonomous networks; however, the services and applications that the users will consume are bound to put more strains on the network tasked with delivering all of this to the users, whether they are private consumers or enterprise customers. Applications such as 3D video, virtual- and mixed-reality applications, and telepresence available all the time and from anywhere impose new requirements. Combined with a growing segment for IoT devices, the autonomous network will have to cope with delivering services to all of them. Users also rely on their access provider to make their services secure. This will also pose new requirements on network operators. Similar to banking, the customer does not want to change the behavior and relies on the bank to protect them from fraud and other security threats. The same requirements will be imposed on the network provider to seamlessly ensure a trusted and secure network. Enterprise customers are likely to enforce more stringent SLA's when subscribing for a network service, but the expectations will be the same for any service anytime and anywhere.

5.4.3 Managing the Services

With the transformation to an autonomous network, the operational staff will move from managing the network elements to managing automation. A critical aspect of this shift is to place the provided service in focus and also how that affects management of that service. A service provides value to the consumer and can be described with a number of attributes. These attributes can be translated into performance indicators, such as latency or delay, service establishment time, availability, data consistency, and service settings. The task of the service provider's operational staff will move toward ensuring that the described performance indicators can be met whilst at the same time consuming the minimal possible amount of resources, such as energy and transmission. This has to be achieved through the entire life cycle of the resources used in the network to deliver the service. Furthermore, AI has a predictive ability, which can enable future service needs to be anticipated. This allows the operator to use this to design and preapprove future services that may be required. Today, the focus is on managing the network, which means using perhaps a different set of key performance indicators (KPIs) to ensure that a customer's SLA is followed. With a change to service-focused management, a different set of KPIs would be monitored, and with smart network control functions interacting better with smart functions in the network, machine learning technologies will provide useful insights for how data and traffic can be handled in order to reach the best customer satisfaction.

5.5 THE FUTURE NETWORK CHALLENGE

5.5.1 It's All about the Data

Today's networks are built from lots of components, from transport through to cloud and to the network, network management, and business management. Whether they are physical entities or virtual functions, they need to operate with data. In order to create a truly automated intelligent network, this data has to be made available for smart functions to operate. Data will exist on various levels in the network. With data, we mean any kind of data that can be produced and exposed, such as (but not limited to) device telemetry, instrumentation, Simple Network Management Protocol (SNMP) statistics, logs, states, current configuration, alarms, user data, Operations Administration and Management (OAM), user statistics, device information, subscription type, data rates, and weather data. With an increase of smart functions in the network, any data that can be used to optimize the network function will be used before it is passed on or discarded. Ultimately, much of this data may end up in a cloud data center or some kind of data lake. Here, data can be used for offline learning to create new functions, long-term learning tasks, trend reporting, etc. This might seem obvious for the reader of this book or anyone who has a background in data science, but without data there can be no learnings from the data. Traditionally, data from nodes and functions in the network stay within this node since the cost of sampling, logging, and exposing data requires additional resources that are mainly used for troubleshooting when things go wrong in the network. This often leaves the network operator without information when problems occur since there are no logs, no recorded data of what was going on in the network when the problem occurred. When designing new functions, data availability should be one of the central functions for each of these nodes. Not only should the network be designed for the possibility to expose data, but one would like to be able to instrument how data is produced for each of these functions. This will make components more future proof than before. In order to achieve this, data exposure should be built into every function designed for the network and streamed in real time. Limiting data movement is necessary to avoid overloading the network. By allowing the network operator to manage data, it would be possible to focus on certain parameters, functions, or services at different times. Typically, this would be helpful in troubleshooting scenarios or when retraining data models. The data produced should also be produced exactly once and read by many services or functions as required. By being able to instrument the data collection before data is published, it will also be possible to manipulate the data during its creation. For instance, one might want to aggregate certain types of data as close to the source as possible. Other functions could potentially also be added directly to the data sources themselves, such as smart filters, functions, or decision models.

As mentioned, when redesigning or creating the new network elements, it should be possible to instrument how data is created and exposed inside and outside the network function. This has the added benefit that new data sets can be created on demand. Since data is associated with a cost, only useful data should be created and maintained. However, in order to try new functions, troubleshoot, or increase understanding of events in the network, it will be a powerful tool to be able to flexibly generate data for research, diagnostics, or other triggering events. It can also be a life-cycle parameter for smart functions where data is turned on and collected for learning during certain periods, only or if performance of current models start degrading.

5.5.2 The Changing Technology Landscape

Artificial intelligence, which is today realized through data science and machine learning, is currently one of the fastest-moving technology areas, enabling new methods, frameworks, and products to be released on a weekly basis. Many of these methods are dismissed as fast as they are produced. However, after some shaking and baking, some of them find their way into the frameworks that become the data scientist's everyday toolkit. In the future network, we will see an equal evolution of smart functions that will either be disproved or evolve to become integral to the networks daily operations. As a result of this change, more powerful networks will be produced. One crucial aspect to increase the power of the network is being able to utilize the data that the network produces. This will mean more computing resources and more memory throughout the network. While Moore's law seems to have slowed down in terms of raw clock cycles per core, the number of cores is increasing at a spectacular rate. Moore's law is still applicable for memory however, which means that the price for memory is halved every eighteen months or so [4]. The combination of increased cores and memory ultimately boils down to more computing power, even if the complexity of the computations increases with distributed computing, more advanced algorithms, and increased complexity of problems to solve. In addition to traditional computing with increased cores, clock cycles, and memory, more tailored hardware is being used for these types of computations. Graphical Processing Units are becoming increasingly popular for deep-learning applications. Custom-built Tensor Processing Units from Google are now available [5], IBM is releasing their SyNAPSE range of neural network processing chipsets [6], and Qualcomm has put a Neural Processing Engine in their latest snapdragon mobile platform [7].

There is a cost associated with increased capabilities in the networks. As cost for this hardware decreases, more services can be handled better, and the ecosystem will eventually balance out the increased investments needed.

5.5.3 The Human Challenge

There are a number of challenges in the field of autonomous networks and AI that are non-technical as well as technical. Network engineers do not trust magic boxes that will solve most of their problems better, faster, and cheaper than they ever could. The quest for acceptance of such methods and models include convincing experienced engineers that machines and algorithms can learn and evolve solutions faster and better than they can. Furthermore, the competence of the remaining engineers will have to shift from understanding the networks to understanding the algorithms and tools used to achieve zero-touch maintenance (as will be described further in the next chapter). In addition, the new generation of network engineers need expertise in Application Programming Interface (API) frameworks, orchestration platforms, and how service deployment and system operations applications interact with the actual physical and virtual components in the network. Another area that will become increasingly difficult is troubleshooting problems. While using advanced machine learning techniques, such as neural networks, can be great for automating certain network functions, understanding the output and intermediate interpretations of this function and why it fails in certain cases can be extremely hard to understand.

In order to overcome the challenge of understanding new ways of presenting results, predictions and models need to be developed. Similar to understandability in other sectors, information needs to be presented in such a way that the user of the system can easily understand the information. As described previously, the users will have to possess a reasonable understanding of the tools and methods that are being used. People working in network management today will have to learn these new technologies in order to maintain relevance. Experienced network management people can play an important role helping in developing and further honing automated methods for autonomous network operations. Of course, not everyone will be able to develop new functionality in such an environment as this; it will require people highly skilled in the field of data science. There will also be a high degree of specialization in various fields and aspects of data science, which in itself will add new specialization tracks for interconnecting several of these various methods. Data scientists will have to work together with subject matter experts (e.g., experienced network operators) and business experts to create the maximum value for new functions for the network.

5.6 AUTONOMOUS NETWORK APPLICATION

The following are example applications envisioned by the autonomous network.

5.6.1 Zero-Touch Operations

The term *zero-touch operations* is rather self-descriptive. That is, the network is operated without human intervention. Still, expectations on the network can vary over time (e.g., optimizing for capacity or optimizing for coverage), and services can be introduced; hence, the service providers' operational staff are managing the networks through managing the required KPIs instead of managing the network equipment itself.

Within the network (covering both the operational support systems and the network functions and devices) the closed-loop control is operating. Closed-loop control involves taking the data from the network, analyzing the data to provide insights on the state of the network to support the services, using policy to decide on the required actions, and actuating the required action through orchestration (refer to Chapter 3 for more information). Artificial intelligence can support the entire close-loop control. The closed-loop control is continuously ensuring the service agreements are met while optimizing the network. The network may identify several ways to optimize its configuration to meet the end-users' expectations, even in the case of a network incident. The decision of which is the best identified alternative to follow will be based on the constraints (what is allowed) and learned history (i.e., which actions are most likely to resolve a given situation). This is illustrated in Figure 5.2.

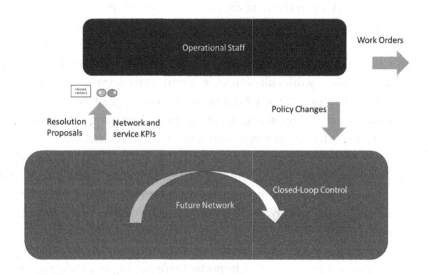

FIGURE 5.2   Zero-touch operations.

In the cases of network incidents, suboptimizations or SLA breaches, the operational staff are both informed of this and provided with suggestions on how to handle this. This may include policy adjustments in the network or creating work orders to fix physical incidents.

One example of this is the following scenario:

Enterprise 1 has ordered connectivity between two buildings, building A1 and building A2. Likewise, Enterprise 2 has ordered connectivity between two buildings, building B1 and building B2. The nature of the agreement is that after an agreed outage time, financial penalties apply. In the case that there is a network incident that implies that transport capacity is insufficient to serve both Enterprise 1 and Enterprise 2, the classical approach would be to program a strategy via policies into the network. This strategy could be, for example, to prioritize traffic for the enterprise that is closest to an SLA breach. This can also have implications if done incorrectly due to constantly changing the configuration of the network. However, with the autonomous network, the network learns that at the time of the network incident, Enterprise A typically uses less than the contracted capacity, hence prioritizes capacity for Enterprise 2, keeping both customers satisfied.

5.6.2 Optimizing the End-User Experience

A special case of zero-touch operations could be the support of voice recognition or video processing capacity for the end-user. As these are computationally intense, the phones generally rely on network support, and the response time can influence the overall experience of the user. It can be expensive to allocate such processing capacity at the edges of the network all the time, in particular for a mobile network. However, an autonomous network can learn a user's behavior. It can learn when and where users rely on such network support and allocate the function and capacity at the appropriate edge sites that need it the most. The autonomous network can also predict when and where the users are going to require this support.

5.6.3 Intrusion Detection

Security of the future network is going to continue to be a big concern. The autonomous networks will understand typical user and network behavior at the time of day, week, month, year, location and how it is influence by external factors such as weather.

A sudden change in either user or network behavior can be a hint of fraud or intrusion. As described before, the observability of the future network will allow the network operator to detect when such a change occurs. The network can then identify the changed behavior and analyze it for intrusion detection, taking actions to inform users, operational staff, and identify and isolate suspect devices or network equipment.

5.7 SUMMARY AND INTRODUCTION TO CHAPTER 6

The future network will be smart. That is, it can learn and adapt to unknown situations to form an autonomous system. This requires smart functions at all levels of the network with on-demand data collection to support diagnostics and closed-loop operation.

This will change the operations of the network from managing networks to managing automation. The potential is exciting, and there are a number of challenges that have to be met along the way, such as access to data, optimal training, and the human transition.

Artificial intelligence is the fundamental aspect of smart. The next chapter is on opensource. Opensource is a key aspect to building sustainable autonomous networks leveraging the global intellectual capital in solving this complex problem.

REFERENCES

1. NGMN 5G white paper. https://www.ngmn.org/fileadmin/ngmn/content/downloads/Technical/2015/NGMN_5G_White_Paper_V1_0.pdf.
2. M. Svensson, M. Agarwal, S. Terrill, and J. Wallin, Open, intelligent and model-driven: Evolving OSS. https://www.ericsson.com/assets/local/publications/ericsson-technology-review/docs/2018/open-intelligent-and-model-driven-evolving-oss.pdf.
3. S.V.D. Meer, Autonomic networks – Challenges in close the loop – IEEE 5G summit. http://www.5gsummit.org/docs/slides/Sven-Meer-5GSummit-Princeton-05262015.pdf.
4. A. Rowstron, D. Narayanan, A. Donnelly, G. O'Shea, and A. Douglas, Nobody ever got fired for using Hadoop on a cluster, *Proceedings 1st International Workshop on Hot Topics in Cloud Data Processing (HotCDP 2012)*. New York: ACM, 2012.
5. Google cloud platform tensor processing units for faster machine learning. https://cloud.google.com/tpu/.
6. SyNAPSE, IBMs neurosynaptic chipset for AI. http://www.research.ibm.com/cognitive-computing/neurosynaptic-chips.shtml.
7. Snapdragon neural processing engine for AI. https://developer.qualcomm.com/software/snapdragon-neural-processing-engine-ai.

CHAPTER 6

Role of Open Source, Standards, and Public Clouds in Autonomous Networks

David Ward and Chris Metz

CONTENTS

6.1 ZEN OF OPEN SOURCE

"We explore a different, more 'open' approach: the system is thought of as offering a variety of facilities, any of which the user may reject, accept, modify or extend…" [1].

As recalled in "A Brief History of the Internet" published by the Internet Society in 2003, Robert Kahn introduced the idea of an open-architecture network in 1972: "The individual networks may be separately designed and developed and each may have its own unique interface which it may offer to users and/or other providers. including other Internet providers…" [2].

With a clear trajectory toward autonomous networks driven by artificial intelligence (AI), it is a must to adopt an open paradigm. For the many challenges to be addressed, any and all innovation is welcome.

6.1.1 Definition and Motivation

The term "open source software" (OSS) was derived from the Debian Free Software Guidelines [3]. These guidelines were posted as a set of principles governing its licensing and distribution. The source code is included, and anybody is free to hack on it. It is absent from vendor or product affiliation and is technology independent. The ethos of OSS was hacking code and sharing it. Open source software inherits the ideals originally laid out by Lampson, Kahn, et al. all those years ago [1].

From those early altruistic ideals, OSS as it exists today has become more organized. Its freewheeling beginnings have been organized into projects, with a spectrum of overlying governance structures. In this context, success is measured by the size and diversity of both those who create and maintain the source code (referred to as committers) and participants (corporations, academic, individuals, and otherwise) who collectively shepherd a project from inception to release. In the best case, the fruits of the project appear in products and services as well as instigating the formation of larger ecosystems.

Open source software has also become a corporate strategic tool in several ways, used to move industries or enhance a competitive position. In this guise, it often democratizes low-value components of a product or solution space to create new opportunities or isolate intellectual property and allow a broader participation.

6.1.2 Open Source versus Private Source

Private source software is distributed under the terms of a bilateral contract between the software provider and software user. The user will pay the provider for a license to use the software under the conditions set forth in said contract. Private source software is not shared with the public (excluding limited function, trial versions), and the source code is not accessible. Roadmap commitments of new feature code drops are entirely at the discretion of a single provider.

Private source software for the most part has usability advantages, including online documentation and for human interactions a well-designed and intuitive user interface (UI). In many cases, it is subjected to rigorous testing and typically ships after beta users have shaken out most of the bugs [4].

Proprietary functions or algorithms owned by an organization, patent holder, or academic institution generally do not find their way into an open source release. Military and government security agencies operating cybersecurity platforms have justifications for keeping software private.

Private software providers may offer software development kits (SDKs) or documented application programming interfaces (APIs) that expose their platforms to third-party applications or developers. While the user/ecosystem cannot contribute to the core Internet Protocol (IP), they may add value around it.

6.1.3 Contributors and Users

In Section 6.1.1, we defined the role of an open source code committer. Committers create, fix, and maintain source code. One measure of success is having a large, active, and vibrant community. However, open source committer profiles differ depending on career aspirations and position in their company.

"Free coders" are an individual or group of developers, volunteers, hobbyists, students, and the like who create a chunk of code and then upload to a Github repository to make it available for users and committers [5]. Their success may include self-satisfaction, a good grade in a class, a hackathon award, and even a mention in one of a many "best open source for" lists that frequently appear. Building on their experiences and knowledge gained, it is not uncommon for free coders to move into the talent pipeline of software engineers recruited by large organizations working on open source projects.

"Organized platoons" is another category of open source committers. They specialize in one or more disciplines backed by organizations with resources (e.g., vendor, service providers (SP), enterprise). Platoons are composed of some or all of the following: coders, software architects, network architects, hardware engineers, sysadmins, lab personnel, test engineers, interns, designers, management, and leaders in the organization. Platoons flourish in an environment where taking risks, failing, trying again, and producing innovation are rewarded.

Platoons typically reside in big companies that are huge catalysts of open source projects. Proof points are seen in foundation membership rosters, GitHub contributor statistics, and job board skill requirements. Many talk openly of their use of open source. It is fair to mention that the majority of big company code for internal tools and external services is composed of some amount of open source software.

For AI-driven autonomous networks to succeed, contributions and innovations from the research community will be required. Service providers will be called upon to deploy the infrastructure and services. Enterprises who wish to grow their market presence will be encouraged to become active open source contributors. Government entities will play a role with one example being the US Department of Transportation (USDOT) Federal Highway Administration's Open Source Application Development Portal (OSADP) site [6]. OSADP is a web-based portal providing access to the Intelligent Transportation System source code and applications with the goal of facilitating community collaboration on projects sponsored by USDOT.

6.1.4 Role of Consortiums and Ecosystems

Consortiums, foundations, and ecosystems have and will continue to play an important role in the success of open source. They host websites, co-sponsor conferences, provide education, and encourage both community and individual participation. Foundations can help jump-start and validate projects and serve as a milestone on the way toward broader industry acceptance. Projects affiliated with a foundation have a certain level of cachet.

The Apache Software Foundation has been in existence for almost 20 years and is synonymous with open source [7]. The "Apache Way" is based on three principles: individual participation, transparent and open project development, and community. This has served as a model for collaborative efforts across the industry for many years. Apache offers a license, and its ecosystem of open source software has been deployed across the Internet. Their influence and contributions cannot be overstated.

The Linux Foundation (LF) was created in 2000 to serve as a home for the Linux OS (including Linus Torvalds and lead maintainer Greg Kroah-Hartman) [8]. It has sustained itself nicely, first by name association and in recent years serving as the "go-to" site for all things open source. Indeed, judging by the number of projects it hosts, it is clear the industry views the LF as the desired location for open source project incubation, growth, accreditation, and release.

But with that growth comes challenges, in particular how the LF can best interact with standards development organizations (SDOs) [9]. The LF published a white paper discussing the need for harmonization between the two. It pointed out that the industry is now software driven—operators design and deploy new services without dependencies on specialized hardware. Technology adoption is moving away from the classic requirements, architecture, standards, and implementations cycle and more toward reference platforms, architecture, and use-cases.

The challenges boil down to the fact that the process of developing consensus-based standards and architectures is time-consuming. The definition of openness is changing—instead of multivendor, we have vendor neutral with the value-add realized through software orchestration and control.

More communications, both informal and formal, organized multi-SDO/OSS projects and a revised technology adoption methodology blending standards, open source, use-case, and vendor contributions.

A refinement of the responsibilities and roles performed by the participating parties can help. It can be a challenge to mix code contributions, dues expenditure allocations, and manage project marketing and support activities into one large bin. Ideally, projects could be organized such that technical members focus on code contributions, and business experts handle expenses and marketing support.

The solution shown in Figure 6.1 consolidates a group of related projects under a uniform network umbrella project. The technical governance of the individual project communities would not change. Business decisions would be handled by the foundation and its board in the background. To achieve this, the LF formed a project called the Linux Foundation Networking Fund [10]. The initial project members are Fast Data Project (FD. io), OpenDaylight (ODL), Open Network Automation Platform (ONAP), Open Network Function Virtualization (OPNFV), Platform for Network Data Analytics (PNDA), and Streaming Network Analytics System (SNAS).

6.1.5 Standards

Standards development organizations like the Internet Engineering Task Force (IETF), Third Generation Partnership Project, Institute of Electrical and Electronics Engineers, and the European Telecommunications Standards Institute (ETSI) have been around for decades. Unlike the OSS projects, SDOs do not necessarily produce code.

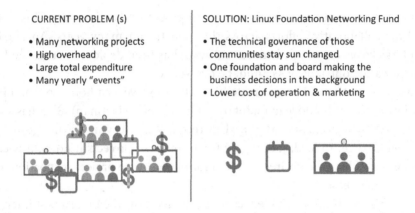

CURRENT PROBLEM (s)

• Many networking projects
• High overhead
• Large total expenditure
• Many yearly "events"

SOLUTION: Linux Foundation Networking Fund

• The technical governance of those communities stay sun changed
• One foundation and board making the business decisions in the background
• Lower cost of operation & marketing

FIGURE 6.1   Linux foundation networking fund solution.

Their contributions include architectures, protocols definitions, interoperability, product compliance, and building vendor/operator coalitions. The evidence of SDO success is obvious in their longevity and the DNA of the Internet and data communications.

A speed mismatch exists between SDOs and OSS communities [11]. The latter moves at a velocity predicated on code development and project committer engagement. Conversely, SDO (let's take the Internet Engineering Task Force [IETF] as an example) time frames are stretched out. The process is composed of written draft text, followed with mailing list discussions and thrice yearly meetings. Birds of a Feather are meetings to debate and decide if there should be formal group meetings—to debate and decide. The end result is a published specification potentially leading to product deployment and operationalization. In turn, a new or modified specification is spawned and the process is repeated. This feedback cycle (good example is the Transport Area Working Group) can occur over a period of years. The authority behind OSS, on the other hand, is in the project community and running code—not a published specification or formal working group structure.

There has been certain progress being made on the SDO front to better reference, utilize, and promote open source. Normative references are provided in IETF Request for Comments (RFC) referencing another standard. In this new scenario, RFCs could provide normative references to an OSS project. OSS documentation including code quality and readability will vary between projects and may not meet the standards of normative references used by the IETF.

A recent development is the release of the YANGCATALOG [12]. It is a catalog and registry of models enabling users to locate and analyze YANG[1] model applicability to their specific use-cases. This application is targeted at several audiences. The first is the YANG module user who wishes to search for a model, double-check the metadata (i.e., organization, maturity, import counts, implementation, service or network element YANG modules, IETF or openconfig tree-type), perform a model impact analysis with dependencies, and generate python code out of the YANG module. The second audience is the YANG module designer

---

[1] YANG is a data modeling language. Other data modeling languages preceded YANG. When it was cooked up, someone in mock resignation referred to it as "Yet Another Next Generation" modeling language, hence the name YANG.

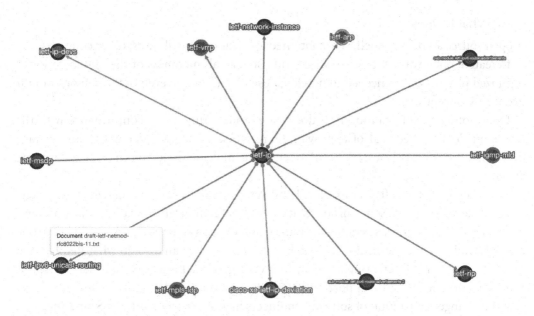

FIGURE 6.2 Example output from the YANG impact analysis tool.

with functions offering a YANG regex validator to play around with W3C pattern statements. It also includes Network Configuration Protocol (NETCONF) and Representational State Transfer (REST) servers to retrieve models for various purposes, including but not limited to inspection, testing, and knowledge building.

Figure 6.2 is an example of the output from the YANG Impact Analysis feature. The figure shows the generation a live tree of the dependent modules based off of the target module (ietf-ip is the example). By clicking on a specific dependent module (ietf-ipv6-unicast-routing is the example), a popup with a URL to the document where it is described will appear. YANG models from different SDOs and vendors are supported. This tool provides the state of complete (and incomplete) YANG module implementations across multiple SDOs. The industry is rapidly moving toward model-driven approaches, and this application can facilitate SDO and OSS cooperation in this important area.

Another area of successful cooperation is the IETF Hackathons [13]. Participants (anyone is invited) engage in coding experimental applications using almost 100% OSS. Prizes are awarded and all efforts are published and available. This is a great way to attract a new breed of programmers, steeped in OSS tooling and development, to IETF meetings and start contributing to the specification process. Better yet, SDO and IETF individuals can meet and talk face-to-face.

And finally, SDOs can emulate the model where a successful transformation and reinvention as an open source project takes place. As a proof point, the Metro Ethernet Forum (MEF) has pivoted from a carrier ethernet service standards body to an open source consortium orientation via the Lifecycle Service Orchestration architecture and their own open source projects (OpenLSO and OpenCS) [14]. MEF is present in the YANGCATALOG tool (one of selectable organizations), partners with the ONAP project and hosts their own hackathon events. They have also stood up infrastructure (i.e., compute, network, storage) where "live standards" experimentation and testing can take place.

6.1.6 What It Does Not Do

Is open source an off-the-shelf, self-contained application? In all cases, other code (private, self-created, open source, or otherwise) and some or all members of the aforementioned organized platoon will be needed to develop a useful application, even of the demonstration/ Proof-of-Concept variety.

Open source is not a standard. It does not mandate functional conformance with the attendant documented seal of approval. There are some that implement industry standards [15]. But alone they are relegated to reference implementation or knowledge-building experimentation.

Open source is not software for sale. However, companies can commercialize an enterprise grade version and sell a product. It is not a stretch at all to claim almost all software (enterprise, consumer) contains a foundation of open source with Android being one example and to a lesser extent is the Apple iOS [16,17]. One can also do what Red Hat has done so successfully by creating a customized version of the Linux OS (Red Hat Enterprise Linux), bundle it up with support and services, and market it to enterprises. Also note that the younger generation of software engineers have experience with OSS, and they will enter the private sector and use these skills to develop products.

6.1.7 Who Benefits from Open Source

Everyone can benefit from open source. Enterprises and operators can involve themselves in the OSS process and use it for learning, development, and testing. They can collaborate with others in the industry (even competitors) to influence OSS project priorities and direction. After all, the desired outcome of any OSS project is that someone will use the software, and may potentially become a code contributor.

Equipment vendors like open source because they can deliver solutions without having to place value-add features inside the hardware. Rather, they can develop hardware platforms using commodity components (e.g., Intel CPUs) and optimize interaction with open source service provisioning and orchestration solutions.

6.1.8 Anticipating Open Source for Artificial Intelligence/Autonomous Networks

What we have learned so far is that open source promotes community collaboration and rapid innovation in the form of committed running code. While more deliberate in pace, SDO architectures and standards have been built into interoperable products deployed worldwide in the global Internet. The advent of AI in software-defined network (SDN) along with the power of OSS and SDO give birth to autonomous networks.

6.2 FROM PIECES TO ARCHITECTURE

6.2.1 Building Blocks

A deconstruction of AI-driven autonomous networks yields nodes of various sizes, shapes, locations, and behaviors. Generally speaking, nodes will operate autonomously, meaning they are not dependent on any external control-plane or data-plane data interactions (unlike IP routers exchanging topology information with each other to determine where to forward packets). Bets are they will run intelligent software or at least through a proxy or server. They could form ephemeral ad-hoc networks and communicate with external entities (e.g., peers, clouds, humans) for application data exchange, telemetry uploads, and software update downloads. One example is our smartphones tethered to our bodies. A more interesting example is the connected vehicle (CV) [18].

Connected vehicles form moving ad-hoc networks that exchange safety and non-safety data wrapped in short messages [19]. Connected vehicles operate sophisticated sensors to receive data from multiple data sources, including in-car, line-of-sight, non–line-of-sight, GPS, road infrastructure, and clouds.

Connected vehicles contain compute resources to run applications, are highly mobile, and require sustained high-bandwidth communications with the Internet over wireless links (LTE/5G). Connected vehicles generate massive amounts of data for internal runtime operations and for telematics export to the cloud. One can consider a CV to be a cloud on wheels.

Data collectors/analytics platforms ingest node-generated data in the form of statistics, states, objects, events, telemetry, and so on, and present it to consuming applications. In some use-cases, the collected data is streamed directly to the application. In other use-cases, the data is stored in a database for offline analysis. A data platform contains southbound plug-ins for communicating with different networks and northbound APIs for external application access. Orchestration/controller platforms support northbound APIs to communicate with the applications and southbound plug-ins to convey program and policy data to the network.

Applications form the brains of the system. They consume data from multiple sources and execute functions where the resultant output in the form of workflow intent is communicated across APIs to the orchestration/controller platforms.

6.2.2 Virtuous Circle

The pattern of reading information from a network, running an application, and (re)programming the network has been a topic of various papers since the early 2000s.

This idea has been applied to autonomic network management called MAPE-K (Monitor, Analyze, Plan, Execute, and Knowledge) that appeared in 2003 [20]. Several renowned Internet technologies described an Internet knowledge plane (KP) as, "a pervasive system within the network that builds and maintains high-level models of what the network is supposed to do, in order to provide services and advice to other elements of the network… is novel in its reliance on the tools of AI and cognitive systems…" [21]

Knowledge-defined networking (KDN) applies the KP to a SDN paradigm [22]. The KDN operational loop depicts the circular flow with AI as a component in the KP, similar to what is described in Section 1.3.4 of this book. RFC7575 outlined the autonomic networking definitions and goals. The IETF Autonomic Networking Integrated Model and Approach working group is chartered to document an overall solution specification.

6.2.3 Big Picture Architecture

Now that the building blocks have been laid out and the notion of the virtuous circle described, we can assemble a big picture architecture. The network and its constituent nodes can take on multiple personalities. Connected vehicles are an appropriate choice for this discussion, given the sheer scale in their numbers and presence of and dependencies on in-vehicle and external compute and network resources (for operating different applications related to safety, infotainment, telemetry uploads to a cloud, etc.). Connected vehicles possess APIs, can be dynamically reprogrammed, and can generate an enormous amount of telemetry data some of which will stay inside the vehicle and some of which will be destined for CV cloud platforms.

There is one other point to make and that is we can have a network of multiple CVs with each being a node; call it an external vehicle network. There can also be a network "inside" the vehicle composed of switch(es) connecting various components (nodes), including electronic control units, head units, and advanced driver assistance systems; call it an internal vehicle network [23].

Data collectors/analytics platforms ingest and possibly process the vehicle data. If the data is being generated from thousands or even millions of CVs and transmitted to a cloud, then that is a big data problem calling for a big data solution. A platform customized for handling internal vehicle data only is present inside the vehicle and is only concerned with internal vehicle network traffic and possibly traffic generated from nearby vehicles or infrastructure (such as safety and non-safety broadcast messages). This data collector/analytics platform, whether cloud based or inside the vehicle, must scale in proportion to the data loads and application processing requirements.

Orchestrator/controller platforms receive workflow orders, intent, a desired predictive or necessary reactive operation, software updates, and so on from applications across APIs—translate that data to configuration and policy commands—then communicate said policy to the network. Connected vehicle clouds will contain large-scale orchestration/controller platform components; those inside a vehicle are smaller and specific to internal vehicle operations.

Different applications, including those employing AI, can exist in the cloud. An example incorporating a big data analytics platform, a machine learning (ML) application and a network controller for automating anomaly detection in a CV network was developed and prototyped by engineers at Cisco Systems. Connected vehicles streamed telemetry to a cloud where a ML application examined the data for potential anomalies. If a candidate anomaly was flagged, the ML application asked the controller to have the CVs increase their telemetry transmission frequency. With additional data arriving to look over, the ML component was able to verify and announce the existence of an anomaly. This closed-loop automation application flow for CV anomaly detection followed the path of the virtuous circle [24].

Note that the big picture architecture typically exists in a campus on up to a large-scale cloud provider environment. However, it can also reside inside in an individual node as is the case with a CV illustrated in Figure 6.3. Connected vehicles are in fact examples of autonomous network nodes, and this notion of nested virtuous circles is a paradigm that will be emulated in multiple domains.

This big picture architecture described in this section is only a high-level abstraction. It can loosely align with the architecture and functions for existing open source implementations with runtime ONAP, discussed in Chapter 3, being a perfect example. Another example can be drawn from the Future Network Architecture vision described in Chapter 5.

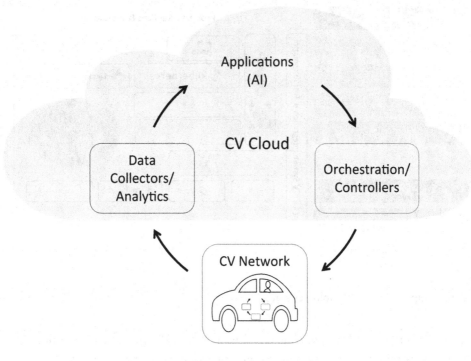

FIGURE 6.3 Nested virtuous circles in connected vehicle networks.

6.2.4 Where Open Source Fits

In principle, open source software can be inserted into any of the building blocks in the CV anomaly detection application described previously, but the amount and roles will vary depending on domain. In the CV space, familiarity and comfort with relatively closed platforms, long development cycles, and necessary caution (i.e., CV safety and security challenges) will delay open source penetration. This is likely not the case in the cloud. It will become standard practice to deploy customized applications such as ML CV anomaly detection on top of an open source cloud platform.

6.2.5 Where Artificial Intelligence/Autonomous Networks Fit

The complexity, scale, and volume of data both for applications and operations will depend on closed-loop automation exemplified by the virtuous circle. Artificial intelligence applications will become commonplace running with, on, and inside of large autonomous networks ranging from the national mobile phone services to automaker clouds communicating with CV fleets out on the road.

6.3 TECHNOLOGIES

There is a universe full of open source packages and platforms. This section will survey a set of open source technologies that individually, or collectively, could be used to build AI-driven autonomous network applications. In the spirit of the classic layered architecture diagrams we are familiar with (i.e., OSI), a modified version of the LF architecture

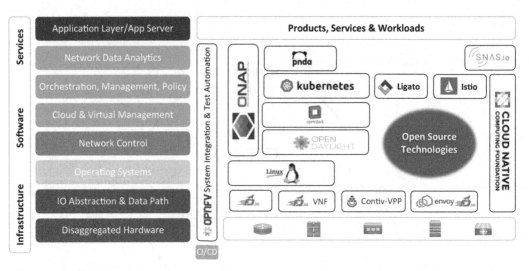

□ THE **LINUX** FOUNDATION

FIGURE 6.4   Open source technologies stack.

stack (infrastructure, software, and services) is shown in Figure 6.4 with the open source platforms and components positioned at their corresponding layer in the stack.

This can serve as a roadmap for the discussions that follow and assist in a recap at the end of this section.

6.3.1 Common Definitions

Acronyms, names, and descriptions of common open source technologies are shown in Table 6.1.

TABLE 6.1   Names and Description of Common Open Source Technologies

Acronym	Name	Brief Description
CN	Cloud native	Encompasses Kubernetes, containers, and microservices
CNF	Cloud native network function	VNFs as a microservice
Container	Container	Lightweight, portable, self-contained executable software package
Contiv VPP	Contiv VPP	Kubernetes network plugin using containerized FD.io as the data-plane
Envoy	Envoy	Invented by Lyft, supports data-plane functions for Istio service mesh
etcd	etcd	k-v datastore for configuration and operations data used in CN environments
FD.io	Fast data project	Open source name for VPP
Istio	Istio	Service mesh software invented by Google
k8s	Kubernetes	Cloud Native Container Orchestration platform
Kafka	Kafka	Message bus using pub/sub pattern
Ligato	Ligato	Platform containing libraries and doc for developing CNFs, a VPP agent, and a CNF Service Function Chain controller

(Continued)

TABLE 6.1 (*Continued*)   Names and Description of Common Open Source Technologies

Acronym	Name	Brief Description
microservice	Microservice	Piece of an application running inside a container
ODL	OpenDaylight	SDN application development and delivery platform
ONAP	Open Network Automation Platform	Reference architecture, framework, and software components for building large-scale cloud deployment platforms
OpenStack	Openstack	Manages compute, network, storage, etc. components in cloud systems
OPNFV	Open NFV	Platform to design, integrate, and test cloud platforms
Plug-in	Plug-in	Software added to any existing system providing additional function
PNDA	Platform for Network Analytics	Open Source Big Data platform
Pub/sub	Publish and subscribe	One application publishes data, one or more subscribers listen and consume it when it arrives
Service mesh	Service mesh	L7 overlay allowing microservices to communicate with each other using sidecars
Sidecar	Sidecar	Container or processes "bolted" to an application microservice container providing additional functions including networking and security
SNAS	Streaming Network Analytics System	High-performance platform for ingesting, storing, and accessing Internet routing system information
VNF	Virtual network function	Virtualized switch, router, service appliance, etc.
VPP	Vector packet path	High-performance packet processing software that can run on physical or virtual systems
ZK	Zookeeper	Configuration and operations datastore, typically used with Kafka

6.3.2 Networking

6.3.2.1 Fast Data Project

The FD.io is a highly scalable programmable application and data-plane platform [25]. It can operate as a virtual switch, router, and service appliance in different environments, including bare metal, cloud, containers, virtual network functions (VNFs), and embedded systems. It runs on a standard suite of commodity CPUs and uses the Intel DPDK (Data Plane Development Kit).

The "special sauce" in FD.io is called vector packet processing (VPP). Figure 6.5 illustrates this process. At a high-level VPP reads a vector of packets from network i/o and runs them through a packet processing directed graph (e.g., one node in the graph is IPv4 input, another might be IPv6 lookup and so on) and then moves on to the next packet vector. Nodes representing different functions can be added, changed or removed thus making it fast and flexible.

The Fast Data Project is a LF project, enjoys broad industry support, has an active and engaged community, and ships in products [25].

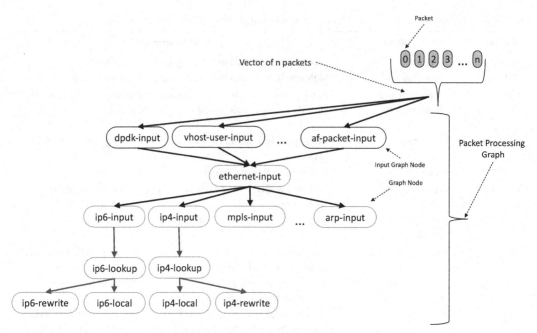

FIGURE 6.5   Vector packet processing graph.

6.3.2.2 Containers

A container can be considered a "lightweight VM" running an application or an individual piece of an application referred to as a microservice [26]. A detailed discussion of containers, microservices, and cloud native (CN) principles is covered in Chapter 7. In this section, we will touch upon the networking aspects of containers.

Containers are deployed across a network of host servers. Containers can be networked together in any number of different ways supported by native or third-party network plug-ins. A container network is a virtual overlay network running on top of a physical underlay network. A network of container-housed microservices is a baseline requirement for application enablement, scaling, and resiliency. A high-performance container network will have a positive impact on overall application performance.

The container networking interface (CNI) is a method for container networking [27]. The CNI defines an API (specification) between the container and a network. The CNI simplifies container networking by grouping one or more containers inside a pod (this is a Kubernetes term discussed in a later section) [28]. Each pod is configured with a unique IP address. Kubernetes employs CNI plug-ins to orchestrate the configuration and establishment of a container network. When a pod is created, a CNI plug-in is installed along with the requisite network configuration information with examples including inter-pod connectivity, encapsulation types, and network policies [29].

As more applications subscribing to the principles of CN are developed and deployed, there will be an even greater need to meet application performance requirements. Improvements in CN container network infrastructure to meet those requirements include:

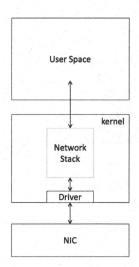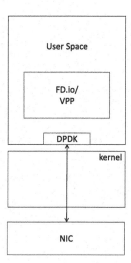

FIGURE 6.6   Kernel networking on the left and user space networking on the right.

- Move container networking functions from the kernel to the user space. Doing so eliminates system call overhead (to the kernel). There is no dependency on the kernel networking community to implement new features. Straightforward to innovate and add new features without touching the kernel. And availability is improved because users space problems will not bring the node down. Figure 6.6 illustrates the differences between the two. On the left, the network stack is implemented in the kernel. On the right, the network functions provided by FD.io/VPP reside in user space and bypass the kernel altogether.

- Build network functions as cloud native network functions (CNFs). CNFs are VNFs implemented as containerized microservices. The same tooling, orchestration, and management systems used for CN application life cycles can be used for CNFs. In essence, CNFs become first-class citizens in a CN application service topology.

The VPP agent provides a control and management plane for VPP-based CNFs [30]. The are several VPP-specific plug-ins (L2, L3, CN-Infra lifecycle mngt) along with northbound API access to external applications and plug-ins. Vector packet processing supplies the data-plane portion. The combination of the VPP agent and the VPP data-plane make up a VPP-based CNF with the architecture depicted in Figure 6.7. The VPP agent is a component of the Ligato open source project [31].

One more example of a VPP-based CNF is Contiv-VPP [32]. This is a Kubernetes network plug-in that abstracts container connectivity and networking. It is implemented in user space and provides high-performance networking for CNFs as well as legacy applications using kernel networking. In addition, applications can bypass the kernel by using a special host VPP Transmission Control Protocol (TCP) stack.

Autonomous networks will place greater scale, performance resiliency demands on CN-based distributed applications operating in any cloud deployment. It is essential to provide the highest possible data-plane performance for container networking.

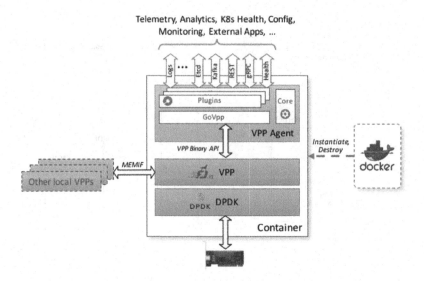

FIGURE 6.7   VPP-based CNF implemented using the Ligato VPP agent.

Container networking interface is supported by the LF and the Cloud Native Computing Foundation [33].

6.3.3 Workflow and Service Orchestration

Workflow is the automation of processes or functions that, when successfully executed, result in the desired business outcome. Service orchestration converts the workflow into tasks that provide and deploy resources to compute network platforms enabling service activation and readiness. This definition could be directly applied to platforms performing these very tasks. One such platform is ONAP, which is discussed in Chapter 3.

6.3.3.1 OpenDaylight

OpenDaylight is an API and development platform supporting application—network interactions [34]. The foundation of the ODL architecture is based on the following:

- Devices, functions, topologies, and services are represented by YANG models.

- Principles of Model-Driven Software Engineering apply. YANG models automatically generate REST APIs. RESTCONF is an example where NETCONF/YANG functions and models are converted into REST APIs [35].

- Supports multiple southbound protocol plug-ins. Examples include Border Gateway Protocol—Link State (BGP-LS), NETCONF, Openflow, and the Path Computation Element Protocol.

OpenDaylight has an active community within the LF. It is fast becoming a cornerstone component in many open source projects such as OpenStack and ONAP.

6.3.3.2 Open Network Automation Platform

Communications service providers (*cloud operators* is another term) are faced with many challenges, including service creation and roll-out, virtual resource optimization, scalability, performance, operation efficiency, and costs. The lack of standards or reference architecture make these tasks very complex.

Operators value services and differentiation. Customers are interested in services and not so much by the infrastructure employed to stand up the service. Thus, it is more cost effective for the industry to solve the problem now in a common way rather than to continue down the road of siloed solutions.

Similarly, vendors see the main differentiation in the virtual and physical devices they provide that create the service, and less so in the way these services are operated. A vendor will be more inclined to support the move toward a common full-service solution stack.

Operators and vendors can collaborate to develop and operationalize cost-effective network stacks that employ the following principles:

- Full-service solution stack that covers service design-time and service runtime for virtual and physical resources. Partial-stack solutions might cover NFV management and orchestration but lack service orchestration and design.

- Full-service solution stack built and architected as a reference platform using existing standards where appropriate. This offers stack "completeness" and avoids costly independent operator solutions.

- Automation to reduce operational expenditures (opex) and deliver faster time-to-market of new services.

- Reference architecture and platform.

These principles are adopted by ONAP [36]. Open Network Automation Platform was born out of a merger between Open-Orchestrator (Open-O) and Enhanced Control, Orchestration, Management, and Policy (ECOMP). ECOMP is the contribution from AT&T and much of what is defined there has been placed under the ONAP project umbrella [37].

The details of the architecture are covered in Chapter 3, and there are supporting references available from the ONAP project repository [36]. The two primary components to note are service, design, and creation (SDC) and the runtime framework [38].

The SDC provides the environment, tools, and systems to define, simulate, and certify assets and functions, including user experience, resources, services, and closed-loop automation. A policy management component enables the creation and deployment of polices governing conditions and expected behaviors to be applied during provisioning of the assets. There are APIs and a software development kit (SDK) offered to encourage ecosystem participation.

The SDC employs a model-driven approach for service definition and orchestration using the Topology and Orchestration Specification for Cloud Applications standard [39]. This offers a set of templates allowing for a straightforward definition of the application (e.g., compute nodes, database, and web app) and deployment life cycle.

The runtime framework executes the functions, rules, and policies defined in the SDC. Included are service orchestration, controllers, and a data collection, analytics, and events (DCAE) component.

ONAP has the distinction of being the first open source platform to realize the vision of automated, closed-loop virtuous circle discussed in the previous section. It is a platform, and as such there is flexibility to incorporate other open source technologies including ODL and FD.io.

ONAP is a LF project and is supported by operators and vendors, somewhat unusual for traditional open source projects.

6.3.3.3 Kubernetes

The use of containers in cloud networks continues to grow [40]. Automation of container life-cycle management and cluster scheduling beginning with their use in development environments all the way through to application and service deployment in production clouds is required. Kubernetes (k8s) is an open source platform providing an automated solution for managing large-scale distributed container deployments [28].

The Kubernetes architecture is composed of several distinct components as shown in Figure 6.8. Pods are where the containerized applications and they are the smallest object that Kubernetes works with. Each pod is configured with a single IP address.

Pods are contained in nodes (also referred to as worker nodes). Nodes consist of a physical or virtual host-enabling container networking and resource management. Nodes communicate with the master node for control plane purposes. There is a kubelet agent that manages nodes and a kube-proxy offering service proxy and load balancer functions for external communications to the Internet as one example.

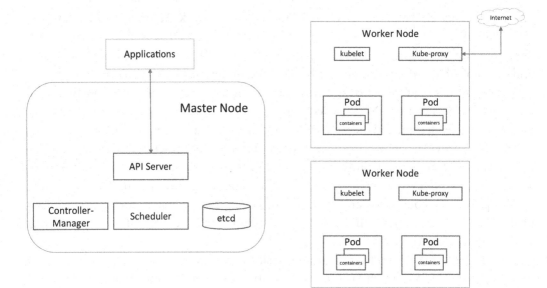

FIGURE 6.8   High-level Kubernetes architecture.

Several different components reside in the master node. An API server offers northbound API support to external applications. Explained in the next section, etcd is used to persist cluster data in a datastore. A scheduler function is responsible for deploying pods and services on available nodes. Controller-manager enables support for multiple controllers including node (monitors node availability) and replication (manages number of pods in the system).

A Kubernetes cluster is defined as a master node and the one or more worker nodes under its control. A Kubernetes namespace value can be assigned to a virtual cluster, thus providing a form of multitenancy. For example, a test group could exist in one namespace and the production deployment group in another. However, inside a namespace, each group could run the exact same applications, services, pod configurations, IP addressing scheme, and so on without knowing about or interfering with the other.

And finally, a Kubernetes service is a logical grouping of pods supporting a specific service entity. An analogy is a front-end load balancer distributing HTTP connections across multiple back-end servers. With a Kubernetes service, there is a pod(s) representing the service (e.g., URL) reachable to external applications and users and one or more back-end pods known only to the front-end pod. Note that back-ends pods can appear or disappear (e.g., for performance or resiliency reasons) without impacting the service.

Kubernetes is supported by the Linux Foundation and the Cloud Native Computing Foundation.

6.3.3.4 Kafka and Zookeeper

According to its homepage: "Apache Kafka is used for building real-time data pipelines and streaming applications. It is horizontally scalable, fault-tolerant, wicked fast, and runs in production in thousands of companies…" [41].

Kafka provides a publisher-subscriber (pub/sub) streaming service message bus inside the cloud, allowing multiple data subscribers (e.g., applications, databases) to consume data from the same data source.

A Kafka-based streaming service requires a topic identifying the stream, a publisher to produce data to the stream, and one or more subscribers to consume data from the stream. There can be multiple topics with different producers and consumers operating on the same Kafka bus.

Kafka leverages Zookeeper to store its metadata. Similar to etcd described in the following section, Zookeeper offers centralized coordination for configuration data of a distributed service, and in this case, for the Kafka cluster.

6.3.3.5 Etcd

Etcd is a distributed key-value store used to store and distribute data across a cluster of machines [42]. Applications can read and write data into the etcd datastore using REST APIs. For example, an etcd datastore could store Kubernetes information about pod and service details, namespaces, and scheduled jobs. These values can be watched, allowing the application to reconfigure itself when these values are updated. Etcd employs the Raft consensus algorithm so that all etcd instances distributed across a cluster of pods can obtain a common view.

Etcd is widely used in the cloud community and in almost all Kubernetes deployments.

6.3.4 Big Data Analytics

The open source community has for some time been part of big data analytics platforms. Apache Spark, Hadoop, and Kafka are common software components found in big data deployments. More recently ONAP has defined the DCAE in the architecture. DCAE and PNDA (described in the following section) are big data analytics platforms. It is possible for PNDA components to operate within the DCAE data platform [43].

6.3.4.1 Platform for Network Data Analytics

Autonomous networks are expected to generate enormous amounts of data for ingestion by cloud platforms. Some nodes present in the network will emit traffic in real time for immediate processing in the cloud. An example is streamed telemetry from an autonomous vehicle critical to safety and security. Other nodes will batch upload data for offline analysis or ML training. An example is an intelligent drone upload of recorded video used for urban planning. The cloud platform must accommodate a diverse set of data sources and applications. The platform must scale and always be available and resilient to application or human failures.

To meet those requirements, Nathan Marz conceived the Lambda Architecture (LA). This architecture is designed as "a robust system that is fault-tolerant, both against hardware failures and human mistakes, being able to serve a wide range of workloads and use-cases, and in which low-latency reads and updates are required. The resulting system should be linearly scalable, and it should scale out rather than up…" [44].

The LA system flow consists of the following:

- Inbound data stream is dispatched to a batch layer and a speed layer.

- Batch Layer (1) maintains an immutable database containing all raw data received by the system and (2) precomputes batch views that can be queried from an application.

- Speed layer handles the most recent data and generates incremental views that can be queried from an application.

- Serving layer can query batch views, real-time views, or merge the two. Note that any errors introduced in the serving layer batch views are overwritten because new batch views are continuously rebuilt from the master data set.

The LA avoids state, data mutability, or data loss. Instead, all raw data is stored in an immutable database and pre- or re-computed as needed. This combination of immutability and computation achieves application and human fault tolerance.

The PNDA is an open source big data platform derived from the LA. Figure 6.9 depicts the PNDA architecture. Beginning on the left there are any number of unique data sources streaming batch uploading information up to the cloud. The data is collected, aggregated, and published to the message bus. The master data store subscribes to and consumes all raw data where it can be processed in batch mode in preparation for historical queries.

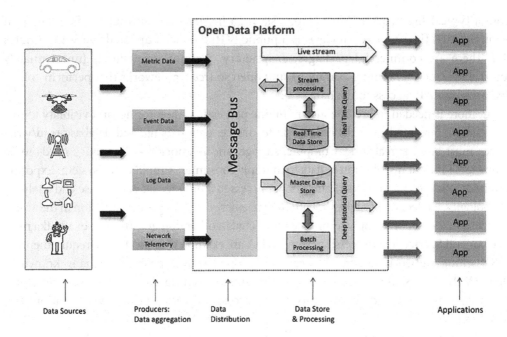

FIGURE 6.9   PNDA architecture.

Stream processing will subscribe to and receive streams requiring real-time processing. In addition, live data can be streamed directly to a consuming application.

The components of PNDA consist of a suite of software packages based on the deployed and mature Apache ecosystem. For example, Kafka/Zookeeper supports the message bus; Hadoop Distributed File System can be set up as the master datastore; Spark could handle the batch processing and real-time stream processing by Spark Streaming. However, PNDA is an open system so developers and operators are free to utilize any component they feel can do the job [45].

The versatility of the PNDA platform is highlighted by the diversity of the implemented applications [46]. PNDA is an open source project supported by LF.

6.3.4.2 Streaming Network Analytics System

The importance of a stable, performant, and secure Internet cannot be overstated. Operator mishaps (benign or otherwise), router software bugs, and poorly engineered networks and route policies impact performance and availability. More ominously, cyberattacks initiated by bad actors could wreak havoc. A critical source of data to analyze and detect potential problems is the Internet routing system data that includes, but is not limited to, the global IPv4 and IPv6 routing tables, AS topology, prefix announcements/withdrawals, prefix address family identifiers (IPv4 and IPv6 among others) details, prefix anomalies, route policies, router telemetry, and network convergence.

Underlying this data is the frequency, velocity, and scale by which it is generated. There are hundreds of thousands of events (e.g., prefix announcements) occurring every day from a typical BGP router. Much progress in gathering Internet routing data has been made through the years. Routeviews is a public BGP data feed updated every 15 minutes [47]. There are commercial packages, proprietary operator scripts/tools (unfortunately automated screen scraping is common), and open source frameworks that perform collection and offer API access to the data [48].

But more is needed to provide instant online processing, monitoring, and visibility to this information. Streamed BGP data ingest performance, data parsing, and database read/write speeds must be near real time. Compute, storage, and memory resource usage needs to be optimized. Efficient distribution of data to multiple consumers simplifies the system. Exposing standard APIs (i.e., REST, Kafka) offers easier access to a broader set of database and analytics technologies. Collection of higher fidelity BGP telemetry enables greater precision in the analysis. It also makes sense to apply techniques perfected in other domains (the use of a Kafka message bus and Spark batch processing from PNDA are examples) to meet these requirements.

Streaming Network Analytics System is an open source project (formally known as OpenBMP) [15]. SNAS collects massive amounts of routing data, maintains, and stores it in a database to provide high-performance access/APIs for tracking, visualization, and analytics [49].

SNAS provides several unique features including:

- Supports a BGP Monitoring Protocol (BMP) collector [50]. A BMP client operates on a BGP router and transmits all BGP routing information bases to the SNAS collector. The collector can also consume public BGP data feed such as routeviews.

- Parses received BMP and BGP information and produces it to a Kafka bus.

- REST APIs, Kafka consumer, and database schemas for rapid application development.

- Support for BGP, OSPF/ISIS, L3VPN, Segment Routing, IPv4/IPv6, and MPLS.

The Internet must absorb the increased traffic loads and billions of end-points with diverse application requirements including low latency, IPv4/IPv6, predictability, ad-hoc connectivity, and security introduced by autonomous network deployments. Online tools for processing streamed Internet routing information and providing API access will be needed. SNAS is supported by LF.

6.3.5 Virtualization

6.3.5.1 Openstack

Back in the day when cloud offerings first appeared, provisioning resources was a cumbersome task driven by scripts, customized network management systems (NMS) systems, and human operators.

OpenStack is a set of components for automating the deployment and management of cloud resources [51]. The classic Openstack projects include compute (Nova), storage (Swift), imaging (Glance), and networking (Neutron) and are probably the most familiar for those who have worked with it for a long time. Openstack is referred to in some quarters as Infrastructure-as-a-Service.

Openstack is backed by the OpenStack Foundation and a large community of vendors and operators. It has evolved into a sophisticated and powerful open source platform. There is now an API for container orchestration, thus enabling hybrid openstack and Kubernetes deployments. Openstack Neutron supports plug-ins for ODL orchestration and high-performance data-plane FD.io components.

6.3.5.2 Cloud Native

The Cloud Native Computing Foundation lays out CN systems as container-based, dynamically managed, and microservice oriented. Chapter 7 provides a detailed discussion on the CN architecture and technologies. High-performance CNFs and Kubernetes orchestration provide the baseline building blocks for CN application solutions.

Smoothing the way for the development and management of VPP-based CNFs (and really any microservice for that matter) is Ligato—an open source platform composed of the following three components:

- CN-infra. This supports different plug-ins, including logging, database, key-value datastore, messaging, APIs (REST and gRPC Remote Procedure Call [gRPC]), and telemetry. Separate application-specific plug-ins can be added, and together with Kubernetes defines the overall platform functionality.

- VPP agent. This was discussed in a previous section but in summary, it provides a control and management plane for VPP-based CNFs.

- Service function chain controller. CNFs, application-CNF containers, can be "stitched" together into a logical service function chain. Kubernetes does not support service chain provisioning, so this is an excellent addition to the CN application service topology deployment tooling.

For clarity purposes, it should be noted that Ligato is not an application [31]. It is a software platform composed of the aforementioned components and libraries that developers can use (some, all, custom in any combination) as they see fit to create and deploy high-performance application service topologies. It is modular, extensible, and written in Golang—the programming language common to CN tools such as Kubernetes and etcd.

A byproduct of CN-developed applications is the placement of their constituent microservices (referred to as services for this discussion) across a large distributed service topology. The advantages include streamlined devops, rapid service deployment, horizontal scale out, and increased fault tolerance. But with those advantages comes a set of challenges related to the application's communication needs. It boils down to the fact that each application (e.g., web services, content server, or business process) is responsible for their own service connectivity, authentication, load balancing, traffic control, monitoring, security policy, and so on. The application must also handle situations when a large number of service workload instances appear/disappear in a short amount of time.

Rather than burden an individual application with all of this complexity, a more optimal approach would be to off-load this work to a separate service that can handle all of the application's service-to-service communication needs. This service is referred to as a service mesh. A service mesh is a dedicated infrastructure layer for handling the application's inter-service communications. It is responsible for the reliable delivery of requests through the complex topology of services that comprise a modern CN application. In effect, a service mesh is performing the role of a L7 overlay.

Some of the functions supported by a service mesh include [52]:

- Visibility enabled by telemetry, traces, and stats reporting. Observability functions where L7 trace and logging functions are activated in the data-plane with the results pushed via a control-plane session to upstream collectors and analytics applications.

- Resiliency and fault tolerance to fluctuations network/application performance and availability. Timeout, health checks, and circuit breakers to detect and if necessary reroute for fast-fail so as to initiate recovery actions.

- Traffic control including load balancing and dynamic traffic reroute. Data-plane functions to optimize resource utilization and deployment efficiencies (via canary testing).

- Enforcement of provisioned application policies. Centralizes policy definitions followed by deployment into the service mesh data-plane.

- End-to-end security. Certificates and keys are deployed in the service mesh to offer secure data-plane communications between the microservices through the use of sidecar edge proxies.

The service mesh shields the developer from worrying about building customized telemetry, security, and network functionality into their applications. Enterprises and operators like service meshes because they finally have observability of the application layer and a means to shift primary policy and networking from the network to the application layer. When coupled with service identity, authentication (e.g., Secure Production Identity Framework for Everyone [53]) and policy-based authorization (e.g., Open Policy Agent [54]), the service mesh promises to deliver consistent, portable security across cloud platforms. The service mesh also provides tunneling and encryption for trusted communications to protect against threats even in a Zero Trust Network (ZTN).

The notion of a ZTN originated out of an internal project at Google with the objective of providing end-user and device access to intranet resources without the use of virtual private network tunneling [55]. Conceptually, a ZTN assumes that all networks are hostile, internal and external threats are ever present, and that network locality (i.e., behind a firewall) is insufficient to decide who can be trusted or not [56,57].

Secure communications between two parties across a ZTN requires that each authenticate the identity of the other at the same time. This is accomplished through a two-way authentication mechanism with Mutual Transport Layer Security (mTLS) being a common approach used in service mesh environments.

In this scenario, certificate/key information is provided to the parties so they can initiate the mTLS handshake, authenticate each other's identity, and establish intersession communications across a secure channel [53]. This can be thought of a two-party trust zone. Of course, it is possible to form a trust zone of multiple parties as long as they are provided with the appropriate certification/key credentials. Thus, a trust zones can be formed between only the parties who require communications with the specific service or services.

A number of web scale companies such as Twitter, Google, and Netflix have for years, used their own in-house service mesh implementations with some contributed to open source projects. Istio is a service mesh solution invented by Google that provides policy definition and deployment, key management, and telemetry/reporting export [52]. It basically is the control plane for the service mesh. Envoy component was developed by Lyft and functions as an edge proxy placed in the service mesh data-plane to intercept all incoming and outgoing traffic. This enables routing, load balancing, access control, stats collection, and policy-based data-plane functionality [58].

Istio with an Envoy edge proxy is deployed using the sidecar model. A sidecar can be viewed as a set of value-add functions supplied to a microservice. It is injected into the microservice by Istio. The functions can operate as processes inside the microservice container or can be housed inside its own container. Since Envoy is in the data-plane, it can incorporate a VPP CNF for maximum throughput and performance. Envoy also works with Kubernetes and the Istio-Auth components to manage certificate/key credential exchange so that secure interservice communications can take place.

Figure 6.10 puts all of these pieces into a complete Cloud Native Network Stack with application service mesh and CNF data-plane functions at the bottom, Ligato service mesh, and CNF controller functions in the middle and overall CN life-cycle orchestration at the top.

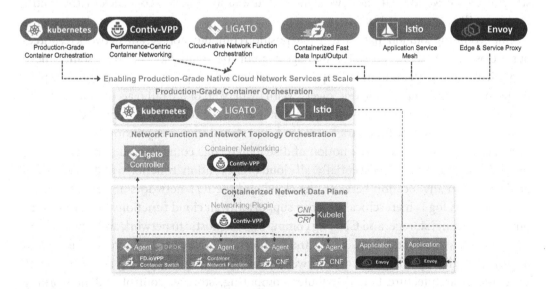

FIGURE 6.10   Cloud native network stack.

With the Cloud Native Network Stack in place, we can begin to think about how it might assist in understanding and building solutions for AI-driven autonomous networks. Consider the following:

- ZTN. We can assume many autonomous networks will be zero trust and nodes will be end-points responsible for communications with trusted parties.

- Service mesh. This polymorphism will be present in autonomous networks. They can be orchestrated or ad-hoc. There will likely be different forms of identity meshes that are put together.

- Cloud portability. CN systems can operate in large public clouds, enterprise clouds, fog clouds, IOT clouds, or hybrids of any combination—generally speaking same architecture, same model, same OSS. Autonomous networks are sure to have on-board or nearby compute resources. Microservices instances could be ephemeral or long-lived.

It is hoped that further CN application innovation, development, and deployments will facilitate more AI-driven/autonomous network solutions.

6.3.5.3 OpenFog

There are a number of challenges introduced by the proliferation and growth of IOT networks and the anticipated arrival of sophisticated autonomous networks. Reduction in size, weight, and battery life constrains the compute and storage resource on small IOT devices—in some cases required to execute AI programs. An unacceptable floor on latency could exist if the distance between the local device and remote entities (i.e., centralized cloud or machine-to-machine) is too great. Networks might become stressed if bandwidth-hungry applications appear in large numbers despite advances in new 5G network infrastructure. One wonders if the low-latency, secure, and reliable properties of the tactile Internet will become a reality.

One promising solution that will help is to position compute, storage, and network resources out as close to the users as possible. This edge compute paradigm has existed for some time—in particular as it pertains to mobile operators who have deployed mobile edge compute platforms in close proximity to the cell towers. With ownership of the radio access and backhaul networks, mobile operators can offer their customers a raft of new and improved functions including faster response times, traffic off-load, and virtual appliance proximity.

Fog computing builds on the notion of distributed edge compute and embeds it inside the cloud architecture [59]. Essentially, all cloud orchestration, functions, and services can be deployed in any location between the cloud and the IOT networks or devices. Unlike edge compute, fog is hierarchical and can support any/all cloud functions including compute, networking, storage, and CN. Fog computing is agnostic to network and device types.

To facilitate understanding, acceptance, product development, interoperability, and deployment, the OpenFog consortium was formed [60]. Fog computing is "a horizontal, system-level architecture that distributes computing, storage, control and networking functions closer to the users along a cloud-to-thing continuum…" Its mission is to develop and deliver a fog-computing architecture that interested parties, including researchers, industry, service/infrastructure providers, and many others, can use to innovate and build new services such as CV-augmented reality.

Example of use-cases and applications that can benefit from closer resources afforded by fog computing are the following:

- Augmented reality
- Vehicle to Anything network, support infrastructure, over-the-air (OTA) download caching
- Local visual security and surveillance
- Factory automation
- Smart grid
- AI applications
- Proximal multitenant application hosting and operations
- Network bandwidth off-load
- Low-latency safety and health applications

The OpenFog consortium has developed and delivered an architecture document.

6.3.6 Systems Integration

6.3.6.1 Continuous Integration/Continuous Delivery

Devops accelerates the time between software development and deployment through the use of tools and automation to streamline the coding, integration, testing, and deployment processes. Continuous Integration/Continuous Delivery (CI/CD) is fundamental to the mission and success of the devops process [61].

Continuous Integration/Continuous Delivery can be depicted as a pipeline as shown in Figure 6.11. The process begins with developers committing their code changes back to the main branch of the application located on a shared repository. Continuous integration is invoked when a commit to the shared repository is detected. A special CI server automatically creates a new build image and performs a suite of automated tests against the build. If the tests fail, then the new commit broke something and the developers can fix it. If the tests pass, then developers can continue their work.

Continuous delivery extends the CI process by preparing and testing the new build for production deployment. This involves pushing the CI-tested build to a staging environment where additional tests (e.g., API, load, and reliability) prior to deployment can be performed. If everything checks out, then the developer manually signs off and the code is ready for deployment to a live production environment. Continuous deployment removes the manual developer sign-off, and the entire release process beginning with code all the way through to production deployment is automated.

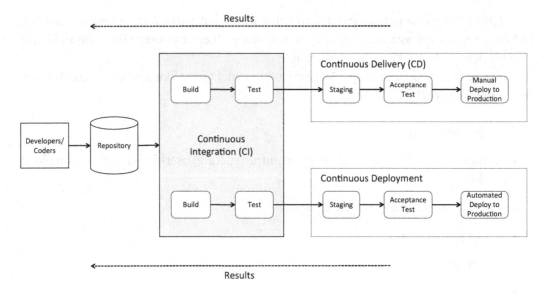

FIGURE 6.11   CI/CD Pipeline.

6.3.6.2 Open Network Function Virtualization

Composing, testing, and validating cloud systems in preparation for deployment can be complex and costly. There are a multitude of considerations to take into account, all of which should be addressed to ensure a successful deployment.

Any one of the following examples could, by itself, be a challenge to complete:

- Requirements spelled out at the beginning of the project with a defined end goal.

- Defined system life cycle and workflow.

- Integration of open source platforms and components.

- Installation, deployment, upgrades, and troubleshooting of VNFs. Recall that VNFs are virtual instances of a networking or service function (e.g., firewall, load balancing) so how to manage and operationalize these components in the cloud environment is important.

- Establishing VNF-based service chains and configuration of the virtual network overlay with the physical network underlay.

- Complete system documentation.

- Use of standard tools and best practices for continuous integration/continuous deployment.

- System security.

Open NFV (OPNFV) is an open source project for addressing these challenges [62]. While the name might imply it is an open source platform for operator deployment of NFV in the

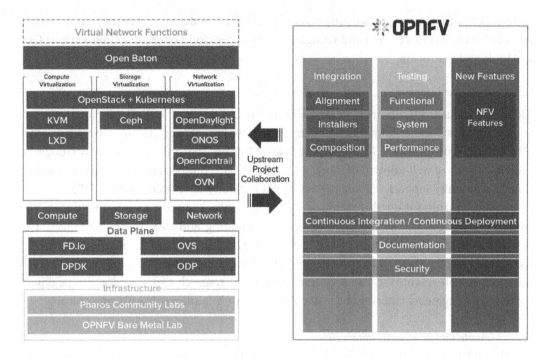

FIGURE 6.12   OPNFV architecture.

cloud, in reality it is not. OPNFV is an open source reference platform available to operators to design, integrate, test, and validate cloud systems composed of NFV components in
support of actual deployment (Figure 6.12).

At a high level, various open source compute, storage, and network virtualization
components are integrated in OPNFV. The idea behind this is illustrated in Figure 6.12. A
particular release of OPNFV will identify what upstream projects are supported. Upstream
means that an open source project has agreed to collaborate with the OPNFV community—
in other words, an operator employing OPNFV to test and validate a system can utilize one
or more of the open source projects (e.g., Kubernetes and containers) identified on the left
as part of their efforts for software development.

On the right are the functional pillars supported by OPNFV, including integration and
testing along with any new features. Cross-community continuous integration is employed
to execute the OPNFV life cycle are utilized. Additional OPNFV value-add features include
the use of automated testbeds, SDO cooperation (e.g., IETF, ETSI NFV, and MEF), and
industry-supported security initiatives via the LF-supported Core Infrastructure Initiative.
Open NFV is a LF project.

6.3.6.3 Tools

The tooling for open source software systems integration (i.e., CI/CD) depends on the
devops workflows employed in the engineering environment. Github is an open source
shared repository used in many development environments. The Jenkins CI server supports hundreds of plug-ins and is versatile enough to operate in any CI/CD pipeline [63].

Netflix Spinnaker supports continuous delivery for CN deployments [64]. And finally, Amazon Web Services (AWS) and Google, among other cloud operators, offer various CI/CD tools and platforms.

6.3.7 Machine Learning

Many open source ML libraries are available and in use today. The PNDA Smart transport application uses Theano. Another PNDA application for security analytics incorporate Apache SPOT. Others include pytorch and Apache Spark MMLlib. Tensorflow invented by Google is probably the most well-known ML library. Developers are comfortable working with it, enjoy broad community support, and are present in many cloud ML service offerings [65].

Machine learning use will continue to grow as networks become more intelligent. We can be encouraged by the fact that vendors are building and shipping ML applications; operators will expand their use of ML technologies. And thanks to automation platforms like ONAP, ML can be used to reduce processing time from data input to output and resultant policy deployment. We also see an increase in AI research and, anecdotally speaking, more young engineers entering the private sector with ML interests, skills, and training.

6.3.7.1 Artificial General Intelligence

Existing AI methods are considered "narrow AI" (a.k.a. weak AI). This means they can perform one task very well, such as buying recommendations or weather forecasting.

Artificial general intelligence (AGI) is considered "strong AI" [66]. Without going into details, it closely approximates human intelligence and reasoning. It can go after the long tail problems—those that have never been encountered and might even seem like a form of creativity or reasoning.

To illustrate the difference between narrow and strong AI, let's assume there is an autonomous network of neighborhood security bots (NSBs). Their purpose is to patrol the neighborhood and stay on the lookout for suspicious activity. If any is encountered, they are to notify the authorities. With narrow AI, the NSBs are trained to look for specific activities classified as suspicious and nothing more. If a break in occurs and the burglars employ tactics the NSB was not trained to detect, the crime goes unreported.

On the other hand, strong AI empowers the NSB to think, reason, and learn. Encountering the burglars employing their new tactics, the NSB, having not seen this before, might now wonder what exactly is going on. It can seek information from other data sources (e.g., police crime blotters, CCTV from other neighborhoods victimized by break-ins), compare recorded normal neighborhood comings and goings with this new activity, or call a neighbor to inquire and confirm that what is being observed is unusual. Taking all of that into account, the NSB can reach the logical conclusion that there is something amiss here and alert the authorities. The NSB will learn from this new experience and will be proactive in reaching out and searching for information to reinforce this knowledge.

6.3.7.1.1 Non-Axiomatic Reasoning System   Artificial general intelligence based on Non-Axiomatic Reasoning System (NARS) is non-axiomatic in the sense that empirical data may at any point override prior beliefs in the system. This is a requirement for any system that must operate in the real world in real time with limited computational resources. Any new sensor data that overrides existing beliefs will update existing knowledge accordingly. One can imagine that sensors operating deep inside autonomous networks will rely on this capability.

There is an open source version of NARS and a growing community of researchers and published papers [67].

6.3.7.1.2 OpenCog   OpenCog differentiates itself by leveraging Cognitive Synergy Theory, which can be thought of as unifying different types of memory. The memory types that OpenCog incorporates includes declarative (i.e., the red ball on the table is larger than the blue ball), procedural (a procedure for stacking a block on top of another), sensory, episodic (e.g., the series of actions that Bill took when he built a tower yesterday), attentional (the set of objects that seem to be important now in the context of a game Bob and Bill are playing), and intentional (the goal of making a tower that does not fall down). Each one of these knowledge types possesses different knowledge creation mechanisms and are interconnected in such a way as to aid each other in overcoming memory type-specific combinatorial explosions.

OpenCog addresses one of the core issues with expert system scaling. If we consider the promise of Web 2.0 with semantically annotated web pages, one clear issue was the need for humans to add this semantic information. OpenCog implements various knowledge creation mechanisms and interconnects them in such a way as to avoid memory type-specific limitations. OpenCog is another community interested in researching and exploring AGI [68].

6.3.8 Summary of Open Source and Artificial Intelligence/Autonomous Networks

Much was discussed in this section on the multiple flavors of open source software. Figure 6.4 at the start of this section laid out the components and their station in the stack. From that and the discussions that followed, there are several interesting take-aways to consider:

- Automation is key to delivering new services quickly. OPNFV and CI/CD streamline the VNF deployment and the software release pipelines.

- Reference frameworks are a must. Large-scale cloud operators can model an architecture and design/deployment/automation pipeline based on ONAP, thus saving time and money.

- Big data analytics must scale in capacity and processing to keep up. PNDA and SNAS are two solutions built to meet that challenge.

- CN exploits containerized microservices for scalable, resilient, and secure application deployments.

And finally, open source AI/ML solutions are available and being used. We expect their use to increase out of necessity (needed in autonomous networks) and because resources and expertise become more easily available for model training and development. The public cloud operators discussed in the next section will help with that.

6.4 CLOUD OPERATORS, ARTIFICIAL INTELLIGENCE, AND AUTONOMOUS NETWORKS

Cloud SPs are instrumental in enabling and supporting AI-driven autonomous networks. They possess massive data collection and processing capabilities to support AI applications (along with compute resources), consume, perform model training, and yield insights, behaviors, and predictions.

Cloud providers perform extensive research and development of new AI functions. Their products support AI-as-a-Service available today. They currently and will continue to provide development environments using the latest open source AI toolsets and frameworks. These tools and environments can expedite progress toward building automated closed-loop systems in autonomous networks.

Cloud providers may develop revenue sharing partnerships with other parties to create new markets and offer new services. The vast amount of knowledge and experience in the AI space can be offered as a consulting service of sorts to help jumpstart customers in their efforts.

There is no argument that current AI-inspired automation, operations, products, and applications are laying the foundation for new AI-driven cloud architectures and services. Heavy recruitment by cloud operators for AI software engineers and data scientists is well underway and not expected to taper anytime soon—perhaps ever.

6.4.1 Amazon Web Services

With its large and seeming bottomless reserves of resources, AWS is aggressively pursuing a "machine learning for everyone" strategy across different markets, many of which will have an impact on domains, including autonomous networks [69].

For enterprises and organizations embarking on the AI journey, AWS offers a multitude of unique offerings:

- APIs to ML-ready services, including speech translation, computer vision, and chatbot interactions.

- AI big data workloads can be integrated with other platform solutions, such as S3 object storage and Redshift data warehouse to investigate and develop new applications.

- Amazon machine learning service, which provides visualization tools and wizards to help guide non-experts through the process of creating ML models without having to learn complex ML algorithms and technology.

- Well-known ML frameworks, including TensorFlow and Apache MXNet, are packaged up in deep learning customized virtual appliances referred to as Amazon Machine Images. Clusters of Amazon Machine Images can be deployed across the spectrum of compute options ranging from GPU resources to off-the-shelf processors.

- SageMaker makes it easy for researchers and developers to construct, train, test, and tune models in applications and workflows.

Of course, all of this and more can be served up on the "pay-as-you-go" platter of secure and flexible AWS services and support.

Another example of AWS AI technologies in action is the deployment of state-of-the-art security services. Amazon Macie, which has been rolled out on AWS S3 storage, is a service leveraging ML to automatically discover, classify, and protect sensitive user data. Macie uses natural language processing (NLP) to parse user data stored in S3 to identify sensitive personal identification information, such as SSN and SSH keys. It automatically classifies data into high-to-low risk levels, and then initiates monitoring of high-risk data access. If data access pattern analysis discovers anomalies indicating potential unauthorized access, Macie warns users through its CloudWatch service. This system could potentially be a life-saver, in particular if unauthorized access credentials for users with top secret clearance are stored in an unfortified location.

Amazon reaches into our daily lives and their AI capabilities will extend out to human/machine communications and transportation. There is Alexa, the home assistant using AI to improve human speech recognition. Unmanned drones delivering goods from an Amazon warehouse will not be 100% controlled by a human pilot. The IoT and connected cars shown in Figure 6.13 can use their Greengrass local compute and ML processing

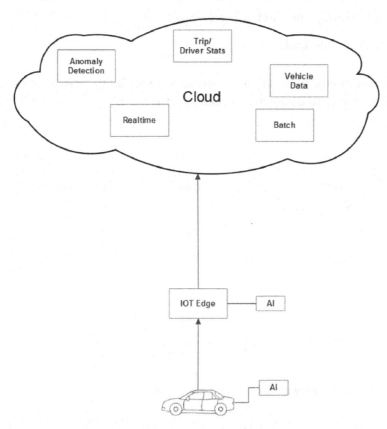

FIGURE 6.13　AWS connected vehicle cloud architecture.

solution and coupled with cloud-hosted applications (data collection, analytics, anomaly detection, and user operations) can maximize utility, lower costs, and deliver the best human experience.

As the largest cloud operator in terms of users and services offered, AWS will play a huge role as autonomous networks evolve. They currently offer and will continue to develop and deliver new ML capabilities. It is clear they intend to project and distribute many of these applications and services as close to the user as possible [70].

6.4.2 Microsoft Azure

Microsoft Azure's ML platform offers a complete set of tools, services, and infrastructure to enable a faster and simpler development cycle for AI developers [71]. The Azure ML platform supports the following:

- Machine Learning Workbench

- Machine Learning Experimentation Service

- Machine Learning Model Management Service

- Machine Learning Libraries for Apache Spark

- Visual Studio Code Tools for AI

Figure 6.14 illustrates the positioning of these services with ML services shown on the left and optional training and deployment options on the right.

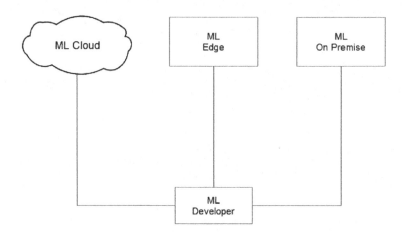

FIGURE 6.14   Microsoft Azure machine learning services.

Visual Studio Code Tools for AI is used for AI application creation. The VS Code Tools is integrated with Azure's ML services, providing a unified view of model training and deployment. Developers could start new Microsoft Cognitive Toolkit projects from VS code, send it to the Azure Batch AI Training service for training, and then deploy the trained models locally, or to the cloud. This addresses the developer's need for the next generation AI Integrated Development Environment (IDE), providing a complete desktop to cloud workflow for AI software engineering.

Another interesting solution that Azure is developing is the IoT Edge platform, which is aimed at extending cloud intelligence to edge devices. By off-loading AI-based data analytics and decision making to the edge, enterprises can reduce bandwidth costs, while still benefiting from insights gained from IoT data.

The Microsoft CV platform is another opportunity for Azure to extend their cloud support down to CV-based autonomous networks. There is ample space for innovation including offering ML-based predictive maintenance service offerings and real-time driver assistance functions. However, there will be many challenges to overcome as these services are rolled out. First, there is security and it must be end-to-end from the components inside the vehicle all the way up to and including inside the cloud. Second, the cloud platform must be capable of handling planned (e.g., OTA updates, normal telematics uploads) and unplanned (e.g., event-driven telemetry bursts, unplanned OTA patches) communication [70].

6.4.3 Google Cloud

Google is an industry leader in developing and introducing AI innovation and solutions [72]. Google Cloud hosts and makes available many of these interesting capabilities:

- Cloud AutoML. This is suite of different products that simplify ML model training and application development. It gained notoriety with the claim that autoML is ML code that can generate ML code.

- Cloud Machine Learning Engine. This is a managed service for building and training models on any data of any type and any size. Tensorflow generated models can be trained on large-scale resource clusters in preparation for deployment of online or batch predictive analysis applications. This service operates in conjunction with other Google Cloud features for production deployments.

Besides software, Google is also invested in AI-optimized hardware. Google Cloud has deployed the purpose-built Tensor Processing Unit (TPU) for maximum ML performance and scale. Google is supportive of the research community by providing a free training service to selected programs on its TensorFlow Research Cloud, which operates a cluster of 1000 Cloud TPUs.

Google's early foray into the self-driving car has pushed the industry and provided them with valuable insights into the technology of autonomous vehicle operation. There is a continuous cycle of data set collection, model training, and model updates occurring between the vehicles and the cloud. Raw data collected from sensors, radar, computer vision, and other data sources must find its way to the cloud for model training.

The data set volumes are highest during development and testing. But the continuous model training cycle will not disappear, and so clouds must provide sufficient resources for data set ingest be it compressed or raw data.

Suffice it to say that Google will continue to push AI-enabled solutions out closer to the user. The Google Home platform is one example—their large investment in autonomous vehicles portends another.

6.4.4 IBM Cloud

IBM's ML cloud service is designed around its Watson platform [73]. Watson ML offers many of the same features as the other cloud operators, including model generation/training, open source libraries, and tools to construct AI workflows to extract and visualize insights.

The Watson platform provides Cognitive Service and Natural Language Processing APIs covered in Chapter 2. Building a workflow using the APIs can be complex, so IBM offers the AppConnect service. This is a graphical configuration tool for users with different skill levels to build a ML application.

For example, a marketer could develop an application that analyzes the tone a customer takes inside a message and determines what action to take next. If the customer uses positive language, a friendly request for a survey could appear. But if Watson determines the tone to be negative, the application locates the customer's account manager and alerts him/her through the IBM Message Hub, suggesting they contact the customer to resolve the issue. Used properly, Watson-supported applications would improve the operational efficiency and enhance customer satisfaction.

IBM supports the notion that ML complexities, costs, and processing requirements can be efficiently exercised in a cloud-based service [74]. Deep-Learning-as-a-Service (DLaaS) provides the flexibility and performance available from a cloud with tools, ML frameworks, models and training data to develop, and test and operationalize ML applications.

The basic DLaaS workflow includes prepare the model, upload the model and training data into the cloud, create, and monitor a training job and then download the trained model.

The DLaaS architecture is shown in Figure 6.15. There exists APIs on top for a UI and application access. The DLaaS core services are a set of microservices supporting the training job workflow from start to finish. The DLaaS platform services are the building blocks for executing and managing training jobs.

When a DLaaS training job is kicked off, the Life Cycle Manager (LCM) will ask Kubernetes to allocate resources. Data is pipelined through set of parallel learner microservices implementing the user's desired framework. Periodically the weights derived from

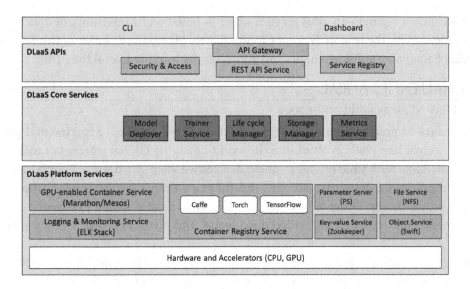

FIGURE 6.15   IBM DLaaS architecture.

the ML computation are pushed/pulled from a parameter server. Zookeeper is the key-value datastore used to orchestrate the training life cycle.

6.4.5 Alibaba

Selected as China's national AI platform for developing the "City Brain," Alibaba Cloud (Aliyun) is one of the pioneers in providing AI as a service [75]. In October 2016, Alibaba initiated the Hangzhou City Brain project, which aims to deploy ML to assist the Hangzhou government in addressing its significant traffic problems. The project is based on image recognition technology, leveraging CCTV cameras to track car and human activities. Through behavior analysis and data inputs, the system analyzes traffic flows as well as detect and predict the likelihood of events resulting in congestion. To close the virtuous circle, the collected knowledge is used to adjust the traffic lights in the city with the objective of improving traffic efficiency in real time. This is a real-world example illustrating the potential of AI in supporting autonomous IoT networks from the cloud.

Besides City Brain, Alibaba Cloud provides other AI services, ranging from social media trend analysis, real-time statistics for NBA streaming, to financial risk assessment and anomaly detection in industrial production [70].

6.4.6 Tencent

Tencent Cloud has been a strong player in AI technologies, such as computer vision and NLP [76]. Similar to Alibaba, Tencent is focused on providing AI-as-a-service on its cloud platform, with most of its services devoted to the areas of medical image analysis, video game AI, and social media.

One interesting example of such a service is their Image to Speech API. This is used by applications to analyze picture content and convert it to natural language speech, thus providing accessibility for those visually impaired. Another interesting service is the

"Wenzhi" public opinion analysis service, which is based on its repository of data for one billion users. With the help of Tencent Cloud's Elastic MapReduce platform, this service is capable of analyzing public opinions and events on the Internet in real time [70].

6.5 CHALLENGES AHEAD

6.5.1 New Markets and Landscapes

It is not easy to predict the future. Who could have foreseen how experimental packet switching circa late 1960s evolved into the world-changing Global Internet of today and tomorrow. Same with smartphones—these devices we seem glued to 24/7 contain orders of magnitude more compute, storage, and memory than their air-cooled, room-size mainframe ancestors. Other innovations and inventions that lacked prescience include social media, music streaming, video downloads, and virtual cryptocurrency with no banks.

Market forecasts and projections offer a view at one point in time. Based on what has been discussed in this chapter and elsewhere in the book, this might be a suitable place to offer commentary on how AI-driven autonomous networks could impact new markets and technology landscapes we foresee down the road.

- Clouds remain at the top of the data food chain. They possess superior compute, storage, memory, and network resources—all needed to consume, store, and process vast quantities of data. It is where content resides and where we as users via smartphones or home appliances go to retrieve it. The social media applications live in the cloud as do enterprise applications and IT infrastructure. Powerful new AI applications operate in the cloud.

  The time and costs for the design and deployment of these and future cloud services will be dramatically reduced via automation and virtualization thanks to new open source platforms such as ONAP and Kubernetes. The platforms, devops, toolchains, and both human and automated software engineering skills will drive new innovations, new markets, and product opportunities.

- Data is king. Clearly there is massive growth in data as pointed out in any and all traffic projections. This will only increase as more IoT devices, sensors, and autonomous nodes come online. It is anticipated that individual CVs will generate O (gigabytes) of data for internal consumption and export to the cloud. In the reverse direction, cloud-sourced OTA downloads, 3D maps, and streaming infotainment will be the norm. Cloud operators will deploy smart sensors, AI pipelines, and algorithms to collect and analyze all sorts of application traffic. Processing and monetization of this data will introduce a whole raft of new opportunities and markets.

- To the Edge. All knowing, all seeing centralized cloud AI acting on uploaded autonomous network data might not be the best fit for some applications if latency is high and bandwidth resources are low. To solve this problem, edge compute can offer an intermediate level of AI located between cloud AI and IoT devices. With local or regional AI resources, IoT devices could obtain faster outputs and insights based on local devices and conditions. This is exactly what the OpenFog consortium espouses, and the case is compelling.

- CVs are outfitted with more compute power. Vehicle AI applications could scrub local data for anomaly detection and enable safer and more efficient driving. Clearly autonomous vehicles are and will continue to utilize in-vehicle AI applications.

  Let's put AI on the smartphone. There are versions of Tensorflow for mobile phones and even AI chips, with the most noteworthy example being Apple iPhone hardware for "on-the-fly" ML applications like facial recognition. In another example, first-time Android smartphone users in India frequently exhausted device storage by sending "good morning" messages to their friends and family every morning. To solve the problem, Google used AI to train a smartphone app to search and remove extraneous data, thus freeing up smartphone storage.

The industry is further looking to broaden the AI landscape. The LF supports project Acumos based on ML [77]. OpenAI is another undertaking looking at ways to introduce AGI to solve real problems [78]. Needless to say, AI is becoming mainstream thanks to open source. This will accelerate deployments of autonomous networks.

6.5.2 Software Engineering

The fundamental challenge for AI software engineering lies in the complex nature of the models. Deterministic software can be tested offline. With a trained ML model, it is almost impossible to forecast precisely how the application will behave before being validated in a production environment. Some hint about the model accuracy is possible during the training phase; nevertheless, uncertainty remains regarding how the model will perform on real data, which is a big challenge.

The popular Agile development method involving a two-week sprint from development team to operations team handoff would be hard pressed to fully vet model performance and accuracy in that time frame, in particular if sufficient training data sets are lacking. While the devops workflow has been automated to some extent, many processes are still performed by humans, creating distractions from the more creative and satisfying aspects of software engineering. Artificial intelligence could relieve engineers from some of the routine work of this devops life cycle.

Fortunately, those vested in AI software engineering and their powerful benefits are delivering solutions such as the following:

- New automated workflows and toolchains forming a "high occupancy vehicle" lane for reducing the devops feedback loop are being developed and deployed. While applicable to any development effort, AI devops can benefit as well.

- ML-based services, including model development, testing, and validation all supported and offered by cloud operators discussed in the previous section will make a big difference. They have customized tools and resources (compute and storage) required to test drive and validate model performance and accuracy. This will shield the application developers from the complexity and mystery of ML and help relieve software engineers from the labor-intensive work, thus enabling faster innovation and development of AI software.

As the population of AI software and devops engineers grows, we can expect more innovations in this space. No question—they will depend on AI-driven automation and life-cycle management [70].

6.5.3 Identity and Privacy

For the purposes of this discussion, let's assume cloud stands for any compute resource a user with required credentials can access. This includes your classic cloud, edge compute systems, and those present inside an autonomous node such as a vehicle.

The most common form of cloud identity management is asymmetric cryptography, where the private key is the only source of identification. In the real world, users don't always secure keys and passwords. Thus, hackers exploit that fact. Having been applied in the field of identification such as facial recognition, AI could be useful in verifying cloud identities. The key to applying AI-based verification is to consider more than just passwords and keys. By constantly monitoring access behaviors from users and differentiating between safe and malicious behavior patterns, AI could discover potential imposters, even though they might possess the correct credentials and access rights. Once a potentially malicious behavior has been identified, the users would be notified and appropriate actions are taken. The accuracy of these systems has not been disclosed at this time, but it does provide another layer of security for those reluctant to apply best practices.

The process described previously provides the hosting cloud with access to user data. This begs the question: can we trust AI clouds with our user data? [79]. We see AI-derived targeted ads all of the time, so there exists financial benefit. Privacy has been signed away once the terms of service is accepted. This bestows the right for the cloud to input or process user data for any purpose, as long as it stays inside the cloud. However, the recent trend in AI is only making the privacy problem worse, since data is a precious resource, which companies are leveraging to fuel their AI models. These models would then be wrapped into products (e.g., home assistants or CVs), which are sold on the cloud via APIs. Although these products do not directly expose user privacy, they do contain insights gained from user data.

While still speculative, it could be possible to build proper privacy access control procedures with the help of AI and blockchain (see Chapter 4). First, instead of storing user data in a centralized database on the company's private cloud, a blockchain could be established between companies and users to store encrypted personal data, which is only accessible via established smart contracts. Second, instead of a terms of service agreement, clouds could use AI to ask user questions in natural language. For example, one question could be, "What is your mother's maiden name?" After a user answers these questions, a customized terms of service would be established between the user and the company.

This new terms of service agreement would then be translated into code and wrapped into a smart contract on the aforementioned blockchain, which could be validated by everyone. Every time the company wishes to use personal data, it has to go through the smart contract, which will only grant access if the scenario meets the requirements of the stated purpose. This procedure would guarantee that companies can access users' personal data for the stated purposes for which users have explicitly agreed upon, thus providing strong and fine-grained data protection for users.

6.6 CAN WE BUILD AUTONOMOUS NETWORKS USING OPEN SOURCE TECHNOLOGIES?

Open Source Software and communities are innovating fast and furious. Based on much of this chapter, it is not a stretch to say open source has formed many of the building blocks for AI-driven autonomous networks. Many advances have been made including automated infrastructure (ONAP, Kubernetes), and advanced data processing/storage platforms (Apache Spark and Hadoop). OSS communities and their projects have emerged as the de-facto industry mechanism for software innovation, much of which will end up in AI-driven autonomous networks.

However, one should be aware that OSS participants and their beneficiaries from academia and industry do hold on to their proprietary components for potential profit. These objectives have created another question: What's the exact role of OSS in building an autonomous network?

To answer this question, we need to first remind ourselves of some of the limitations of OSS collaborations.

- Lowest common denominator. OSS is built by different companies and individuals that make up the project community. Maintaining this participation means that it should meet a minimal set of requirements common to all. As a result, successful OSS often has a tendency to stay generic to be useful in a variety of scenarios. It offers "pretty good" functions for most. For example, Linux is successful because it can be used in different industries including automotive, cloud, and mobile. The flexibility of Linux has made it one of the most heavily invested open source projects in the world.

- Specialization out of the box. The "pretty good" philosophy encourages broad participation, but this tendency introduces specialization challenges making it unsuitable for certain environments. For example, Linux is not suitable for real-time applications, thus for the embedded system, engineers have to develop the RT patch [80]. Linux is not suitable for the corporate laptop population since it is not fully compatible with the Microsoft applications. It is a long way from replacing Autosar as the OS operating inside CVs—not withstanding automotive grade Linux, which might turn out to be a good fit for infotainment purposes [81].

That said, OSS should never be considered the ultimate solution for all, rather it should be considered as a building block for cloud operators delivering their own

Software-as-a-Service. It can also be a good opportunity for providers to offer OSS maintenance and support subscriptions, thus staying out of the fray of business software competition.

For the foreseeable future, autonomous networks will be developed with a mix of OSS layers and proprietary software. Artificial intelligence frameworks such as TensorFlow and Acumos will benefit community participation, and certainly when deployed, will leverage large automation platforms such as ONAP.

In conclusion, open source software will play a huge role in the evolution of AI-driven autonomous networks. The cloud will rely on these technologies to scale out, deploy new services, and introduce ever more sophisticated AI/ML solutions in an automated closed loop. Large-scale automation platforms along with applications and networks developed using CN principles will be common.

The next chapter entitled "Machine Learning, Containers, Cloud Natives, and Microservices" will provide more details and insights into these topics.

REFERENCES

1. Lampson, B. W. and Sproull, R. F., An open operating system for a single-user machine, *ACM Operating Systems Review*, 11(5), 98–105, 1979.
2. Leiner, B. M., Cerf, V. G., Clark, D. D., Kahn, R. E., Kleinrock, L., Lynch, D. C., Postel, J., Roberts, L. G., and Wolff, S., A brief history of the Internet, 2003. Retrieved from https://www.internetsociety.org/internet/history-internet/brief-history-internet/.
3. https://www.debian.org/social_contract
4. https://www.coredna.com/blogs/comparing-open-closed-source-software
5. https://github.com/
6. https://www.itsforge.net/
7. https://www.apache.org/
8. https://www.linuxfoundation.org/
9. Examples are Internet Engineering Task Force (IETF), Institute of Electrical and Electronics Engineers (IEEE), European Telecommunications Standards Institute (ETSI) and Third Generation Partnership Project (3GPP).
10. [LNF], https://www.linuxfoundation.org/projects/networking/
11. 3 years on: Open standards, open source, open loop. Retrieved from https://blogs.cisco.com/sp/three-years-on-open-standards-open-source-open-loop.
12. https://yangcatalog.org/
13. https://www.ietf.org/how/runningcode/hackathons/
14. http://www.mef.net/mefnet/mefnet
15. https://github.com/OpenBMP/openbmp
16. https://source.android.com/
17. https://techcrunch.com/2017/10/01/apple-open-sourced-the-kernel-of-ios-and-macos-for-arm-processors/
18. https://www.its.dot.gov/cv_basics/cv_basics_what.htm
19. IEEE Standard for Wireless Access Vehicular Environments (WAVE) Networking Services, IEEE 1609.3, 2016, IEEE Standard for Wireless Access Vehicular Environments (WAVE) Networking Services, IEEE 1609.3, 2016.

20. Movahedi, Z., Ayari, M., Langar, R., and Pujolle, G., A survey of autonomic network architectures and evaluation criteria, *IEEE Communications Surveys & Tutorials*, 14(2), 464–490, 2012.
21. Clark, D. D., Partridge, C., Ramming, J. C., Wroclawski, J. T., A knowledge plane for the Internet, *ACM SIGCOMM Proceedings*, 2003. Retrieved from https://conferences.sigcomm.org/sigcomm/2003/papers/p3-clark.pdf.
22. Mestres, A. et al., Knowledge-defined networking, *ACM Sigcomm Computer Communications Review*, 47(3), 2–10, 2017.
23. http://www.sae.org/images/books/toc_pdfs/B977.pdf
24. https://pndablog.com/2017/04/17/smart-transport-connected-car-cloud-analytics-with-machine-learning-using-pnda/
25. http://fd.io
26. https://medium.com/flow-ci/introduction-to-containers-concept-pros-and-cons-orchestration-docker-and-other-alternatives-9a2f1b61132c
27. https://github.com/containernetworking/cni
28. https://kubernetes.io/
29. https://kubernetes.io/docs/concepts/cluster-administration/networking/
30. https://github.com/ligato/vpp-agent
31. https://ligato.github.io/
32. https://ligato.github.io/mydoc_container_net_vpp.html
33. https://www.cncf.io/
34. https://www.opendaylight.org/
35. RESTCONF protocol, RFC8040. RESTCONF is an HTTP-based protocol providing APIs to data defined in YANG models.
36. https://www.onap.org/
37. http://about.att.com/innovationblog/041116ecomparchitect
38. [onaparch], https://www.onap.org/wp-content/uploads/sites/20/2017/11/ONAP_CaseSolution_Architecture_FNL.pdf
39. SDC TOSCA AID v2.0/ECOMP data model specification. Retrieved from https://wiki.onap.org/download/attachments/10784241/SDC_TOSCA_AID_1710%20v16.docx?version=2&modificationDate=1501658412000&api=v2.
40. http://blog.kubernetes.io/2017/03/scalability-updates-in-kubernetes-1.6.html
41. https://kafka.apache.org/
42. https://coreos.com/etcd/
43. Brockners, F., Telemetry and analytics for the NFV world: IOAM, PNDA, DCAE, *ONAP Beijing Release Developer Forum*, December 2017. Retrieved from https://onapbeijing2017.sched.com/event/D5pJ/telemetry-and-analytics-for-the-nfv-world-ioam-dcae-pnda.
44. http://lambda-architecture.net/
45. http://pnda.io/
46. http://pnda.io/blog
47. http://www.routeviews.org/
48. https://bgpstream.caida.org/
49. http://www.snas.io/
50. https://datatracker.ietf.org/doc/rfc7854/
51. https://www.openstack.org/software/
52. https://istio.io/
53. https://spiffe.io/
54. http://www.openpolicyagent.org/
55. https://cloud.google.com/beyondcorp/

56. Gilman, E. and Barth, D., *Zero Trust Networking*, O'Reilly Media, Sebastopol, CA, 2017.

57. Entities connecting into a ZTN must establish basic connectivity. To accomplish this, entities can employ "plug-and-play" (PnP) functionality to bootstrap IP addressability and retrieve data for communications across a ZTN. PnP embeds a "call home address" along with secure credentials at creation (i.e., assembly complete), so once attached to the network, it can establish a secure session with a PnP server to retrieve configuration information [82]. A PnP server has been implemented in ODL. Autonomic Networking enables devices to automate self-management, network discovery, and secure connectivity across an autonomic network without central control. And finally, Universal PnP (UPnP) is another protocol supporting plug-and-play but extended to a broader set of solution domains including cloud [83].

58. https://www.envoyproxy.io/

59. Chiang, M., Ha, S., Chih-Lin I, Risso, F., and Zhang, T., Clarifying fog computing and networking: 10 questions and answers, *IEEE Communications Magazine*, 55, 18–20, 2017.

60. https://www.openfogconsortium.org/

61. https://www.atlassian.com/continuous-delivery/ci-vs-ci-vs-cd

62. https://www.opnfv.org/

63. https://jenkins.io/

64. https://netflix.github.io/

65. https://www.tensorflow.org/

66. https://medium.com/intuitionmachine/from-narrow-to-general-ai-e21b568155b9

67. https://github.com/opennars/opennars

68. https://opencog.org/

69. https://aws.amazon.com/machine-learning/

70. Co-Authored with Andrew Li, Cisco Systems

71. [azureml], https://azure.microsoft.com/en-us/overview/machine-learning/

72. https://cloud.google.com/products/machine-learning/

73. https://www.ibm.com/cloud/machine-learning

74. Bhattacharjee, B. et al., IBM deep learning service, *IBM Journal of Research & Development*, 61, 10:1–10:11, 2017.

75. https://www.alibabacloud.com/

76. https://cloud.tencent.com/

77. https://www.acumos.org/

78. https://openai.com/

79. https://en.wikipedia.org/wiki/Facebook%E2%80%93Cambridge_Analytica_data_scandal

80. https://www.linuxfoundation.org/blog/intro-to-real-time-linux-for-embedded-developers/

81. https://www.automotivelinux.org/

82. [network-pnp], https://blogs.cisco.com/enterprise/introducing-pnp-connect

83. [UPnP], https://openconnectivity.org/foundation/faq/upnp-faq

CHAPTER 7

Machine Learning, Containers, Cloud Natives, and Microservices

Eyal Felstaine and Ofer Hermoni

CONTENTS

7.1 INTRODUCTION

This chapter considers some implications of applying artificial intelligence (AI) and particularly machine learning (ML) to cloud-based communication networks providing complex computing services. From one aspect, applying AI, and particularly ML, to the network includes two fields: AI in the network management, and AI-based network services.

Artificial intelligence in the network management is based on several assumptions that are considered facts, but they are not. It is assumed that a cloud-based network enables flexibility, complexity, and dynamics beyond the abilities of humans to control the network in real time. Here, flexibility refers to the ability to customize or configure the network services to users' needs. Complexity refers to the number of configurations of the network services running in parallel with possible direct and indirect interaction. And dynamics refer to the rate of change of these configurations, for whatever reason. It is assumed that the combination of flexibility, complexity, and dynamics (as well as other similar features) requires automation, for example in the form of a closed-loop control (see Chapter 3). It is also assumed that procedural automation is insufficient, and therefore AI is required. It is further assumed that humans may be too slow to code the AI rules manually, and therefore ML should be used to learn the network behavior and automate the creation of network management rules.

Developing, testing, deploying, and securing AI-based communication services for cloud-based autonomous networks is challenging and complex. Cloud technology, including containers, cloud natives, and microservices, enables reusability of applications, reduced time to market, optimal use of infrastructure, and detailed adaptation to users' needs; however, the administration complexity calls for AI.

Facilitating AI and ML requires massive training data, and in many cases target labels particularly for supervised learning (See Chapter 2). The training data should be collected, cleansed, organized, and provisioned very carefully. The data quality and data excellence of the training data is obviously crucial to the network's performance and resilience.

On the national level and on the international level, the telecom network is a very complex system. The cloud-based communication network is even more complex, and even more so is the cloud-network complex, as will be further detailed in the following section. The AI-based closed-loop control of the network is, therefore, practically a network of numerous closed loops, where none of the loops is really closed.

Artificial intelligence in the network services refers to network entities, such as AI-based microservices, which may behave very differently for different customers or situations. Activating, monitoring, predicting (the behavior), and managing AI-based microservices are complex challenges by themselves. One may obviously envisage a third field that covers AI-based management of AI-based services.

As we experienced with stock algo-trading allegedly exacerbating the 1987 stock market crash [1] as well as several later "flash crashes," a simple AI failure may quickly degrade into a total network outage. Probably even worse, a simple AI failure may develop into an intermittent "traveling" network failure. This traveling failure may have a very different temporary effect for different services. For example, traveling-increased latency may delay just some of the inputs of an industrial Internet-of-Things (IoT) system causing temporary miscalculation, which changes as the failure travels through the network.

7.2 THE ADVENT OF CLOUD COMPUTING AND COMMUNICATION

From one aspect, engineering is the art of optimization, trading unnecessary deficiencies for necessary deficiencies. Optimization considerations develop and change as the underlying technology changes, and then return in a slightly different form.

The basic goal of the operating system (OS) is hardware transparency (what is now termed "virtualization"), additionally supporting multiprocessing and multiprogramming. In cloud technology, a process in multiprocessing (or a task in multitasking) is termed a *server*. It refers to the ability to break the software into processes that may be processed in parallel. Multiprogramming refers to concurrently running several different programs on the same computer. The OS provides hardware reuse and software reuse at the cost of context-switching and the danger of thrashing, where the computer is processing OS code more than it processes application code. These principles are carried to the cloud environment.

With a single processor, parallel processing is virtual, and the processor executes processes alternatingly (with context-switching in-between). A multiprocessor system may actually execute processes in parallel if the entire system is built for distributed processing. Aside for multicore processors, client-server is the most commonly used distributed-processing architecture [2]. Distributed processing introduces connectivity, communication bandwidth, latency, network architecture, etc. The Internet introduced globalization to computing, so that processing can be done anywhere, online. With mobile computing, distributed processing has reached to our pockets (in the form of smartphones) and most of the client software is now processed on the move, taking roughly half of the Internet traffic.

Software layering, or stacking, is very common as a mean of abstraction, enabling upgrading a layer without affecting the other layers. Open Systems Interconnection (OSI) is a conceptual model of a network developed at the International Organization for Standardization (ISO) as ISO/IEC 7498-1 [3].

Cloud computing took information technology (IT) into extreme economy of scale. It is assumed that reducing cost will increase consumption to the point that resources are always in short. Organizations move to the cloud for three main advantages: reduced Capital Expenditure (CAPEX), scalability, and the ease or speed of deployment and acquisition of software-based services. Obviously, there are further reasons, mostly based on these three cloud advantages. Cloud computing is based on sharing, which means that everybody is affecting everybody else. The goal of the autonomous network is to minimize the perceived effect while hardware efficiency, software efficiency, and service flexibility are increasing.

7.2.1 Cloud Computing as a Business and as a Service

From afar, the concept of what we now know as cloud computing is as old as digital computing. However, we are more interested in understanding the patterns of the current revolution. From one aspect, economy may be divided into added value (products and services) and intrinsic value. Added value economy is based on cost sharing, and the price of the product or service is based mainly on the cost of providing it. Intrinsic value economy (also known as the outcome economy) is based on revenue sharing, and the price is based on the benefit to the customer. These two types of economy have been around for ages and will obviously persist; however, it seems that intrinsic value economy is currently gaining, and the revolution of cloud computing as well as the autonomous networks should be investigated from this aspect.

We may observe the wish of telecom operators to move into intrinsic value economy. Instead of providing a basic bit-moving infrastructure, operators would like to provide sophisticated services specifically customized to the users' needs. Bandwidth, latency, and similar network (and computing) terms will be replaced by user-particular business and lifestyle terms. The idea is not new at all, but it seems to gain momentum.

Computing technology has evolved from few huge mainframes worldwide to a super-computer in everybody's pocket. However, the real development is the migration toward serving a user's need on demand. The business is not the computing infrastructure, not the software, and not the processing; it is the outcome, the intrinsic value, and the solution to the user's current problem in real time. The service may involve any number of input devices and various types of output devices. Possibly the particular computing configuration is one time, unique, ever. Apparently, such service cannot be provided by any single business entity, and therefore, possibly, the particular business configuration providing this one-time service is also established on demand.

There is no way to achieve such intrinsic value services other than by the cloud, or rather, by an autonomous cloud-based network. As stated earlier, the combination of flexibility, complexity, and dynamics requires AI-based automation of service provisioning using ML and similar technologies.

7.2.2 Cloud Concepts and Components

CAPEX is a major reason for organizations to move to the cloud; however, this rather narrow financial point of view is somewhat misleading. The private data center requires long-term and complex planning, procurement, installation, and maintenance. Moving to the cloud and to Operational Expense (OPEX) allegedly simplifies matters. Practically, a solution migrates the center of weight of a problem into another part of the overall complexity, which may seem, for a time, more comfortable and lenient to a particular need. However, in the long term, the core of the problem persists.

The reliance of businesses on their IT operation is growing, requiring a highly reliable system and rigorously tested software. The telecom network is one example of a highly reliable service. However, reliability comes with a financial high cost and even higher operational cost. The IT center becoming a major cause of business latency, which is a major cause for losing market share and profitability.

Businesses are under increasing demand for agility, and the IT center is under special pressure to support business agility. Cloud computing's foremost promise is agility, supported by collaborative development and collaborative computing. However, intricate collaboration and cross dependencies have their price, introducing intermittent and unstable stochastic effects. Still, undoubtedly, the cloud offers faster scaling, at least where "horizontal" scaling is a valid solution.

The consistency, availability, and partition (CAP) tolerance theorem (a.k.a. Brewer's theorem [4]) states that it is impossible for a distributed data store to simultaneously provide more than two out of the three guarantees of data consistency, data availability (or latency), and partition tolerance [5]. Data consistency means that any read operation retrieves the most updated value. Data availability means that any operation is served immediately. Tolerance means that the data service is "tolerant" to load (albeit the partitioning). Practically, CAP theorem states that partitioning degrades either data consistency (to provide for data availability), or data availability (to provide for data consistency) or both (e.g., an optimized configuration). Any data store is partitioned; however, the cloud glorifies partitioning (e.g., horizontal scaling), making the CAP theorem acute.

For simplified examples of what CAP theorem refers to, we may think of transaction processing, and particularly situations like double ordering the same airplane seat, or the same hotel room, or the same slot of a hospital operating suit, turning the "tolerance" issue into a business call. Mission-critical control systems (e.g., trains coordination or air traffic control) are obviously intolerant to any aspect of data consistency and availability.

The broad sense of data consistency can be divided into consistency of a single data item regarding different parallel processes, and data coherency (or concurrency) considering the consistency of a plurality of different and interrelated data items. For example, a database is coherent when all the transactions are completed. Tolerance may refer to the intrinsic error of any calculated value due to incoherency due to multiple transactions executed in parallel, thus introducing data uncertainty as a phenomenon rather than as a fault.

Nevertheless, cloud computing with its indispensable advantages and its particular troubles is here to stay and proliferate. The communication network is also migrating to the cloud, and the cloud-network complex is about to use AI to manage its complexity in real time. In Section 7.3, we will try to describe a few aspects of this developing mix of AI, fuzzy logic, continuous ML, intrinsic data uncertainty, and CAP trade-offs.

7.2.3 Cloud Natives

Cloud native is a concept whereby software is designed, developed, and optimized to exploit cloud technology [6,7]. Cloud technology is primarily a distributed architecture, and cloud natives are particularly designed for distributed processing and distributed data store.

Another way of considering cloud natives is the methodology of the twelve-factor app developed at Heroku (https://12factor.net/). The goal is to break the system into as many as possible independent processing entities that collaborate via the cloud infrastructure. Therefore, each cloud processing entity makes as few as possible assumptions about its environment. Thus, allowing simple and automated provisioning, upgrading, scalability, graceful shutdown, and obsolescence. Cloud natives also assume being stateless, relying on backing services for any aspect of "long-term memory" such as state and data.

The Cloud Native Computing Foundation, founded in 2015 and now counting over 550 members, promotes the concept of cloud natives and particularly the use of containers as a means for rigorous boundaries.

According to the Cloud Native Computing Foundation, cloud-native systems should have the following properties:

1. Container packaged. Running applications and processes in software containers as an isolated unit of application deployment, and as a mechanism to achieve high levels of resource isolation. Improves overall developer experience, fosters code and component reuse, and simplifies operations for cloud-native applications.

2. Dynamically managed. Actively scheduled and actively managed by a central orchestrating process. Radically improve machine efficiency and resource utilization while reducing the cost associated with maintenance and operations.

3. Microservices oriented. Loosely coupled with dependencies explicitly described (e.g., through service endpoints). Significantly increase the overall agility and maintainability of applications.

7.2.4 Microservices

Microservices represent cloud modularity and a typical implementation of the cloud-native concept [8,9]. A microservice is a piece of software that can be deployed and removed, allegedly without affecting the operation of the entire software system. One microservice may apply for a service from any other microservice via the cloud interprocess communication infrastructure. A microservice is protected from its environment, and vice versa.

Breaking the software system into independent microservices enables several important advantages of cloud computing:

- Independent development of each microservice, enabling short development cycles and rapid release of new versions. New computing technologies (e.g., software languages, management support software, and methodologies) may be gradually introduced to the system, and the system may easily and safely include several computing technologies.

- Scalability, flexible system configuration, and ease of migration of microservices between hardware and software platforms.

- Resilience of the entire system against failure of a particular microservice.

While it is easier and faster to develop and deploy a single microservice (than a monolithic system), it is much more difficult to manage the entire system of numerous microservices with their various versions running in parallel.

To achieve their advantages, microservices require rigorous boundaries. Microservices cooperate using Application Programming Interface (API) protocols, preferably Representational State Transfer (REST) oriented (REST is a set of constraints and properties based on HTTP supporting interoperability between computer systems on the Internet) and preferably being stateless. If not absolutely stateless, microservices also advocate decentralized data management where each microservice manages its own data store. If any other microservice B is in need for data managed by microservice A, it must use the microservice A's API to call it to get the required data. While robust, remote calls are inherently slow, and rigorous boundaries increase latency, as well as bandwidth and processing requirements, hence increasing topology and configuration complexity too. While each microservice is easier to understand, the complexity is shifted to the interconnections between the microservices, increasing debugging and operational complexity such as associated with transaction processing, data locking, deadlock detection and recovery, and critical races.

Few three letter acronyms, such as Enterprise Application Integration (EAI), Service-Oriented Architecture (SOA), and Enterprise Service Bus (ESB), are intended to provide adequate solutions to the problem of interprocess communication [10,11]. Such solutions solve the need to define, develop, and test an API between any two interacting microservices. An effective implementation of EAI/SOA/ESB acts as a bridge between any two interacting microservices, thus increasing context-switching, processing load, communication load, latency, and a single point of failure, as well as forming a programming bottleneck. Implementing EAI/SOA/ESB as an absolutely stateless microservice and instantiating microservices according to load may help with the load issue. On the other hand, the EAI/SOA/ESB solution may also be used as a data-locking facility, which is absolutely not stateless.

Having rigorous boundaries, microservices are advantageous for continuous integration and continuous delivery (CI/CD) discussed in the following section. A rapid release indicates a very limited testing, and the expectation that the system is tolerant to single microservice failure. However, complex systems, and particularly complex databases, are not tolerant at all. Returning to the issue of data coherence, a software fault may leave the database incoherent creating proliferation of data inconsistency and repetitive crashing.

Another aspect of microservices is cybersecurity, and the dilemma whether it is safer to keep the assets in a single place having ultimate protection, or whether a security breach of a single microservice does not compromise the entire system. On one hand, rigorous boundaries, if set appropriately, are good against cyberattacks; however, a fast-changing topology and less-predictable system behavior make cybersecurity much more difficult. Again, AI may offer a solution, though still increasing the costs of processing and latency.

7.2.5 Virtual Machines and Containers

Virtual machine is an old computing technology used as a layer between the OS and the hardware, thus virtualizing the hardware. The concept has been further developed as a layer between a base (or hosting) OS and a guest (or hosted) OS. This technology, also known as hypervisor, enables several hosted OS to run concurrently over the same hardware, via the shared (base, hosting) OS.

Virtual machines became a very useful, if not essential, cloud infrastructure tool, enabling flexibility where an application may run anywhere, irrespective of the underlying hardware and OS. However, this virtualization also means that the application cannot be optimized to any particular hardware architecture or OS. Consequently, when an application is migrated to a different hardware architecture or OS, its performance may considerably degrade.

Running each application over its own guest OS also provides effective isolation between the applications. However, as with any heavily stacked software system, this isolation is costly, as context-switching takes a heavy toll.

Running each application over its own guest OS and its own virtual machine requires extensive system administration. The concept of the container has been created to simplify matters. Instead of stacking and administrating several layers of software, the application is packaged together with all its system tools, libraries, settings, etc., and only those that the application needs.

A container may run directly over the kernel OS. Therefore, containers are managed and migrated more easily, however, reducing the ability to optimize the software to the particular hardware and OS.

Another advantage of the container is size. Using a virtual machine per application also requires memory for the full virtual machine and the full guest OS, most of which is not used. The container takes just those parts of the OS that the application uses and is therefore much smaller. Consequently, more containers may run on the same server, as far as processing needs and context-switching allow.

However, this is a somewhat misleading comparison, as it assumes the cloud-native approach where each part of the application is an independently containerized microservice. If a system is designed as a plurality of subsystems (applications, microservices) running over a shared operating system, then the size comparison may tilt as containers pack the same operating-system code again and again.

A third advantage of containers results from the simplicity of instantiation and the speed of instantiation, which enables faster response to changing demands, such as processing load, latency, and communication bandwidth. Faster reconfiguration of the system topology means better utilization of the hardware infrastructure, lower costs, and a better service, as well as faster fault recovery. It is noted that the shared-OS system approach presented in the previous paragraph is usually much less flexible.

The processing load and processing latency associated with context-switching should be compared between a plurality of containers and a virtual machine carrying a shared operating system and a plurality of subsystems. Such comparison may show an advantage for the virtual-machine solution.

Security is generally considered a disadvantage of the container approach, as the underlying kernel may be susceptible to security breaches and thus provide a back door to the containerized applications. Means to overcome such security problems are being developed, however, adding complexity and reducing flexibility. Again, the virtual-machine approach gains further advantage when a plurality of subsystems is protected by a shared OS.

The Open Container Initiative (OCI) was established in 2015 under the auspices of the Linux Foundation to develop an industry standard for a container format and container runtime software for all platforms. The project's sponsors include Amazon Web Services, Google, IBM, HP, Microsoft, VMware, Red Hat, Oracle, Twitter, HP, CoreOS, and Docker that donated about 5 percent of its codebase to the project to get it off the ground.

7.2.6 Management and Orchestration Systems

Docker [12] is perhaps still the most popular tool for packaging a microservice code in a container, but there are several other tools gaining popularity [13]. Above the containerization tools there are tools for managing containers, such as Kubernets and Docker Swarm [14]. There are also similar tools for managing virtual machines such as VMware vSphere suit [15]. Practically, every cloud platform has its own virtual-machine management suit as well as several third-party tools. Similarly, as container technology gains popularity, more containerization tools and container management tools enter the market, and the need for standards becomes viable.

A system management tool should display and administrate all the host servers (hardware) and all the virtual machines and containers operating within a particular infrastructure. Various management systems offer automatic services, such as generating alerts, consolidating virtual machines onto the fewest number of host servers when possible, detecting unused storage, code, etc. Such features usually rely on some software hooks within the virtual machine or container.

The OCI promotes standards and specifications for container technology to achieve interoperability for container technology and management tools [16]. Currently, the effort is more toward an open source project than a standard. A first release of image format and specifications issued in July 2017 defines minimal requirements for a container that is portable across different OS, hardware, CPU architectures, public clouds, etc., with a planned formal certification process. Currently, there are no plans regarding networking, intercontainer communication, and distribution.

The Cloud Native Computing Foundation also promotes the container network interface (CNI) [17] and the container storage interface (CSI) standards [18]. CNI standardizes the network underneath multihost container deployments enabling cooperation and interchangeability between proprietary networking tools (e.g., Weave, Contrive, Docker Network); CSI is a similar standard for the data infrastructure (e.g., Rook [19]).

7.2.7 Network Function Virtualization

Network function virtualization (NFV) promoted by the European Telecommunications Standards Institute is basically a cloud architecture for telecom services creating a network that is more flexible and dynamic than the current conventional communication network. In an NFV-based network, services that can be implemented in software are executed over generic cloud hardware as virtual network functions (VNFs). In this respect, a VNF is like a microservice operating over a virtual machine or container. Like microservices, VNFs are easily installed, removed, and migrated between hardware facilities, on demand, under the control of an NFV orchestration software (NFV-O).

From the telecom operator's standpoint, NFV moves the network to cloud technology. From the IT point of view, the public network interconnecting cloud sites or a hybrid cloud is virtualized. The variety of cloud management software systems should now cooperate with respective NFV-Os, and each NFV-O should consider respective cloud management software systems it interconnects. As telecom networks are interconnected, their respective

NFV-Os should coordinate their functionality and activities. Therefore, NFV dynamics add to the complexity of cloud-computing dynamics.

Network function virtualization promotes decomposition of the functionality of a network node as much as possible. The packet flow is vertically decomposed into signaling, control, data, streaming, etc., each handled in a different plane. Processing these elements in each of the planes is decomposed to enable horizontal distribution over a plurality of hardware units, enabling optimized scalability, etc. Communication-related application are decomposed into selectable functions to enable separate instantiation of each function to optimize customization, reduce costs, etc.

As a rule of a thumb, in terms of performance per dollar, hardware is more efficient. In terms of flexibility, software is more efficient. Hence, for business purposes, operators would have to exploit software flexibility by continuously consolidating software functionality (e.g., VNFs, microservices) over shared hardware, while continuously considering service-level agreements (SLAs), quality-of-service (QoS) requirements, availability, security issues, etc.

Additionally, NFV should develop into an effective platform for newly developed sophisticated communication services enabling business differentiation and competitive advantage in the market. Understanding that cloud technology and NFV promote business agility and faster technology development, it is expected that new functions and features are delivered continuously at an increasing rate, practically exceeding the ability to disseminate knowledge and assimilate it.

7.2.8 DevOps, Continuous Integration, and Continuous Deployment

Business agility is the main driver for moving to cloud technology and NFV. Business agility means shortening time-to-market while reducing the cost of delivering a new function, from function definition to billing. Carrying a function from definition to billing involves many disciplines having an intricate network of motivations and considerations. The two common approaches are "built-it-right-the-first-time" and "quickly-repeated-prototyping." Considering that manpower and budget are always limited, it is obvious that only a fraction of the projects taking the quickly-repeated-prototyping venue will end up in profitable business. However, this venue has two important advantages: "let the market decide" and "bury the dead," both contributing to the business bottom line.

DevOps and CI-CD are concepts promoted by research and development (R&D) to increase the rate of function definition-to-deployment. DevOps promotes tight integration of software development, quality assurance, and data-center operations, which are traditionally deliberately separated. Integrating these business functions tends to enable a faster and automated cycle of coding-integration-testing-delivery-deployment with the goal to complete as many as possible cycles per day. The basic difference between continuous integration, delivery, and deployment is how far in the cycle does automation reach. Practically speaking, DevOps attempts to reorganize the business to enable R&D to push features to customers at a faster rate without compromising the service quality. Fully automated cycle (as in CD) means that the deployment to the customer is initiated by the programmer without further intervention or consideration, of course, if the automated testing approves.

DevOps and CI-CD go well with software decomposition, microservices, and the cloud-native concepts. However, where NFV is considered, it is yet to be seen that a telecom operator allows a vendor's programmer to push a new release of a microservice directly to the production of a major client having a rigorous and highly detailed SLA.

One important element of DevOps and CI-CD is continuous monitoring. If a module, for example, VNF or microservice, is released few times a day, with enough such modules in the system and a continuous deployment process that takes enough time, versions of the system are released in parallel. Online log analysis, monitoring, and reporting upstream the DevOps CI-CD process becomes critical.

7.2.9 A Glimpse on Edge Computing

On one hand, edge computing defies the centralized concept of cloud computing as a global data center. On the other hand, edge computing is the culmination of the cloud's concept of horizontal distribution and migration dynamics. In this later sense, edge computing manifests all the problems of cloud computing for the benefit of reducing latency, processing turn around, and bandwidth. (Also cost of performing local data processing without moving large data to core.)

There are two main aspects of edge computing:

Network edge computing such as C-RAN and V-RAN, which are edge functions intrinsic to the telecom/network/site operator.

Cloud edge computing, where the telecom/network/site operator does not own and is not responsible for the edge software other than providing the processing, storage, and networking infrastructure (e.g., Infrastructure-as-a-Service). There are also on-premises white boxes, which are a form of mini edge clouds.

One major question is how does network edge computing differ from NFV, other than mobile network edge computing being subject to terminal mobility (e.g., roaming).

Cloud edge computing, operative on much smaller and limited computing infrastructure, is less efficient than central cloud computing, and therefore costlier. Cloud edge computing is also more risky than central cloud computing, particularly when roaming. Therefore, unless something changes in the infrastructure, applications may migrate to the edge only if central cloud computing cannot provide the required service due to limitations, such as bandwidth, latency, and turn around.

Infrastructure change that may cause cloud edge computing to be more efficient than central cloud computing is the rising cost of communication, which, at this time, seems unlikely. Infrastructure change that may cause cloud edge computing to be more efficient than terminal computing has improved power efficiency (J/bit) of the radio access network. This may suggest using cloud edge computing to reduce battery power consumption of battery-based client devices.

Cloud edge computing facilities may reside between the core network main switching facilities and the client, anywhere the network operator has any type of "real estate," including base stations, curbside closets, and building basements, with distributed processing power and storage varying on demand. Examples of real-estate buildings may include central offices and regional and national data centers.

7.2.10 Antifragility

The concept of antifragility was introduced by Nassim Taleb in his book *Antifragile* (Random House/Penguin) as the quality of a system that gets stronger when subjected to stressors. This is similar to the human immune system, which gets stronger when exposed to pathogens. Practically speaking, antifragility may be manifested by stochastic load emulation. The Chaos Monkey submodule of Netflix Simian Army project injects random failures into production components to identify weaknesses in the software architecture and subsequently eliminate them.

7.2.11 Enters Artificial Intelligence

As discussed earlier, the goal of the cloud network complex is business agility through system complexity. Increased vertical stratification, increased horizontal distribution, and faster CI-CD, all add to the complexity and system dynamics, making the use of AI technologies mandatory. However, considering the scope of the challenge, AI technologies are still nascent. The basic problem, as will be further discussed in Sub-section 7.3.4, is that AI-based cloud-network orchestration, when combined with AI-based cloud processing management, creates a web of interconnected AI-based management systems.

7.3 A LEARNING NETWORK OF MICROSERVICES

The push for business agility promotes technologies enabling processing (cloud) and network dynamics. Huge numbers of microservices are intricately coupled between themselves, with data stores of various types, and by shared processing, storage, and networking infrastructure, and obliged to various constraints, such as SLAs. These microservices may be continuously upgraded or replaced, while the customers' needs, service requirements, and loads continuously change too, with fault maintenance (as well as predictive maintenance) adding to the unpredictability of the overall system. On top of this very complex problem, there is a constant burden to reduce the overall cost, in terms of both CAPEX and OPEX.

The growing dynamics of the cloud and the network require sophisticated management and orchestration systems, understanding that these systems are practically coupled between them. No single management or orchestration system is an island. Any reconfiguration decision has immediate implications on processes managed by neighboring management and orchestration systems, which will immediately respond and affect each other again and again.

The question is whether sophisticated conventional automation may solve the problem or whether AI is essential. For this purpose, automation uses man-made algorithms or rules, while AI systems learn the cloud network and automatically generate their own rules (e.g., without human intervention). One aspect of this difference is the likelihood of the rule base of different management and orchestration systems to converge, or diverge, as well as the question, What is better for their respective likelihood to crash? In other words, what may be the better way to antifragility?

Artificial intelligence in the microservices adds to the complex situation described previously. The IoT is expected to engage AI intensively and may provide a glimpse of the resulting complexity. The IoT may be viewed as a huge distribution of devices, such as sensors and actuators where each device reports, directly or indirectly, to several processors. Each processor continuously analyzes data collected from a large number of inputs to make a decision. A processor may, therefore, maintain its own data store but may also access other data stores. Assuming that some of these processors employ AI, data access is intensive, and the scope of the data accessed may change "unexpectedly."

The complex cloud network environment managed is, therefore, practically coupling a plurality of cloud network management and orchestration systems (and so does the ecosystem of AI-based microservices) then obviously, the AI of these management and orchestration systems is coupled. This coupling affects both the data analyzed and the rule base created. Other than the question of "who owns what?" there is a need for some "standardization" of the data, data quality, and data excellence, as well as similar features of the rule bases.

Cloud native refers to efforts aligned with the Cloud Native Computing Foundation [20]. Its mission is to drive alignment across containers and microservices that leverage one of several frameworks to simplify the design, creation, and deployment of scalable distributed applications leveraging clouds. A key aspect is how the applications are organized to allow different parts of the application to be optimally deployed to match performance, cost, and scale requirements. When a cloud native architecture is considered in the design, development, and deployment, the utilization of the underlying cloud resources can be as much as 70% more efficient.

7.3.1 A Use Case of a Learning Network of Microservices

Artificial intelligence is becoming the brain driving cloud native. Software developers are embedding microservices with AI-driven intelligence. This capability is important AI for autonomous networks to allow key microservices to be optimally placed and scaled to meet the requirements of the application. Artificial intelligence microservices can be first broken down into smaller functional technologies (e.g., regression, classification, and prediction). These functional blocks/microservices can then be containerized and dynamically deployed in a cloud-native environment. Interactions between these microservices are typically facilitated using a message bus.

If we look to the Open Network Automation Platform (ONAP) for example, there are several places—such as the Data Collection, Analytics, and Events section and Policy and Control Loop Automation Management Platform section—that are distributed [21]. Specifically, control loops (CLs) are where we can find applications of AI for autonomous Telcom networks.

As part of service assurance, different types of CLs monitor network functions for performance and fault management. These CLs span different parts of the network to complete their needed functions. For high-speed actions, the CLs often needs to be distributed close to the edge. For complex services, CLs often span multiple sites and

ONAP Control Loop

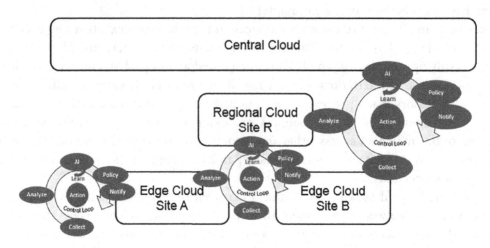

FIGURE 7.1   ONAP control loop example showing edge, regional, and central cloud deployments.

regional centers. For complete service monitoring, the CLs can span across edges and regional- and central-distributed components (Figure 7.1).

Reasons for leveraging cloud native for AI microservices are that many of the different CLs and AI analytics have different kinds of requirements. The CLs need to be efficient while scaling and distributed as the service or network are requested. Other requirements for AI and predictor models include processing of large data sets, moving the data or the analytics to the data as needed. It often requires leveraging special performance hardware (e.g., GPU/TPU) and linking to accelerators for AI, such as deep learning. The cloud-native frameworks [22] and runtimes assure execution in a manner that is vendor, provider, stack, location, and technology agnostic while providing vital intelligence back to ONAP to reinforce its "decide" role.

Let us walk through an example of ONAP Virtual Machine (VM) Resource Predictor. There are a number of data sources and collectors. Data is processed and aggregated to prepare it for the analytics containerized as microservices. In this case, there can be three classes of predictors (CPU, Network, Traffic) which are built in SciKit Learn and TensorFlow libraries (See Chapter 6). Each is a specific AI model trained using real data. Classifiers identify the specific devices to map the actions to the correct part of the service. The recommender works with policy to determine the specific action to be taken (Figure 7.2). There may be different options depending on location or other circumstances that need to be accounted for during the decision process.

For cloud native, this means each collector can be placed in a container by its data source forming an efficient package aligned with the resource need (low overhead).

The predictors are made of multiple artifacts leveraging the cloud native fabric for functional elasticity, connectivity, and infrastructure abstraction.

For example, the data preprocessing can also be placed by the data and collector to minimize the movement of extra data. The learning model can be placed and run in a

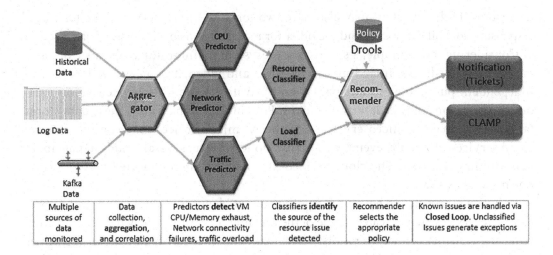

| Multiple sources of data monitored | Data collection, aggregation, and correlation | Predictors **detect** VM CPU/Memory exhaust, Network connectivity failures, traffic overload | Classifiers **identify** the source of the resource issue detected | Recommender selects the appropriate policy | Known issues are handled via **Closed Loop**. Unclassified Issues generate exceptions |

FIGURE 7.2   Data flow pipeline.

container where a group of specific cores are assigned to meet the model's needs and guarantee performance requirements. The training could be placed in a container that is leveraging GPU resource to handle the deep learning requirements. Then the reporting can be place in a container in the central cloud to simplify access, interconnectivity, and logging requirements.

In summary, cloud native will allow a higher level of efficiency and management of a distributed microservice solution to be deployed in containers that closely match the processing needs. With the growth of microservices, their efficiencies and manageability will be very important to scale the solutions.

7.3.2 Network of Data-Powered Microservices That Are Continuously Learning

Consider an AI microservice that is analyzing big data. In most cases, the big data is an independent data store, and probably a plurality of data stores. Each such data store is managed by a single microservice, which is responsible for all data access to the particular data store. In some cases, the data store is a database shared by a plurality of processes sharing the same VM. Each such data store may be part of several big-data collections. Each collection of data stores may be analyzed by several AI microservices. Hence, the network should carry an immense amount of data being analyzed by a very large number of AI microservices.

Having analyzed their respective big data and producing analysis results, such as actionable rules, the microservices should again analyze real-time data, make decisions, and communicate the decision via the overloaded network.

Mirroring is a costly brute force solution. Another possible approach that is consistent with the cloud-native concept of decomposition is to separate the AI learning analysis process from the AI real-time analysis process, and possibly from the control section too into two or three "loosely coupled" microservices. Similarly, data stores may be divided into long-term data and short-term data stores, respectively, serving the long-term learning microservice and the real-time analysis microservice, co-located with their respective data stores. Each data store may also have two (or more) microservices, one (or more) responsible for collecting data and the other (or more) responsible for disseminating data.

Considering, for example, a smart-city ecosystem maintaining a plurality of databases and repositories, including image stores and video streams, as well as several independent public (i.e., municipality) and private AI applications feeding on various combinations of this data and content. Possibly, if not plausibly, these data stores (and their managing microservices) and the AI microservices may run on separate cloud services. Probably, even for the same cloud service, several cloud-management software may be used. The cloud service sites may be interconnected by more than one network operator.

Each city is expected to have a similar, though not identical, ecosystem, where many of the microservices are replicated. Some of the learning results may apply in different cities, requiring exchange of analysis results, which makes the sharing of raw data between cities useful too. Exchanging raw data requires some level of standardization of data quality, data excellence, and similar measures of the value of the analyzed data.

There is, therefore, a network of "systems." Each system includes several subsystems, some may be AI based (and the other involve regular IT processes). The AI subsystem may include several AI processes, such as big-data analytics, to create rules and short-term analysis using the rules in real time. These processes may be implemented as independent microservices that may be instantiated in co-location with their data stores, as well as replicated for different customers (having different data stores). Microservices of the same system may, therefore, be instantiated under different cloud management software as well as in different cloud sites and interconnected by more than one telecom network.

When an AI-based cloud management software system "learns" the behavior of its cloud, and when a network orchestration software analyzes the network traffic, they actually learn a behavioral combination of the AI microservices in their territory, the effect from AI microservices outside their territory, and the overlying effect of the neighboring cloud management and network orchestration systems. While a successful new consumer-oriented application may take at least months to develop and affect the cloud universe and network, a network of AI-based microservices may have a considerable effect within hours, if not minutes. The challenge is that this interrelated learning process converges, rather than explodes. The challenge can be met, for example, by means of a "negative feedback" exchanged between cloud management and network orchestration systems.

7.3.3 False Alarms Handling in a Multitier Learning Network

So far, we have touched some problems associated with agile business, agile cloud, and agile network. We considered exemplary issues of data processing, data stores, and communications, associated with the dynamics of a cloud and network designed for business agility. We also briefly touched on issues of the intricate management cloud structures and their intermediating networks. We then considered some aspects of AI, as it may be implemented within cloud applications, network applications, cloud management, and network management (or orchestration). One aspect of the cloud and network management is the generation and handling of alarms, both are (independently) subject to AI technology, big-data analytics, ML, etc. Handling alarms is a highly sensitive and very costly business. False alarms, both false positive and false negative, may trash a business.

From the point of view of a monitoring system, the complex of the agile cloud(s) and agile network(s) is inherently unstable, particularly when monitoring a part of the complex. We may expect a large number of (fault) monitoring systems generating various types of alarms (e.g., hardware related, software related, load related, security related, or content related). Each cloud management instance, and each network management instance, is associated with a different plurality of alarms generating systems, each handling respective types of alarms.

Due to the overlapping and interconnected nature of the cloud and network management tasks, a single cause may generate many alarms. A single cause may affect the behavior of modules of different cloud layers and different network layers, as well as vertically decomposed or multi-instantiated modules and cloud and network components shared by different management systems. There may be a plurality of similar types of alarms, generated by monitoring systems of a similar type, associated with their respective management systems. The same cause may also initiate a plurality of alarms by monitoring systems of different types serving the same cloud or network management system. Therefore, it requires a supervising alert monitoring layer consolidating the various alarms and making sure that alarms are handled efficiently.

Some types of alarms are initiated directly by the monitored unit (hardware or software). However, fault detection systems tend to use AI to analyze and detect inconsistencies as means for predicting the development of a fault, anticipating load development, detecting covert security breach, etc. Such mechanisms should understand the dynamics of the cloud and network, as they are changed by their respective management systems.

Other than the common problems of false positive alarms and false negative (lack of) alarm, there is also the problem of the untimely alarm, which may be premature or late. False positive and untimely alarms are obviously costly, but also cause "alarm fatigue" (or alert fatigue) of the response teams, which degrades efficiency, adding to the overall cost. Changing the alarm threshold increases the probability of false negative event, which is even more costly.

The goal of all the predictive fault analysis systems is to grade the events associated with faults and provide more accurate and timely alarms that are based on a plurality of indications. Such indications may result from a time series of events of the same type or from a plurality of different but related events. The purpose of AI and ML in fault detection is to determine such relations between different events and possible faults and grade them accordingly. Grading denotes statistical parameters of fault occurrence, such as the probability of a fault occurring with a time frame (e.g., mean time between failures).

The relations between events and faults are obviously tightly linked to the dynamics of the cloud and network environments requiring a tight handshake between the management systems and the fault detection systems. Management systems report general maintenance, such as log compression, garbage collection, and data reconstruction, as well as deployment and migration of microservices, while fault prediction analysis systems report fault probability grading to enable the management system to plan ahead.

Considering AI and particularly ML, it is obvious that the entire cloud-network complex is continuously learning, as a web of coupled independent learning machines. It is noted that this web is undesigned in the sense that no particular business entity or organization is responsible for the topology of this web. Therefore, cybersecuring the operation of the web becomes a challenge of its own type.

7.3.4 Debug a Learning Network in a Continuous Deployment Microservices Environment

Testing a system has three aspects. One aspect, relatively simple, is testing that the system is doing what the specification requires. Another more complicated aspect is testing that the system is *not* doing what the specification forbids. The third, problematic, aspect is testing for "unspecified faults." Such faults usually result from a particular sequence of operations, more likely two or more concurrent sequences of operations, as well as load-related situations, such as affecting data-locking mechanisms or critical races.

Unlike "specified faults" that tend to be stable and localized, "unspecified faults" tend to be erratic, intermittent, and "traveling." Such fault may cause data inconsistency that degrades into database incoherence that travels through the system while spreading garbled data that may be difficult to locate and difficult to recover.

The cloud-native approach—horizontal and vertical decomposition of processing tasks and data stores, augmented by CI-CD—increases the possibilities for the "unspecified faults." Testing a microservice or even a system in an isolated sandbox would not generate the complex scenario leading to an "unspecified fault." Eventually, considering unspecified faults, microservices are tested "live," while providing service. Hence, cloud management systems, network management systems, fault monitoring systems, etc., while supervising the cloud-network complex, also monitor the effect of a testing system testing a live microservice or system.

However, the supervision systems have to identify and separate the testing effects from the rest of the cloud network behavior. Obviously, monitoring data used for ML should not include testing effects. Therefore, log records should indicate whether the source is real or test generated. As an unspecified fault results from a complex sequence of operations, or even a plurality of sequences, it is difficult to associate a fault to any particular source. However, such source identification is essential to the debugging, to the runtime management, and to the ML process.

The testing system is also expected to use AI to develop testing data sequences that are likely to cause unspecified faults. On one hand, the testing system analyzes the code to locate possible vulnerabilities, and on the other hand, the testing system analyzes log files of fault detection systems to determine situations that may cause unspecified faults. The testing system then injects testing data while simulating hardware-related problems, load related problems, etc.

It can be expected that every system of microservices may have at least one and probably more than one automatic AI-based testing system operative in runtime. These systems interfere with the runtime operation and in the learning phase, requiring tight coordination.

Considering the stratification of the cloud-network complex, the processes described previously for the application processing layers repeat at the network level. Networking microservices as well as network orchestration microservices are continuously released, tested in runtime, and supervised for fault detection, while providing crucial networking services to numerous applications.

7.4 SUMMARY: HOW IS THE FUTURE OF CLOUD-POWERED ARTIFICIAL INTELLIGENCE NETWORK GOING TO LOOK?

From a slightly cynical point of view, the autonomous network manifests the "inverted" *Fallacies of distributed computing* [23]:

- The cloud network is *un*reliable. There is at least one fault now initiated somewhere.

- Cloud-network latency (communication and processing apart) is considerable, changing, location variable, and unpredictable.

- Cloud-network bandwidth (communication and processing apart) is limited, changing, location variable, and unpredictable.

- The cloud network is insecure and has just been compromised.

- An unknown number of poorly coordinated administrators (mostly automatic and somewhat unpredictable) are now managing the cloud network. The cloud-network topology is being changed now, by more than one administrator.

- Transport cost in the cloud network is considerable, changing, location variable, and unpredictable (regarding latency, security, reliability, etc.). The same applies to migration (regarding time of change and resulting bandwidth, latency, security, reliability, etc.).

- The network is not homogeneous in any aspect of the term.

The cloud network is, therefore, inherently unstable, and the data consistency-availability-tolerance is unknown (or known with some limited uncertainty). The purpose of the autonomous network is to resolve these issues in real time, while decreasing the overall cloud-network instability (and data uncertainty), and **reduce costs**.

While the world may seem to become less predictable, the promise of the autonomous cloud network is that when an adverse effect is sensed, the remedy is already in process.

7.5 LOOKING FORWARD: THE ENTERPRISE ON THE EDGE

At the edge of the public telecom network lies the enterprise network, and the edges of the two networks tend to blur into each other. The operator of the public telecom network may provide the enterprise with services such as the virtual private network, network slicing, and edge computing; manage on-premise hardware and software entities; and provide local breakout mobile computing.

The edges also blur from the enterprise's point of view. With the enterprise applications running on smartphones and connected devices, and communicating with home-based IoT devices, the border between enterprise computing and customers' premises blurs. Similarly, the borders between enterprise computing environments may blur where, for example, different computing services may communicate with the same public IoT (e.g., municipality) and industrial IoT devices.

Artificial intelligence enters into the enterprise digital transformation, and the internal disciplines of planning, production, promotion, and provisioning blur as well. As all borders blur into each other, AI itself dissolves into these blurred borders, both in the computer processing sense, and the business processes sense. The next chapter is all about AI in the digital transformation of the enterprise.

REFERENCES

1. A Brief History of the 1987 Stock Market Crash, Federal Reserve Board, lists program trading as the second factor contributing to the severity of the crash. https://www.federalreserve.gov/pubs/feds/2007/200713/200713pap.pdf
2. https://msdn.microsoft.com/en-us/library/dd129906.aspx
3. http://ieeexplore.ieee.org/document/1094702/
4. https://people.eecs.berkeley.edu/~brewer/cs262b-2004/PODC-keynote.pdf
5. https://groups.csail.mit.edu/tds/papers/Gilbert/Brewer2.pdf
6. https://www.cncf.io/blog/2017/05/15/developing-cloud-native-applications/
7. http://www.oreilly.com/programming/free/files/migrating-cloud-native-application-architectures.pdf
8. http://www.oreilly.com/programming/free/files/microservices-antipatterns-and-pitfalls.pdf
9. http://www.oreilly.com/programming/free/files/microservices-vs-service-oriented-architecture.pdf
10. https://www.innovativearchitects.com/KnowledgeCenter/business-connectivity/ESB-EAI-SOA.aspx
11. http://hosteddocs.ittoolbox.com/enterprise%20integration%20-%20soa%20vs%20eai%20vs%20esb.pdf
12. https://docker-curriculum.com/
13. https://www.datadoghq.com/docker-adoption/
14. https://caylent.com/containers-kubernetes-docker-swarm-amazon-ecs/
15. https://www.vmware.com/pdf/vsphere4/r40/vsp_40_intro_vs.pdf
16. https://www.opencontainers.org/
17. https://www.cncf.io/blog/2017/05/23/cncf-hosts-container-networking-interface-cni/
18. https://github.com/containernetworking/cni
19. https://rook.io/
20. https://www.cncf.io/
21. https://www.onap.org/wp-content/uploads/sites/20/2017/12/ONAP_CaseSolution_Architecture_120817_FNL.pdf
22. D. Linthicum, What being cloud-native really means, *Infoworld*, January 24, 2014, https://www.infoworld.com/article/2610438/cloud-computing/what-being-cloud-native-really-means.html
23. A set of assertions Originally by made by L Peter Deutsch and others at Sun Microsystems (ca 1994).

CHAPTER 8

Artificial Intelligence Software and Hardware Platforms

Rajesh Gadiyar, Tong Zhang, and Ananth Sankaranarayanan

CONTENTS

8.1 INTRODUCTION

Artificial intelligence (AI) plays a pivotal role in fueling autonomous networks with capabilities such as self-healing and closed-loop automation. Artificial intelligence requires significant investments in both hardware and software platforms to enable fast, scalable, and cost-effective solutions. This chapter will describe emerging hardware platforms, such as graphics processing units (GPUs) and Intel's high-performance Xeon processors, and industry standard software frameworks, such as Hadoop, TensorFlow, and Spark. Additionally, we will discuss opportunities for fixed function acceleration of AI workloads.

Section 8.2 presents an overview of AI system architecture, including statistical machine learning and deep-learning principles along with key use cases. Section 8.3 introduces the art of data science and end-to-end workflows. Section 8.4 shows machine- and deep-learning software frameworks, libraries, and primitives. Section 8.5 describes various hardware capabilities and their architectural fit for key use cases. Section 8.6 explores how AI software interacts with hardware for key workloads. And Section 8.7 summarizes new innovations and future research work in this area.

8.2 ARTIFICIAL INTELLIGENCE

Machine learning and AI have arrived in the data centers. The unprecedented compute capabilities and hardware acceleration techniques provide more computing horsepower to train machine learning systems, a process that involves enormous amounts of data crunching. Artificial intelligence is now transforming how data centers are built and operated while also powering every aspect of the Internet, and machine learning is transforming how developers build intelligent applications that benefit customers and consumers touching almost every aspect of our everyday lives.

One of the most exciting aspects of AI is that it has the potential to revolutionize not just the computing industry, or the software industry, but really every industry that touches our lives. It will transform the society in much the same way as the industrial revolution—the technical revolution and the digital revolution altered every aspect of daily life. For developers, the expansion of the AI field means that you have the potential to apply your interest and knowledge of AI toward an industry that you're also interested in, like music or sports or health care.

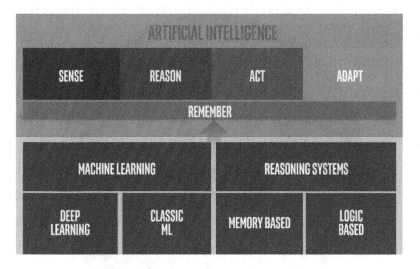

FIGURE 8.1   AI taxonomy.

In this chapter, we will start by describing the AI system architecture. However, before that, let's first familiarize ourselves with the following AI taxonomy (Figure 8.1).

While there are a lot of different ways to think about AI and a lot of different techniques to approach it, the key to machine intelligence is that it must be able to sense, reason, and act, then adapt based on experience. Each of these data processing stages is explained as follows:

- **Sense:** Identify and recognize meaningful objects or concepts in the midst of vast data. Is there a stoplight in the video? Is it a tumor or a normal tissue in the image?

- **Reason:** Understand the larger context and make a plan to achieve a goal. For example, if the goal is to avoid a collision, the car must calculate the likelihood of a crash based on vehicle behaviors, proximity, speed, and road conditions.

- **Act:** Either recommend or directly initiate the best course of action. For instance, based on vehicle and traffic analysis, it may brake, accelerate, or prepare some other safety mechanisms.

- **Adapt:** Finally, we must be able to adapt the algorithms at each phase based on experience, retraining them to be ever more intelligent. Autonomous vehicle algorithms should be retrained to recognize more blind spots, factor new variables into the context, and adjust actions based on previous incidents.

Two of the most popular approaches that developers take to program machines to do the earlier tasks are statistical machine learning and deep learning (Figure 8.2).

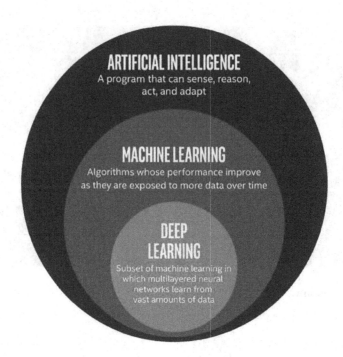

FIGURE 8.2 The concepts of artificial intelligence, machine learning, and deep learning.

8.2.1 Statistical Machine Learning

In machine learning, learning algorithms build models from data. These models can continuously improve as they are exposed to more data over time. There are four main types of machine learning: supervised, unsupervised, reinforcement, and continuous learning (see Chapter 2). In supervised machine learning, the algorithm learns to identify data by processing and categorizing vast quantities of labeled data. In unsupervised machine learning, the algorithm identifies patterns and categories within large amounts of unlabeled data. Reinforcement learning allows the machine or software agent to learn its behavior based on feedback from the environment. And continuous learning (also called lifelong learning) is built on the idea of learning continuously and adaptively about the external world.

Statistical machine learning merges statistics with the computational sciences. It is a scope within machine learning that is concerned with the development of algorithms and techniques for the purpose of learning from observed data by constructing stochastic models that can be used for making predictions and decisions.

8.2.2 Deep Learning

Deep learning is another subset of machine learning in which multilayered neural networks are trained with vast amounts of data. Deep learning (also sometimes referred to

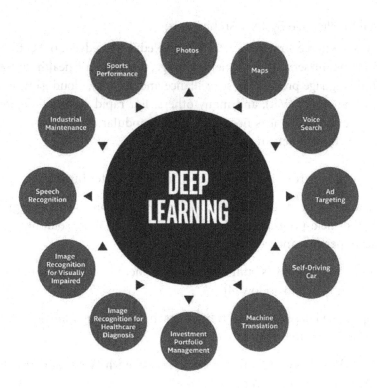

FIGURE 8.3   Example use cases of deep learning.

as deep-structured learning or hierarchical learning) is one part of a broader family of machine learning methods that are based on learning data representations, as opposed to task-specific algorithms (see Chapter 2). All four types of machine learning methods as mentioned previously may include deep learning models in the implementation (Figure 8.3).

8.2.3 Reasoning Systems

In contrast to machine learning systems, a reasoning system is a software system that generates conclusions from available knowledge using logical techniques, such as deduction and induction [1]. Reasoning systems play an important role in the implementation of AI and knowledge-based systems. There are two types of reasoning systems: (1) memory-based reasoning and (2) logic-based reasoning. Memory-based reasoning is to identify similar cases from past experience or memory, and to apply the information from the past experience to the problem at hand. Logic-based reasoning aims at learning rule-based knowledge, called hypotheses, from observations (positive and negative), using existing background knowledge and integrity constraints.

8.2.4 Artificial Intelligence System Architecture

The next few years will see a rapid growth of AI fueled by the advent of 5G technology and the new applications and services at the network edge, such as retail, health care, autonomous driving, natural language processing, surveillance and security, cloud gaming, augmented reality (AR)/virtual reality (VR), and many others. For rapid creation, deployment, and adoption of AI applications, it is necessary that a modular and scalable architecture is defined with a few basic tenets in mind:

- General purpose hardware to reduce cost and drive faster innovation cycle

- Software and hardware accelerators, such as application-specific integrated circuits (ASICs) [2] or field-programmable gate array (FPGA) [3] are solutions where there is a significant performance and cost benefit

- Ability to utilize AI models built with various different software frameworks, such as Caffe2, Theano, or TensorFlow [4]

- Enable optimized deployment of trained machine learning models on various hardware platforms through inference engines

- Create an "AI models community"—a marketplace where developers contribute and perfect AI models and software

- Fuel faster application and services innovation with open source software

Following is a high-level modular AI system architecture (Figure 8.4).

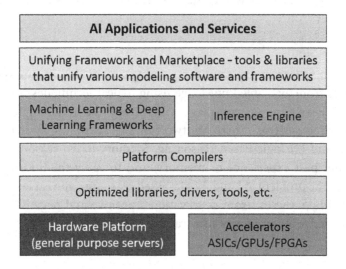

FIGURE 8.4   Modular AI system architecture.

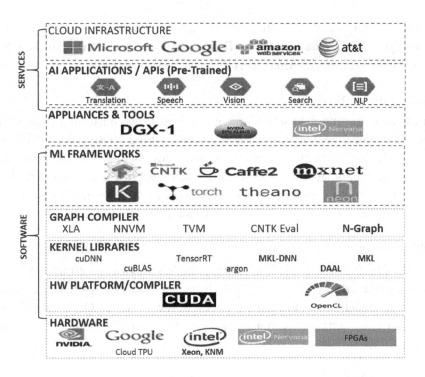

FIGURE 8.5 Hardware and software solutions for deep learning.

The above is a mapping of the earlier system architecture to hardware and software solutions used for building machine learning applications today (Figure 8.5).

The next sections will provide more details on the hardware and software architecture.

8.3 ART OF DATA SCIENCE

Data science is a blend of expertise in data interpretation, algorithm development, and software programming to solve computationally complex analytical problems.

The art of data science involves four major steps: (1) Data acquisition, (2) Data preparation, (3) Model development/validation, and (4) Model deployment and inference (Figure 8.6).

8.3.1 Data Collection

Billions of users and devices generate large amounts of data on a daily basis in a variety of formats at different velocities. The first step in the data science process is to acquire

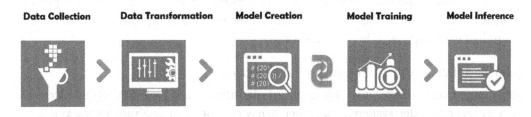

FIGURE 8.6 Data science workflow.

meaningful and impactful data from those various sources, for example, sensors in Internet-of-Things (IoT), cloud, and Web. Data scientists typically store data sets in private or public cloud stores, such as Amazon Web Service S3 buckets [5].

8.3.2 Data Transformation

Aggregating and curating data sets is one of the most time-consuming steps in the data science workflow pipeline. For supervised machine learning, those collected data sets will need to be labeled and formatted. As an example of data labeling, to detect corrosion levels of bolts in oil rigs automatically, data scientists will need to create a data set of training samples by extracting frames from video recordings, draw bounding boxes around each bolt with coordinates, and manually assign corrosion intensity levels.

8.3.3 Model Creation

Next, the data scientists will explore existing models to swiftly extract value from the data set. Oftentimes, they end up using models from a model zoo (which is a collection of already trained models) and tuning them to best fit their data set. Once the right model is identified, they use a certain percentage (by convention, usually about 70%) of their input data set to train the model.

8.3.4 Model Training

Model training is one of the most compute intensive steps in the workflow pipeline. CPUs or GPUs are generally used to support the training step, which can run for several hours to days depending on the complexity of the model and the training data set size. Once the expected level of accuracy is reached, the model is expected to be ready for validation. The remaining of the input data set (e.g., the rest 30%) is typically used for model validation.

8.3.5 Model Inference

Once the expected accuracy level of the model predictions is verified with a validation data set, the next step in the workflow pipeline is model inference. Depending on the solution under development, the models are either deployed at the server side or at the edge devices, such as phones or smart cameras. Depending on the processor architecture of the edge devices, techniques such as quantization may be applied on the trained model to shrink its size to fit within limited memory footprint without losing their prediction accuracy levels. An inference step takes in a new data sample into the model and derives a prediction score with accuracy and confidence level. As more data is processed, the model is refined to become more accurate. For instance, as an autonomous car drives, the application pulls in real-time information through sensors, GPS, 360-degree video capture, and more, which it can then use to optimize future predictions.

8.3.6 Distributed Artificial Intelligence at Hyperscale

Many large cloud service providers apply AI algorithms in several of their applications, such as recommender systems, consumer behavior/sentiment analysis, operational efficiency improvements, and advertisement placements. Usually, their AI models are complex and sample data sets are several terabytes in size. Training AI models with those large data sets on single CPU or GPU to high accuracy levels takes several days or weeks. In order to reduce the time to train, several AI software frameworks have been enabled with multi-CPU or GPU support.

These multiprocessor implementations employ distributed computing principles such as message passing interface as shown in Figure 8.7 or remote procedure calls as shown in Figure 8.8 to enable multinode all-to-all communications and/or master-slave architectures [6].

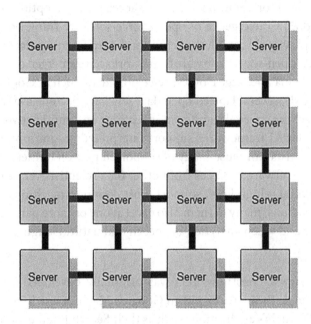

FIGURE 8.7   All-to-all communication, using message passing interface.

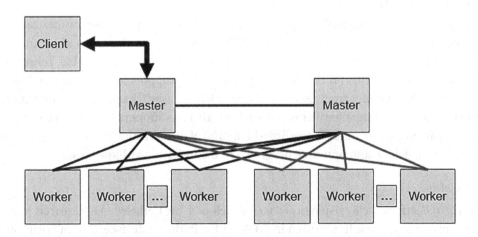

FIGURE 8.8   Master-slave architecture, using remote procedure calls.

8.4 ARTIFICIAL INTELLIGENCE SOFTWARE FRAMEWORKS

The art of AI has enticed our imagination since the middle of the twentieth century, inspiring computer scientists to create increasingly complex computing technologies, while inventing new customer facing solutions to enhance people's everyday lives. Advances in the following three areas have fundamentally changed the AI computing landscape and empowered democratization of machine learning: (1) Unit cost of computing has been going down year-over-year making AI more affordable; (2) Democratization of data where institutions and governments willingly share data (under certain compliance and data privacy conditions) for common goodness, accelerating adoption of machine learning algorithms; and (3) Convergence of open source software frameworks has simplified implementation of previously complex machine and deep learning algorithms.

Several popular AI open-source software frameworks have emerged in the last three years, especially from academia and large cloud service providers, such as Google, Facebook, and Microsoft. Additionally, several labeled open data sets have become available, for example, the ImageNet data set has spurred significant inventions on neural network topologies [7].

Most of the popular AI frameworks support interpreted programming languages such as Python. Data scientists can reuse many of supported python numeric computing modules and also import software modules from other data scientists very easily. While these software frameworks, at a high level, support most common machine and deep learning algorithms and operations, many of them also excel at one or more particular implementations, such as image and video analytics, or speech and natural language processing.

8.4.1 TensorFlow

TensorFlow (https://www.tensorflow.org/) was originally developed by researchers and engineers on the Google Brain Team within Google's Machine Intelligence research organization. Several of Google's applications such as their Search Engine, YouTube, Home and Advertisement services use TensorFlow heavily for the purposes of conducting machine learning and deep neural networks research and driving model development and deployment. Use cases include recommendation, natural language understanding, speech recognition, image classification, etc.

TensorFlow is implemented in Python and uses data flow graphs for numerical computation. Because of its broader adoption within Google and in the external community, TensorFlow is currently the best documented open source framework available. TensorFlow has modular architecture and easy-to-use frontend with support for convolutional neural networks (CNN) and recurrent neural networks (RNNs) (see Chapter 2). In addition to a number of deep learning algorithms, TensorFlow also has support for selective statistical machine learning algorithms. TensorBoard is a suite of visualization tools that can be used to understand, debug, and optimize programs that run on TensorFlow code.

8.4.2 Caffe

Caffe (http://caffe.berkeleyvision.org/) was developed by Berkeley AI Research and by community contributors. It is written in C++, with a Python interface. It is an open source project hosted at GitHub. Caffe is widely used in academic research projects and start-up prototypes, as well as large-scale industrial applications in vision, speech, and multimedia. In April 2017, Facebook announced Caffe2 (https://caffe2.ai/), which includes new features, such as RNNs.

8.4.3 Neon

Neon (https://www.intelnervana.com/neon/) is Intel Nervana's reference deep learning framework that is designed for extensibility and ease of use.

Neon is an open sourced framework that supports Python and several deep learning implementations, such as CNNs, RNNs, long short-term memory models, and deep auto-encoders [8]. Neon will be one of the first frameworks to offer support for the Intel Nervana deep-learning ASIC hardware product that is currently in development.

8.4.4 Hadoop

The Apache™ Hadoop® (http://hadoop.apache.org/) project develops open-source software for reliable and scalable distributed computing. The Apache Hadoop software library is a framework that allows for the distributed processing of large data sets across clusters of computers using simple programming models.

The Hadoop framework supports several statistical machine learning algorithms through the Mahout Software library and is designed to scale up from single servers to thousands of machines, each offering local computation and storage. Hadoop is designed to handle hardware instability and by bringing redundancy through software techniques such as triple data replication, delivering a highly available service on top of a cluster of computers, each of which may be prone to failures.

The Hadoop project includes several modules (Figure 8.9). Hadoop Common: The common utilities that support the other Hadoop modules. Hadoop Distributed File System (HDFS™): A distributed file system that provides high-throughput access to application

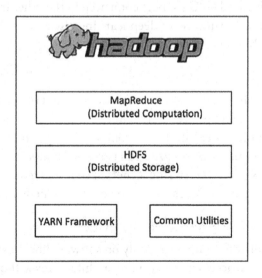

FIGURE 8.9   Hadoop framework modules.

data. Hadoop YARN: A framework for job scheduling and cluster resource management. Hadoop MapReduce: A YARN-based system for parallel processing of large data sets.

8.4.5 Spark

Apache Spark™ is a fast and general engine for large-scale data processing. It is built by a large community of developers from over 200 companies (with committers from 19 organizations). Since 2009, more than 1000 developers have contributed to Spark.

Spark offers over 80 high-level operators that make it easy to build parallel apps. And you can use it interactively from the Scala, Python, and R shells. Spark powers a stack of libraries including SQL and Data Frames, MLlib for machine learning, BigDL for deep learning, GraphX, and Spark Streaming. These libraries can be seamlessly combined in the same application. Spark runs on Hadoop, Mesos, standalone, or in the cloud. It can access diverse data sources, including HDFS, Cassandra, HBase, and S3 [9], offering the ability to bring compute to the node that has the data, thus minimizing or eliminating the need to move the data.

8.4.6 Scikit-Learn

Scikit-Learn (http://scikit-learn.org/) is a machine learning framework in Python, built on libraries like NumPy, SciPy, and matplotlib. It provides simple and efficient tools for data analytics tasks, such as classification, regression, and clustering, as well as data preprocessing, dimensionality reduction, and model selection. It is open source and commercially usable.

8.4.7 MXNet

MXNet (https://mxnet.incubator.apache.org/) is a deep learning framework developed by collaborators from various companies and universities including the likes of Microsoft, Nvidia, Baidu, Intel, Carnegie Mellon University, University of Alberta, and University of Washington, which is currently an Apache incubator project. MXNet supports multiple programming languages, including R, Python, Julia, and Scala.

MXNet has more advanced GPU support compared to the other frameworks and is also relatively fast with regard to runtime of deep learning algorithms. MXNet has modeling capabilities for both CNNs and RNNs.

8.4.8 H2O

H2O (https://www.h2o.ai/) is open source software for big data analytics. It is written in Java, Python, and R. The H2O project claims to develop an analytical interface for cloud computing, and its graphical user interface is compatible with most commonly used internet browsers. H2O allows users to analyze and visualize whole sets of data and has statistical algorithms, such as K-means clustering, generalized linear models, distributed random forests, gradient boosting, naïve Bayes, and principal component analysis.

8.4.9 Libraries (Intel MKL/MKL-DNN, Nvidia CUDA)

Artificial intelligence software frameworks rely on software libraries from silicon vendors, such as Intel and Nvidia, to access instruction set architectures without having to program at assembly level.

As a common practice, silicon vendors create low-level libraries that include a number of mathematical and numerical kernels (assembly code) and expose them to higher-level applications through common application programming interfaces.

Intel Math Kernel Library (MKL) has highly optimized, threaded, and vectorized functions for dense and sparse linear algebra (BLAS, LAPACK, and PARDISO), Fast Fourier Transforms (FFTs), vector math, summary statistics, deep neural network (DNN) primitives, and more. MKL is offered as a binary format that higher level programming languages can link to while compiling to take full advantage of Intel silicon capabilities.

Intel MKL-DNN is an open source performance library for acceleration of deep learning frameworks on Intel® architecture. This includes highly vectorized and threaded primitives for the implementation of DNN with C and C++ interfaces.

Nvidia offers a collection of GPU libraries (e.g., cuDNN, cuFFT, cuSPARSE, cuBLAS, cuRAND) that are targeted for machine and deep learning applications. All popular machine learning frameworks link to these CUDA libraries to take full advantage of GPU hardware capabilities [10].

8.4.10 Platforms

There are quite a number of AI software platforms available these days, each having its unique features and application domains. Among them, Amazon Machine Learning, Microsoft Azure Learning Studio, and IBM Watson are some of the most well-known ones. The recently announced Acumos platform (https://www.acumos.org/) is aimed at creating an industry standard for making AI apps reusable and easily accessible to any developer.

Figure 8.10 illustrates the full AI solution stack, which includes (from low level to high level) hardware systems, low-level libraries, frameworks, platforms, and applications.

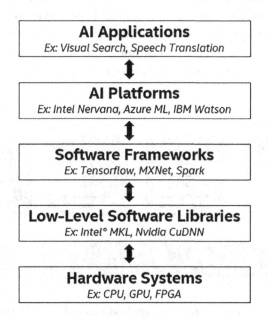

FIGURE 8.10 Artificial intelligence platform solution stack.

8.5 ARTIFICIAL INTELLIGENCE HARDWARE CHOICES

Artificial intelligence applications demand powerful computer hardware, which means the market for AI chips is potentially enormous. That is why so many companies, from semiconductor giants to start-ups, are jumping into the mix. The various hardware choices can be categorized into the four basic device types: CPUs, GPUs, FPGAs, and ASICs (Figure 8.11).

Heuristically, data collection, transformation, and model creation steps in the AI workflow pipeline are run on general purpose CPUs alongside web and database applications. For the compute-intensive training step, data scientists may choose from the earlier four types.

The majority of statistical machine learning applications can run on general purpose CPUs. Deep learning training frameworks require intensive in-memory computation (in particular, matrix multiplications), and GPU architectures are often more suitable solutions.

8.5.1 CPU (x86 Architecture)

CPUs are the most flexible and easy-to-use platform, which serve as the "brain" of a wide range of computing systems, from mobile, tablet, consumer (laptop/desktop), to enterprise servers. Today, CPUs are the most commonly used platform for classic machine learning (both training and inference), as well as deep learning inference (i.e., run-time deployment).

The two stages of training and inference in deep learning are quite different, and each requires a different style of processing. In particular, inferencing is essentially a sequential calculation (although some parallelism can be achieved during a single inferencing operation, it is limited by the data dependencies defined by the network architecture and the degree of parallelism is generally low) [11]. Most data scientists will not need inferencing optimized devices unless they plan to perform volume processing of data in a data center. Applications such as autonomous driving, real-time surveillance, and those running on IoT edge devices will perform sequential rather than massively parallel inferencing. Inferencing of individual data items will be dominated by the sequential performance of the device. In such cases, CPUs are a much better choice than massively parallel devices like accelerators.

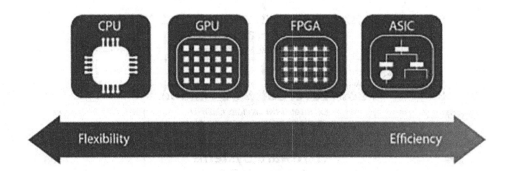

FIGURE 8.11 Hardware choices for AI applications. (From https://www.napatech.com/age-of-fpga/.)

At the training side, CPUs can deliver higher performance than GPUs on many training problems, especially when the training data size is relatively small. Accelerators achieve high performance when they have large numbers of concurrent threads to execute. When training with data sets containing only hundreds to tens of thousands of examples, only a small fraction of the accelerator parallelism may be utilized. In such situations, better performance may be achieved on a many-core processor with a fast cache and stacked memory subsystem like an Intel Xeon or Xeon Phi processor [11]. Therefore, it is important to consider how much data will be available for training when selecting your hardware.

Another important factor to consider is that it often turns out training performance is limited by cache and memory performance rather than floating-point capability, because once the memory and cache systems are saturated, any additional floating-point capability is wasted. Given the dependence of gradient calculations on memory, users need to be careful about what the real (not peak) floating-point performance is when the calculation is dominated by memory and cache bandwidth performance. With this consideration, CPUs with larger memory may be a more preferred choice than GPUs for certain use cases.

New generations of Intel CPUs have evolved to accommodate AI workloads. Even without specialized hardware, it has been proven that the inclusion of the wider AVX-512 vector instructions and extra memory channel can more than double both training and inference per core performance on the Intel Skylake processors without requiring an increase in data set size to exploit parallelism [11]. Using more cores should provide an additional performance increase (there are up to 28 cores on each CPU). Both Intel Xeon Phi and Intel Xeon (Skylake) product SKUs offer on-package Intel Omni-Path interfaces, which should decrease system cost and network latency while increasing network bandwidth. This is good news for those who need to train (or perform volume inferencing) across a network or within the cloud. Figure 8.12a shows the current Intel server roadmap, and Figure 8.12b shows the most recent Purley platform.

8.5.2 Graphics Processing Units

Graphics processing units have become the most popular option for deep learning training where the goal is to speed training to achieve the shortest "time-to-model." All hardware on the market uses parallelism to speed training. Accelerators achieve high floating-point performance when they have large numbers of concurrent threads to execute. GPUs have taken the multicore trend to the extreme by adding thousands of smaller control cores onto a single device. Additionally, GPUs have large amounts of arithmetic logic unit resources compared to the CPUs. A typical Nvidia GPU has thousands of cores, allowing for fast execution of the same operation across multiple cores. At the heart of deep learning is huge amount of matrix multiplications (general matrix multiplication) and convolutions that can be done in parallel, which makes GPUs an excellent option [12].

In general, for inherently parallel workloads with heavy matrix operations requiring high bandwidth to memory, GPUs can offer better performance than CPUs if the workload can fit within the GPU memory, typically 16GB. However, if the workload involves larger than 16GB data set sizes, GPU devices will need to fetch data from memory through CPUs,

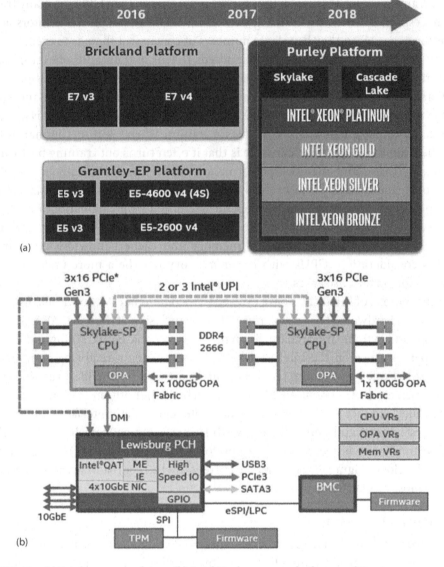

FIGURE 8.12 (a) Intel server roadmap. (b) Intel Purley server platform architecture.

which can substantially slow down job performance. For example, medical equipment manufacturers handle high-resolution 3D images in gigapixels, and leading pharmaceutical companies have 1024 × 1024 images with more than 10 channels for drug discovery related CNN implementations. Deep learning training time is directly proportional to the image batch-size each processing node is able to hold within its local memory. For high-resolution images, as the batch size increases, current GPUs do not have large enough memory to hold the data, thus resulting in longer time to train.

One challenge in using GPUs is the larger distance from the main memory of the server, hence causing delay in data movement (it is often done through the PCI Express or PCIe protocol). To speed this up, companies like Nvidia have developed a faster inter-connection called NVLink [13]. Other challenges with GPUs include lack of scalability across cards and across servers, usually higher prices and their need for higher power consumption. For example, Nvidia rates their Titan X graphics card at 250W, and recommends a system power supply of 600W [14].

8.5.3 Field-Programmable Gate Arrays

Field-programmable gate arrays are integrated circuits whose logic blocks can be programmed and reconfigured using a hardware description language. The most significant advantage that FPGAs have over CPUs and GPUs is computing efficiency, which means faster operations that consume less energy in many applications. It is observed that FPGAs offer much higher performance/watt than GPUs, because even though they cannot compete on pure performance, they have much less power usage (often tens of watts). In addition, FPGAs may exhibit some of the lowest inference latencies, plus they are field upgradable [15].

The flexibility of the FPGA fabric enables direct connection of various inputs, such as cameras, without needing an intermediary. This eliminates unnecessary data movement, allowing even lower system latency so that the system can process data and make decisions in real time. Meanwhile, FPGAs also have exceptional power efficiency, for applications like hyperscale data centers where the total cost of ownership is a key factor. Off-loading deep learning algorithms, such as AlexNet (a CNN model), can reduce the power needed by up to 80% [16]. For power sensitive edge devices, FPGAs can be preprogrammed to support various statistical machine learning and deep learning algorithms.

Moreover, the flexible fabric and reconfigurability of FPGAs allow users to future proof their hardware. In a field as fast paced and evolving as AI, this maximizes customers' return on investment, enabling outstanding performance for both today's and tomorrow's needs. For example, one can run both current and whatever future neural network topologies on the same hardware. FPGAs also are flexible to any precision type, allowing one to optimize accuracy, performance, and speed to his/her exact needs. Finally, FPGAs can be deployed for both inline and offload processing.

As neural network implementations continue to evolve, redefining silicon architectures for each evolution can be extremely cost prohibitive. FPGAs due to the nature of reprogramming capability are better alternative platforms, especially for deterministic, real-time, inline processing of streaming data without buffering. However, one major drawback with FPGAs is the difficulty in programming (requiring register transfer level development expertise), which has prevented FPGA from becoming a general computation solution (Figure 8.13).

8.5.4 Application-Specific Integrated Circuits

Application-specific integrated circuits are the least flexible, but highest performing, hardware option. They are also the most efficient in terms of performance/dollar and performance/watt but require a huge investment and non-recurring engineering costs that make them cost-effective only in large quantities. ASICs can be designed and hard-coded for either training or inference. Although single purposed, ASICs have the highest computing efficiency of all. Neural networks can run faster and consume less power

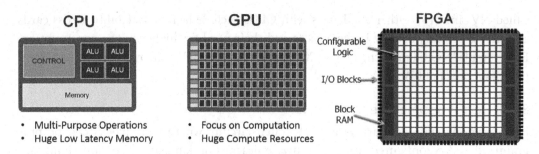

FIGURE 8.13 Characteristics of CPU versus GPU versus FPGA. (From https://channels. theinnovationenterprise.com/articles/9781-accelerating-computing-of-the-future.)

when paired with chips specifically designed to handle the massive array of mathematical calculations that AI systems require.

Recent announcements on custom AI hardware (e.g., Google tensor processing unit [TPU] and Intel neural network processor [NNP]) have raised awareness that custom solutions might leapfrog the performance of both CPUs and GPUs for some neural network applications. However, users may want to consider the types of network models that will be trained when they make the hardware choice. For example, benefits of special-purpose hardware that performs tensor operations at reduced precision apply to only few types of neural architectures like CNNs. It is important to understand if your work requires the use of those specific types of neural architectures.

Google's TPU1 targeted inference only, and their TPU2 or "cloud TPU" supports both training and inference [17]. Each TPU2 chip supports 45 Tera Floating Point Operations per Second (TFLOPs) and comes in a board of four, which has a total of 180 TFLOPs (for 16-bit half-precision floating point). The TPUs are not to be sold commercially but will be accessible through Google's cloud computing platform.

Intel's NNP chips, built from the ground up for AI, is the first of its kind (i.e., designed specific for deep learning) that is commercially available. It eliminates standard cache hierarchy and uses software to manage on-chip memory to achieve faster training times for deep learning models. This hardware specializes in flex-point architectures, which will be exposed to multiple deep-learning software frameworks such as Neon, TensorFlow, and MXNet via a graph compiler layer called Nervana Graph [18]. Multiple generations of Intel Nervana NNP products in the pipeline have been recently announced, which will deliver higher performance and enable new levels of scalability for AI models [19].

At the same time, vendors are also building chips to help execute neural networks on smartphones and other devices. For example, IBM is building such a chip [20]. And Intel has recently acquired Movidius, a company that is already pushing chips into devices.

8.6 WORKLOAD CHARACTERISTICS

In general, AI workloads can be divided into two classes: classical machine learning and deep learning. Classical machine learning is the overwhelming majority, which includes the most common algorithms used by data scientists, such as linear models, k-means clustering, and decision trees (see Chapter 2). Such methods are widely used in fraud detection, marketing personalization, key performance indicator prediction, cybersecurity, etc. Typical deep learning applications include image recognition, voice recognition, automatic game playing, and autonomous vehicles.

8.6.1 Performance and Latency Examples

At the inference stage of AI, the paramount performance goal is latency. To minimize the network's end-to-end response time, inference typically batches a much smaller number of inputs than training to support near real-time processing. For example, the latency requirement for the entire Google Autosuggest pipeline is less than 200 milliseconds. The workflow includes the frontend, load balancing, query understanding, and auto-complete suggestion powered by deep learning, as well as a full search stack traversal to display what the result would be if users actually search for one of the autosuggested queries [21]. Mission-critical applications like autonomous vehicles put an even stricter latency requirement on the processing pipeline where deep learning is used as one component of the pipeline. Fast processing time for these applications influence people's safety and lives. For another instance, speech interfaces require speech recognition and synthesis models to return a result without a delay that is noticeable to a user.

To help developers better leverage their hardware, venders have provided a series of inference optimizations for GPUs or CPUs (e.g., Nvidia's cuDNN library and Intel's MKL-DNN library). As an example, the latest versions of cuDNN include improvements on small batch inference by splitting in an additional dimension. This reduces the amount of computation per thread block and enables launching significantly more blocks, increasing GPU occupancy and performance [21].

Another major improvement is made by reduced precision floating point operations. In recent years, researchers have found that using lower precision floating point or even integer point representations (FP16 or INT8) for storage of layer activations and higher ones (FP32) for computation does not sacrifice classification accuracy. Such reduction of precision remarkably improves performance in bandwidth-limited situations and reduces overall memory footprint required to run the deep neural networks.

Algorithmically, one promising approach to reducing inference latency and memory requirement (and hence power consumption) is model compression, which has been a hot research topic lately [22].

An important trend to mention is that as AI continues to grow in the cloud, the industry will experience a shift in the inference stage from using high-end specialized servers to general processors at the cloud edge of the network. This trend is fueled by the necessity to reduce latency on a bandwidth-bottlenecked network and address the heated issue of privacy and compliance (that is, processing data locally instead of sending it to the cloud in order to control access to the data).

8.6.2 Time to Train

For the training stage of machine learning and deep learning algorithms, "time to train" is a critical metric in many use scenarios, in addition to accuracy. This metric is determined

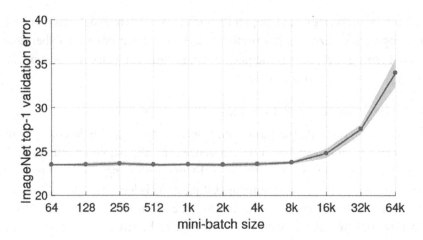

FIGURE 8.14   ImageNet top-1 validation error versus mini-batch size. (From Goyal, P. et al., Accurate, large mini-batch SGD: Training ImageNet in one hour, https://research.fb.com/wp-content/uploads/2017/06/imagenet1kin1h5.pdf.)

by a number of factors, for example, the network model, hyperparameter setting, the framework, library optimization, and hardware platform. There exist a number of algorithmic tricks that can accelerate the training process. From a hardware perspective, peak floating point capabilities (i.e., TFLOPs, the metric for machine learning hardware, basically the number of floating point operations the hardware can support per second) are often regarded as the most important spec. However, memory and cache performance, as well as I/O bandwidth, can be equally critical in most circumstances.

Scalability across multiple servers and multiple accelerators is another key factor in achieving breakthroughs in time to train. It was published that a Facebook team reduced the training time of a ResNet-50 deep learning model on ImageNet from 29 hours to one—which they did so by distributing training in larger mini-batches across more GPUs [23]. Previously, batches of 256 images were spread across eight Tesla P100 GPUs, but today's work shows the same level of accuracy when training with large mini-batch sizes up to 8,192 images distributed across 256 GPUs (Figure 8.14).

On November 7, 2017, UC Berkeley, U-Texas, and UC Davis researchers published their results training also ResNet-50 in a record time of 31 minutes and AlexNet in a record time of 11 minutes on CPUs to state-of-the-art accuracy [24]. These results were obtained on Intel® Xeon® Scalable processors (codename Skylake-SP). The major drives of these performance speeds are: (1) The improved compute and memory capacity of Intel Xeon Scalable processors over earlier generations; (2) Software optimizations in the Intel® MKL-DNN and in the popular deep learning frameworks; and (3) Recent advancements (e.g., Intel® Machine Learning Scaling Library) in distributed training algorithms for supervised deep learning workloads.

8.6.3 State-of-the-Art Model Accuracy

With groundbreaking improvements in deep-learning algorithm developments during the last five to eight years, state-of-the-art model accuracy has been increased dramatically,

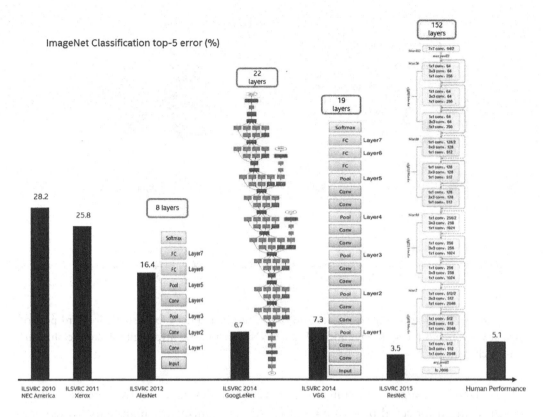

FIGURE 8.15 Convolutional neural network models for image recognition—improvement in accuracy.

even surpassing human accuracy in some applications. For an instance, the following figures show the evolvement of convolutional neural network models for the image recognition task and their accuracies indicated by top-1 and top-5 errors. Top-1 accuracy is the conventional accuracy where the model answer (the one with highest probability) must exactly match the expected answer and the top-5 represents your model's five highest probability answers must match the expected answer. As shown in Figure 8.15, the accuracy achieved with the ResNet-152 model is a top-5 error of 3.5%, which is significantly better than the human error of 5.1%.

Figure 8.16 illustrates popular CNN models—their accuracy (y-axis), amount of operations (x-axis) and their model size (indicated by the size of the bubbles).

8.6.4 Performance Bottlenecks and How to Alleviate Them

Deep-learning performance bottlenecks lie in the following areas:

- Compute and memory: This remains a challenge even as we are getting customized chips, as there is continued demand for more. Memory is one of the biggest challenges in current deep neural networks. Researchers are struggling with the limited memory bandwidth of the Dynamic Random-Access Memory (DRAM) devices that have to be used by today's systems to store the huge amounts of weights and activations

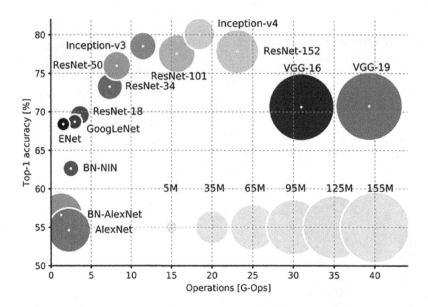

FIGURE 8.16 Top-1 accuracy versus amount of operations required for a single forward pass of popular CNN image recognition models. (From CNN benchmarks: https://github.com/jcjohnson/cnn-benchmarks.)

in DNNs. Computer architectures have been developed with processor chips specialized for serial processing and DRAMs optimized for high-density memory. The interface between these two devices is a major bottleneck that introduces latency and bandwidth limitations and adds a considerable overhead in power consumption. Researchers have applied various memory-saving techniques to obtain reduction in memory requirements. For example, a memory-reuse approach has been developed by researchers at Google DeepMind with RNNs (see Chapter 2). RNNs are a special type of DNN that allow cycles in their structure to encode behavior over sequences of inputs. For RNNs, recomputation has been shown to reduce memory by a factor of 20 for sequences of length 1000 with only a 30% performance overhead [26].

- Data sets: With the current algorithms being largely supervised, there is the need for larger data sets to continue to push the envelope on new research. Companies like Google have been working to generate and publish more data sets (e.g., they released a video data set and two data sets for robotics recently). On the other hand, unsupervised learning, which doesn't require labeled training data, has been an active research topic.

- Algorithms: Existing algorithm advancements, such as the ideas of ReLU, Dropout, Sequence to Sequence, and GANs have brought in big changes [27]. However, it is not likely to get a 1000X improvement in compute with the traditional, pure hardware improvements. It will need co-design of algorithms and compute. For example, it would be a game changer to create a model with a 1000X more parameters, but using only 10X more compute.

- Expertise: Experimenting configurations used for improving performance as shown in the previous section are considered as tricks. These configurations may not be general enough that can be applied to other data sets and network topologies.

8.7 SUMMARY

We live in a data economy. There is a huge amount of data everywhere—personal devices, such as smartphones and PCs, enterprise servers and data centers, network infrastructure, and the private and public clouds. The advent of machine-to-machine communications and IoT devices is further adding to the data deluge. As such, deriving intelligence from all the structured and unstructured data can enable new applications and business models in this data economy. In this chapter, we have described machine learning and deep learning as foundation elements enabling AI. We have described how models can be created to emulate a human brain, and we can use various types of historical data to "train" these models. Once trained, these models are akin to a human brain and can draw inferences to make intelligent decisions. We also discussed hardware architecture that enable such training and inferencing solutions—general purpose x86 platforms, GPUs, FPGAs, and custom-built ASICs all have a place in the solution continuum. We also discussed open source and popular software frameworks, such as Tenserflow, Caffe, H2O, Scikit Learn, Neon, Hadoop, Spark, and MXNet, as well as the Acumos platform, which are enabling the next generation of developers to build AI applications. We also briefly touched upon key performance and latency considerations for various workloads. As 5G wireless technology rolls out and drives deployment of edge clouds, AI will continue to evolve over the next decade. There are bound to be new innovations—both technology and business model innovations.

The next chapter describes how AI can be applied to make network infrastructure smarter. The last few years have seen the virtualization of network infrastructure with Network Function Virtualization (NFV) and Software Defined Networking (SDN) technologies on standard high-volume server platforms. As the network infrastructure becomes homogenous and software defined, there is an opportunity to apply machine learning, make smart and real-time decisions, and drive closed-loop automation of networks. This will bring significant operational efficiency to network deployments in the future. Applying AI techniques to drive this efficiency is the main focus of the next chapter.

REFERENCES

1. Reasoning system: https://en.wikipedia.org/wiki/Reasoning_system
2. ASIC: https://en.wikipedia.org/wiki/Application-specific_integrated_circuit
3. FPGA: https://en.wikipedia.org/wiki/Field-programmable_gate_array
4. A survey of deep learning frameworks: https://towardsdatascience.com/a-survey-of-deep-learning-frameworks-43b88b11af34
5. Amazon S3: https://docs.aws.amazon.com/AmazonS3/latest/dev/UsingBucket.html
6. Remote procedure call: https://en.wikipedia.org/wiki/Remote_procedure_call
7. Deep learning datasets: http://deeplearning.net/datasets/
8. Deep learning algorithms: http://deeplearning.net/tutorial/
9. Spark: https://spark.apache.org/

10. CUDA libraries: https://developer.nvidia.com/gpu-accelerated-libraries
11. R. Farber, Technology requirements for deep and machine learning.
12. GPU for deep learning: https://themerkle.com/why-gpus-are-ideal-for-deep-learning/
13. NVLink: http://www.nvidia.com/object/nvlink.html
14. Titan-X power consumption: https://www.geforce.com/hardware/desktop-gpus/geforce-gtx-titan-x/specifications
15. Real-time FPGA numerical computing for ultra-low latency high frequency trading: https://www.eetimes.com/author.asp?section_id=36&doc_id=1325724
16. Can FPGAs beat GPUs in accelerating next-generation deep learning: https://www.nextplatform.com/2017/03/21/can-fpgas-beat-gpus-accelerating-next-generation-deep-learning/
17. Google TPU: https://cloud.google.com/tpu/
18. Intel nGraph: https://ai.intel.com/intel-ngraph/
19. Intel NNP: https://www.theverge.com/circuitbreaker/2017/10/17/16488414/intel-ai-chips-nervana-neural-network-processor-nnp
20. AI chips: https://www.wired.com/2017/04/race-make-ai-chips-everything-heating-fast/
21. Deep learning in real time—Inference acceleration and continuous training: https://medium.com/@Synced/deep-learning-in-real-time-inference-acceleration-and-continuous-training-17dac9438b0b
22. Y. Cheng, D. Wang, P. Zhou, T. Zhang, A survey of model compression and acceleration for deep neural networks, *IEEE Signal Processing Magazine*, Vol. 35, Issue 1, pp. 126–136, January 2018.
23. P. Goyal et al., Accurate, large mini-batch SGD: Training ImageNet in 1 hour: https://research.fb.com/wp-content/uploads/2017/06/imagenet1kin1h5.pdf
24. Y. You et al., ImageNet training in minutes: https://arxiv.org/pdf/1709.05011.pdf (November 2017).
25. CNN benchmarks: https://github.com/jcjohnson/cnn-benchmarks
26. J. Hanlon, How to solve the memory challenges of deep neural networks: https://www.topbots.com/how-solve-memory-challenges-deep-learning-neural-networks-graphcore/
27. T. Eduard, Deep learning: Advances of the last year: https://www.slideshare.net/Eduardyantov/deep-learning-advances-of-the-last-year

CHAPTER 9

Artificial Intelligence for Network Operations

Jennifer Yates and Zihui Ge

CONTENTS

9.1 INTRODUCTION

In this chapter, we explore the role of artificial intelligence (AI) for network operations. We define and discuss the zero-touch network and identify how software-defined networking (SDN) and AI are together providing the core technology and intelligence to make such networks a reality.

Network operations is the typically well-hidden role of making networks and services operate to deliver seamless service experiences to customers. Network operators are the oftentimes magicians who silently and seamlessly take high-level network designs and technologies and make them real—identifying where capacity should be deployed and expanded, deploying network technologies, and making it all operate smoothly and seamlessly—even in the face of tremendous traffic growth, continual technology changes, diverse technologies, complex software, hardware and software failures, and even natural and man-made disasters.

There is a tremendous amount of network operations automation in large-scale networks today, although there is also still a fair amount of human intervention. The network itself has a considerable amount of automation and intelligence, such as routing protocols [1] and intelligence within network functions to automatically recover service by re-rerouting traffic in the event of failures. Today, however, humans are engaged in complex tasks associated with designing and planning the network, updating the network (adding new network functions, updating software, and updating how the network is configured), and repairing impaired network functions. As networks continue to scale, it will become increasingly impossible to scale human engagements in these functions. Instead, advanced network automation and AI will increasingly permeate into network operations tasks, taking us increasingly closer to the vision of an autonomous or *zero-touch network*. In a zero-touch network, all day-to-day tasks are automated, with AI and machine learning enabling decision-making. Network operators provide high-level guidance to the automation—describing their *intent* and *operations policies*. The automation and AI take it from there—translating the intent and policies into decisions and actions that scale out the network, enable new services and features, recover network and services in the face of failures and impairments, and safeguard the network against potential attacks and external influences.

This chapter describes how AI and SDN will together be used to drive toward the zero-touch network goal. Section 9.2 presents a background overview of the tasks involved in operating a network. In Section 9.3, we present the "zero-touch network" vision—how AI and SDN are revolutionizing how networks are operated. Section 9.4 discusses the technologies required and the journey that the industry is on to realize this vision. Finally, Section 9.5 describes the impact that this has on operations teams, and how their role evolves as the zero-touch network is realized.

9.2 WHAT IS NETWORK OPERATIONS?

We start by first defining network operations tasks. *Network operations* is the process by which networks, applications, and services are deployed and maintained. The network operations team is responsible for ensuring that the network has appropriate capacity installed and operational, for executing updates in the network and for managing the network functions and services, such that desired service performance levels are attained.

We categorize these functions as network provisioning (providing the quantity of network elements configured appropriately to deliver economical and quality service), network maintenance (executing planned activities and preventing and correcting faults and impairments), and network administration (ensuring that the network delivers on predefined service objectives, even in the face of changing external influences).

Network provisioning includes the network planning, engineering, and implementation of network functions and services. Its primary goal is to determine how the network will evolve, determine where capacity should be deployed, and then to realize this plan in the network. *Network maintenance* refers to the tasks involved in servicing network functions and their interconnections, both reactively (when issues arise) and preventatively (to prevent issues). Finally, *network administration* relates to managing how the network topology and the traffic routing are adapted to deliver on predefined service objectives, even in the face of changing external influences (e.g., changes in incoming traffic), network activities (impairments and maintenance activities), and disasters.

9.2.1 Network Provisioning

For service providers who provide a range of different services—wireline Internet, virtual private networks (VPN), mobile voice and data, voice over Internet protocol (IP), and TV services—there can be hundreds of different types of network functions (also traditionally know as network elements). These network functions typically constitute equipment and/or software provided by multiple vendors even for the same network function role. There may be tens of different types of network functions supporting a given service—for example, a mobile user's data path can traverse up to 50 unique types of network functions between a cell site and the Internet. As the industry advances along the path of virtualizing an increasing number of network functions, networks will also consist of both physical and virtual network functions (VNFs). Over time, VNFs are expected to become increasingly prevalent. However, physical network functions will always remain, as it is impossible to virtualize all functions (e.g., fibers and radios). All of these different types of network functions along the service path must be provisioned, with sufficient capacity on each for services to be supported.

We focus here on network provisioning and assume that the provisioning of customer connectivity and services is outside the scope of this chapter. Network provisioning is the process by which network operators decide where and when to deploy new software and hardware into the network (network capacity planning), and then execute on this deployment—turning the capacity up and configuring it so that it becomes part of the network. The network provisioning process assumes as input network technology choices and a basic network design; these are typically decided by network engineers outside of the network operations team.

Network capacity planning must determine how much capacity of each network function is to be deployed in each location and how to connect the network functions within and between locations. Where long time intervals are required to deploy capacity, planners must forecast capacity needs out into the future before performing capacity planning.

Once capacity is planned, it must be deployed. Traditional, physical network functions require physically deploying equipment on location, requiring that technicians be dispatched.

Such deployments typically take up to months, and thus capacity planning had to forecast out demands and plans months or more in advance. However, VNFs can be spun up remotely—on demand—providing that there is sufficient cloud capacity (server, storage, and network interconnectivity) available. Thus, capacity planning can also be performed "on demand," with capacity moved around as the demand shifts over time and even during the day.

Whether physical or virtual, network functions must be logically configured and then be validated before they can be used to carry traffic and deliver services. Configuration includes things like specifying the network function's identities (e.g., IP addresses), specifying the routing protocols to use to communicate with other network functions (where routing is performed within the network functions), and configuring policies such as what traffic to carry or block. Once configuration is completed, "test and turn up" validates that the network function is ready to support traffic and then updates network configurations to start routing traffic through the network function.

9.2.2 Network Maintenance

Network maintenance is much like car maintenance—preventative maintenance needs to be performed on an ongoing, proactive basis to reduce the risk of issues, and it needs to be performed when problems arise. Responsible car owners take their cars in to be serviced on a regular basis, changing the oil, updating the car's software, and checking the health of the car by replacing parts before catastrophic failures may impact the car's ability to operate. They also respond to recall notices—maintaining the vehicle in response to issues that have been identified by the manufacturer. However, despite the best efforts of even the most responsible car owners, failures of critical components or external influences can cause the car to perform poorly or even fail. The car owner then needs to have reactive maintenance performed—troubleshooting what the problem is and then repairing or replacing the failed components.

Networks have traditionally been managed in much the same way—with operators performing both preventative and reactive maintenance. Routine preventative or planned maintenance is performed to mitigate the risk of failures, for example, backup generator runs are executed to ensure that they will be able to perform their functions when required and software updates are deployed to fix software bugs. Reactive network maintenance, often referred to as fault management, deals with recovering from impairments within the network. This includes both hard and soft failures—hard failures refer to when network functions have failed and are completely out of service whereas soft failures refer to when the network functions are degraded, that is, they may be dropping or corrupting traffic, but not completely failed. A key goal of both preventative and reactive maintenance is service quality management—ensuring minimal impact on the service experienced by customers.

9.2.2.1 Planned Maintenance

For large-scale networks, maintenance activities are an ongoing reality, with typically thousands of activities happening on a monthly basis. Planned maintenance activities are required to roll out new software to introduce new network and service features and to provide fixes for software bugs. Device configurations are changed, with changing network topologies, to work around software issues and remediate misconfigurations and to activate new services. Regular maintenance is also required to ensure that idle hardware, such as generators and batteries, are working—we don't want to risk finding out that something is awry when the network functions fail and the generators are activated.

Planned activities need to be designed, scheduled, and then executed across potentially very large numbers of network functions. Activities need to be managed across network functions to minimize customer impact—for example, maintenance activities need to be coordinated amongst themselves and take into account current network conditions to minimize the risk of interrupting network services. The maintenance activities also need to be closely monitored, with restoration actions such as roll backs (going back to the previous state) executed should the activities go awry.

9.2.2.2 Reactive Maintenance

Failures and impairments of network functions are occurring on an almost continual basis in large-scale networks—software bugs, hardware faults, and weather are just some of the causes of such concerns. Network operations need to first detect and identify such failures and impairments—looking for signatures indicating issues within the vast amounts of alarms, logs, and measurement data received from the network and service-monitoring devices. Once a problem is identified, network operations have two main goals here: (1) mitigate service impact for customers and (2) permanently repair the issue and return any recovered capacity back into the network.

For much of the network, there is built-in redundant capacity that can carry traffic in the face of failures and impairments. If there is a failure, or a significant impairment in a network function or the connectivity between two network functions, then the network will typically automatically recover customer traffic by re-routing it. Thus, services may experience minimal impact as the network automatically recovers. The operations role is then to repair any failed network functions so that capacity is returned to the network. And importantly, from an operator's point of view, this means that there is less pressure to perform a rapid repair—so long as the failed network functions are repaired before something else goes wrong in the same region that may become customer impacting if there is insufficient available capacity after the initial failure.

However, not all failures or impairments can be recovered automatically today. In some rare cases, the network function may fail to recognize the failure and may silently drop traffic without the failover mechanisms being activated. In other scenarios, there may not be sufficient available restoration capacity to recover service—either there is no recovery mechanism (e.g., edge routers or customer routers may not be configured with redundancy due to the cost and complexity of providing such failure recovery mechanisms), the outage may be too large, or at the network edge there may not be capacity that is usable (e.g., customers at the mobility network edge may not be able to fail over to alternate towers if there is insufficient signal strength at the neighboring towers or if the failure is too large geographically). Complex interactions between network functions can also trigger unexpected failure modes that can be extremely complicated to understand, or operator error or even malicious behavior in configuring network functions can result in them failing to carry traffic as expected. In such scenarios, network operators have to detect, rapidly localize, and troubleshoot the issue and then execute actions to restore service. In the meantime, customers are potentially experiencing service degradations. Depending on the complexity of the issue at hand, localizing and troubleshooting issues can be a particularly time consuming and oftentimes an extremely challenging task, performed under immense time pressure.

For physical network functions, recovering the network function after *hardware failures* typically means repairing the physical hardware if it has failed or is impaired. Temporary measures may be required to recover service where permanent repairs may be longer in coming. For example, traffic may be re-routed around the failed network function, or either fixed or portable generators may be used in situations where power has been interrupted. Many of these hardware repairs necessitate having a technician onsite with the failed equipment—which is typically costly. Either technicians must man offices 24 × 7, or technicians must be deployed to the offices when hardware needs to be repaired, which has associated delays. If the response must be rapid (e.g., where customers will be impacted until the repair is completed), then this can be particularly costly.

However, in a virtual world, VNFs can be recovered even in the face of hardware failures (servers, storage, and underlying network failures) by spinning up a new VNF to replace the failed or degraded VNF. This becomes purely a remotely managed function—detecting a failed VNF and then reinstantiating it on new hardware. Although failed hardware must eventually be repaired, this can be scheduled on a semiregular basis, with many such repairs/replacements being scheduled in a common location, say, once per month. This significantly reduces the operational overhead and associated cost of dealing with hardware failures. In fact, in many failure scenarios, this can become a fully automated (software based) function without human operator engagement, in contrast to the physical network functions where the hardware failure needs to be accurately localized and isolated to a specific root cause, and a technician needs to be dispatched (if not already in the office) to rapidly replace the failed hardware.

Software failures can typically be recovered remotely—both for physical and virtual network elements. For physical network elements, the software is inherently tied to the hardware, and thus the operator is limited to rebooting devices or line cards, or changing configurations of the device. Such repair actions and more are also available for VNFs.

9.2.3 Network Administration

Network administration ensures that the network delivers on predefined service objectives, even in the face of changing external and internal influences. Specifically, we focus here on how the network topology and the traffic routing are adapted to maintain service levels where possible. We discuss three core functions—traffic management, special event handling, and disaster recovery.

A core part of network administration is traffic management, which ensures that the network remains well behaved (delivering on service objectives) even in the face of traffic abnormalities (e.g., sudden traffic surges) or network failures and impairments. Network operator tasks may include re-routing traffic in response to network outages, maintenance activities, special events, and disasters. Such responses may be performed either reactively or proactively, depending on whether prior knowledge is available or not. In an extreme case, network operators need to respond to disasters as they strike a region. In such situations, there can be a sudden influx of traffic hitting the network, potentially when capacity has also been reduced by the disaster. Traffic management controls are used to ensure that congestion does not spread to other areas of the network, and that network capacity is utilized effectively to manage communications within and in/out of a disaster area. For example, controls are typically put in place to ensure that calls originating from a disaster area get preferential treatment over calls originating outside the area but seeking to terminate there.

Many traffic management controls are automated today—particularly where rapid responses are vital to minimizing customer impact. However, some controls still require human intervention, particularly where human judgment is required (e.g., disaster recovery).

In some situations, simply re-routing traffic within the network is not sufficient for handing temporary increases in traffic demand. Large social events, such as concerts, sports events (e.g., marathon) and political events (e.g., presidential inaugurations or protests/marches) can attract large populations to an area for a short period of time. Given the sudden influx of people—and their associated mobile networked devices—the mobile network risks becoming overloaded at the network edge. To avoid this, mobile network operators go to great lengths to identify upcoming events and to then introduce temporary network capacity, using technologies such as cell towers on wheels or COWs [2] (Figure 9.1). Significant planning is involved here—identifying and predicting where such events will occur, determining how much capacity is required, and then scheduling the necessary resources.

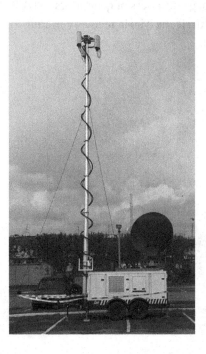

FIGURE 9.1 Cell tower on wheels.

For each event, COWs need to be transported to the relevant location(s) and connected to the network, and then be appropriately monitored and managed.

Similar deployment of on-demand capacity can be required in response to disasters. Communications services are vital to the functioning of society and cannot simply disappear even in the face of massive natural or man-made disasters. Thus, service providers such as AT&T go to great lengths to ensure that they can rapidly recover services even in the most dire of circumstances, such as after tornadoes, hurricanes, and terrorist attacks. This is known as *disaster recovery*.

Disaster recovery requires significant planning and complex execution. Disasters are of course hard to predict, but the network operations team is responsible for performing careful scenario planning and for creating comprehensive disaster recovery plans. As part of its disaster recovery planning, AT&T has created portable offices—built on trucks—that can be transported around the network and hooked up as needed. These disaster recovery trucks carry physical network assets—Reconfigurable Optical Add-Drop Multiplexers (ROADMs), routers, voice switches, and more—that need to be connected in the event of a disaster to recover network services. These are complemented by generators and COWs so that the network can be re-created in the face of disaster (Figure 9.2).

The operations teams are responsible for devising disaster scenarios and creating plans to respond to these, along with executing such plans in the event of a disaster. The teams execute regular practice drills to ensure that they are ready when disaster strikes. And of course, the operations teams are responsible for network recovery when such plans are called into action. As an example, more than a thousand technicians were deployed during the US hurricanes of 2017 to rapidly recover services—along with cells on light trucks with satellite backhaul, COWs, and large numbers of generators. AT&T also deployed its first "cell on wings" helicopter during Hurricane Maria recovery in Puerto Rico, depicted in Figure 9.3.

FIGURE 9.2   Disaster recovery trucks arriving in Puerto Rico after Hurricane Maria in 2017.

FIGURE 9.3   Cell on wings (also known as flying COW) in action in Puerto Rico after Hurricane Maria (2017).

9.3 THE ZERO-TOUCH NETWORK VISION: AN EXPANDED WORLD OF AUTOMATION AND INTELLIGENCE

As network traffic loads and corresponding network capacities continue to grow at a tremendous rate, it is imperative that we automate network operations functions. What would it take to get to a zero-touch network? And how does AI play into this?

Let's imagine a world in which the network is fully autonomous, where network designers and operators provide key inputs (intent/policies) to guide how the network operates and then the automation takes over. The network automatically and autonomously decides where and when capacity is needed and spins up and/or physically deploys the new network capacity, and then makes the desired changes across the network to realize business goals. Capacity that is not required is automatically taken out of service, and hardware is either turned off or "put to sleep" to save energy when it is not required. The network monitors network and service conditions, and automatically and rapidly repairs network and service issues with minimal customer impact. Where feasible, the network also predicts and remediates impending network impairments before they even occur. Emerging technology in the form of autonomous cars and drones deliver physical network functions where needed and without human intervention—e.g., cells on wheels that are used today to augment capacity for special events or to replace failed network capacity. Robots even deploy and repair physical equipment, installing and repairing servers, installing fibers and hooking up physical connections or repairing fiber cuts. Just think about what humanity has already achieved with robots—we've been able to deploy robot technologies on remote planets millions of miles away [3]! Robots repairing fibers and deploying equipment is not unimagineable.

As the zero-touch network vision is increasingly realized, operations efficiency will be increased. Network functions will be deployed as and when they are needed, thereby efficiently using capital expenditure as just-in-time capacity is matched with real-time needs. Customers will benefit from superior service quality enabled by fast, automated responses to network impairments and rapid capacity augmentations. Power consumption will be improved with subsequent environmental implications. And finally, continual service innovations are enabled, through rapid rollouts of new software, technologies and services.

Software-defined networking technologies (Chapter 3) will be core to realizing the zero-touch vision. Given the diversity and complexity of service provider networks and services today, it is imperative that network control technologies that intelligently automate operations functions leverage reusable intelligence across different network functions and services. It is also imperative that operators can define how such network operations activities are performed for any given network function and service by specifying their intent via policies. For example, policies could be used to specify how VNFs are placed—including affinity rules. Other policies specify what issues should be detected and how they should be responded to. Network operating systems, such as the Linux Foundation's Open Network Automation Platform (ONAP) [4] enable this.

A sophisticated level of "thinking" and "learning" will need to complement the policy-based network automation to realize the zero-touch network vision. Artificial intelligence will predict future customer demands, translating this to network demands and intelligently deciding where and when to spin up and deploy new capacity. Algorithms will watch vast amounts of network data in real time, predicting likely future impairment conditions and remediating these before they occur. Machine-learning algorithms will also be vital to learning what are normal network and service conditions and identifying anomalous conditions that require remediation. And ultimately, the network intelligence would have to automatically learn how to deal with anomalous situations, including failures and planned maintenance fallout, to instigate self-repair. The following sections delves further into this vision.

9.3.1 Autonomous Network Provisioning Vision

In a zero-touch network, network provisioning is a fully automated process—determining where and when network capacity should be deployed, deploying the network functions and then executing "test and turn up" before declaring the network functions ready for carrying production traffic.

Parts of this process is automated today—human operators forecast traffic demands into the future, collecting current demands and extrapolating on growth across different services carried over a network. Operators execute various runs of capacity planning tools to determine where to deploy new capacity. Physical network functions are deployed by technicians—manually screwing in hardware into bays in a central office. Configuration of these devices may be automated or at least semi-automated—especially where there is significant scale. And finally, operators will typically execute a set of scripts to test network functions before introducing new network functions and capacity into the network via routing configuration updates.

9.3.1.1 Capacity Planning

We first start by considering network functions that can be dynamically established or configured in near real time, such as VNFs and connectivity between network functions established as "bandwidth on demand." Virtualization radically changes the capacity planning process compared with historic physical network elements; assuming that there is sufficient cloud capacity within the data center, new network functions can be spun up in minutes or less. If networking capacity between offices can also be provisioned rapidly to interconnect VNFs, then the historical need for traffic forecasting out months or even years is eliminated for the VNFs. We thus assume here that there is sufficient spare capacity available such that when these new network functions are required, they can be instantiated by leveraging spare server or bandwidth that is lying idle or being used by services that can be pre-empted. The VNF capacity needs here can thus be identified on demand. Traffic loads are monitored and trended over time to predict near-term future traffic demands, with decisions automatically made as to when new capacity should be automatically spun up (instantiated) on predeployed data center or network capacity. Machine learning is critical to deciding when and where to spin up new VNFs, taking into account available server and interconnecting network capacity, customer requirements (e.g., latency requirements), and more.

We all know that predicting the future can be challenging, and this is true for traffic forecasting too. Thus, eliminating this lengthy forecasting process for these network functions reduces or even eliminates the forecasting errors. This thus means that we can reduce or even eliminate the potentially large amounts of stranded capacity that forecasting errors can cause in specific locations, whilst scrambling for capacity in other locations. Similarly, traffic can be routed on the optimal routes if network capacity is available in the desired locations, contrasting with where historical errors would force traffic to be routed on suboptimal paths, resulting in longer latencies for customer traffic and inefficient capacity utilization for service providers.

Virtualization also opens up the opportunity to delete network functions when not required for a period of time or to migrate functions over time—potentially even on a time of day basis for functions supporting services that are not delay/location sensitive (assuming that sufficient interconnecting capacity is available). All of this requires machine learning—sophisticated algorithms to learn traffic patterns and make intelligent decisions. The virtual network can also be regularly reoptimized, dynamically rehoming VNFs to maintain efficient utilization of resources.

Virtual network functions and dynamic interconnectivity are established by using spare, physical capacity that is available in the network as required. These physical assets need to be predeployed so that they are available when needed. Deploying physical assets—including cell tower carriers (capacity), servers, storage, and ROADMs—is a much longer process than spinning up VNFs and can take weeks to months (or even longer). Buildings, fibers, and cell tower locations must be procured and deployed on even longer time scales—these can take even years to procure or lease real estate and negotiate rights of way and cell tower locations.

User-demand forecasting provides the starting point for the physical asset network provisioning process. Such demands are created by predicting future loads based on historical demand growths and injecting known or predicted aberrations from this growth rate. Artificial intelligence and machine learning will be instrumental here in terms of predicting future traffic demands—including looking at external factors which could cause high variations on the basic, trended demand. Example external factors could include specific customers that could bring in massive step functions in the demand at a given location or major population shifts in a given city due to large industrial changes that could be predicted by monitoring industry trends. Such learning requires analysis of data from well beyond the network—including social, population, and economic-related data.

Capacity planning in future networks will be a fully automated, highly optimized function that simultaneously takes into account multiple network layers. Server and storage capacity, local networking capacity, physical network functions (e.g., cell towers) and interoffice connectivity (e.g., fiber/Dense Wavelength Division Multiplexing demands) needs are predicted based on forecasted user demands across the range of different services that a service provider supports; these are in turn translated to capacity needs for different technologies (equipment) in specific locations within the network(s).

9.3.1.2 Deploying, Configuring, and Turning Up Network Functions

Network automation implemented through a network operating system platform will provide the mechanisms for automatically spinning up the virtual network capacity, without human intervention. The network automation would also initiate the provisioning of physical network functions. The identity and other configuration details of network functions will be automatically determined, translating a high-level description of the network operator's intent [5], which is then translated to device-specific configuration. The automation will install the configurations on the network functions and then validate the successful instantiation of network functions through a battery of automated tests, before making the newly deployed capacity available for carrying production traffic.

Machine learning can complement operator-specified tests to identify anomalously configured or anomalously behaving network functions. By analyzing the configuration and behavior of already deployed network functions, we can learn what is normal for a given type of network function; comparing this normal with newly instantiated network functions may identify situations where the network function is misconfigured or not performing or behaving consistently with existing network functions. In fact, this type of comparison can be performed on an ongoing basis—not just as new network functions are instantiated.

9.3.2 Autonomous Network Maintenance Vision

Easily the most time-consuming and complex network operations tasks performed today is network maintenance—and particularly reactive maintenance. We believe that this is where there are also the most significant opportunities for both automation and AI.

9.3.2.1 Planned Maintenance

Planned maintenance is a critical part of network, application, and service life cycles—it is required to both introduce new services and features and to prevent certain failures. Many common failures can be avoided if proper monitoring/diagnostics and preventative/planned maintenance are exercised.

Historically, planned maintenance activities were often planned by network engineers who provided written, high-level specifications of what was required from each maintenance activity and the list of network elements on which a given maintenance activity was to be executed. From there, network operators created local schedules for executing the change over the relevant network functions, based on available human resources and network function-specific constraints (e.g., time intervals over which customer agreements allow maintenance on the network functions to be performed). The operators then had to work across operations teams to "deconflict" schedules—ensuring that activities on different network elements do not conflict. This last step has typically been a very manual and time-consuming process. Finally, the execution was typically either fully or partially automated—especially where there are large numbers of network elements on which the maintenance was to be executed, such as at the network edge.

Planned maintenance activities in the future will take on a life of their own—a network operator specifies the intent of the maintenance and the scope, and then the automation takes over. The automation coordinates across activities—intelligently scheduling (and rescheduling) different activities on different network functions, taking into account a range of customer, network topology, and service constraints. At the scheduled times, the automation executes the maintenance activity—automatically deploying new software releases, changing network configurations, validating the effectiveness of changes, and handling fallout.

The planned maintenance activities are, at least in the foreseeable future, likely to be initiated by network operators. These operators will decide what maintenance needs to be performed, describing this at a high level to the automation system which then takes over to schedule and execute the activities. However, there may even become a day when the network has the intelligence to decide what maintenance needs to be performed on its own—and then goes ahead and schedules and executes these activities.

Once decisions have been made about what maintenance needs to be performed, the automation needs to schedule the activities and execute them. An important goal of these functions is to minimize customer impact during the maintenance—thus, activities that will cause the network function to be unavailable are carefully scheduled to ensure that they are performed at times that minimize customer impact, and such activities are coordinated in such a way to minimize customer impact. For example, a single cell tower could well be taken out of service for maintenance without any negative customer impact—customers on the cell tower are automatically connected to neighboring towers when the tower under maintenance is not available. However, if too many towers are all taken out of service in the same location, then there may not be any cell towers to pick up the customer demand, and thus customers may not be able to make phone calls, watch videos, or connect to the Internet. Thus, minimizing the customer impact requires careful planning on which network functions can simultaneously have maintenance activities performed. Note that if maintenance can be performed without any downtime on network functions, such as is promised with network virtualization and the hitless migration of VNFs, the sophisticated scheduling of activities will become less critical.

The coordination of different maintenance activities is achieved through the scheduling of activities across different types of network functions and across the same type of functions (e.g., different cell towers). The scheduling algorithms take into account the time periods available, customer constraints, topology and service paths, predicted customer impact, and the expected duration of the activities to identify when maintenance should be performed on the different network functions. However, unexpected interruptions and issues during maintenance can occur, and thus rescheduling of maintenance activities can be required. Algorithms to achieve all of this can be quite complicated, especially when working across multiple network layers and with complex network topologies and service paths.

Machine learning can be used to determine whether activities that are being rolled out networkwide are causing potential customer impact during the execution of the change—information that can be used to decide when such activities should be performed (e.g., do they need to be executed during periods of low customer traffic, typically at night?). Machine learning and advanced analytics can also be used to predict the customer impact when network functions will be out of service during maintenance activities—for example, predicting if neighboring towers can service the traffic impacted by a set of cell towers undergoing maintenance. Machine learning can also be used to determine when the best time period is on a per location basis to perform such maintenance activities—these are typically when traffic is at its lowest, often late at night, although other factors such as specific critical customer activities may also be taken into account. Such prediction would need to take into account normal activity in the location, which can be obtained from network data, along with information obtained from non-network sources about activities that may be occurring in or around the impacted region (e.g., social events that may introduce unusually high demand). Similarly, machine learning can use external, non-network data to predict when external factors could impact the maintenance—for example, if there is bad weather predicted.

The execution of planned activities will be automated—including checking current network conditions to determine if it is "safe" to proceed with the planned activities, and also dealing with when things go awry (what we refer to as fallout). The second of these is the most complex to automate—a simple solution is to simply roll back the changes, but this is not always possible nor a solution. Machine learning can be used to learn what the most appropriate actions are to deal with unexpected fallout.

Fallout is often very easy to identify—if we are unable to reach the network function, or execute the desired change or if the network function fails as a result of the maintenance activity, it is immediately clear that there is fallout. However, sometimes the change may be executed and more subtle negative impacts are induced. Machine learning is thus used to determine whether the network changes are having an unexpected longer-term negative impact, which may be indicative of software bugs or misconfigurations. This can be identified by comparing performance before and after changes—either on a single network function or across a range of network functions that have all been subjected to similar changes. Such comparison needs to take into account normal fluctuations in performance, such as time of day or seasonal changes.

9.3.2.2 Reactive Maintenance

Significant operator resources are typically involved in reactive maintenance today. Operators typically respond to tickets, which are typically created by automated systems that detect and (largely) localize network conditions. Process automation systems [6] populate additional information into tickets, simplifying data collection and analysis for the operators, and thus speeding troubleshooting investigations. Operators delve into the collected data and information and further investigate the issue to identify what is happening and determine potential restoration actions. The operators take appropriate actions—sometimes having to try different alternatives to execute the repair.

We instead envision a world in which machines automatically detect, isolate, and take restoration actions in response to and in advance of predicted network and service impairments. Such *closed loops* are implemented using the network automation platform, where the automation monitors network and service conditions, detects and localizes issues makes intelligent decisions regarding what actions to take and then executes these actions (see Chapter 3).

In a zero-touch network, all issues are automatically resolved through closed-loop actions without any human intervention. However, we expect that not all issues will be automatically resolved in the near to medium term, leading us to more general *control loops*, which enable open- and closed-loop control. Open loops refer to when the automation falls out and a human operator is engaged. Open loops may result because the system is unable to determine an appropriate closed-loop action to try, or because the closed-loop actions attempted do not successfully resolve the issue. Open loops are also used whilst closed-loop (automated) actions are being considered—the automation systems recommend actions that are then validated (or not) by the network operators before the action is taken; enabling network operators to gain confidence in new closed-loop actions before automation is fully leveraged.

Artificial intelligence and machine learning will be integral to future control loops. As illustrated in Figure 9.4, machine learning and other analytics will continually monitor vast

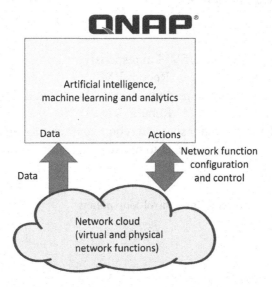

FIGURE 9.4   Machine learning-based closed loops.

volumes of data related to network and service conditions to detect anomalous conditions and predict future impairments. Artificial intelligence will be used to automatically diagnose root causes of detected conditions (as needed), and machine learning-based analytics will quantify the service (customer) impact of detected impairments. And finally, we expect that machine learning will also be key to intelligently learning what signatures indicate issues and what actions the system should execute in response to detected issues. The automated learning will need to adapt to changing conditions, such as when network function software is updated—introducing new software bugs with different restoration actions.

In the ultimate future vision, the system will complement learning based on historical experience with automated active experiments of alternative restoration actions, just as a human operator would do when faced with impairments with no clear and obvious resolution. The system will also learn as to when to take different restoration actions—learning over time what the customer impact caused by the restoration action is and trading this off during any given event with the customer impact currently experienced and predicted to be experienced as a result of the impairment that is to be remediated. For example, if restoration actions are planned in response to conditions that are having minimal to no customer impact, then restoration actions that are expected to interrupt traffic flows (e.g., rebooting a network function) may be delayed until traffic is low (e.g., during night hours). However, immediate restoration may be taken in response to serious customer-impacting impairments.

However, in the near to medium term, machine learning would be complemented and even subsumed by human domain knowledge, as network operators provide information described as policies (or eventually as more abstracted intent) regarding signatures that define events of interest and restoration actions that should be taken in response to known network and service conditions. For example, if the operator knows that there is a particular software bug that causes the virtual machine (VM) to become unresponsive and can be resolved simply by rebooting the associated VM, then this can be expressed by the operator as a policy as illustrated in Figure 9.5.

> If VM unresponsive
> Reboot VM
> If VM unresponsive and reboot failed
> Rebuild VM
> If VM unresponsive and reboot and rebuild failed
> Open ticket to network operator

FIGURE 9.5 Example operator-specific control-loop policy.

As machine learning-based intelligence becomes increasingly comprehensive, human domain-knowledge-based policies would reduce to one of the data sources from which machine intelligence derives the action decisions. This is analogous to a child growing up and the "rules" enforced by his or her parents subsiding over time, being replaced by his or her own experience and judgment.

As each restoration action is attempted, the system must determine whether it was effective in resolving the issue at hand. This typically equates to determining whether the symptom that triggered the control loop has been eliminated and that service performance is good after the resolution action. In some services, such as mobility, service performance varies over time and across locations. Thus, machine learning is used to determine normal performance at any given location and time and can be compared with conditions after restoration actions are taken to validate successful repair.

Many repair actions can be executed entirely without human engagement—for example, network functions (physical or virtual) can be rebooted and configurations updated. However, VNFs introduce a whole new level of opportunity, where new VNFs can be spun up rapidly and traffic migrated over to quickly alleviate failure conditions. Taking a leaf out of a cloud providers' book, when impairments or failures are detected for a given VNF, a replacement VNF can be rapidly spun up and traffic migrated to it. For example, consider a virtual provider edge router (vPE)—a VNF that sits at the edge of a service provider's network and to which Internet customers connect. In the event that the vPE fails, or an impairment is detected, we can spin up a new vPE on a different server, and then migrate the customers over to this new vPE. Achieving this requires configuring the new vPE with matching functional settings to the failed vPE, such as the Virtual Local Area Network, the access control list, and the quality of service configuration. It also requires that traffic be re-routed to the new vPE. Similarly, if network functions are congested—even if this congestion is unexpected and may be a result of a software bug that is causing erroneous overload conditions—rapidly spinning up additional VNF capacity may be a simple and very rapid way of mitigating the customer impact, even if the actual underlying root cause of the issue is unknown.

Virtual network functions are thus opening up new opportunities to rethink the traditional, manually intensive and oftentimes painful approach to troubleshooting network issues. The ability to spin up new instances of a failed or impaired network function promises to simplify or even eliminate the troubleshooting process in advance of network and service repair. Rather than spending an inordinate amount of time trying to localize an issue and determine the root cause, with customers potentially experiencing a service impact, we can simply spin up a new or additional instance of a network function in a bid to recover service. This could save hours of effort from large teams and associated customer impact, and is aligned with how traditional cloud providers typically manage services. However, this is typically a considerable change in thinking for network service providers!

Similarly, being able to spin up new VNFs in response to hardware failures eliminates the need for rapid dispatches to replace failed hardware, vastly simplifying and streamlining field operations. Instead, failed cloud capacity can be replaced on regular intervals—for example, monthly—without time pressures and expensive out of hours technician dispatches.

However, not all network impairments will be able to be handled without real-time intervention at the physical location. Fiber cuts and physical network function failures would both likely require onsite attention—if there is limited hardware and capacity available, customers may be impacted until onsite repair has been completed. This imposes time pressures on dispatching for restoration. In the future, dispatches will not always require human beings. With the advent of drones, autonomous cars, and even robots, we envision a world in which resources can be dispatched and even integrated into the network with full automation. For example, cell sites on wheels or cell sites on wings (drones) can be dispatched autonomously to deal with power failures, disaster scenarios, and to provide capacity augmentations for special events. Where not feasible, human technicians will complement autonomous dispatches.

Whether dispatches are automated or not, automation and machine learning are still vital in managing the dispatches; analytics within the automation platform analyze network data to localize the issue and identify appropriate restoration actions. The prioritization of actions should be performed based on customer impact—issues with high customer impact must be dealt with immediately, whilst issues that have no customer impact can be handled with lesser urgency. This requires quantifying the customer impact of outages and other issues—the complexity of which varies with different network technologies. Advanced machine learning analytics will quantify the customer impact across different technologies, so that service providers can determine when and how to prioritize dispatches (and issue resolution in general), and so that the service providers can in general understand the customer impact of network outages.

The policies associated with the automation leverage information about the customer impact and other factors to decide what actions need to be taken, if any. In addition to automatically triggering the dispatches, AI integrated into the system would optimize all of the field visits according to physical geography, priorities (based on customer impact), and available resources. The automation will then be responsible for monitoring the effectiveness of such dispatches on different time scales.

The earlier discussion focuses on real-time or near real-time responses to network conditions, with a focus on repairing service for customers. However, it is also important that we identify issues that keep reoccurring, and, where possible, find ways to permanently eliminate or at least reduce their frequency of occurring. For example, if a software bug requires that network functions be regularly rebooted, then we need to ensure that the software vendor fixes the associated bug and that the software is rolled out across the network to permanently eliminate the issue. Such heavy-hitting issues are identified through long-term trending and analysis of network and service impairments. Machine learning can further collate information regarding the conditions that trigger those issues and identify the patterns for trouble diagnosis and bug fixes.

9.3.3 Autonomous Network Administration Vision

Traffic management, special event management, and disaster recovery are all areas that have historically been fairly dependent on human intelligence and judgment. Human operators execute the detailed planning of special events and disaster responses and determine how to manage traffic in advance of special events and in response to unusual situations. Technicians are responsible for deploying equipment in response to disasters. Figure 9.2 depicts some of the complexity where equipment has to be transported to locations that can sometimes be challenging to get to (e.g., remote islands such as Puerto Rico in 2017). Artificial intelligence provides the potential to transform some of these functions.

As machine learning advances, the technology is expected to be available to enable automatic decision-making and execution of activities supporting traffic management. Sophisticated intelligence will be able to detect and predict anomalous traffic based on network and social data (e.g., news events, social media) and determine how to re-route traffic to manage load. Network automation will make the necessary changes to the network functions.

In the fully autonomous network vision, community, convention center and arena calendars and social media will all be automatically mined to identify and predict large social events that would cause significant increases in traffic load on the network, and to predict the magnitude of these increases. Using these predictions, network intelligence will automatically determine the additional network capacity needs and where to deploy the capacity. Network intelligence will then automatically dispatch capacity at the relevant time and monitor and react to network conditions during the event, finally decommissioning the capacity once the event is over. A closed-loop feedback mechanism will enable the intelligence to continue to learn and refine event and capacity predictions, based on measurements made during such events.

Finally, SDN, virtualization, and AI have the potential to transform the disaster recovery process. Disaster recovery would be greatly simplified in a virtual world compared with recovering physical network assets. A data center may be recovered by dynamically rehoming VNFs to one or more different data centers—this requires the ability to either backup VNF images and dynamically spin up new VNFs in locations based on the backup images, or the ability to dynamically recreate the VNF images. It also requires sufficient spare network capacity to appropriately re-route traffic. In the event that spare capacity is not available in other locations, data centers on wheels can be deployed locally to the disaster and the VNFs migrated accordingly. Artificial intelligence will make decisions according to how and where to migrate the capacity. Machine learning and AI will also be vital to managing physical resources deployed during disasters, as such COWs. Equipment can be predeployed in advance of natural disasters such as hurricanes, placed in locations optimized to simplify and speed the deployment of network functions during and after the event. Weather forecasts, predicted customer impact of equipment outages, and information about battery lifetimes can together be leveraged to optimize where equipment is deployed in advance of a natural disaster, whilst measured customer impact and equipment information can together be used to prioritize, design, and coordinate deployments once a disaster has occurred.

9.4 REALIZING THE VISION: A JOURNEY TO THE FUTURE

There is a tremendous amount of automation that is available in the network today—vital to enabling a relatively small operations team to manage massive international networks and services. However, there is also a fair amount of human intervention required in all aspects of operations, particularly when it comes to scheduling activities, troubleshooting and remediating network issues, and managing special events and disasters. The automation available today leverages a combination of multiple systems, ad hoc scripting, and is heavily dependent on development activities. As network services continue to grow in scale and complexity, and as customers and technology demand rapid innovation, traditional systems and automation will not suffice.

The telecommunications industry is thus embarking on the journey toward policy-enabled, SDN-based network operating systems. This will provide the foundation of the zero-touch network. The Linux Foundation's ONAP is a "comprehensive platform for real-time, policy-driven orchestration and automation of physical and virtual network functions that will enable software, network, IT, and cloud providers and developers to rapidly automate new services and support complete life-cycle management" [4]. Put in our context here, ONAP and associated recipes, policies, and analytics will provide the foundation on which we can automate network provisioning, maintenance, and administration.

New types of VNFs are onboarded onto the ONAP platform by service designers who work in tight collaboration with the network operators. The onboarding process specifies the VNF role, and how new instances of the VNF should be configured, connected to other network functions (virtual or physical), and life-cycle managed. This would include specifying how the ONAP platform should instantiate new instances of the VNF and how the ONAP platform should respond to different network conditions associated with the VNF. These initial specifications are modulated by the operations teams once the newly designed VNFs have been handed to them, based on field experience.

We will now review the technologies required and the journey that we are on to create an ONAP-based network that leverages AI in a march toward a zero-touch network.

9.4.1 Realizing Autonomous Network Provisioning

As discussed earlier, there are many physical assets required in future networks—servers, fibers, and cell towers being examples. Even large backbone routers may not be virtualizable in the near future, until servers can achieve the kind of throughputs required. Service providers may also choose for other business reasons to virtualize only some but not all of their network elements. Such physical assets require long lead times and thus forward-looking planning; capacity planning tools are required to support this.

Capacity planning takes network designs, traffic forecasts and other constraints as input to determine where to deploy future capacity. Assuming that the basic network design already exists, then the process toward accurate network capacity planning breaks into a few key components—traffic demand matrix estimation or measurement and growth modeling and forecast are used together to create the traffic forecast, whilst network routing design and optimization algorithms form the basis of the capacity planning tooling.

Artificial intelligence that streamlines the entire process can seamlessly take measurement data from the operating network and produce capacity augmentation plans to be executed.

Let's first start by estimating traffic demands, focusing here on IP networks. Our ability to accurately estimate a traffic demand matrix has evolved significantly as network measurement technologies and data infrastructure have matured. Simple Network Management Protocol (SNMP)-based traffic volume measurements do not provide the source and destination information of the network flows. Hence, to compute the traffic matrix requires combining the SNMP measurements and a network routing matrix, which can be derived from control (a.k.a. routing) plane measurements and solving underconstrained linear equations. This tends to lead to high estimation errors. Where flow-based measurements such as NetFlow are available, the traffic matrix can be directly computed with only a small statistical error (due to the flow sampling process). Enhanced with deep packet inspection [7] measurements, the traditional source-destination traffic matrix can be further decomposed into different component traffic matrices by application classes (such as video streaming, web, and Internet-of-Things) and user devices (such as smartphone, tablet, and PC), which would enable finer-grained growth modeling and forecast. Traffic growth modeling involves trending the traffic demand over time and fitting it to a data model, for example, estimating the compound annual growth rate. As different classes of traffic grow at different rates, finer-grained growth modeling achieves better forecasting accuracy.

Mapping traffic demand to a network capacity plan requires solving routing simulation and optimization problems. For a large-scale network, the complexity for doing this far exceeds the processing capacity of human intelligence, even for the most experienced network planners. While finding the shortest path routing or equivalently the least-cost network design among candidate sets of nodes and paths is a tractable problem, practical constraints such as capacity increments being in discrete bandwidth units quickly turns the problem into a combinatorial optimization, greatly adding to its computational complexity. Additional considerations further complicate the capacity planning analytics. One example is designing for resiliency—accounting for link and node failures. Sophisticated probabilistic models can account for component failure rates—such failure rates can be measured from the production network and modeled according to historical data. Another example is designing robust networks that are resilient to inherent traffic demand forecasting errors. Capacity planning tools have become increasingly intelligent over the years, producing more efficient capacity plans with less human input.

However, traditional capacity planning tools tend to take into account one layer at a time, which leads to inefficiencies across network layers. Cross-layer optimizations, which incorporate multiple network layers (e.g., jointly optimizes optical, IP, and mobility network layers) improve the efficiency of resource utilization, improving both network latency and capital expenditure. Cross-layer optimization can be extremely challenging. For this, new algorithms and their careful implementations are necessary.

Besides physical network capacity augments, capacity planning and optimization for other physical resources, including compute, storage, memory, power, and cooling, present similar challenges and opportunities for machine learning-based intelligence. The same set of principles apply—taking fine-grained measurements (e.g., breaking CPU measurements by network functions), constructing multivariate forecasting models with trends, seasonality, and external business factors accounted for (e.g., modeling workload for video streaming during holidays), and performing what-if analyses and optimizations (e.g., rack optimization and resiliency optimization).

In contrast to physical assets, which require long deployment times and thus forward-looking forecasting and planning, VNFs can be spun up on demand, and thus new capacity can be deployed when and where it is needed—assuming that there is available underlying cloud capacity as discussed in the previous paragraph [8]. This is a game changer in terms of realizing an autonomous, zero-touch network—reducing operator overheads and speeding responsiveness to changing network demands.

The design and planning for VNFs can then become a real-time decision process and does not require the lengthy lead times and long-term traffic demand forecasting that are necessary for their physical peers. However, the complexity associated with the resource optimization remains. The VNFs are composed of one or more resource groups and VMs, as described in OpenStack Heat templates. The efficient placement of the VNFs on the physical resources requires solving a complex multidimensional bin-packing problem [9]. Coming to the rescue, there exist several algorithms for machine intelligence to identify efficient solutions to this class of problem, with or without additional placement affinity constraints and/or options to migrate already deployed VNFs. ONAP includes the VNF placement optimization automatically in its VNF instantiation decisions.

Network functions must be interconnected to enable end-to-end services. This requires that capacity between offices be established automatically if we are to realize the zero-touch network vision; technologies such as Ethernet (for lower speed connectivity between locations) and ROADMs [10] are making capacity available "on demand."

Once network capacity is deployed, we need to configure, test, and then activate it into the network. Much of the configuration and test and turn up of legacy network elements has historically been automated to differing extents in large-scale service providers. However, ONAP provides a platform to deliver consistent and integrated mechanisms for achieving these functions and can enable driving to a fully automated process.

Whether physical or virtual, network functions must be logically configured and then be validated before they can be used to carry traffic and deliver services. Configuration includes things like specifying the network function's identities (e.g., IP addresses), specifying the routing protocols to use to communicate with other network functions, and configuring network function policies, such as what traffic to carry or block. One of the biggest challenges faced by network operators is the diversity of different types of network functions and the tremendous differences in how they are configured and operated. One of the primary goals of the ONAP effort and beyond is to provide consistent interfaces across different network functions from the network operators' point of view. Standards such as NetConf and RestConf are being increasingly adopted across network function vendors, which greatly accelerates the convergence to such a consistent configuration interface.

The data models via the configuration and management interface are described in a modeling language, such as Yet Another Next Generation (YANG) [11]. There are two sets of widely deployed and supported YANG models. The Internet Engineering Task Force

(IETF) standardizes a data model for each protocol, for basic routing functionality, and for common equipment management requirements. The OpenConfig group maintains another set of data models, largely overlapping, and often coordinated with the IETF data models. Beyond these models, each vendor also supports a vendor- and equipment-specific model set that can often be downloaded from their support sites. Using these YANG models enables model-driven management controllers such as those in ONAP.

Once configuration is completed, "test and turn up" validates that the network function is ready to support traffic and then updates network configurations to start routing traffic through the new network functions. The "test and turn up" is achieved through a battery of tests designed to validate the configuration and health of the network function and the services passing through it. Each network function will require different tests, depending on where they are located in the network, the specific role that the network function performs, and the services carried. Initially, the set of tests that are to be performed would be indicated by a network operator—specified as intent or policies in the ONAP system. As the industry continues to mature, machine learning could take this role over—automatically learning what tests should be performed based on information inferred from the network, service designs, and past experience regarding effective monitoring.

The earlier discussion focuses on introducing new capacity to the network. However, as networks grow incrementally over time, they typically become suboptimal. Historically, with physical network assets, it has been extremely expensive and time consuming to rearrange the network to reoptimize how capacity is used. However, given that VNFs are intended to be readily migrated, we now have an opportunity to be able to regularly reoptimize capacity. In addition to the ability to be able to migrate VNFs and their associated traffic in a seamless fashion managed by ONAP, sophisticated reoptimization algorithms will be required to decide when and where to migrate capacity.

Similarly, conditions can occur where traffic subsides—either temporarily or permanently in a location. In such situations, VNFs can be turned down or reduced in size, and physical resources can be turned down or reduced in capacity. Regions with seasonal demand—such as popular summer vacation locations—may demonstrate very high traffic demands during one season (e.g., the summer), but low demands for the remainder of the year. In such situations, it is possible to reduce network capacity or to either temporarily shut down or put some of the network resources (e.g., carriers on cell sites) to sleep. Machine learning is instrumental here to learn the normal traffic conditions, so that decisions can be made regarding capacity that can be temporarily removed from the network to save operating costs and/or energy (with associated environmental benefits).

9.4.2 Realizing Network Maintenance

Once network functions have been deployed, they need to be managed. We now examine network maintenance and how it is evolving toward the autonomous network vision.

9.4.2.1 Planned Maintenance

ONAP provides a consistent way of automating the change management process. Service designers and/or network operators design change activities by constructing a *change workflow* for a given change activity. Executing a change activity for a given network function typically involves first determining if the current network state is such that it is "safe" to proceed with the maintenance, and then executing a suite of tests (pre-checks) to capture pre-maintenance network function configuration and state, and service performance—to be used as a baseline for comparison after the maintenance activity. The change activity is then executed, and post-checks are performed to verify that the change has been successfully executed without any unexpected negative consequences. Such post-checks need to be performed across services—for example, if maintenance is performed on a router, then all services that are carried through that router (e.g., Internet access, mobility services, Voice over LTE [VoLTE], and TV services) should be monitored and validated. Should issues arise, such as network functions failing to come up after rebooting or key performance indicators (KPIs) being degraded, appropriate actions should be executed. The series of actions that should be performed to execute the change, what tests should be performed before and after the activity to capture issues, and how issues should be remediated should they occur are captured in recipes, which are "glued" together as desired using a graphical interface.

Once the maintenance activity has been designed, it needs to be scheduled. The service designer and/or operator defines the set of network functions on which a given change is to be executed, and other policies that prescribe how these should be scheduled. Change scheduling is then an automated process, leveraging optimization algorithms and heuristics implemented within the ONAP optimization framework.

Finally, change execution is automated via ONAP, executing the change workflow that the service designers have specified on the set of network functions according to the calculated schedules. The execution will typically also handle automation fallout, when the change activities fail. A common restoration technique is to simply roll back the change (e.g., reverting back to the old software during a software update procedure).

Artificial intelligence permeates the change management process—from optimization algorithms used to calculate and recalculate schedules to the execution and validation of the effectiveness of change activities. One particularly challenging area that AI is addressing is the change scheduling. Maintenance activities that are potentially customer impacting are typically performed during the maintenance window—typically night hours when traffic is low and thus customer impact is low. This gives a limited window in which activities can be scheduled; with complex network topologies, multiple different maintenance activities making changes to network functions and with the large network scale, such scheduling can be complex. Customer impact must be minimized—thus coordinating across different network functions of different types and across different network layers is crucial to ensuring that redundant service paths are not simultaneously impacted. As higher priority activities arise, or as maintenance activities go awry or network impairments interfere with maintenance activities, schedules need to be reworked, adding to the complexity. Such scheduling is a complex coordination problem to determine across change activities which times are available for activities on a given network function. Algorithms to schedule change activities are implemented in ONAP on top of the optimization framework—these algorithms take into account service paths and other constraints to ensure that change activities being simultaneously executed on different network functions do not cause unnecessary customer impact.

The effectiveness of change activities is ideally monitored on multiple time scales; tests immediately before and after the maintenance activities check for significant issues that are readily detected. However, some issues do not appear until traffic load increases—typically several hours or more after the change activity. Thus, the impact of changes on both service and network metrics should be monitored for a period of time after the maintenance, and compared with performance before the activity. Advanced machine learning-based analytics such as Mercury [12] take into account time of day and location-specific performance to quantify the intended service and network function performance improvements and capture any unintended consequences of the upgrades. The output from both the immediate post-change validations and the more advanced Mercury analytics drive the decision on whether repair or restore (e.g., rollback) actions are needed and when to perform the actions.

Before rolling out a common change networkwide, such as deploying a software upgrade or patch to all cell sites across the network, network operators typically execute a first field application (FFA) phase, where a subset of devices is chosen for deploying the change. Detecting even very subtle unexpected degradations during FFA is crucial for preventing a service impact on a wider scale. Advanced machine learning algorithms such as those used in long-term Mercury [13] provide the intelligence to look across different instances of a common change activity to identify persistent impact amid normal variations of service performance. Further advanced intelligence [14] can distinguish service performance impact due to external factors that are independent of the deployed changes versus impact that is intrinsic to the changes. This is achieved by uncovering the regression structure among instances that are both within and outside of the FFA deployment. The regression structure is then used as the basis to "predict" the service performance indicators during the post-change time interval and in the post-change environment if the planned change had not happened. Finally, by comparing the predicted and observed performance, the analytics quantifies the service impact resulting from the deployed change.

If an unexpected service degradation is detected during FFA, the change deployment would typically halt or revert back. Meanwhile, all data during the FFA would be analyzed for root cause investigation. Machine learning is useful in identifying the common characteristics of the instances where service degradations are observed, such as common configuration settings or common environmental or traffic patterns. The dimensionality of such a characteristic space is typically too large for human intelligence to effectively explore and reason about.

In the earlier process, FFA deployment and issue investigation are performed in iterative and separated steps. However, an AI system such as described in [15] may jointly optimize and orchestrate the FFA planning and the analysis of issues identified during the FFA. This is achieved by adaptively rolling out a next batch of FFA deployments at locations that are deemed more likely to capture any unexpected service degradation. Such locations are determined based on the characteristics learned from earlier FFA deployments validating the same change. For example, if an initial rollout of a new software to cellular base stations observes slightly increased dropped calls at low-traffic and high-mobility sites (e.g., along a highway), an AI system may choose to deploy the new software at additional low-traffic and high-mobility sites to confirm or disprove the observation. Such an AI system would also govern the network wide rollout of any given change and intelligently make the decision on when and where to deploy more changes and whether to halt and revert back any prior deployments.

9.4.2.2 Reactive Maintenance

Network functions generate a tremendous amount of data—alarms, syslogs, workflow logs, performance measurements, and more. Service level measurements are also captured— from records of individual calls and transactions, to metrics aggregated at different levels, including by call status, location, service type, customer device model, and other factors. There is a vast wealth of data—overwhelming if not managed carefully. A large part of the challenge in reactive maintenance is detecting important issues whilst minimizing false alarms, which historically waste operator resources and in future networks could cause unnecessary actions to be initiated. Processing the massive onslaught of network data to find those needles in the haystack—the issues that need to be investigated and the underlying root cause—is the role of event detection and alarm correlation systems.

Event detection may be as simple as listening to alerts from network functions— for example, a "link down" from a network function is a clear and simple indicator. Performance impairments may be detected by listening to KPIs generated by network functions and determining when KPIs are above/below a predefined threshold or are anomalously degraded. And service degradations are identified by looking at service measurements—aggregated in different dimensions (by different service types, location, etc.)— and similarly identifying anomalously degraded conditions. For example, we may want to alarm when IP network latencies have exceeded their normal values or when throughput in a cellular environment has dropped compared with normal—for the given location and time of day. Latency in IP networks varies by locations, depending on how far apart they are. Similarly, throughput in cellular networks varies by location and also with time of day. Thus, we cannot use simple threshold values to define when something is awry and must instead use more sophisticated anomaly detection mechanisms to determine when something has changed negatively and thus should be analyzed and remediated. Argus [16] is such an advanced time-series anomaly detection capability that is used to detect anomalous and actionable network and service conditions.

Advanced anomaly detection analytics often utilize built-in learning modules to automatically extract normal profiles from historical data so as to alleviate human network operators from the complexity of determining and setting the anomalous conditions to be alerted on. Such normal profiles may be univariate numerical time series of traffic volume or performance measurements with seasonality that vary by location, such as the profiles learned by Argus [16]. Alternatively, the normal profiles may be structural patterns capturing the relationship among different entity locations and across different metrics, such as those captured by the covariance matrix in [14]. Machine learning technologies are key enablers to these analytics. Moreover, integrating domain understanding in these machine learning-based analytics can typically help improve their effectiveness. Argus, for example, tailors its learning for network and service performance data by explicitly ignoring any significant short-term pattern changes (anomalies) while rapidly adapting to sustained pattern changes. This design of the algorithm is based on the understanding that network and service performance data typically contain anomalies due to transient failures, maintenance activities, or flash crowd traffic demands, and the network state would return to its normal behavior afterward as if the transient issues had not occurred. Meanwhile, permanent upgrades or traffic engineering changes would lead the network to a new state where prior history before the pattern change bears little value going forward. The same cannot be said for financial data, such as trade volumes or prices in stock market. Consequently, Argus has proven to produce high-quality results (e.g., low false alarm rates) in network operations applications compared with other general purpose univariate time-series anomaly detection techniques.

Arguably, the most complex tasks involved in operating networks today are associated with troubleshooting complex network and service issues—to determine where the issue is stemming from, and what is causing it. Any given network issue will typically result in multiple symptoms that are alarmed on; the challenge here is identifying what the underlying root cause is amongst the set of observed symptoms. With such a wide variety of failure modes, large numbers of different types of network functions deployed across a large geographical set of locations, multiple network layers and complex software with even more complex interactions across network functions, it can be extremely challenging to isolate where a problem is occurring and what is causing the problem—two steps that are often tied to taking recovery actions.

Let's illustrate this with a simple example where a single link between two routers is experiencing high bit error rates; we also assume that the link is not configured to fail on such error rates (as may be the case where there is little redundancy). Let's also assume that this link is providing transport connectivity between a mobility cell site and the mobility packet core network, as depicted in Figure 9.6. In this scenario, the routers on two ends of the impaired physical link will detect the errors and alarm accordingly. End-to-end

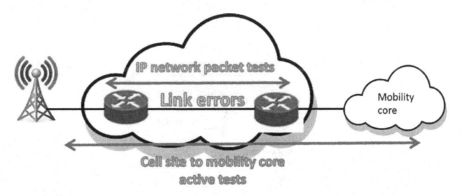

FIGURE 9.6   Event correlation example.

packet test transmissions executed in the IP network will also alarm, as will active measurements performed on the relevant segment(s) of the path between the cell site and the mobility core. And finally, customer measurements may also capture the impairments, with degraded customer experience being reported in the region. Without appropriate massaging (or correlation) of these alarms, operations teams will be inundated by alarms for even the simplest of issues, with multiple teams and individuals looking into different aspects of what is inherently a single underlying event (in this case, the impaired link between the two routers). This is clearly inefficient, resulting in wasted operator resources, and can elongate customer impact.

It is the responsibility of AI, particularly the *correlation engine* [17], to collate related alarms together into a common event, so that they can be processed accordingly. Correlation engines form the heart of the fault and performance management processes deployed today, reducing the volume of alarms by many orders of magnitude to create a manageable volume of tickets that require operator attention.

In addition to detecting and isolating issues, we need to understand the customer impact of issues so as to prioritize investigations and repair actions. Advanced, machine-learning analytics can quantify the current [18] and predicted customer impact [19] of network issues. Such customer impact quantification is used for prioritizing repair activities and even for deciding whether a dispatch for a physical network function is necessary for certain types of conditions. AT&T's TONA [18], for example, uses advanced machine learning-based analytics and service level data (e.g., call blocks, drops, and throughput) to assess the customer impact of network failures by comparing the observed performance after the failure with expected or learned performance before the failure so as to determine the severity of the issue.

As discussed in Chapter 3, AI in the form of control loops provides the core mechanism for enabling reactive maintenance within ONAP. Figure 9.7 depicts a simple control

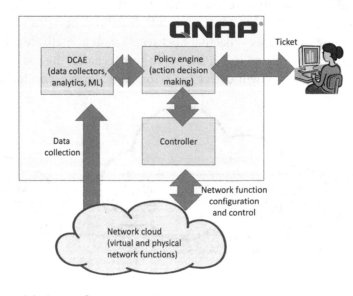

FIGURE 9.7 Simplified event flow on ONAP.

loop—collectors deployed on ONAP's Data Collection and Analytics Engine (DCAE) gather vast amounts of diverse data from network functions and end-to-end services. Analytics on the DCAE then process the incoming data to detect and correlate events to localize issues, and to quantify the customer impact of issues. Such analytics include simple thresholding, anomaly detectors (e.g., [16]), correlation engines [17], and TONA [18]. The localized events are passed to policy to decide what to do with them; either an action or set of actions are attempted via the SDN application controllers or the issue is ticketed for human analysis and restoration.

Human operators have historically been responsible for executing repair actions—events output from correlation engines are ticketed and human network operators delve into these to identify what the most likely root causes of issues are and how best to repair issues. Even once an issue is identified and localized, recovery steps may be less than obvious—an operator may need to try a few different options before finally resolving the issue. Process automation systems [6] automate a tremendous amount of data collection and event analysis, populating tickets to considerably speed human investigation. Machine learning technologies, such as AT&T's Mercury [12]—originally envisioned for evaluating the effectiveness of planned maintenance—can also be used to determining if restoration actions were effective.

However, automation is now advancing to the point of *automatically repairing network conditions* that would have previously been handled by human operators—automatically taking actions, such as migrating failed or impaired VNFs to new servers, rebooting VMs, and rebooting physical network functions and line cards. Such automated responses are an integral part of the ONAP vision; operators specify policies within ONAP that define what automated actions should be attempted and when to ticket to initiate human investigation. The ONAP policy engine, as illustrated in Figure 9.7, can also leverage additional data collected on demand regarding the observed condition, aiding in deciding what action to take. In a truly zero-touch network, all repair actions are automated and do not require human intervention. However, such a vision is a distance away today—and may never be fully realizable—and thus the policy engine will automatically populate tickets to instigate human analysis and restoration.

Service designers and network operators are expected to initially be responsible for specifying the policies that define the ONAP control loops—the events to detect, corre-lations to be performed, the restoration actions to be attempted and when to ticket for human investigation. However, the domain knowledge that defines these control loops is not always readily available; for mature network functions, this domain knowledge may be distributed across multiple network operators, and for new network functions, this knowl-edge may simply not exist. Where network operators are rapidly rolling out large numbers of different types of VNFs in a short period of time, it may be near impossible to scale the manual lab testing and detailed analysis that were historically executed and documented to identify a complete set of initial policies in advance of network deployment. Even for mature network functions, new software releases and changing external conditions may require the introduction of new control loops.

Machine learning can aid the identification of control-loop policies, creating a strong set of initial policies for new network functions in advance of field deployment and continually refining and maturing policies for network functions deployed in the field. Thus, policy learning may be executed in lab environments and/or based on field data. Policy learning for open loops (no automated repair actions) focuses on what events to detect, how these different events are related (correlated), and identifying their associated root cause (where possible)—thus defining the policies for event detection and correlation rules. Policy learning for closed loops also incorporates learning policies for the actions being automatically taken.

Policy learning for open loops aims to identify events that consistently co-occur and thus are likely symptoms of the same underlying event. Unsupervised learning applies here; the labels used in supervised learning would equate to the correlation rules we are aiming to identify and thus would defeat the point of using supervised learning. The unsupervised learning process aims at reducing large volumes of alarms, logs, network state, and performance measurements to actionable events by finding common patterns in the data. There is an abundance of algorithms and technologies for general clustering and pattern recognition, ranging from procedural Association Rule Mining [20] to AutoEncoder deep neural networks [21]. However, network and service path topologies are key to event correlation; the unique challenge in open-loop policy learning is in incorporating network and service paths in the learning by constructing a graph-based time series pattern recognition problem. Such a domain knowledge model and data representation are also critical for closed-loop policy learning. The graph-based time series patterns can be inspected by operators and automatically translated into ONAP correlation rules (policies). One can further apply causal inference techniques, such as Granger causality tests [22], to derive understanding for event localization and troubleshooting.

The effectiveness of unsupervised learning grows with the scale of the data set. For pre-field-deployed network functions, manually driven testing data from lab environments can be limited, both in volume and in diversity. This can be addressed by automation systems that systematically or randomly inject faults or simulate failures and adverse conditions, such as a sudden increase of traffic demand, in the environment. Repeated controlled experiments can then supply sufficient data to bootstrap machine learning. The failure injection control actions should be captured—these give us known failure root causes, which can also be used by the learning engines to refine the correlation signature and even appropriate repair actions for closed loops.

Closed-loop policies—the signatures and actions taken to detect and automatically remediate an issue—can be learned either in a lab environment, or by "watching" the actions taken by human operators in the field. Supervised machine-learning techniques are a natural fit for learning from network operators to derive the intelligence that governs the closed loops. While operators investigate each individual problem scenario and apply their domain understanding and experience in determining a suitable restoration action, they also provide a "training label" for supervised machine learning. Using such labels, machine learning evaluates the events and network states and performance conditions, together with the topological models, to construct rules in applying such restoration actions.

Introducing machine learning into closed loops will require building experience and trust in the technology—especially when the machine learning is related to actions that are to be automatically taken within the network. Building this experience and trust for network operators will be easier if they can understand what the system is recommending and doing—for example, if they can interpret the policies that are being recommended by the closed-loop machine learning. Such understanding of the closed-loop policies also provides operators with valuable insights regarding the root cause of the underlying issue, such as a software bug that is triggered by some specific condition, which they can use to eventually drive the root cause (bug) out of the system. Different supervised learning techniques produce rules that vary significantly in interpretability for human understanding. Decision tree-based technique such as Random Forests have readily interpretable rule logic, while neural networks-based techniques such as long short-term memory are highly obscure in the reasoning logic, and graph-based techniques such as Hidden Markov Model and Bayesian Belief Networks are in between. Machine learning technologies such as those in the DARPA Explainable AI program suit the mission well as they aim to produce more explainable models and enable human users to understand, appropriately trust, and effectively manage the emerging generations of artificially intelligent partners, while maintaining a high level of learning performance (accuracy) [23].

Depending on the intrusiveness of the restoration actions, the requirement on the machine learning performance varies. Some restoration actions have minimal service interruptions, such as clearing the cache content in a proxy server, while others may have to be exercised with extreme caution, such as rebooting an edge device where customers are single-homed. When tuning the desired operation point for closed-loop policy learning, operators need to determine the balance between potential false negatives (missing conditions where a restoration action should be applied) and potential false positives (unnecessary attempted restoration actions causing undesirable service impact). While such tuning can be initially provided by human operators based on domain knowledge, it is also conceivable that over time a separate machine learning intelligence can evaluate service performance impact of restoration actions and feed the result into closed-loop policy learning.

Treating human operators' restoration actions as training labels or ground truth may suffer from the label contamination problem, as human operators do not always take the "right" action. In many cases, operators have to explore different alternative actions using trial-and-error to resolve an issue. Machine learning-based intelligence should evaluate the effectiveness of the restoration actions to de-noise the training labels. For reactive closed loops, automated evaluation of the effectiveness of restoration actions may utilize the "reactive" assumption that the performed actions were aimed at clearing the triggering events or restoring a degradation in service quality, which is captured by KPIs. By monitoring the events and KPI time series before and after the actions, machine learning intelligence can infer the effectiveness of the actions, which helps further improve its learning performance [24].

A closed-loop policy may also be proactive, where a predictive signature is detected and a closed-loop action is taken before service impact is incurred. A memory leak can be addressed using a proactive closed-loop policy, where a process restart or migration action would prevent a potential system failure when memory utilization starts to approach the system limit. Machine learning for a proactive closed-loop policy can utilize the same class of supervised learning techniques as in reactive policy learning, with some desired lead time separating the feature conditions and the action or impact events. However, such early warning patterns do not always exist in operational environments, and it remains a challenge to quantify the effectiveness of actions, particularly quantifying the false positives—unnecessary actions taken where no system impact would happen.

The earlier discussion assumes that ONAP closed-loop policy learning is passively observing what actions human operators take in the network. However, in many situations, the human operators need to try out multiple actions before landing on an action that remediates a given issue. We can go a step further with machine learning and let the machine do this exploration of appropriate restoration actions. This takes us to an online machine learning model, where the learning system itself is continuously updating its knowledge based on active experiences exploring different actions in the network.

Adapting the closed-loop policies online is typically modeled as a reinforcement learning process (Chapter 2), which involves finding a balance between the exploration on assessing the effectiveness of different restoration actions and the exploitation of using known policies that have been acquired over time. While a human's comfort level for letting machine learning identify the right balance may grow over time as technologies mature, the journey may start with machine learning taking minimal to no exploration. As comfort levels grow, machine learning can automatically learn and adopt repair actions where there is high confidence that these are the appropriate actions. However, whenever the confidence level of taking a closed-loop restoration action is low and the cost associated with the action results in customer impact, machine learning would (at least initially) engage human operators through ticketing systems. After human operators act upon the tickets, machine learning analyzes the actions and results and evolves its closed-loop policies accordingly.

Thus, ONAP control loops as defined today leverage policies that define signatures (events to detect and correlations) and actions. However, machine learning can be advanced to a whole new level, where the machine learning simply monitors the incoming stream of data and then decides what actions to attempt—without explicit signature and action definitions.

Chronic issues are ones that keep reoccurring—these typically need to be identified and permanently eliminated, where possible. Long-term trending on different temporal, spatial, network function, software version and configuration aggregates of network and service performance metrics, and restoration actions being performed is needed to identify and troubleshoot such chronic issues. Such analysis can reveal software bugs in network functions, and even issues with customer devices that are impacting network and service level metrics. Consider, for example, our earlier scenario where ONAP reboots or migrates a VNF to avoid a predicted failure caused by a memory leak. Although the automation may be able to minimize or even hide the effects of this memory leak, if it is a regular issue, then the software should be fixed. As these issues are identified, network function and customer device vendors are engaged as appropriate to fix the software to provide permanent repairs.

9.4.3 Realizing Autonomous Network Administration

As discussed earlier, many traffic management controls are automated today—for example, networks automatically re-route traffic in response to failures. However, as self-adaptive networking protocols, elastic network functions—which can dynamically grow and shrink in size in response to changing traffic loads—and policy-enabled closed-loop automation become increasingly prevalent for automatically managing traffic, machine learning will be leveraged to enhance the parameter setting and to automatically learn policies (rules) in a similar fashion as described earlier for network maintenance. Offline (i.e., batched model adaption) and online (i.e., continuously model adaption) unsupervised and supervised learning techniques as well as active-exploration-incorporated online reinforcement learning techniques are applicable.

Machine learning is also key to enabling proactive traffic management—enabling the network automation to respond to impending traffic conditions before they arise. The key to proactive traffic management is the ability to predict traffic volumes and patterns. Machine learning technologies such as Argus [16] can be used to identify seasonal patterns and trends, such as how peak traffic demand varies across different days of the week and how it grows week by week. For short-term temporary increases in traffic, which can result from events in the physical word, such as a concert, or from events in the virtual world, such as the release of a new popular game, operators can leverage machine learning to derive the parameters of a traffic increase model at the beginning of the event. The network intelligence can then leverage the model to project the peak traffic demand in the hours/days to come. Based on this load prediction, the operator or network automation can adjust short-term capacity accordingly. Where short term spikes occur repeatedly over time—such as might occur at concert venues or sports arenas—machine learning will be used to learn the magnitude and distribution of the traffic for such events, thus enabling accurate predictions of required capacity for these events. This capacity can be proactively deployed and monitored—leveraging (automatically mined) calendars available for such locations to identify when events that may result in high traffic loads would occur, and the traffic load predictions to determine how much additional capacity would be required to service the increased traffic demand.

The rate at which natural disasters are occurring on our planet is increasing [25], and this impacts the frequency at which network operators need to respond to disasters. Network automation and AI help streamline the disaster management process, improving responses and reducing associated costs.

Much of the disaster planning and responses have historically been handled manually. However, AI and automation are increasingly being used to more effectively plan responses to disasters—for example, to determine where to predeploy equipment in advance of a disaster to enable faster recovery. Weather reports associated with impending storms and hurricanes can be intelligently combined with network and traffic data, historical failure data, and social data (e.g., map data that captures where hospitals and emergency responder centers are located) to predict the most effective locations to place equipment (e.g., generators for cell sites) in advance of an event. Such preplacement of equipment can significantly reduce the time required to deploy the equipment after the disaster, minimizing the time involved in recovering critical services. Advanced intelligence can also be used to prioritize restoration events after a disaster has occurred—again taking into consideration network and traffic data, along with social data (e.g., locations of hospitals and emergency responder centers). Machine learning and intelligent automation can also be used to prolong the availability of equipment during an outage—for example, intelligently putting carriers to sleep to conserve energy during a disaster to prolong the life of a battery and thus delaying the need for a generator dispatch.

As we drive toward a zero-touch network, ONAP can be leveraged to manage capacity and dispatches, and to deploy additional network capacity in disaster scenarios. The ONAP workflows will be responsible for determining when and where to deploy new capacity and will automatically monitor the customer impact of recovery actions using machine learning analytics [18] running on ONAP's DCAE.

9.4.4 Data Quality

All of the earlier network management tasks are fundamentally dependent on timely, good quality data. If data is missing, incomplete, or incorrect, then erroneous decisions, including intrusive network actions, could be triggered by ONAP, risking unnecessary customer impact or worse. Thus, it is imperative that we pay careful attention to data quality—rapidly detecting failed data feeds, detecting bad and missing data, and carefully designing analytics logic so as to effectively deal with missing, delayed, and erroneous data.

Much of the operations data leveraged for the tasks discussed in this chapter require near real-time data on which decisions are being made. For activities such as reactive maintenance in particular, establishing data feeds with low latency is key to achieving fast responses to network and service impairments.

Tackling data quality demands countermeasures from many fronts. Let's first start by considering data feeds—this is data that is flowing in, either as streams or as files to ONAP or equivalent. We need to be able to rapidly detect when one or more feeds fail, when feeds have been corrupted or are losing data, or when they are excessively delayed. This requires a feed management system that monitors the incoming data feeds, detects anomalous behavior (e.g., a drop below the normal volume of data associated with a feed) [16], and then executes repair actions. Repair actions should ideally be automated, just like with network control loops; human operators would be required where the automation falls out.

However, different data sources inherently arrive with different delays and have different levels of time aggregation. Some data sources are associated with points in time (e.g., a link going down), whilst others represent aggregates over time intervals (e.g., number of packets carried in a 15-minute interval). Correlation rules (policies) that join these different types of data are inherently challenging to manage, as we need to be able to specify how to deal with these different timings. Identifying when data is delayed to the point of being unusable, missing, or incorrect, is even more challenging.

In addition to monitoring data feed volume, we can also examine the contents of the data feeds. Changes in data formats can be automatically identified, flagged, and shared with applications that leverage the data so that they can adapt accordingly in processing the data. Similarly, data can be validated on the fly—for example, detecting values that are outside acceptable ranges (e.g., CPU that exceeds 100% or is less than 0%, throughput that exceeds capacity or is less than zero). Issues can be flagged and reported back to the application generating the data for longer-term restoration and to the application using the data to indicate that such values should not be used or used with caution.

Missing data can be most easily detected via sequence numbers—the sequence numbers need to be injected by the source application layer. However, where sequence numbers are not available—as is the case for most data sources today—complex inferences can sometimes be used to detect missing data. For example, where performance measurements are reported on roughly regular time intervals, missing data can be inferred by looking for intervals without reported measurements.

At data aggregation points where multiple data streams are processed to produce output data streams, such as event correlation and performance metrics computation, the analytics should be designed to expect delayed and missing data. As different inbound data streams may experience different delays, the analytics would most likely be required to wait for a period of time for the different data to arrive before calculating results. It is typically a design choice to strike a trade-off between the timeliness of the output data (as for time-sensitive applications such as event detection) and the completeness of the output data (as for accuracy-sensitive uses such as billing).

In places where computation and storage resources permit, an aggregator analytic may produce both a near real-time result, that is, with a short holding time based on data that it has in time, and a more accurate, delayed result as more data becomes available. Thus, applications that need to react very quickly leverage the less accurate, more timely aggregator result, whilst applications that require more accurate results must wait for the data to be available. In all cases, it is a good practice to include not only the aggregation result but also a data quality indicator associated with the result and propagate it to the downstream analytics (e.g., how many collector data streams was the output based on).

While each individual application should determine its desired trade-off between data latency and data completeness and accuracy, the overall data movement and analytics flow design bounds the minimum latency that applications can achieve. Moving from centralized data processing toward distributed data analytics and intelligence at the edge (local to where network or service data are collected and controls are actuated) would reduce the lower bound latency when ultra-real-time control is needed. In some cases, measurement data are "too big to copy," that is, it is undesirable to transmit the data over wide area networks either due to wasted bandwidth or prolonged data latency. A hybrid approach should be considered where edge processing through aggregation, anomaly or event detection, or intelligent sampling significantly reduces the volume of the data stream and a centralized intelligence makes further analytics and controls based on the reduced data stream.

Finally, on the application analytics side, it is important to explicitly represent and handle missing and erroneous data. A common mistake is to carelessly treat missing data as being a data value of zero, polluting the result and potentially wreaking havoc with the network. Similarly, data that is clearly erroneous, such as CPU values exceeding 100%

utilization or link utilization exceeding capacity, must be appropriately identified and handled (rounded or dropped entirely). Catching these data errors early on minimizes the so-called "garbage-in, garbage-out." Furthermore, depending on the application, it can be helpful to leverage robust analytics where applicable: using median statistics is less subjective to occasional erroneous data than mean statistics; using robust regression is a better alternative to least-squares regression when data are contaminated with outliers or influential observations.

9.4.5 Safe Policies

ONAP leverages policies to enable users to define how the system behaves. Policies are, for example, used to configure how the system instantiates VNFs (e.g., policies define where to place VNFs), how to schedule planned maintenance events, and control-loop signatures and actions. Thus, ONAP policies place tremendous power into the hands of users—eliminating custom development, thereby speeding responses to changing network conditions and reducing development costs.

However, with such power comes risk. Errors introduced in policies by network operators or malicious policies can cause tremendous harm, unless safeguards are put in place to override them. Even bad data combined with poorly authored policies risk causing harm. And as machine learning replaces explicit, human-defined policies in control loops and beyond, we need to make sure that this does not risk the network. ONAP leverages *safe policies* [10] to minimize the risk associated with human-defined and machine-learnt policies.

As with any new technology, policies and machine learning for control loops will need to be introduced with care into the network. Extensive testing and evaluation in lab environments is performed. However, lab environments and offline simulations cannot introduce the diversity, noise, and scale of production networks. New technologies are thus typically introduced incrementally into the production network—for example, as FFAs with limited scope (e.g., associated with a small number of network functions). Such technologies can also be introduced into parts of the network where they can have lesser impact should something go awry (e.g., at the network edge).

One example of technology that can be used to protect against bad policies is the policy guard [10]. As an analogy, guardrails on mountain highways are placed at the edge of the highway to provide protection against cars catapulting off the edge of a cliff. Under normal conditions, cars should not hit the guardrails. However, should a car spin out of control and hit the guardrail, the guardrail is designed to prevent a catastrophic outcome. Policy guards are similar; they are essentially overriding policies, which, when they detect a violation of an invariant condition (a condition that should always be true), prevent further relevant actions from being taken.

As an example, consider a policy guard that limits the number of network interfaces that can be shut down by the system at any given point in time. The guard policy can be specified according to Figure 9.8, which translates to saying that if the number of interfaces shut down at a given point in time exceeds a predefined threshold, T, then no more interfaces should be shut down until the condition has been resolved. This guard policy thus overrides all other system policies that are attempting to shut down interfaces.

If (Num_interfaces_shut_down > T) then
do not shut down more interfaces

FIGURE 9.8 Example guard policy.

If (interface utilization <= 100%)
shut down interface

FIGURE 9.9 Example "bad" policy.

Policy guards can be used to protect against errors from both human and AI or against malicious intent. For example, if an operator had either deliberately or erroneously entered into the system a policy, such as that defined in Figure 9.9, which effectively attempts to shut down all interfaces in the network, then the guard policy in Figure 9.8 would override it once the number of interfaces shut down has exceeded T, protecting the network infrastructure.

Considering control loops in particular, policy guards can also provide a level of protection as we evolve to autonomous control loops in which the system learns signatures and actions on its own without intermediate operator validation. Policy guards can limit what the autonomous learning can do, particularly limiting the rate of actions and the extent that actions operate on the network. This can provide network operators with a level of confidence as such cutting edge technology is deployed.

9.5 IMPACT ON OPERATIONS ROLES AND RESPONSIBILITIES

We now look beyond the technology and consider the effect that automation and AI has on the network operations teams.

9.5.1 Network Operations Structure and Roles

The network operations team's roles and structure have continually evolved over time, as technology has advanced and as network management tasks have become increasingly automated.

In a large service provider such as AT&T, with many diverse networks and technologies, operations teams have historically been organized according to roles and network technologies. There are teams who plan the network, technology-focused reliability centers that manage different network technologies and segments of the network, service management centers that manage end-to-end services (e.g., Internet and VPN services, voice service, and video/TV distribution), and field teams that work in central offices, customer premises, and in the community at large executing work that cannot be accomplished remotely.

The network maintenance team are tiered, with the level of skill and responsibility increasing with increasing tiers. Tier 1 responsibilities have largely been automated in service providers today and include executing tasks such as reviewing and storing log files, verifying port configurations, and verifying circuit connectivity. Tier 1 personnel have low levels of technical skill and require minimal domain knowledge. The Tier 2 organizations perform most of the network maintenance and administration work that is not already automated. Tier 2 technicians are more skilled than Tier 1; they are the primary teams responsible for routine planned and reactive maintenance and provide the first line of defense for network issues.

The Tier 3 organization provides both operations support and network and service operations design and planning. Tier 3 personnel are enlisted to assist in resolving complex network issues—issues that the Tier 2 team could not resolve on their own in a timely fashion. They perform the deep, technical forensics required to determine the root cause of complex network impairments, and they perform detailed post-issue analyses to create action plans that address any gaps revealed by major events. This team is also responsible for resolving chronic or systemic problems, partnering closely with the network function vendors as required. The Tier 3 team also works closely with the engineers that design network services and the network itself, particularly regarding the network management plan that defines how networks and services should be operated. In particular, Tier 3 personnel design and certify the complex procedures that are required for deploying new network technology, replacing network functions, and upgrading network software.

The Global Technology Operations Center (GTOC) is a single, site-redundant network operations center that provides an overall oversight and coordination function. Figure 9.10 depicts AT&T's GTOC. The GTOC manages outage escalations and provides operational oversight and coordination across the various technology-focused reliability centers, customer care, and external bodies such as the FCC. It is responsible for traffic management,

FIGURE 9.10   Global technology operations center (GTOC).

including responses to disasters and special events. It also serves as the single communications channel to internal senior leadership so that consistent and accurate information on network events reaches all stakeholders. In addition, the GTOC develops and maintains critical processes used across the entire operations organization.

9.5.2 The Changing Network Operations Role

Despite the fact that traffic volumes continue to grow exponentially, revenue growth for service providers does not follow the same curves. Thus, operations teams typically cannot be significantly expanded, even in the face of new services, new network and control technologies (e.g., introduction of VNFs) and the continual expansion in the number of network functions being managed.

The introduction of VNFs into the network changes the roles which operations teams perform. The operations role becomes more closely aligned to that of a traditional software company, such as Google or Facebook. However, there still remains a very strong role for networking expertise as the applications running on the "cloud" are network functions that provide networking capabilities and leverage networking protocols.

As automation continues to advance through ONAP and associated AI, lower operational tiers (Tier 1, Tier 2) will continue to be reduced. The ultimate vision of a zero-touch network eliminates these roles entirely—tasks previously performed by humans will be handled by ONAP and other automation. The introduction of network function virtualization is also reducing the need for onsite work forces and rapid, on-demand visits to central offices. However, the increased complexity and reliance on software drives an increase in Tier 3 skills, where personnel are required to perform sophisticated debugging of complex software-based issues. Depending on organizational structures, roles, and responsibilities, the operations teams may also have a greater need for advanced software skills and for policy developers who can use ONAP's policy interface to enable new automation.

As discussed earlier in the chapter, machine learning is expected to be increasingly used for learning policies that are leveraged in policy-based network automation platforms such as ONAP. Operators will need to be on a journey to work with the AI as it evolves—commencing in a parent role where the operator is responsible for policy authoring and workflow management, moving toward a mentorship role, where AI imitates and learns from human activities and decisions, and finally to a counselor role where human operators provide corrective guidance and feedback to the AI controls. Machines and humans will need to meet partway to make this journey—human network operators will need to become increasingly comfortable with machine learning and increasingly trust the machine, whilst machines need to provide humans with a level of understanding on what the machine learning and automation are spitting out to help gain that increasing level of comfort.

A natural progression for human operators to gain trust on machine learning-based intelligence is reflected in the three classes of use scenarios of machine learning technologies: (1) machine learning producing models and data to improve human's understanding of complex data, (2) machine learning presenting recommendations for human decision-making, and (3) machine learning realizing complete automation, bypassing human operators. An example of the first class of applications is operations ticket mining, which includes parsing and understanding both structured and unstructured data (such as the operators' notes in the tickets), generating statistics of common failure patterns or network elements, and determining the effectiveness and efficiency of different issue response procedures and actions. As operators gain insights from the machine learning-based ticket mining, their confidence in "consulting" machine learning for recommendations increases. Here, machine intelligence compares ongoing/given network tickets and identifies the response actions and procedures that are likely to successfully resolve the issue. These are provided to the network operators as recommendations; it is up to the human operator to decide whether to follow the recommendations (or not). Such a recommendation system is called an expert system. While the underlying technologies for expert systems may vary, ranging from rule-based decision logic to deep neural network-based intelligence, it is always helpful for the expert system to expose the factors that lead to the recommendation and the "confidence" score of the recommendations to human operators. Helping human operators to pass through their vetting process helps machine learning intelligence to evolve to the third application scenarios where machine learning-based decisions directly connect with the control platform to actuate control activities; human operators only need to occasionally inject some corrective feedbacks to the machine learning intelligence.

As AI and increasing network automation are introduced into the network, it is up to the network operations team to ensure that this automation is working effectively and as designed. This is typically achieved by carefully and incrementally rolling out the automation and judiciously monitoring the automation and its impact on the network. Advanced technology can also be leveraged first at the network edge, where any issues with the automation would most likely have significantly lesser impact and where the automation often provides greater operational and service performance improvement impact.

9.6 CONCLUSIONS

Network operations roles and responsibilities will continue to evolve as we advance toward the autonomous network vision. A rapid technology transformation is currently underway, with virtualization, machine learning, and policy-based SDN control technologies such as ONAP rapidly maturing and making inroads into scaled network deployments. The networking community and AI community need to work closely together to effectively forge forward to achieve the autonomous network vision.

In the following chapter, we delve into cybersecurity—an area that tightly relates to network operations.

ACKNOWLEDGMENTS

The authors wish to acknowledge Irene Shannon and Isaac Rodriguez for the insight and wisdom that they contributed to this chapter.

REFERENCES

1. D. Medhi and K. Ramasamy, *Network Routing: Algorithms, Protocols, and Architectures* (The Morgan Kaufmann Series in Networking), Morgan Kaufmann Publishers, San Francisco, CA, 2007.
2. https://en.wikipedia.org/wiki/Mobile_cell_sites
3. https://en.wikipedia.org/wiki/Mars_Exploration_Rover
4. https://www.onap.org/
5. R. White and E. Banks, *Computer Networking Problems and Solutions: An Innovative Approach to Building Resilient, Modem Networks,* Addison-Wesley Professional, Boston, MA, 2018.
6. A. Cichocki, H. A. Ansari, M. Rusinkiewicz, and D. Woelk, *Workflow and Process Automation: Concepts and Technology,* Springer Science & Business Media, New York, 2012.
7. S. Dharmapurikar, P. Krishnamurthy, T. Sproull, and J. Lockwood, Deep packet inspection using parallel Bloom filters, *Proceedings of the 11th Symposium on High Performance Interconnects,* IEEE, Stanford, CA, 2003, pp. 44–51.
8. K. Futamura, A. Karasaridis, E. Noel, P. Reeser, A. Sridharan, C. Johnson, and P. Velardo, vDNS closed-loop control: A framework for an elastic control plane service, *IEEE SDN-NFV Conference,* San Francisco, CA, November 2015.
9. F. Lopez-Pires and B. Baran, A virtual machine placement taxonomy, *Proceedings – 2015 IEEE/ACM 15th International Symposium on Cluster, Cloud, and Grid Computing, CCGrid 2015,* 2015. doi:10.1109/CCGrid.2015.15.
10. J. Donovan and K. Prabu (Ed.), *Building the Network of the Future: Getting Smarter, Faster, and More Flexible with a Software Centric Approach,* CRC Press, Boca Raton, FL, 2017.
11. M. Björklund, YANG - A data modeling language for the network configuration protocol (NETCONF), IETF. doi:10.17487/RFC6020.
12. A. Mahimkar, H. H. Song, Z. Ge, A. Shaikh, J. Wang, J. Yates, Y. Zhang, and J. Emmons, Detecting the performance impact of upgrades in large operational networks, *ACM SIGCOMM,* New Delhi, India, August 30–September 3, 2010.
13. A. Mahimkar, Z. Ge, J. Wang, J. Yates, Y. Zhang, J. Emmons, B. Huntley, and M. Stockert, Rapid detection of maintenance induced changes in service performance, *ACM CoNEXT,* Tokyo, Japan, December 6–9, 2011.
14. A. Mahimkar, Z. Ge, J. Yates, C. Hristov, V. Cordaro, S. Smith, J. Xu, and M. Stockert, Robust assessment of changes in cellular networks, *ACM CoNEXT,* Santa Barbara, CA, December 9–12, 2013.
15. A. Mahimkar, L. Qiu, Z. Ge, S. Puthenpura, N. Mir, and S. Ahuja, Automated test location selection for cellular network upgrades, *IEEE ICNP,* 2017.
16. H. Yan, A. Flavel, Z. Ge, A. Gerber, D. Massey, C. Papadopoulos, H. Shah, and J. Yates, Argus: End-to-end service anomaly detection and localization from an ISP's point of view, *INFOCOM,* Orlando, FL, March 25–30, 2012.
17. M. Hasan, B. Sugla, and R. Viswanathan, A conceptual framework for network management event correlation and filtering systems, *IFIP/IEEE International Symposium on Integrated Network Management,* Boston, MA, May 1999.
18. Z. Ge, M. Kosseifi, M. Osinski, H. Yan, and J. Yates, Method and apparatus for quantifying the customer impact of cell tower outages, U.S. patent 9426665.

19. S. Yang, H. Yan, Z. Ge, D. Wang, and J. Xu, Predictive impact analysis for designing a resilient cellular backhaul network, *Sigmetrics'18*, Irvine, CA, June 2018.

20. R. Agrawal, T. Imieliński, and A. Swami, Mining association rules between sets of items in large databases, *Proceedings of the 1993 ACM SIGMOD International Conference on Management of Data*, Washington, DC, May 26–28, 1993.

21. Y. Bengio, Learning deep architectures for AI, *Foundations and Trends in Machine Learning*, 2, 1–127, 2009.

22. C. W. J. Granger, Investigating causal relations by econometric models and cross-spectral methods, *Econometrica*, 37(3), 424–438, 1969.

23. Explainable Artificial Intelligence (XAI). DARPA. https://www.darpa.mil/program/explainable-artificial-intelligence

24. S. Deb, Z. Ge, S. Isukapalli, S. Puthenpura, S. Venkataraman, H. Yan and J. Yates, AESOP: Automatic policy learning for predicting and mitigating network service impairments, *KDD 2017*, Halifax, Canada, August 13–17, 2017.

25. United Nations Office for disaster risk reduction website. https://www.unisdr.org/we/inform/disaster-statistics

CHAPTER 10

Artificial Intelligence for Cybersecurity

Anestis Karasaridis, Brian Rexroad, and Pat Velardo

CONTENTS

10.1 INTRODUCTION

In this chapter, we will discuss some consideration for use of automation, machine learning (ML), and artificial intelligence (AI)—for example, neural networks (NN)—in the context of network security. We will describe challenges and technologies in combating cyberattacks and describe some examples where aggressive use of automation technology can be used to improve security capabilities in a software-defined network (SDN) environment. Opportunities exist in many areas, such as identity proofing, authentication, security policy management, security posture assessment, and threat analytics. It can be applied to improve scale of operations beyond human capacity, improve currency of security configuration, reduce problems due to errors, and reduce times for detection and responding to events. We will discuss more on these topics and others in the following sections.

10.1.1 What Is Network Security?

For this discussion "network security" is primarily focused on assuring the network itself is resistant to cyberattack. To some extent, network security may also assure that the network service is resilient and relatively impervious to attacks on routing or attempts to monitor network traffic. Network security can apply to networks provided by a service provider, for example, an Internet Service Provider (ISP). Or it could apply to an enterprise network provided by a business in a building, campus, or across multiple campuses. Figure 10.1 shows a general network reference model that helps to identify some of the infrastructure needed to provide network function. The illustration also introduces the notion of virtualized network functions (vNF). Virtualization or SDN provides some new security opportunities that will be discussed later. There are network functions of various types within the enterprise network, interfacing with the ISP, within the ISP, and within mobility network services. Each of these functions need to be protected from attack. Many of these functions can be virtualized.

The illustration also shows a "micro-perimeter" as a means to help provide security controls of the vNF. A micro-perimeter is a set of software-driven functions that help to protect the function [1]. Controls may include network policy controls, security compliance audit, encryption, activity data collection, and other security functions. Finally, there are security orchestration functions in the enterprise as well as the service provider. The security orchestration functions serve to manage the collective set of capabilities

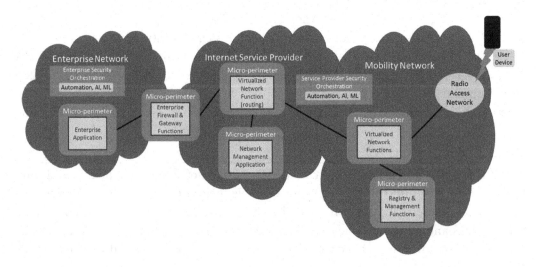

FIGURE 10.1 General network infrastructure model shows security controls moving closer to virtualized network functions (vNF) as well as enterprise applications.

across the respective entities in a cohesive and holistic manner. Since the security orchestration function is the primary means to manage security, it is useful to logically think of automation, AI, and ML functions as part of this function. There may be other supporting functions that have complex logic as well, but ultimately, they should probably be thought of as subordinate to security orchestration.

Network security does not intend to imply that users of the network, systems that use network services, or applications transiting traffic over the network will be impervious to some sort of cybersecurity attack. Things connected to a network can still be attacked, and only certain types of attacks can be identified through analysis of network activity. For example, if a user connects an infected USB device to a computer and infects the computer, there is little the network can do to protect that computer from attack. However, if that infected computer connects through the network to attack other computers, there are measures that the network can potentially do to help minimize the attack or prevent the attack from being successful. To do that, the network needs to know which traffic is attack traffic, and it needs to have the capability to selectively filter the bad traffic without unnecessarily disrupting the good traffic. These are some of the measures that become opportunities for applying AI for network security. The opportunities fit into the following categories:

1. Monitoring the configuration of many systems and the network to identify weak points and apply appropriate controls, which can minimize the attack profile.

2. Monitoring the impact and benefits of security controls to help minimize the burden of security controls on the network and applications.

3. Cumulatively learning a wide variety of attack scenarios and monitoring the network indications of threats and minimizing time to respond.

These are good fits for AI and ML, largely because they are complex and require significant scale and dynamics. As large complex networks are changing, the security configuration needs will need to change with it continually and dynamically. We will investigate more about this later.

10.1.2 Trends in Cyberthreats

The objective of this section is to help establish the need for more advanced methods to manage cybersecurity. Generally, the motives of cyberthreats are the following:

- Monetary gain: Cybercriminals have developed technology methods to steal and sell nearly anything of value in the cyberworld including electronic funds, retail purchasing, media content, credit cards, identity information, and online services. An entire ecosystem has developed with specializations in development of malware, data theft, reselling, laundering, and shipping. Distributed denial of service (DDoS) attacks (i.e., traffic flooding attacks), data theft, and system destruction are popular methods of extorting money from victims. Distributed denial of service attack services have become a commercial industry facilitating thousands of attacks worldwide on a daily basis for a fee.

- Political influence: Nation states as well as terrorist groups (or nations) can gain an advantage against adversaries by manipulating their media, manipulating elections [2], and gaining control of critical infrastructure. Of course, one of the critical infrastructures is telecommunications. In many cases, this becomes an asymmetrical threat since the cost to prevent successful attacks can be much greater than the investment needed to successfully conduct attacks.

- Nuisances: Some people hack for fun. While this is not the most formidable threat, it can have unexpected consequences. Some new attack methods are developed through independent experimentation.

The threat landscape is becoming increasingly more complex. As new attack technology and methods are developed, the old attack techniques do not go away. So long as humans are involved, there will be mistakes. So long as solutions are constrained by budgets, older systems may remain in service. Consequently, known vulnerabilities will exist and the older attack techniques will continue to be useful to attackers. This may not be the case in mainstream system or network operations. But there may be activities on the fringes of enterprises and networks that also need to be considered.

For businesses (including network service providers), breaches or outages are increasingly devastating as more automation is incorporated into business processes. Implications include:

- Operational impact and downtime

- Damage to brand reputation

- Lost revenue

- Lost customers and competitive advantage

For consumers of these services, this can have sustained effects if customers' private information is exposed.

As systems and software become increasingly complex, the frequency of vulnerabilities has also continually increased as illustrated in Figure 10.2. The growth of Internet-of-Things (IoT) (i.e., autonomous network connected devices) has its own set of ramifications on security:

- **IoT is being applied to all kinds of applications.** As of the writing of this book, it is nearly impossible to determine how the wide variety of applications of IoT translates into life or death situations, but many scenarios that are not obvious today most certainly will have an impact on life or death.

- **There is no longer a human at a monitor and keyboard to make good judgments** about what can happen. Remotely controlled things will act as they are commanded (right or wrong). Information will be provided by devices (right or wrong). We depend

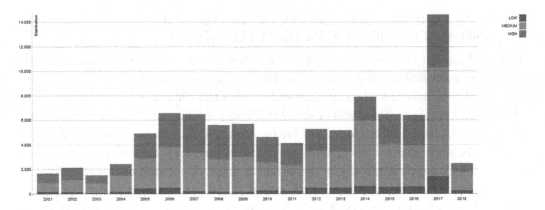

FIGURE 10.2   Common Vulnerability Scoring System (CVSS) vulnerabilities by year shows an increase in reported vulnerabilities over the years. (From National Institute of Standards and Technology, Gaithersburg, MD. https://nvd.nist.gov/general/visualizations/vulnerability-visualizations/cvss-severity-distribution-over-time#CVSSSeverityOverTime.)

on the security of devices (as well as good design decisions) to assure they can make the right decision at least most of the time. If devices are compromised, they are going to do what the attacker wants them to do.

- **IoT is changing the scaling parameters of networks.** While networks have generally been designed to accommodate byte capacity, now networks must be designed to accommodate the number of connected devices. The world is still in the infancy of understanding how small actions by many, many devices can affect the security of the network and the users. What happens if someone steals a little bit of information from a million places?

- **IoT devices are designed to be cheap (sometimes really, really cheap).** This cannot equate to weaker security. Therefore, the most efficient and effective means possible is needed to assure devices are secure. This is a significant challenge, and it needs to be a very high priority objective.

- Invariably, **massive amounts of devices will be found to have security problems**. There must be methods and tools to correct vulnerabilities, to block attacks, and remediate compromised devices. It is no longer sufficient to be able to remediate (or eliminate) the security issues or devices manually. There will need to be means to remediate issues automatically and potentially massively and very quickly.

Collectively, we have noted a variety and growing set of motivations to conduct cyberattacks, the threat landscape becoming cumulatively complex over time, growing implications for businesses that are victims of breaches, and a growing set of vulnerabilities with software and yet to be determined implications of IoT. These security demands cannot be tackled with conventional methods. Highly automated solutions need to be created to help improve and simplify security.

10.2 CONSIDERATIONS FOR ARTIFICIAL INTELLIGENCE AND AUTOMATION OF SECURITY FUNCTIONS

We have discussed the basic security problems that exist and established that they will need more automated solutions. In this section, we will focus on the foundation topics that should be considered when applying automation techniques, such as ML and AI to solve security problems. There will be many challenges to solve. In the current state of the art, the use of advanced techniques to solve problems requires some specialized skills on behalf of the implementers. These skills are relatively rare, and there are many problems to be solved. Consequently, it will be important to target opportunities that will have the most benefit for the least amount of technical risk. It will also be important to try to generalize solutions as much as possible, so they can be applied to a wide variety of needs with minimal change. For example, there are many types of security-related events that can be identified through some variation of volumetric anomaly detection, so perhaps a relatively generic form of detection that leverages ML and NN can be applied to a variety of situations with good results. The quest for a generic form of analysis is the holy grail in automated security. Meanwhile, the quest for variety and unexpected attack methods is the holy grail for attackers. As you might surmise from this, it is going to continue to be a difficult challenge.

10.2.1 Role of Software-Defined Networking

Software-defined networking [3,4] is the use of cloud computing technology to minimize the dependency on specialized hardware (see Chapter 3). By reducing dependency on hardware, network functions can be "virtualized" (i.e., run as software functions on commodity computer hardware). There are several advantages of this virtualization that relate to security:

1. **Security issues can be corrected quickly.** Since a generally common infrastructure is used instead of specialized hardware and software, many types of security issues can be corrected with software changes across the infrastructure in a relatively consistent manner. No longer are software patches specific to a unique model of networking equipment. Automated cloud management technology can be used.

2. **Security data acquisition can be modified.** Generally, it is difficult to predict the type of data that is needed to detect, quantify, characterize, investigate, and remediate attacks. This is particularly true if the attack has not been invented yet. There are generic data types that are useful, such as flow data, and access logs. However, invariably, there will be needs that we cannot anticipated in advance. Software-defined networking can allow modifications to vNFs more dynamically than a hardware appliance-based, infrastructure. Data acquisition can be accomplished through modification of existing vNFs. Alternatively, data acquisition functions can be accomplished through service-chaining [5] with functions that are designed specially to generate, collect, and analyze appropriate network activity data. For example, we introduced micro-perimeters in Figure 10.1. Micro-perimeters represent an example of a service chaining solution that

can help collect data and provide security controls for virtualized functions. Since the functions are virtualized, they can be inserted into the path of appropriate network activity when needed and removed when not needed through remote methods. If it isn't already obvious, it is impractical and undesirable to collect, store, and analyze all network activity. Software-defined networking provides an opportunity to be as efficient and effective as possible. This allows specific SDN data acquisition and analysis capabilities to become a differentiator between providers of network services. And the flexibility provides many opportunities that will be useful for closed-loop [6] (i.e., automated) control (see Chapter 3).

3. **Security controls can be changed.** As new security controls are needed to deal with specific types of network attack activity, new controls can be implemented as part of vNFs or (again) through service-chaining of specialized network functions. For example, it may be practical to segment certain protocols to a function that can filter for specific signatures of malicious traffic. Software-defined networks provide an opportunity to be as efficient and effective as possible by tailoring the processing function to the specific need at that time. This allows specific SDN control capabilities to become a differentiator between providers of network services.

Software-defined networks provide an important framework for greater automation in security controls [3]. SDN can be configured to generate the data needed to use AI and ML techniques as part of the security solutions. SDN also provides the means to programmatically control and adapt network and system capabilities in response to AI and ML direction. When we use automated methods to observe conditions and activity, compute corrective actions or adjustments, and introduce the changes without human intervention, this is sometimes referred to closed-loop control.

There are practical considerations as well. Changing vNFs can introduce changes in performance behaviors of the network functions. Adding new functions will consume likely more CPU resources or more memory resources. Service-chaining functions will likely introduce more latency and complexity to network flows. For these reasons, it is important to balance the value of introducing the security controls and consider whether there are other, more efficient methods to accomplish needed security goals. In other words, the network is an important part of good security, but the network may not be the best answer to all security problems.

10.2.2 Evolution of Enterprise Security Strategy

We have discussed the benefits of SDN as part of the network security solution. However, enterprises are transforming as well. In the legacy enterprise, most applications were hosted within enterprise data centers. Controls around the enterprise network perimeter were used to protect the applications from the Internet. And the communications with those applications to and from enterprise clients (e.g., employees) were confined to access within the enterprise network. Modern enterprises have become much more complex. Applications are hosted in partner networks. Applications are provided as hosted public

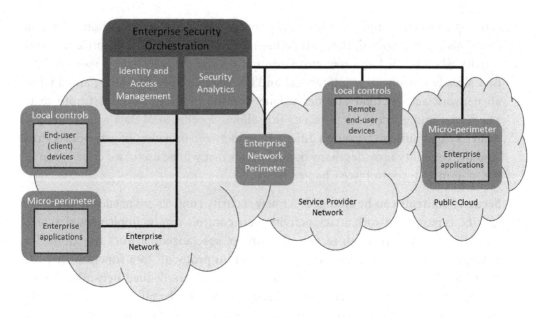

FIGURE 10.3 Security orchestration provides holistic management of security across enterprise assets.

cloud services on the Internet. Enterprise employees work remotely and use mobile devices to access enterprise applications, which translates to making enterprise applications accessible from the Internet. The structure and security approach for enterprises is forced to change to accommodate these changes in enterprise structure. Whereas there will continue likely to be a concept of an enterprise network for some time [7], the role and effectiveness of the enterprise network perimeter of the network continues to deprecate. General areas of emphasis to accommodate these changes are illustrated in Figure 10.3, which include:

- **Security Virtualization:** Security controls must move closer to the applications (a la micro-perimeter), to cloud infrastructure (a la micro-perimeter), into connected clients (e.g., anti-malware tools), and to the network (a la Software Defined Wide Area Network [SD-WAN]).

- **Strong authentication and access management** is necessary to control application access permissions regardless of where or how applications are hosted. Password-based access control is too susceptible to protect sensitive applications.

- **Security Analysis:** Security analysis is needed to holistically facilitate detection of risky security status and behavior (a la verify security controls are as expected and effective). It also serves to detect, investigate, and respond to threats across enterprise infrastructure, applications, and data assets. We have traditionally called this "threat analysis," but there are many opportunities to search network activity data to find security relevant activity that is not associated with a threat. For example, identifying and removing equipment on the network that is unknown by compliance systems is helpful to assure there are no unnecessary vulnerabilities.

- **Security Orchestration:** As the enterprise diversifies, the security controls in place also diversify. To manage security for the enterprise, a centralized set of security controls are needed to manage the security posture of the enterprise. This is often referred to as "security orchestration." For example, as micro-perimeter firewalls are introduced to protect applications, these controls need to be configured in conjunction with legacy enterprise firewalls and security controls in the cloud. This needs to be done consistently and dynamically to support the needs of businesses in conjunction with good security posture.

10.2.3 Motivations for Artificial Intelligence Automation in Security

Our primary objective is automation. Use of AI and ML are means to this end. Let's discuss some of the things we will want to look for in AI security automation opportunities.

1. **Scalability:** Some jobs can be done manually on an individual basis, but they do not scale effectively if there are thousands or millions of scenarios or instances to consider. For example, we previously discussed the need to be able to keep up with the new attacks that are being developed while at the same time keeping track of old attack methods. This is a scalability objective. We also noted the increase in IoT devices that will be connected to networks, that will increase the scale of security events and issues that may occur. There are also other types of scalability that will lead us to AI solutions. We will discuss this in terms of preventative security measures later.

2. **Talent Amplification:** It is well known in the industry that cybersecurity talent is at a premium. This is a fact that will remain for some time. And in the current state of the art, effective application of ML and AI technology remains a relatively focused discipline. In other words, we do not yet have the capability to use AI as a means to interpret new cybersecurity challenges and automatically determine appropriate ML technology to apply to specific needs. However, the use of available cybersecurity talent to help direct how and where to apply specific ML techniques is achievable. If applied effectively, this allows that talent to apply efforts to new problems without having to frequently resort to maintaining existing capabilities. We can amplify the capabilities of a few to solve and adapt to many more security challenges.

3. **Practical Complexity:** Some problems are simply too complex for typical humans to comprehend or solve. As a simple example, consider dimensions of a matrix. People are typically capable of comprehending a two-dimensional matrix and many can visualize three dimensions relatively well. Most humans are incapable of considering how tens or hundreds of dimensions translate to specific solutions. However, the use of directed ML can help develop reliable relationships to scenarios and help determine what attributes of data or dimensions are relevant without the need for human comprehension. When considering security problems such as malware analysis, it can be very difficult for a human to comprehend the many branches of activity and to recognize the coding techniques used by malware developers. This complexity lends itself to use of rules-based and perhaps cognitive analysis methods.

4. **Expediency:** There are limits to what can be done with humans because they can only work so fast. In some cybersecurity scenarios, expediency of response to an attack can be the difference between a nuisance and a major breach. It is important to act fast when responding to an incident. Systems that devise a response (at least a recommendation) have the potential to be much more expedient and comprehensive than depending on humans to collect, interpret, and analyze data—and subsequently craft pieces of a response. Automated methods for detection and response are frequently used to mitigate DDoS attacks. In most circumstances, attacks can be detected by measuring activity relative to normal and maximum capacity of the protected resource (e.g., a website). Mitigation can generally be performed by recognizing patterns in standard attack types and dropping packets that match that pattern. In cases like this, even a crude mitigation capability that is performed automatically and quickly has value. If the attack persists, it is then possible for humans to review the mitigation and adjust to any nuances in the attack activity for optimal service restoral.

5. **Accuracy:** Assuming a ML model is appropriately calibrated and can learn appropriate responses to a given scenario, it will at least behave **consistently**. Humans on the other hand are prone to errors. This is especially true in cases where humans have had only limited opportunity to practice. The capability of humans is dependent on the knowledge, experience, and skills of each individual. And there is only limited capability (through training) to transfer knowledge from one human to another. This is particularly important for security, as actual targeted attacks may be quite rare. A given person may only encounter a particular type of threat a handful of times. If a machine is taught a response, it will remember that response and will tend to execute that response consistently—even if it is the incorrect response.

As you can see, there are plenty of motivators for using advanced automation methods to solve security problems. As we select candidate activities for applying the automation, it will be beneficial to understand what advantages will come from the effort.

10.2.4 Considerations for Driving of Artificial Intelligence Automation Opportunities

The following additional and somewhat random considerations may be helpful to establish practical security automation activities:

1. **Routine should never be routine:** Any time security practitioners are performing routine activities, this is an obvious opportunity to consider how automation can be introduced. Look at the activities your team is performing most and consider what aspects of those activities are similar on a day-to-day basis. With the maturation of AI technology, the scope of candidate activities that can be considered for automation can expand. No longer is it necessary to define specific rules or procedures for performing automation.

   For example, anytime an alert is generated by a system that needs validation or more investigation, there are relatively standard steps that an analyst is going to perform.

The objective of the analyst will be to determine if the event is a true-positive (i.e., assure there is really a security event that requires response), develop an interpretation of what is happening, determine whether more investigation is needed, and determine the appropriate response. The analyst will start by gathering information about the potential target and source of the attack prior and after the detected event(s). Further contextual information will be gathered. And the information will be interpreted for additional leads. These steps (to a point) are relatively standard and can be performed by the system automatically and immediately upon detection of an alert. The process can continue to monitor and report on the target and source. Rules-based analysis in conjunction with cognitive ML can be used to help develop an interpretation. The capability can also evolve to recommend and perhaps initiate responses. All of these things can save significant labor, improve accuracy of response, and perhaps most important, improve expediency of response. Most standard detection and response processes can be automated. This allows security practitioners to focus on the more complex activities as well as development of new types of capability.

2. **Attackers are creative, AND they are good at automation:** As we have discussed previously, attackers are continuously developing new attack techniques. Attackers have also proven to persistently evolve the capabilities of their attack tools. For example, it is common to see new malware that exercises one exploit method to gain access to escalate privileges on a system. As the malware matures, the malware developer(s) continually evolve the malware to incorporate, prioritize, and exercise new exploit methods. Most exploits today are automated, where networks are scanned for potential vulnerable systems, potential targets are profiled for weakness, an appropriate exploit is conducted. After that, foothold is established by automatically loading command and control malware. The target system may be profiled for capability (e.g., memory, storage, interesting software tools, data), which is reported back to the attacker. All of this happens in seconds and can recruit thousands of devices into a botnet within hours. There are only rare circumstances where attackers revolutionize attack strategies. Generally, they are making small incremental changes and improvements over time—improving what they know already works. Organizations that are automating security protection functions can benefit from following the lead of the attackers. Continuously seek opportunities to automate. Consider new tools to facilitate automation. Start by solving small and simple problems and grow in complexity over time. Continue to improve the level of automation in solutions. Never stop automating.

3. **Workers will tend to have limited domain knowledge:** Generally, **security** practitioners will be knowledgeable in cybersecurity topics and will practice cyber-security. That does not mean they are necessarily knowledgeable in ML, AI, or even programming skills. Similarly, personnel who are knowledgeable in programming, ML, and/or AI are not likely to be security experts. Each of these areas of technology are highly complex and involve a significant amount of effort to learn sufficiently. Further, it is not unusual for organizations to be biased in their hiring practices and neglect the need for diversity in workforce skills.

For example, a hiring manager in a security organization might have significant experience and knowledge in security. They will tend to identify with others who have similar background and skills. Deliberate effort is needed to assure organizations develop appropriate skills diversity and include data science and software engineering candidates to work alongside security practitioners. Recall the previous consideration where we need to never stop automating. These new roles and activities are permanent and should not be treated as consulting activities.

4. **Machines don't know everything:** At least not yet. It is important to study the details of how decisions are made when attempting to automate activities. This is especially important when attempting to use advanced automation such as cognitive AI to make decisions. In some circumstances, AI can help to identify characteristics that are not immediately noticeable to humans.

   For example, it may be readily possible for AI to recognize network packet characteristics that are invalid and can be considered for blocking. However, the opposite situation is often the case as well. Determining that the invalid packets are part of an attack can be much more difficult to determine through analysis of the data. It is often necessary to use other data sets and information to conclude the cause of the situation and the level of threat it presents. Because some conventional analysis steps are manual, it allows humans to go to other systems for information, make phone calls, and interview other people. This leads to a need for security analysis systems that are applying AI. These systems may need to collect a much broader set of information to aid in the automated diagnosis of events. It may be necessary to have system configuration data, system owner information, vulnerability data, and exploit information available to help make more conclusive decisions. This does not necessarily mean that security analysis systems need to collect all data all the time, but they may need a very broad set of information to be available on an as needed basis.

5. **Expert attackers don't create big anomalies:** We need to recognize that there is a wide spectrum of attack types that exist for a variety of motivations. Some attackers intentionally grab attention. Some attackers go through great lengths to avoid being caught. We should avoid the temptation to over generalize attacks and the methods needed to effectively detect the variety of attacks that exist. Further, we need to expect that highly sophisticated advanced attacks are deliberately designed to look like normal activity and may be practically impossible to detect through activity analysis. This suggests that the best method may be to prevent attacks from being successful rather than attempting to detect and respond to attacks. Focus on prevention first. And consider a wide variety of integrity checks in infrastructure as cooperative and complementary to activity analysis.

   For example, the holy grail of an attacker is to gain access to the user credentials (username and password) of a legitimate user on a system, and to gain access to systems that are exposed to the Internet via remote access protocols such as secure shell (SSH) or remote desktop protocol (RDP). With these capabilities in hand, it is very easy for an attacker to look like a legitimate user. No intrusion detection system will detect an exploit. With a little care, no network activity anomaly will be triggered. How does one protect against threats like this? Tools like two-factor authentication, limiting access from the Internet—for example, restricting access to needed Internet protocol (IP) address space—can prevent an attacker from stealing and using legitimate credentials respectively. Integrity checks within systems can help identify changes or activities within systems that are inconsistent with expected use. Machine learning can be used to profile the normal access points (source IP addresses) for users, and this can be used to help create more restricted and safer access policies, thus denying attacker access. Machine learning can be used to profile the normal configuration of systems, which can help flag changes that are outside normal. Neither of these types of profiling would be practical for hundreds of thousands of systems without significant automation.

6. **Attackers have an objective to be subversive:** As we strive to automate security and implement closed-loop controls (i.e., automated implementation of security controls), it is undesirable for an attacker to be able to use closed-loop security controls to achieve their own goals. Attackers may attempt to intentionally create activity that appears to be attack activity to activate closed-loop counter measures and thus cause impact to legitimate activity. Conversely, attackers may attempt to use a subtle and long-term attack-like activity with a goal of training attack detection tools to accept attack activities as normal activity. Use of AI and ML techniques need to take this into consideration. Is it possible for an adversary to train the system to accept the malicious behavior as normal? What are the countermeasures for this?

For example, if a solution is intended to block malicious activity upon detection of that activity, an attacker might inject activity into the "normal" activity stream that intentionally looks like malicious activity. The object might cause the closed-loop automation to block the malicious activity but also block legitimate activity. This can result in a disruption in normal service.

It is interesting to note that this consideration is not only applicable to security controls. An attacker might manipulate normal performance indicators to create a desired result. For example, if an attacker can create an illusion that vNFs are under heavy load (even if they are not), a closed-loop response might cause more resources to be allocated to this function. Since there are only a finite amount of resources available, the closed-loop operation may be forced to manage priorities and disable some ancillary functions in favor of avoiding service disruption. Perhaps one of those ancillary functions is fraud detection, usage accounting, or threat detection.

10.2.5 General Implementation Methodology

Agility in security applications is critical to success. There is only limited benefit to security controls that lag significantly behind the technology that threat actors have at their disposal. Therefore, the processes used to develop security protection technology need to

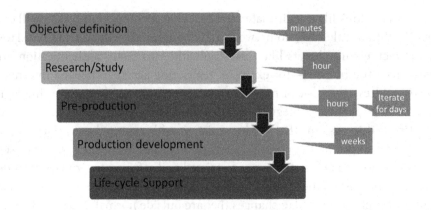

FIGURE 10.4   General process for rapid implementation and adoption of new security technology.

be able to adapt quickly and effectively to new situations. The illustration in Figure 10.4 is a model that can be used to help rapidly implement solutions—particularly in the context of threat analysis.

The objective of the process is to get new security functionality into a usable state as soon as possible. It consists of the following steps:

- Objective Definition: This step is to define a need or requirement. For example, suppose new exploit method has been identified, and there is a need to detect attempts to use the exploit. The objective statement may hypothesize what relevant data would be used to detect it, the general method that would be used, what is intended to be done if the exploit is detected, and how the results of analysis should be presented. In an urgent situation, the process to develop and objective may take only minutes. It does not need to be formal, but there needs to be an objective in mind.

- Research/Study: The purpose of a research study is to determine how viable the objective statement really is. It is a one-off analysis—prior to coding any automated solution. It is usually helpful to start with a known sample set of data for study. This data should include nominal activity data as well as data that represents the type of activity that needs to be identified. Typically, actual "labeled" data is not available, so it may not be possible to fully verify that the detection method will work. It may be necessary to synthesize data to verify detection. A study using nominal data can also help to determine if there will be many false positive detections (i.e., alerts that do not represent the actual exploit). If there are too many false positives, the detection method will need to be refined or revised. In an urgent situation, the study may be performed in a matter of hours. However, for more general problems, larger data sets and more studies may be needed. This may require weeks of effort.

- Pre-production: Once a successful study has been conducted, the next step is to code the solution in a skunk-works manner. The solution may not be polished or nicely formatted. But it may prove to be useful. This step is very much akin to a typical agile development process where the objective is to prove the solution early (or fail early).

Further, the objective here is to get the solution into actual use with real data. It may be a matter of reproducing the one-off study in repeated small batches and generating periodic output reports for inspection. In many cases, we have successfully implemented new detection capabilities in a matter of hours and are able to monitor for new threats on a 24 × 7 basis with relative confidence that we are able to detect and respond to the threat.

A pre-production solution may remain in operation for days, weeks, or perhaps months depending on need. Adjustments and improvements may be performed along the way to further refine the solution. In the meantime, if desired, the full-production solution can be engineered to accommodate long-term operational needs.

- Production Development: Based upon the pre-production solution, requirements for a production solution can be much better understood. There are always opportunities for improvement (e.g., more real-time results, improved granularity in the analysis, self-adjusting thresholds, collection of supplemental details, and refinements to minimize false-positives, more reliable operation). Perhaps some of the code from the pre-production solution can be reused in the production solution.

- Life-Cycle Support: Any solution that is put into place requires life-cycle support to remain viable. This is particularly true with threat detection solutions, where new variations on the exploits are added or adjusted in the attacks. The algorithm/methods for detection must also adjust to accommodate the changes. The operating environment also changes with time. New legitimate applications may introduce false-positive detections. If the production solution is designed well, the methods will be general enough to accurately detect new variations of attack. However, this cannot always be the case.

10.3 EXAMPLES OF MACHINE LEARNING AND ARTIFICIAL INTELLIGENCE IN SECURITY

10.3.1 Preventative Controls Based on Normal Application Behavior Modeling

For this example, we will focus on network security policy controls. Generally, there seems to be a tendency to apply ML to identify threats (a la look for behavior of bad guys). Indeed, we will discuss the application of ML in looking for threats (a la threat analytics). However, any security program should emphasize methods to prevent attacks from being successful in the first place.

One way to prevent threats is by allowing the things that are desirable to happen with applications and using layers of controls (e.g., firewall rules, user access permissions, file permissions, accessible software features) to help block the things that are undesirable. The concept of establishing firewall rules that are as restrictive as possible without inhibiting the function of applications is commonly recognized best practice for security. However, growth of development abstractions, plug-in tools, and complex development libraries have isolated application developers from the network functions. Consequently, application developers do not know which ports, protocols, and address are needed to make their application operate. Consequently, something as basic as firewall rules generally are not well crafted to be as restrictive as possible. With thousands of applications in an enterprise and interactions between applications, it is an impossible task for firewall administrators to effectively manage firewall rules in the most restricted way possible. Recall our discussion on security virtualization, where we have an opportunity to apply firewalls in microperimeters around individuals' workloads in the enterprise and in network infrastructure. There will be thousands (perhaps hundreds of thousands) of available micro-perimeters to configure. This further creates a scaling challenge, which is an opportunity for ML to aid in observing behavior, formulating control, and establishing controls that are based on normal behavior of applications.

We stated earlier that an important characteristic for the use of ML is to have observable data to learn from. Characterizing normal behavior of applications is (or at least should be) the most common activity that is available to observe. The best opportunity for the use of ML is to profile normal behavior for applications, formulate and implement preventative controls, and minimize the need to detect and respond to threats.

Normal application behavior is much more observable, which is a critical component of ML. Observation of common threats may be observable, but advanced threats are not readily observable. Expecting a machine to understand and expect an advanced threat is tenuous and risky. It is impossible to predict when a new bad guy will show up and what that bad guy will attempt to do. However, it is possible to "learn" what is normal behavior for an application, system, or network.

Machine learning should be applied to define what is normal behavior for systems and using that information to **tighten the allowed operating rules of systems** (block unneeded ports, control permitted IP addresses to/from, identify accepted packet content patterns, apply volumetric limits, restrict running processes, flag deviations for validation).

There are nuances to this concept. For example:

1. There is invariably "normal" abuse activity in any system—especially if it is exposed to the Internet. In other words, systems are always under attack (e.g., log-in prompts will be subjected to password guessing). The "normally bad" activity should not be included in the model for acceptable.

2. There will be exception cases that are valid operational scenarios for a system (e.g., sales volume will be higher in the holiday season). A good definition of acceptable should account for acceptable differences from normal behavior.

The question becomes, can we make ML processes that are smart enough to filter out the "normally bad" and allow the "abnormally valid"? This is an easier problem than attempting to predict the new attack or detecting an exploit of an unknown vulnerability (zero day).

Characterizing normal behavior for automated applications is likely much more predictable than characterizing normal behavior for human behavior. Humans (and the activities they need to perform) are less predictable and will change outside normal configuration management controls.

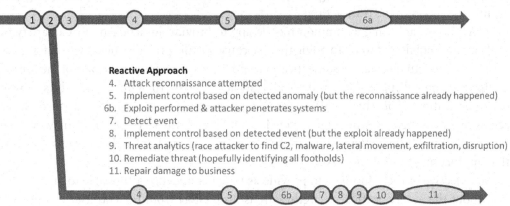

1. Application defined & created (with unknown flaws)
2. Activity to/from application profiled with machine learning (define normal)

Preventative Approach
3. Policy controls implemented (block unnecessary accesses to enforce normal)
4. Attack reconnaissance attempted (countered by policy controls)
5. Exploit attempted (countered by policy controls)
6a. Life-cycle analytics for validating adjustments to allowed policy

Reactive Approach
4. Attack reconnaissance attempted
5. Implement control based on detected anomaly (but the reconnaissance already happened)
6b. Exploit performed & attacker penetrates systems
7. Detect event
8. Implement control based on detected event (but the exploit already happened)
9. Threat analytics (race attacker to find C2, malware, lateral movement, exfiltration, disruption)
10. Remediate threat (hopefully identifying all footholds)
11. Repair damage to business

FIGURE 10.5   Preventative approach has fewer steps is less complex, does not force responders to race the attacker, and has less impact on business.

Figure 10.5 presents two comparative timelines that consider a preventative approach and a reactive approach to security. This is intended to further reinforce the earlier discussion. In particular, the timeline in a reactive approach is dictated by the attacker, which is undesirable. Further, the amount of work needed to protect against a threat is much less when using a preventative approach.

The fundamental difference in the two is when policy controls are implemented in the solution. In the reactive approach, we are racing the clock to block an undesirable event that may already have happened. In the preventative approach, the policy controls are applied as soon as the "normal" behavior is identified. Improving protection is much better than waiting for a threat to find holes in the protection. Subsequently, threat behavior should be blocked inherently.

10.3.2 Dynamic Authentication Confidence (Risk-Based Authentication)

Dependence on passwords as the primary basis for authentication is a source of many security compromises. Phishing attacks, social engineering, system breaches, and other methods are routinely used by attackers to collect user ID and password information, Credential "stuffing" is used to see if passwords captured from one account are also used on another accounts by the same user [8]. There is a need toward multifactor authentication, where user credentials cannot be compromised simply through phishing sites, keyboard logger malware, or social engineering. It is generally desirable to verify a user based on something they have (e.g., a device), something they know (e.g., a password), and ideally include something they "are" (e.g., biometrics). However, most methods tend to create a greater burden on users since users generally need to take additional steps to authenticate.

There is an industry concept called "risk-based authentication" that is emerging. With the aid of rules-based solutions in combination with ML, it will be possible to perform dynamic risk management. The objective is to minimize the burden on users when performing transactions by assessing the authentication status of the user and balancing that against the stakes of the transactions.

At AT&T, we are using a common mobile app to provide authentication to a variety of applications (mobile and web). In doing this, we can generally provide single sign-on for users with high-strength multifactor authentication, and little to no effort on the part of the users.

However, not all applications and not all transactions have the same needs. The strength of authentication to view personalized weather information may not need to be as robust as access to a banking app, which may allow large financial transactions. There may even be the possibility of different levels in a single app (e.g., viewing a bank balance is less sensitive than performing funds transfers).

An objective of the solution is to provide as much confidence as possible to an application about the authentication strength with as little effort from the end user as possible. This may include considering things like recent mobile device account changes, device location, time since actively authenticating, other factors, and perhaps even feedback from applications that suggest a problem may have occurred. The objective is to provide a centralized authentication function that takes advantage of the binding relationship between mobile devices and the network, minimizes special action by users, and allows applications to be in control of their own destiny relative to authentication risk.

This does not need to be limited to mobile applications only. It will be possible to use this solution to authenticate to web applications on other devices (e.g., a laptop) as well. For example, if we consider a standard single sign-on process that is used for typical web applications, the process might be like this:

1. User visits a single sign-on enabled website and is prompted to login.

2. User select(s) the mobile-app authentication option from the single sign-on prompt (which can be a memorized option).

3. User enters user ID into a single sign-on prompt (which may also be memorized) and submits.

4. The single sign-on application prompts the mobile app (on the user's mobile device) with an authentication request and specifies a minimum required confidence.

5. The mobile authentication app responds back to the single sign-on application with an authentication result and measured confidence.

6. Assuming success, authentication success message is presented.

7. User proceeds to application.

This may look like a lot of steps, but the user doesn't need to do much, and won't need to enter a password. They may just touch (or look at) their mobile device to verify

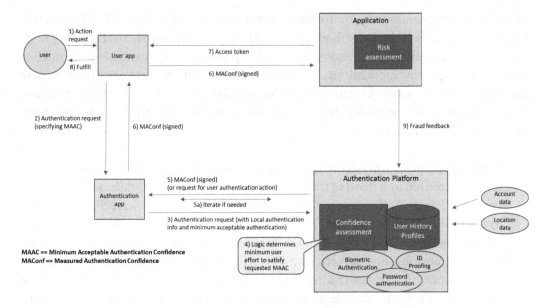

FIGURE 10.6 Authentication risk management allows use of a mobile device to minimize the effort on behalf of the user while establishing necessary authentication confidence.

possession, and the result is a high confidence, multifactor authentication that is very difficult for attackers to defeat. Credentials cannot be social engineered or phished. Users will get immediate notification anytime someone attempts to access their account.

There is an opportunity for AI here as well. The steps in an authentication process are illustrated in Figure 10.6. As authentication activities take place, and as applications provide feedback on potential issues with user accounts, the methods required to authenticate to applications can be ratcheted upward for users that appear to be at risk. For example, did an application report a suspicious event? Is the device located in an unusual place? The mobile authentication app should be able to dynamically prompt the user for more information to assure the correct person is in possession of their device and the needed authentication confidence is satisfied.

10.4 APPLICATIONS IN THREAT ANALYTICS

10.4.1 Generalized Network Anomaly Detection

Use of anomaly detection on networks is a popular trend. A search on the phrase "network behavior anomaly detection" reveals this. We at AT&T have had good success using ML to develop baseline references for many attributes of network activity and to detect anomalies on networks. This is used as a means detect events that might have impact to services that AT&T provides to customers. Early detection is the first step to rapid correction and minimal impact to service. This sounds relatively easy, but it can be complex to detect events that are relevant since the network is continually evolving. Routes change, systems change, user demographics change, and applications change. It is not sufficient to simply detect anomalies. Relevant anomalies must be detected among the many parameters or attributes of network activity (e.g., byte volume, ratio of flows/connection to bytes, volume of activity on specific ports). Useful interpretations of the anomalies are necessary to devise appropriate responses. Most anomalies are normal (e.g., new applications are created, routing on the network changes, new customers join the network). However, there are certain types of anomalies that are security relevant and are readily detected as well as interpreted with anomaly detection. Examples of these include:

- Distributed Denial of Service Attacks: There are many types of DDoS attacks, but most are characterized by a flood of traffic toward one or more target addresses from many source addresses. Different types of attacks manifest in different ways. For example, a Transmission Control Protocol (TCP) SYN attack, which is a flood of TCP SYN packets with no connection follow-through, is generally notable as many, many flows with very few (often just one packet), with SYN flag set and only 40 bytes of traffic. There are variations on this, but this relatively simple set of rules can isolate SYN attacks most of the time. An example of such a detection is illustrated in Figure 10.7. There are many other types of DDoS attacks that can be identified with similar types of rules. However, there are new attack variations developing all the time as attackers attempt to create attack methods that are not automatically characterized and/or are more difficult to mitigate (i.e., drop attack packets and pass good packets).

- Worm and Botnet Detection: Generally, worms are characterized by a growing number of source IP addresses that are scanning the network on one or more specific IP protocols and/or ports. The objective is to find vulnerable target hosts to infect and enlist in the search for more vulnerable target hosts. This analysis requires detection of patterns of activity that are indicative of scanning activity (i.e., a source IP address that is

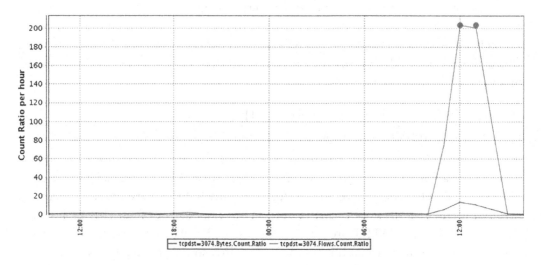

FIGURE 10.7 The change in ratio of flows associated with a DDoS SYN attack shows most prominently in the graph whereas an increase in the ratio of bytes relative to normal is notable but less prominent. The dots at the top of the graph represent alarms generated by the anomaly.

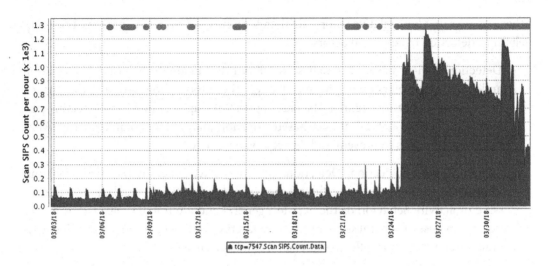

FIGURE 10.8 Detection of botnet activity targeting port 7547/tcp (CPE WAN Management Protocol). The graph shows the number of unique source IP addresses scanning on the port. Markers across the top of the graph indicate alarms generated by the anomalies.

attempting many connections to many, many different target IP addresses). Based on detection of scan activity, anomaly detection is used to identify changes in the number of scanning sources over time. Generally, increases in the number of sources scanning over time is indicative of an Internet worm. If the increase in unique source addresses is abrupt, this is generally indicative of botnet activity. An example is illustrated in Figure 10.8, where an abrupt increase in the number of sources scanning port 7547/tcp is indicative of a botnet attempting to enlist vulnerable Internet Customer Premise Equipment (CPE) such as Digital Subscriber Line (DSL) modems, into the botnet.

For these events, interpretation is important. Detecting DDoS attacks is not all that difficult or notable. Isolating characteristics that are anomalous and can be used to help mitigate the attack in the network is the true value proposition. For each of the alarms in the earlier examples, a full set of "post detection analysis" details are published to help provide an interpretation of the event and to identify specific entities (source addresses, target addresses, ports, protocols, counts) that can help with formulating response. However, this represents some new opportunity for advanced automation. It is desirable to have the interpretation generated more automatically as new variations on threats are detected. This can perhaps be performed through human-directed ML. Or perhaps some cognitive analysis can be used to associate known vulnerabilities or exploit publications with detected activities.

Generally, detection of advanced actors using exclusively behavioral analysis detection network level has been unsuccessful. There are some suggestive signs of advanced actor attacks (e.g., detection of large data transfers, periodic check-in activity, or very long flows of activity). However, there are many, many legitimate network activities that share these same characteristics. After all, what makes advanced actors "advanced" is their ability to behave in ways that look relatively normal. Therefore, two additional factors have been very helpful in detection of advanced actors:

- Detection of Host-Based Anomalies: Recall our discussion on security virtualization and micro-perimeters earlier in this chapter. These tools allow profiling the normal behavior of applications (and hosts that support those applications) and detecting patterns that are unusual. Local host-based behavior analysis can complement network behavioral analysis to prevent and detect advanced actors.

- Signature-Based Detection: Detection signatures have generally had two problems. They tend to be either two specific and can be easily bypassed by small changes in malware or activity behavior, or they are too general and are fraught with false-positive detections. Use of general signatures in conjunction with behavioral patterns has generally been much more effective at detecting advanced actors.

As you can imagine from this discussion, there are a few things that are somewhat challenging in this strategy so far:

1. Many Attributes: One must determine what attributes are most useful for detecting security relevant events in network activity, given the many attributes that are available, the number of combinations of attributes that could be measured, and the types of anomalies that might manifest in security relevant event detection. As we introduce specific patterns of activity (e.g., periodic check-in, scanning activity), the number of available attributes expands further. We discussed a few types of attributes, but there are literally thousands, which is much too many for humans to effectively evaluate.

2. Context Matters: The vantage point on a network changes how anomalies should be interpreted and how sensitive the detection likely should be. For example, any scanning activity in and of itself within an enterprise network should be noted. However, it is regular practice for researchers, would-be attackers, and botnets to scan on the Internet. In fact, there is still a reasonable amount of noise on the Internet associated with the Conficker worm, which dates back to 2008. Analysis methods need to accommodate these differences.

3. Signatures Are Labor Intensive: While useful, development and maintenance of relevant signatures is difficult and labor intensive. It will be beneficial if we can reduce the need for good signatures through improved context awareness and behavioral analysis.

This suggests it is desirable to create more generalized analysis that can be applied to a variety of data sets with minimal modification (e.g., firewall logs, proxy logs, authentication logs, flow data) in multiple contexts, and to have the analysis adapt to the needs of the environment.

Figure 10.9 introduces a general functional model for network anomaly detection that can potentially be applied to a broad set of contexts.

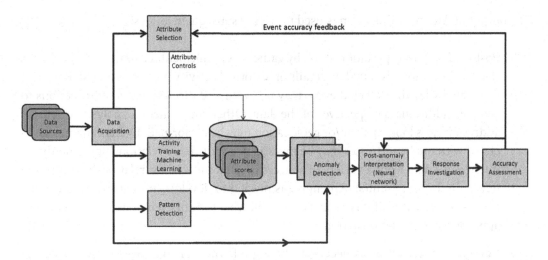

FIGURE 10.9   General application of machine learning and artificial intelligence to threat analysis.

Once data is acquired through Data Acquisition on the left of the illustration, there are four parallel paths the data feeds to:

- Attribute Selection is a non-real-time path. It assesses the data that is available and selects attributes that are likely to be relevant to security. There may be some experimentation involved to determine if new attributes are complementary to existing knowledge of security events. Important to this function is the feedback path from Accuracy Assessment, which helps to indicate true-positives (i.e., good detection), false-positives (i.e., bad detections), and false-negatives (i.e., missed detections). Accuracy assessment may initially need to be primarily fed by humans or associated with trouble ticketing. Other contextual information may be provided to help Attribute Selection make its decisions (e.g., information about applications, infrastructure and their address assignments).

- Activity Training: Based on attributes that are identified by Attribute Selection, Activity Training is used to generate profiles of activity for relevant attributes. For example, it may be necessary to track the amount of byte traffic on per-minute intervals associated with a group of addresses on specific ports. The output of this will be profiles or Attribute Scores that will be stored for comparison with future activity.

- Pattern Detection: We discussed some patterns earlier that are helpful to detect events. For example, patterns of scanning activity are useful. They are not signatures, but they are strong behavioral indicators. These too are recorded as Attribute Scores for baselining and anomaly detection.

- Anomaly Detection: Current data activity is fed into an anomaly detection engine that compares current activity relative to prior activity that is recorded in the Attribute Scores data. Anomalies are noted.

The output of Anomaly Detection is used to trigger subsequent analysis.

- Post Anomaly Interpretation starts by gathering supplemental details associated with the detected anomaly. Further details of historical activity may be gathered. Raw data associated with the detected event may be sliced and diced in different directions to generate additional perspectives of the data. Other supplemental analysis such as IP address WhoIs look-ups and/or geolocation may be performed. Domain names associated with the IP addresses may be investigated for further relationships. And threat intelligence data from a variety of sources may be checked for relationships with the newly discovered event(s). An engine is needed to develop an interpretation of each event—to determine if it is security relevant, what type of event it is, and recommend appropriate remediation actions.

- Response Investigation is needed to help guide the learning process. Given we are attempting to create something that is general and will know little about the context and environment to start, there will need to be further investigation into events to guide the learning process.

- Accuracy Assessment is intended to represent a manual process that is facilitated through tools. As more events are learned, the need for manual response investigations and corrections should decrease and true-positive detection rates should rise.

Note: Many people ask about using AI for prediction of attacks. Unless there is a means for machines to read the minds of attackers, it is not practical to predict an attack. The best we can expect to do is to prevent attacks from being successful (through proactive preventative controls). Alternatively, we can detect and resolve attacks quickly—before they have an adverse impact to business.

10.4.2 Isolating Anomalous Domain Name System Activity

This section takes the concept of anomaly detection and investigates a more specific example. As with the previous example, the main task in designing threat analytics is to establish a baseline as a model of "normal" activity. There is usually no strict definition of what is normal other than it should not include known attacks and any special events in the network, such as outages or unscheduled maintenance. The baseline should incorporate factors, such as diurnal patterns, busy vs. non-busy hours in a day, weekday vs. weekend variations, or other seasonal patterns. It should also consider typical error conditions in a network or applications that are parts of the daily operation of various services.

For network activity, one simple model consists of selecting a set of atomic metrics, such as number of packets or number of bytes, incoming to and outgoing from an application or network, and a set of basic statistics such as mean, median, and standard deviation over a period of time (e.g., 5 minutes, 1 hour, 1 day, or 1 week). An anomaly is then flagged when one of the metrics of interest exceeds the mean or median plus or minus x number of standard deviations. The variable x can be used to label the size of the anomaly: for example, $x = 3$ for a minor, $x = 4$ for major, and $x \geq 5$ for a critical anomaly. While this approach is simple and commonly applied, it is not very precise, as it looks only at a small number of statistics and assumes that the distribution of the metrics selected is normal (i.e., Gaussian) and therefore follows a "bell" curve.

More advanced data models capture periodicity, seasonality, and overall trends. These models are more accurate than the "flat" models described previously, especially for network traffic that is driven by humans either at home or work or while they travel. For example, Internet access traffic generated by consumers can be three to four times higher during evening hours versus business hours. While a flat model (across a day) would likely flag incorrectly the evening traffic as anomaly, a data model that captures hourly variations throughout the day will correctly identify it as normal. Similarly, as the popularity of a service increases or wanes, there are longer-term activity trends that change, which need to be captured as part of the baseline. The corresponding increases or decreases in total customers or customer visits at different seasons (e.g., summer vs. back to school) drive different network and application demands. For traffic that shows these characteristics, it is important that the anomaly detection is based on deviation from models that capture periodicity, trending and seasonality as described previously.

Flagging a data point as anomaly is equivalent to applying a decision function. In the previous discussion, the decision is made based on one-dimensional data, but more frequently such decisions must be made on data that are multidimensional. For example, for a single point in time, our data can contain the number of incoming packets, outgoing packets, packets with a certain protocol, packets with certain types of flags, etc. So, the decision at any given point in time related to the classification of the data as anomalous can depend on any number of these data elements or a certain combination of them. Neural networks have long been used to model classes of multidimensional data, such as images or human voice. They simulate the behavior of a human neuron that takes inputs from other neurons, combines them, and produces an output that can be fed to other neurons. Depending on the various inputs these neurons can learn certain patterns and recognize them again if they reappear or even if they are slightly different.

The increased availability of data in structured or unstructured form and low cost of computing power has brought a resurgence of ML techniques based on NN—see Chapter 2. While NNs have been used since the 1950s for voice recognition and image analysis, they are also gaining popularity and applicability in cybersecurity tasks to classify and recognize different security types of events, such as reconnaissance and various types of denial-of-service (DoS) attacks. The attractiveness of NNs is that they can capture previously unknown relationships between different variables in high-dimensional data. They allow also a lot of flexibility in terms of their architecture to perform better in certain categories of problems, and they can be used for supervised or unsupervised classification of data.

For example, a special type of recurrent NNs, called Long Short-Term Memory networks, has been found very effective in classifying Domain Generation Algorithm domains used by botnets to communicate with their controllers [9]. These NNs, as the name suggests, are designed to learn a long duration pattern, while also able to forget certain anomalies in the training data. They are also relatively easy to train using implementations that are available as open source.

Autoencoder NNs have been also very useful in learning the essential features from multidimensional data with unsupervised training using a small number of hidden nodes. To detect anomalies, the output is reconstructed from a hidden layer with a small number of nodes, and an error is calculated between the input and the output. Anomalies can be flagged for high error output while clustering of the states of the hidden layer nodes can be used to classify the anomalies. This has been tested in AT&T for resource exhaustion attacks that are frequently observed commonly in Domain Name System (DNS) traffic.

To securely operate large networks, detection and interpretation of anomalies is essential. Security analysts and operators need to understand the nature, the severity, and if they need to act on the anomaly. Is the anomaly a single short event or is it part of a growing pattern? For example, detection of a single or few scans of certain ports may be useful for situational awareness, but a growing number of scan sources may be an indication of a new infection growing, taking advantage of a zero-day vulnerability discovered in the wild. Getting a summary of the data during and around the anomaly, and aggregating summaries of multiple anomalies, can be very useful to enhance our understanding of the state of the network. This essentially is a meta-analysis that can improve the situational awareness or lead to certain actions by analysts or operators. Meta-analysis can focus on features of the anomaly or can focus on orthogonal features. For example, if the anomaly is a scan across multiple targets on a particular port, meta-analysis can focus on the number of unique sources of the scans over time or can focus on traffic of those sources that is not related to the scanning to see what other activities are taking place.

Machine learning can facilitate the interpretation of the anomalies and attribution to known attack types by architecting the algorithm as an auto-encoder NN and training it with normal traffic. Figure 10.10 shows an outline of how DNS anomalies

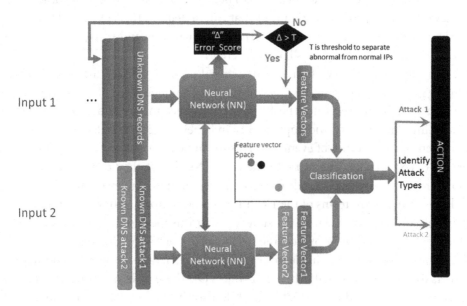

FIGURE 10.10 Auto-encoder formulation for detection of anomalies and attribution to known types of attacks.

can be detected and classified using an auto-encoder NN. Initially, normal traffic can be used to train the auto-encoder NN. Known attacks can be used as input to the NN (Input 2 in the figure) and create signatures in the feature vector space. During the testing phase, anomalies can be detected when the error score between the input and the reconstructed output is high. When the NN detects anomalies, the corresponding feature vectors can be compared to the feature vectors of known attacks (e.g., using K nearest neighbor clustering). The algorithm can be used to detect other unknown anomalies, which can be presented as logs or metadata to analysts for further investigation.

Figure 10.11 gives an example of the hidden layer feature data set for two known types of DNS attacks and one that is unknown (unlabeled). In this example, the initial 30-dimensional data set is compressed to 2 dimensions in the hidden layer of the encoder stage of the NN. The values of the 2-d vectors are shown in the figure for a DoS attack (single source), a DDoS attack, and for an unlabeled anomaly. Any subsequent attacks that have similar characteristics exhibit feature vectors that are clustered accordingly.

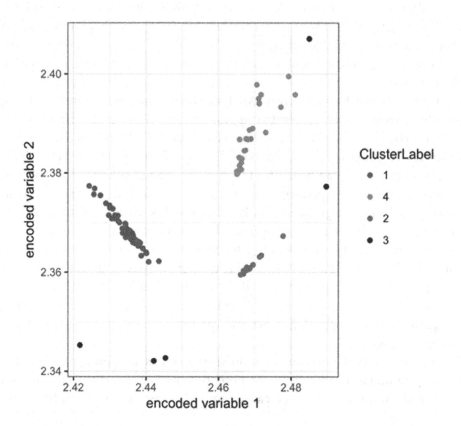

FIGURE 10.11   DNS traffic anomalies as represented in two-dimensional feature space of an auto-encoder neural network.

10.4.3 Insider Threat Analysis—User Event Behavior Analysis

Generally, an insider threat is a person(s) with malicious intent that has access to an organization's assets. Their objectives may be to steal property, disrupt business, or expose information to the public domain. Some also consider inadvertent impact to organizations that are caused by personnel with authorized accesses as insider threats as well. In other words, if there are insufficient controls in place to minimize the opportunity for personnel to make honest mistakes that impact the business, this too is sometimes considered an insider threat. These threats may be employees, former employees, contractors, or business associates. Finally, if an outside attacker can obtain valid user credentials and log into systems with the appearance of a normal user, the means to detect such a threat has significant overlap as an insider threat. An insider threat misuses his/her privileges to perform activities that are not intended to be allowed. The awareness of the threat posed by trusted insiders has greatly increased in recent years because of recent high-profile insiders incidents, (e.g., Snowden [10] and Manning [11]), where large amounts of very sensitive information has been exposed to the public domain. Information technology and digital assets can allow insiders threats to conduct their activities remotely, which may make them feel safer.

Organizations that support sensitive projects such as Department of Defense contracts handling classified information are now required to have a defined Insider Threat Prevention Program [12]. Facets of a complete insider threat program include policy that helps to define acceptable behavior and obligations of personnel, controls that limit access to sensitive or critical systems, awareness training, investigation activities, and finally detection.

Application of User Event Behavior Analysis (UEBA) methods to insider threats has been evolving from traditional reactive approaches [13]. Traditional insider threat programs have relied upon someone reporting suspicious behavior or discovery of a breach before an investigation was launched. New detection technologies are being developed to identify anonymously candidates for investigation. Some leading indicators of insider threat include: poor work performance, financial distress, sudden financial gain, odd work hours, unusual disagreements with policies and/or coworkers, unusual overseas travel (associated with foreign espionage), and leaving the company [12]. It is important to consider that the technology is attempting to use passive observed behaviors to determine the intent or objective of an individual. This type of analysis is not fully deterministic, so as long as there is no capability to read the minds of individuals, UEBA to predict or detect insider threats will be either fraught with false positives or it will not find much of anything. However, the technology when used properly can help to identify certain types of insider threat activity.

The technology typically uses a cumulative risk-based approach to identify the most likely candidates/individuals for potential further investigation—in hopes of preventing or minimizing damage caused by an insider threat. Much like was done with threat analytics. The types of indicators that an insider threat detection tool might look for include the following:

1. Individuals can be profiled based on their past behavior, and analysis used to identify change in their behavior. Long-term and short-term behavior pattern profiling along with anomaly detection can be used to detect changes in individual behavior.

2. Individuals' behaviors can be compared with others in their organization, where presumably there are others who need the same system and data accesses, and they perform similar or the same job functions. This might include advanced methods to profile the activity of a group and use that as a basis to detect anomalies in individual behavior.

3. Activity can be identified that is defined as a violation of accepted business practices. The methods may be based on learned activity of the populous and/or may be based on some baseline policy rules. This sort of detection is generally going to be more useful if there is a strong awareness training program—where violators of the policies will generally know they are violating policies.

4. Patterns of activities that are generally associated with insider threats can be detected. For example, someone who is stealing data may use a USB memory stick on systems, may upload large amounts of data to public cloud sites, or may use unusual encryption methods. These are effectively rules and/or preprogramed behavior patterns that can be compared with the behavior of individuals.

5. Some personnel who work with particularly sensitive data or critical systems may be considered a higher risk target for extortion or bribery and might be treated with special attention. In effect, personnel with access to sensitive data will generally have a higher risk score.

6. Of course, if someone reports suspicious behavior associated with a person, that person might be treated as a higher risk relative to others. Like earlier, reports will certainly raise the risk score of individuals. The types of reports might have some weighting associated with the risk.

Generally, it is accepted practice that any one of the types of indicators above are not sufficient grounds to launch an investigation. The risk score for an individual will be ranked relative to functions of all the risk behaviors or characteristics that are being observed. As more relevant types of indicators are incorporated into analysis, we might expect to see an increased accuracy in risk scores.

As can be seen, there are many aspects of this detection that can make use of advanced analytical techniques to collect indicators and assign a risk score to the behavior of individuals. At this stage in technology, it is generally not possible to set a threshold for detection of an insider threat. However, the individuals with the highest scores are generally worthy of some additional investigation.

The specific methods in use are generally proprietary and beyond the scope of this chapter. Hopefully this description of insider threat detection technology helps to establish a basis for advancements in analysis technology to detect insider threats. However, we still do not have a means to read the minds of the actors.

10.4.4 Understanding Vulnerabilities and Exploits

To understand the security threat landscape, organizations need to accurately evaluate the vulnerabilities and risks of the software, firmware, and hardware for each manufacturer equipment and version type installed in their network. A vulnerability can be exploited by an adversary by building and deploying an exploit—remotely or locally in the network. Availability of known exploits and outstanding vulnerabilities poses a high but calculable risk. Typically, the discovery of a vulnerability is quickly followed by the crafting of exploits in the black market, especially if the potential gain breaking into the application or network can lead to high rewards (e.g., obtaining access to a customer identity and contact database, competitive data, blueprint designs etc.). Artificial intelligence can play a significant role [14] to assess the risk of newly published vulnerabilities and predict the creation of successful exploits by scouring different public databases and analyzing known vulnerabilities. This can be very helpful for overburdened administrators and operations personnel in prioritizing which patches they need to apply first. Delays in applying critical patches can be devastating, as they can lead to massive breaches of private data for millions of subscribers (e.g., Equifax [15]) that can severely impact the financial viability of the affected companies.

A ML approach in cybersecurity can help detect an anomaly, predict an outcome, or assess a risk. The analysis can help operations by creating logs or alerts if the severity of an anomaly is high or there is a high-confidence prediction for a high-risk event. If the classifier determines that a certain anomaly is of known type, and there is a mitigating action that can be taken, then a software controller can use the output of the ML module to remedy the situation. This can facilitate automated patching and testing in the lab, or reconfiguration and verification in the field. Automated actions should only be taken if there is well-defined action for the type of anomaly that is predicted and that the action would not cause other peripheral issues in the network. An untested patch, for example, may cause other applications to break, so automation in this case should only be extended to patching in the lab and running automated tests, while deployment in the field should be taken care by operations after reviewing the automated test results or running additional regression tests to verify that the patch solves the original problem without breaking anything else in the system.

In the cases where mitigation of the security event can be done with reconfiguration, one of the main concerns is not to harm any legitimate traffic, even if this can be a very small fraction. In business, a single large customer complaint may override a configuration change that aims at protecting the service for all customers such as rate limiting, as this transaction rate limiting can affect network throughput.

Also, blocking an Internet-facing IP address based on an assessment that a source of traffic could be malicious is risky, as the source may be a Network Address Translation (NAT)

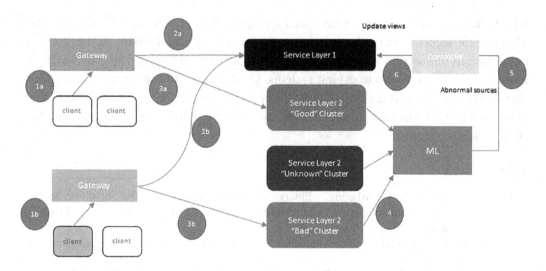

FIGURE 10.12   Using ML and a software-defined controller to reconfigure a multi-tiered system to allocated dedicated resources to trusted clients.

gateway in front of many different users and devices. A NAT gateway allows many devices on the LAN side of the gateway to share a single IP address on the Internet side of the gateway. To minimize risk of accidentally blocking sources of traffic, one approach is to serve all traffic but dedicate different pools of resources to different risk classes of traffic demand (benign, attack, or unknown). Figure 10.12 shows an example where ML algorithms combined with a software controller can adjust the service demand originating from different gateways to different pools of server clusters, thus allowing well-behaving gateways (and all their clients behind them) to access dedicated resources.

In the illustration, the steps are as follows:

1. (a) Request from a "good" client or (b) Request from a "bad" client.

2. Query routed to the first layer of service (e.g., HTTP or DNS) cluster that redirects or refers the client to the appropriate cluster in the second layer.

3. Client is referred to the second layer and to the appropriate cluster.

4. Requests are continuously analyzed through a two-stage NN.

5. Output of ML module provides sets of source IP addresses that need to be reclassified.

6. Controller applies a reconfiguration script (e.g., Ansible playbook) to reconfigure the first layer of the service cluster.

10.5 SUMMARY

In this chapter, we have looked at the need for security to help protect networks from attack, corruption, or disruption. We have looked at related technologies such as virtualization that are enabling factors for automation of security functions. We have looked at the considerations for how to select appropriate security tasks to be automated. And we have looked at some examples where security automation and AI can advance the state of the art for security management in networks and enterprises. Perhaps the most important lesson in this section is to consider the fact that the need for security is driven by the motivation of threat actors to exploit systems. Until the cost to exploit systems is greater than the gain of the threat actors, there will be a continuing need to improve security. It is an arms race. Use of automation is a tool that can help to drive more efficient and cost-effective security controls.

REFERENCES

1. Ed King, VP Product Marketing – Emerging Technologies, Axway The Shrinking Security Model: Micro-perimeters https://blog.cloudsecurityalliance.org/2013/03/20/the-shrinking-security-model-micro-perimeters/.
2. Schneier, B., Crypto-Gram, March 15, 2018. https://www.schneier.com/crypto-gram/archives/2018/0315.html.
3. Open Networking Foundation, SDN architecture—A primer, September 2016. Online: www.opennetworking.org.
4. AT&T domain 2.0 vision white paper, November 2013. Online: https://www.att.com/Common/about_us/pdf/AT&T%20Domain%202.0%20Vision%20White%20Paper.pdf.
5. A. M. Medhat, T. Taleb, A. Elmangoush, G. A. Carella, S. Covaci, and T. Magedanz, Service function chaining in next generation networks: State of the art and research challenge, *IEEE Communications Magazine*, 55(2), 216–223, 2017.
6. Control theory, https://en.wikipedia.org/wiki/Control_theory.
7. De-perimeterisation, https://en.wikipedia.org/wiki/De-perimeterisation.
8. Credential stuffing, https://www.owasp.org/index.php/Credential_stuffing.
9. J. Woodbridge, H. S. Anderson, A. Ahuja, and D. Grant, Predicting domain generation algorithms with long short-term memory networks, *preprint arXiv:1611.00791*, 2016.
10. Wikipedia, Edward Snowden. Online: https://en.wikipedia.org/wiki/Edward_Snowden.
11. Wikipedia, United States vs manning. Online: https://en.wikipedia.org/wiki/United_States_v._Manning.
12. DoD insider threat information, http://www.dss.mil/it/index.html.
13. User event behavior analysis, https://en.wikipedia.org/wiki/User_behavior_analytics.
14. M. Bozorgi, L. K. Saul, S. Savage, and G. M. Voelker, Beyond heuristics: Learning to classify vulnerabilities and predict exploits, *KDD'10*, July 25–28, 2010, Washington, DC.
15. Equifax Breach 2017 https://www.equifaxsecurity2017.com/.

CHAPTER 11

Artificial Intelligence for Enterprise Networks

Sandeep Gupta, Kathleen Meier-Hellstern, and Michael Satterlee

CONTENTS

11.1 INTRODUCTION

Artificial intelligence (AI) is a key enabler for the digital transformation that is shaping enterprises across all sectors of the economy. Digital transformation is defined as a continuous process by which enterprises adapt to or drive disruptive changes in their customers and markets (external ecosystem) by leveraging digital competencies to create new business models, products, and services [1]. Digital transformation enables enterprises to seamlessly blend digital and physical business and customer experiences while improving operational efficiencies and organizational performance. Lowering operational costs and enhancing customer experience is at the core of digital transformation [2]. Successful digital transformations focus on creating, collecting, and analyzing customer and operational data so that data-driven decisions can be taken to improve the processes. Artificial intelligence is at the core of this automated process improvement.

By the end of 2019, spending on digital transformation will reach $1.7 trillion worldwide—up 42% from 2017, according to a new report from the International Data Corporation [3]. New business paradigms are emerging as legacy businesses are being displaced by new more efficient models. Not that long ago, consumers visited a store to rent DVDs. Today, the video rental business has been completed displaced by online businesses like Netflix. The taxi business has been disrupted by Uber and Lyft, and in the not-to-distant future, drivers may be replaced by self-driving vehicles. Brick-and-mortar shopping malls need to establish a value proposition that entices customers to visit in person rather than shop online. When customers do visit stores, inventory needs to be available and easy to locate.

In addition to driving fundamental changes in how enterprises serve their customers and improve their operational performance, the digital transformation is also driving changes in the networks that serve enterprises. Customers desire to be in the driver seat in the design, scale, and automation of their networks. These characteristics provide them with the ability to be agile and offer on-demand services anytime and anywhere. Artificial intelligence enables a new generation of software-defined networks (SDN), through which business customers can build virtually any network, optimize their bandwidth capacity, reduce their transport cost per terabyte, and dynamically respond to network events. They can harness the power of network data that will be available to them to better understand their customers, increase the effectiveness of marketing, and internally understand the demand for product/feature prioritization.

In this chapter, we address AI for both facets of the digital transformation: the transformation of the enterprise and the transformation of the networks that serve enterprises.

11.2 ENTERPRISE ARCHITECTURE FOR THE DIGITAL TRANSFORMATION

Figure 11.1 shows a network architecture for a digitally transformed enterprise where data and data-driven decision-making drive business processes and operations. Network functions that reside at enterprise locations are virtualized, so that a typical location contains white boxes serving as small clouds hosting virtual routers, firewalls, Internet-of-Things (IoT) gateways, and limited AI functions [4]. The term "white box" refers to commodity hardware that can be used to host a variety of virtual applications, such as routers and firewalls. White boxes located on customer premises are also sometimes referred to as Universal Customer Premises Equipment (UCPEs). Artificial intelligence functions that can be performed on the UCPEs will tend to be those that require low latency, limited compute and storage, and limited external or network data.

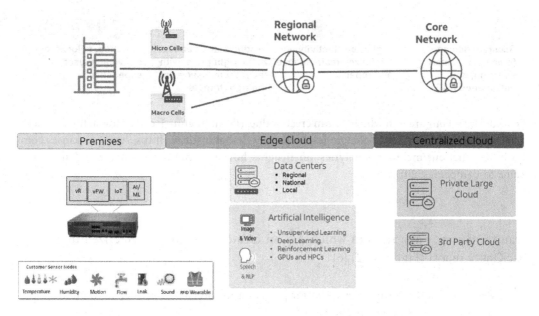

FIGURE 11.1   Architecture for a digitally transformed enterprise.

Enterprise locations connect to regional networks using fixed or wireless access. Regional networks will host local and regional datacenters that host network functions, such as virtual routing, together with processing for network functions. Regional datacenters may also host enterprise AI applications of moderate complexity.

Finally, the core network will provide high-speed transport as well as hosting for large private and third-party clouds. Intensive AI tasks, such as model training and storage of large amounts of data, will be performed in the core, whereas the AI models will run locally and at the network edge. The most successful enterprise AI solutions will combine enterprise-collected private data with network-collected data. Artificial intelligence solutions that require both enterprise and network data will likely reside in secure regional or core network datacenters that guarantee privacy.

11.3 THE ENTERPRISE TRANSFORMATION AND ARTIFICIAL INTELLIGENCE

Enterprises leverage the architecture shown in Figure 11.1 for data-driven decision-making to create efficient, frictionless, customer experience and operations. In this section, we provide examples of how AI is transforming enterprises.

11.3.1 Examples of Artificial Intelligence in Digitally Transformed Enterprises

A recent study by PWC [5] scored industry verticals with respect to AI potential. The top verticals were health care, automotive, financial services, transportation logistics, technology, consumer products, oil and gas, and industrial manufacturing. Although there are different opportunities to apply AI across the industry verticals, the opportunities can be categorized according to common areas that are conducive to the digital

Project	Produce	Promote	Provide
Accurate demand forecasting, smart sourcing, and enlightened R&D	Higher productivity and minimized maintenance and repairs	Products and services at the right price, with the right message, to the right targets	Enriched, tailored, and convenient user experience

FIGURE 11.2 Four areas in which AI can create value. (From Bughin, J. et al., How artificial intelligence can deliver real value to companies, McKinsey Global Institute, https://www.mckinsey.com/business-functions/mckinsey-analytics/our-insights/how-artificial-intelligence-can-deliver-real-value-to-companies, 2017.)

transformation. Four areas in which AI can create value are characterized in a recent McKinsey report (Figure 11.2) [6].

1. **Project**: Enable companies to better project and forecast to anticipate demand, optimize R&D, and improve sourcing.

2. **Produce**: Increase companies' abilities to produce goods and services at lower cost and higher quality. Improve productivity and minimize maintenance and repairs.

3. **Promote**: Promote offerings at the right price, with the right message, and to the right target customers;

4. **Provide**: Provide rich, personal, and convenient user experiences.

In a similar study, Cisco [7] categorized the areas impacted by AI into asset utilization, supply chain and logistics, sustainability, innovation, customer experience, and employee productivity, which cover the same type of areas presented in the McKinsey report. Regardless of the classification, the message is clear. Data-powered digital transformations are transforming customer experience and operations, reducing costs, and increasing revenue. The most successful enterprises are using AI to differentiate themselves from their competitors.

In the remainder of this section, we demonstrate how AI can be applied in enterprises across each of the four areas defined by McKinsey: Project, Produce, Promote, Provide. Wherever possible, we highlight ways in which network-collected data can be combined with enterprise-collected data to maximize the potential of AI. The requirement to maintain privacy and security drives the enterprise AI architecture, which will have both local and network components working together in a secure private manner.

11.3.1.1 Project

"Project" focuses on accurate demand forecasting, smart sourcing, and product improvement [6]. It allows enterprises to ensure that they have appropriate inventory available when consumers need it, without having excess inventory. In the procurement and manufacturing process, it helps to make sure that the best suppliers are selected based on cost and quality needs, and it can be used to identify product improvement opportunities.

The retail industry is particularly well suited to AI-driven demand forecasting. In the online shopping era, customers are quickly discouraged by unavailability of inventory in brick-and-mortar stores. Lack of inventory in online stores translates to immediate lost sales. Artificial intelligence can be used to analyze historical sales data to predict when inventory needs to be refreshed. Network location data, such as number of shoppers in specific areas of the store, number of cars in the parking lot, or trends in traffic on surrounding roads, can be used to anticipate future demand. This can be combined with population demographics to identify types of products that are likely to be in demand. For in-store shopping experiences, retailers can use AI to reallocate staff to parts of the store that are experiencing more traffic or add or subtract personnel using historical trends as well as in-store location analytics.

Large enterprises who procure network services from multiple vendors can use network usage and fault data as part of AI-driven predictive analytics to estimate future usage, trade-off suppliers, and negotiate rates to minimize cost. More broadly, network data can be used to evaluate the quality of networks and suppliers, to negotiate contracts and Service Level Agreements, as well as to predict future maintenance events. This approach is not restricted to network services; it can be applied to any supplier negotiation and contracting, for example in the automotive industry. In the automotive industry, sensors can be used to identify the age of parts, impending failures, and failure modes. This can in turn be used to drive parts manufacturing, maintenance, or vendor selection.

In the health-care industry, location demographics and insurance claims can be used to identify people who are likely to become ill, and pre-emptively treat them or prepare for increased demand (such as when flu season starts). With appropriate privacy permissions, location data could be added to identify individuals who may have been exposed to contagious diseases. The health-care sector is also starting to see exploration in data-driven diagnostics and more personalized treatment. This can be targeted to more effective prevention, and may lead to long-term benefits, such as intelligent implants [5].

Service providers can capture network data combined with customer care data to improve the customer experience. Artificial intelligence can be used to anticipate conditions that will lead to customer dissatisfaction and can recommend improvements or proactively contact impacted users. This use-case is not restricted to network data. The same methods can be applied in any service-oriented enterprise.

11.3.1.2 Produce

"Produce" focuses on increasing companies' ability to produce goods and services at lower cost and higher quality [6]. This may include improving asset utilization by minimizing maintenance and optimizing repairs, energy management, optimal use of space, factory automation, or supply chain and logistics to improve inventory management and tracking. There are many applications of AI in the "Produce" area, mostly associated with cost reduction. A key opportunity to utilize network data in this space is the data generated by IoT sensors.

Sustainability and energy management is a large expense for many businesses. According to the National Foundation of Independent Businesses' Energy Consumption poll, energy costs are one of the top three business expenses in 35% of small businesses [8]. The primary energy costs for small firms are:

- Operating vehicles, for 38% of small firms
- Heating and/or cooling, for one-third of small firms
- Operating equipment, for one-fifth of small firms

A small business has relatively few levers to deal with increasing energy costs. It can be prohibitive to make a large price changes to compensate for increased energy costs, and small businesses cannot afford frequent upgrades of their equipment. For large businesses, manufacturing, or datacenters, energy costs may be even more substantial. There is a significant opportunity for enterprises to use smart metering to measure energy, water, or natural gas consumption. Internet-of-Things sensor data, gathered from the enterprise network, can be used to improve forecasts and streamline power consumption and reduce energy theft [9]. In an office setting, AI can be used in building automation controls to dynamically adjust temperature or lighting settings to minimize energy consumption. A corporate office provides and manages many support services to help ensure employee productivity, comfort, and safety. Many of these support service costs (security guards, food services, network bandwidth, heating/cooling, custodial staff, etc.) are directly proportional to employee occupancy metrics. Known seasonal and general weekday patterns will be replaced with new AI algorithms that also consider a given day: employee outlook calendars, reserved meeting space, connected car GPS destination settings, location-based analytics from macro-cellular data traffic, construction, news, and weather events. The same principles can be applied to large or small enterprises, datacenters, and utility companies to optimize energy consumption.

Another rich application in the "Produce" area is in the tracking inventory using IoT sensors. For example, in the maritime shipping industry, sensors help track the location of a ship at sea. On a smaller scale, they can provide the status and temperature of individual cargo containers. Temperature sensing can be used to ensure that correct temperatures are maintained in refrigerated shipping containers to ensure freshness. Or if the refrigeration system fails, operators can be promptly notified so that repairs can be made before the goods perish [9]. In a restaurant setting, IoT sensors can be integral to quality management and cost minimization. For example, oil temperature and viscosity can be managed so that fried food comes out just right. Oil viscosity can be checked to determine the optimal time to change the frying oil, which in turn can be used to efficiently drive the oil replenishment policies.

Factory automation will be one of the top uses of AI. Robots will be used to replace humans for tasks, such as picking, sorting, and loading stock for shipping, and they will also be used for product assembly. Artificial intelligence-enhanced camera-equipped logistics robotics can be trained to recognize empty space and correctly place objects [6]. All of these applications will be driven by wireless network data.

Finally, self-driving and connected cars represent an extremely challenging application of AI that requires network data. Self-driving cars that can avoid accidents require extremely low latency network data and complex AI models to operate reliably. Artificial intelligence can be used to optimize and adapt vehicle routes to minimize drive time and fuel consumption. These same technologies can be applied to human-driven cars in an enterprise fleet, or by network operators to optimize dispatch and truck rolls.

11.3.1.3 Promote

"Promote" creates offerings at the right price, with the right message, and to the right target customers [6]. Examples of digital transformation with AI include in-store analytics and insights, personalized engagement, promotional effectiveness, insight-driven customer experience, and the ability to monetize buyer insights. On a consumer-permitted basis, many of the AI applications in this category make extensive use of mobile network data, such as shopping or browsing history and customer location.

By combining knowledge of customer preferences with recent browsing history and customer location inside of a store, AI can be used to send coupons or targeted ads to a customer as they are passing by a display containing information that they might want to purchase [10]. Pricing of products can be adjusted based on traffic patterns in and outside the store and external factors, such as weather, time-of-day, or day-of-week. Sephora [10] allows customers to "try on" their products. After uploading a picture, a smart chatbot will help the customer visualize difference makeup styles and products, provide personalized suggestions, and offer some items the customer may want to purchase.

In the health-care sector, network data generated by health and environmental sensors can be used to encourage healthy behavior (such as walking more or eating less), to identify personalized medicine recommendations, or in the early detection of illness.

In the energy sector, customized pricing can be created using data collected from smart metering devices. Artificial intelligence can be used to combine this data as well as demographic data and usage data from other customers to create customized pricing incentives for users who conserve energy.

The financial services industry is being revolutionized by AI. Many of the use-cases do not require network data. For example, the industry is using AI-powered robo-advisory services that recommend personalized portfolio changes based on a client's financial goals or risk tolerance [11].

11.3.1.4 Provide

"Provide" uses AI to create rich, personal, and convenient user experiences. These experiences increase customer engagement, increase upsell opportunities, and reduce the friction between online and offline experiences. Artificial intelligence applications in this space can also be used for training or giving customers or enterprise employees access to personalized interactive learning.

Discussion of the "provide" function would not be complete without addressing customer care. There is a tremendous opportunity to use AI chatbots to handle routine tasks like answering standard questions or handling returns. This frees up employee time to handle more complex tasks and may lead to a reduction in the overall number of employees required [12]. Artificial intelligence can help automate the customer care process by developing and deploying a conversational computer program that interacts directly with customers without human intervention (or use a human customer service representative who is supported by AI technology).

In many industries, particularly in the financial industry, using AI for improved security is essential [12]. As the number of security breaches increases, users will expect features like voice/facial recognition, fingerprint identification, and iris scanning to augment identity management. Security cameras that feed video to an AI application that identifies individuals requesting entry represent a major opportunity for AI. Many of these applications will require advanced networking.

An intriguing application that requires network data is in the insurance industry [12]. Insurance companies are experimenting with drones that fly over damaged cars and take the necessary pictures, to avoid having to send a staff member or disrupt the car owner's schedule [11]. These applications may generate significant amounts of network data.

Another key application of AI is personalized training. This may be training for enterprise operations staff on how to operate network equipment and services, or it could be training aimed at customers. Artificial intelligence can be used to modulate the training based on user behavior. Augmented reality applications will further enhance the customer experience and can be both personalized and delivered at a time that is convenient for the user.

In the retail space, a prominent use of AI is in the recommender systems implemented by Amazon and Netflix that recommend items a customer may enjoy based on their preferences and shopping patterns [10]. Panera Bread has a mobile app that allows customers to order in advance. Rebecca Minkoff stores [7] allow shoppers to select items from a digital screen and have the items placed in a fitting room. Artificial intelligence could be used to suggest additional items or place them into the fitting room for customer consideration. If an AI app had additional information on the customer, such as age, past preferences, or body type, these could be used to tune the suggestions.

11.3.2 Example of an Integrated Experience—The Smart Store

In this section, we give an example to demonstrate how the capabilities in the previous section can be integrated to redefine the customer experience, using a "Smart Store" as an example. The key capabilities used in the example are shown in Figure 11.3.

The Smart Store experience begins when the user downloads a mobile app for the store and registers their identity and payment information, as shown in Figure 11.4. The user profile and payment information would likely be stored in a private cloud, where it can be accessed securely by the Smart Store when the user enters or pays. The user can upload a variety of information for subsequent authentication, such as photos, fingerprints, and voice prints. Credit card transaction activity can be used to identify possible fraud using AI or other technologies.

Key Capabilities

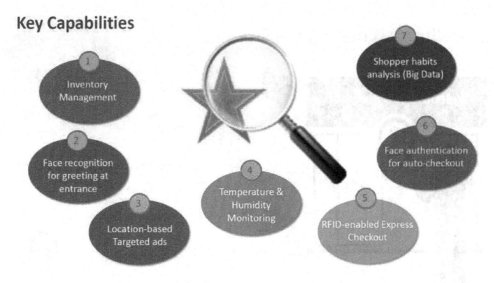

FIGURE 11.3   Key capabilities demonstrated in the Smart Store.

Smart Store – Registration via Mobile App

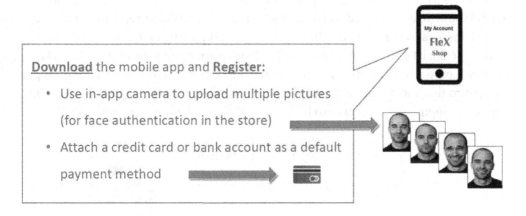

FIGURE 11.4   Smart Store registration via a mobile app.

When a user enters the Smart Store as shown in Figure 11.5, AI is employed for facial recognition using a model that is implemented locally on a UCPE at the store, having been trained on a public or private cloud in the core. Artificial intelligence algorithms could also create multifactor authentication algorithms that use customer location profiles to strengthen the authentication. The customer can be given a personalized greeting and perhaps recommendations of special offers on products they may be interested in based on their purchase history and preferences of similar customers. If the store is unstaffed, security may be set to that only registered customers can enter the store.

FIGURE 11.5   Using facial recognition with AI when entering the Smart Store.

Back at the warehouse, inventory is tracked using Smart Labels as shown in Figure 11.6. Artificial intelligence is used to identify when items need to be replenished and to keep track of the location of items within the warehouse. If picking and placing is performed by robots, the Smart Labels can be used to locate inventory and identify where to place new inventory on the shelves. By tracking the freshness of items in the warehouse, suppliers can ensure that the oldest items are shipped first, while ensuring that stale items are not shipped. Shipping policies can also be tailored to the individual store sales characteristics.

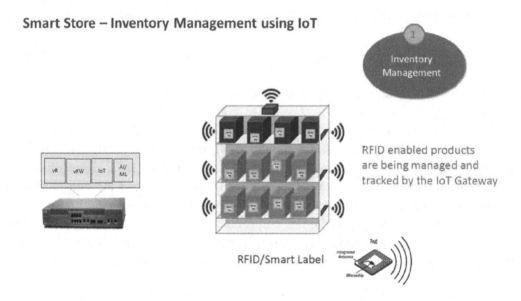

FIGURE 11.6   Smart Store inventory management using IoT.

Smart Store – Shop in Store

Targeted ads will pop up on the mobile device as shopper approach to each aisle

Temperature sensitive items can be monitored b Flexware IoT Gateway

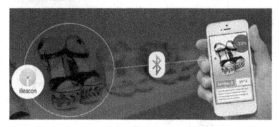

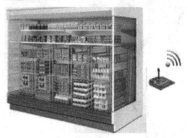

FIGURE 11.7   Using IoT for advertising and monitoring.

Artificial intelligence can also be used to improve the quality of in-store shopping experience as shown in Figure 11.7. Customer demographic and marketing data can be combined with network location data and radio-frequency identification sensor data to deliver in-store targeted ads. With the advent of online shopping, the importance of in-store product quality is increased. Temperature sensors can be monitored to continuously adjust to optimal temperatures, and freshness can be tracked so that old goods are promptly removed from the store shelves. Employees or customers can quickly locate items through an app that keeps track of the location of all merchandise, and employees can quickly locate out-of-place items. Artificial intelligence can be applied to predict when new inventory should be added, to determine which items are selling well, and to determine optimal placement of inventory within the store.

Finally, Figure 11.8 shows the checkout experience. Artificial intelligence is used for user authentication, and purchase history is stored in a private or network cloud where AI can be applied for future sales and marketing purposes. Artificial intelligence chatbots can be used to process routine returns, and the return data can be analyzed to refine future orders.

11.3.3 The Enterprise Transformation and Artificial Intelligence—Putting It All Together

As discussed in the previous sections, the digital transformation has created new opportunities for AI to transform enterprises, leading to increased operational efficiencies, reduced cost, and personalized customer experiences. It is transforming the very nature of businesses, disrupting how customers engage with enterprises. Some of the AI use-cases discussed in this section will be offered through vertical applications that account for the unique customer needs within a sector. These applications will need to seamlessly integrate data from many sources—customer profile data, demographic data, marketing and sales data, industry data, public data, and network data. Network data may be gathered from customer private networks or service provider networks, encompassing sensor data,

FIGURE 11.8   Smart Store checkout experience.

mobile location data, network usage data, and network-collected customer transaction data. Collecting and managing the wealth of data required by these applications will pose a significant challenge for enterprises, and the AI applications themselves may require significant computational power. Large enterprises will have to choose between managing the AI applications themselves or paying for a service that performs these functions for them. Smaller enterprises who desire to take advantage of the benefits of AI may not have the expertise or resources to undertake the AI investment on their own.

The cloud will play a central role in enabling AI in the digital transformation. Enterprises will make use of private clouds, public clouds, and provider clouds to store and process data, as shown in Figure 11.1. Resource-intensive computations, such as training AI models, may be deployed on a large public or provider cloud, while execution of the trained model may be performed at a smaller on-site private cloud. Network and service providers will need to accommodate multiple clouds, working together to achieve the digital transformation goals.

The digital transformation also requires network and service providers to deliver more agile and adaptive services. They will also need to employ AI to deliver the agility and quality that enterprises require to keep pace with rapid innovation. The enterprise network transformation is the topic of the next section.

11.4 ENTERPRISE NETWORK TRANSFORMATION AND ARTIFICIAL INTELLIGENCE

To facilitate the digital transformation of an organization, the enterprise first must transform its network and its architecture to be more flexible, secure, and dynamic to handle the needs of new digital processes and workflows. Competitive pressures, increased expectations in terms of response time, and the need for cost-effectiveness require networks to be highly available and provide self-service management for administrators to respond to business needs more quickly. These new requirements represent significant changes for the existing networks within an enterprise. Enterprise networks and services of the future require very different terms of procurement, implementation and operation where network as a component can quickly and easily be plugged into a specific use-case of digital transformation.

The network transformation began several years ago with the adoption of SDN, virtualization, and cloud principles [13]. Enterprise Chief Information Officers are developing strategies that "software define" different aspects of their network architecture, processes and organization, and are adopting new operational processes that are nimbler, more automated, and provide better total cost of ownership.

Artificial intelligence and related technologies, such as machine learning, deep learning, and chatbots, are further enhancing these transitions by leveraging the huge amounts of data that can be gathered and integrated across the software components. The following sections will explain the current industry transition in various parts of enterprise networks and how AI will further boost these transitions.

Figure 11.1 showed a high-level enterprise architecture. The aspects of the enterprise architecture that most benefit from AI are given. These are also discussed in the previous chapter.

- Datacenters and the Cloud Transformation

- Wide Area Network (WAN) transition to Software-Defined WAN (SD-WAN), including virtualization of the Premises network

- Wired and Wireless Local Area Networks (LAN)

11.4.1 Enterprise Datacenter and Cloud Transformation with Artificial Intelligence

When one considers the most valuable and most costly asset of enterprise information technology (IT) infrastructure, datacenters almost always take the top spot. Datacenters are often considered as the backbone of enterprise IT infrastructure that run all the enterprise applications and store internal or customer data. Any interruptions to the datacenter can bring enterprise operations to a halt. Thus, organizations across the verticals continuously demand increased reliability, optimal utilization, and reduced cost associated with datacenter operation.

Cloud transition started because even with the adoption of virtualization, the current datacenter environment is costly to operate and manage. Many enterprises started using the external cloud infrastructure for transient workloads and adopting software-as-a-service models for many applications instead of dedicating costly compute and storage in private datacenters. However, from an enterprise perspective, while running the applications in an "off-premises" cloud provides simplification of the internal IT environment, the overall requirements of reliability, utilization, and cost still apply. It is just that they now require cloud providers to meet the same requirements.

Artificial intelligence and related technology promise to solve many of the core issues irrespective of enterprise datacenter strategy. Early examples of AI solving some of these core issues came into existence when Google started using technology from an AI start-up "DeepMind" to slash costs and improve the efficiency of computing devices. According to [14], Google reduced its datacenter power consumption by 15% and cooling power usage by 40% by discovering and monitoring inefficiencies across 120 datacenter variables, including fans, cooling, and windows, thus saving the company hundreds of millions of dollars over several years.

Today, all datacenter solution providers, such as Cisco, Aruba, HP, and others, are leveraging AI and related concepts such as machine learning to enhance cost-effectiveness, ease of operations, and to improve reliability [15]. Some of the problems that AI can potentially solve in datacenters include:

- Improved uptime, reliability, and optimized utilization of computer servers and storage infrastructure by generating more telemetry information for AI algorithms to spread the load.

- Reduced energy and power consumption in elastic datacenter environments, achieved by instantiating the applications and server nodes on an on-demand basis.

- Technical resource allocation using predictive analytics and intent-based networking principles whereby technical resources can just communicate their intent to an orchestrator, which in turn converts their intent to product-specific policy.

- Reducing the operational risk by monitoring the computer and storage nodes on a continuous basis and redirection of traffic to other available nodes based on the probability of overloaded nodes for certain time of the day or day of the year.

- Reducing the security risk by monitoring the application flows while comparing with the continuously evolving baseline and alerting the users for key deviations.

In the future, we believe many AI tools will be integrated into traditional datacenter infrastructure management solutions provided by the vendors. It is also conceivable that an AI toolkit can be integrated within datacenter solutions as a value-added service that enables enterprises to perform operations, such as automated data-mining, data analytics, and data-security, for the applications that run on the compute and server nodes. From the perspective of cloud providers, a similar move could allow them to offer new value-added services to further augment the business case of moving additional applications to the cloud environment.

To summarize, enterprises will benefit from AI in the cloud in multiple ways.

- Large enterprises with private clouds can take advantage of the same AI techniques used by datacenter operators to improve efficiency and resiliency using scale-in/scale-out and application migration.

- Enterprises can use AI to forecast workloads and migrate transient peak loads to external cloud providers, saving the cost of expensive capacity that is rarely used.

- AI depends on the cloud. Enterprises will make extensive use of the cloud for data storage and processing, utilizing on-site private clouds, regional network clouds, and third-party clouds to balance the needs of cost, capacity, security, and privacy.

- Enterprises can leverage AI tools as they become available as cloud services.

11.4.2 Artificial Intelligence-Enabled Predictive Software-Defined Wide Area Network

An enterprise WAN is basically a fabric connecting many different network segments of the enterprise, such as branch locations, headquarters locations, regional offices, home offices, and mobile endpoints. Traditional enterprise WANs are based on static designs and proprietary or specialized WAN technology. Software-defined WAN is an emerging solution that allows enterprises to meet many of the requirements associated with cloud transition and mobile adoption in a cost-effective manner. The SD-WAN is a specific application of SDN technology applied to WAN connections, which are used to connect enterprise networks over large geographic distances [16]. SD-WAN aims to replace traditional branch routers with appliances that use virtualization, application-level policies, and network overlays to make several consumer-grade Internet links behave like a dedicated circuit. The intention is to simplify setup so that the only thing branch office personnel need to do is plug in a cable for the appliance to "phone home" and automatically receive its configuration from a central controller [17].

Gartner has defined SD-WAN as having four required characteristics [18]:

- The ability to support multiple connection types, such as multi-protocol label switching (MPLS), frame relay, and higher-speed LTE wireless communications

- The ability to do dynamic path selection, for load sharing and resiliency purposes

- A simple interface that is easy to configure and manage

- The ability to support virtual private networks (VPNs), and third-party services such as WAN optimization controllers, firewalls, and web gateways

Figure 11.9 shows the evolution of WAN connectivity. Traditional WAN networks rely on dedicated branch routers and other premises equipment that is interconnected using static WAN connections, typically MPLS or private lines. With SD-WAN, the branch routers are replaced by UCPEs. UCPEs are a form of "white box," commodity hardware that can be used to host a variety of virtual applications, such as routers and firewalls. (see also Figure 11.1). Static WAN connections are replaced by multiple connection types, including consumer-grade internet connections that are managed to create reliable connectivity. Predictive SD-WAN uses AI to optimize bandwidth in the SD-WAN network.

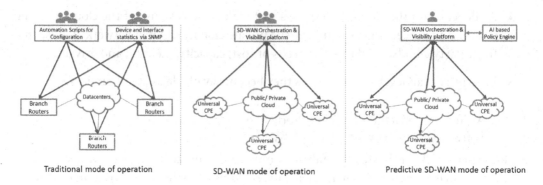

FIGURE 11.9   WAN modes of operation—traditional, SD-WAN, and predictive SD-WAN.

Three key aspects of SD-WAN solutions save costs:

- Zero-touch provisioning: SD-WAN solutions enable cloud-controlled deployment of the WAN edge (UCPE) without requiring prestaging of routers or on-site technicians, thus avoiding the costs associated with truck rolls for CPE deployment.

- Transport independence: SD-WAN uses software control to add new features, such as packet retransmission, path quality-based routing, and packet duplication, for making Internet or broadband an acceptable transport for enterprise-grade traffic instead of requiring MPLS transport for security and Quality of Service.

- Management and orchestration: SD-WAN provides a simple graphical policy interface for visualizing the network telemetry and simpler application-based policy model, avoiding the need for high-skilled workers and specialized tools for policy management.

With the use of a simplified policy interface and network data analytics enabled by SD-WAN, it has become easier for network administrators to design and operate the network. Admins can use a simple graphical interface to design the network and visual interactive graphs to monitor operations, and they can define much more granular policies for application-level traffic flows.

Artificial intelligence will further transform the existing SD-WAN solution into "predictive-SD-WAN." While today's SD-WAN solutions provide simplified policy interfaces, they are mostly static and manually controlled. While SD-WAN provides network telemetry, its primary use is limited to report generation to understand network topology, application traffic behavior, and usage.

Predictive SD-WAN will embed continuous learning within the WAN ecosystem to pave the way for popular concepts, such as self-healing and self-defending networks. Many SD-WAN providers are currently evaluating how they can leverage AI to augment their SD-WAN solutions to gain a competitive edge. Following are some of the examples of how AI technology can be used for enterprise SD-WAN.

- Using AI to create dynamic VPN topologies. In today's SD-WAN solution, VPNs and Internet access networks are configured statically with fixed bandwidth by highly skilled engineers who are responsible for creating and managing the overall network design. Using AI, it could be possible to create the network map of the underlay fabric where overlay services such as VPN need not be persistent and can be created dynamically based on traffic demands. This capability will reduce the complexity of network design significantly.

- Intent-based policy interface. Intent-based policy refers to a concept where an administrator can define and communicate the desired policy to a network orchestration platform without having to understand the network topology [19]. In general, this concept presents a stark departure from the way enterprise networks are managed today where user intent is translated to network design by the network design experts and sometimes gets implemented without proper validation of original intent. Recent advancements in concepts such as network data-modeling (i.e., ability to organize network elements, interfaces, attributes, etc. in a structured format and as addressable objects) along with advancement in chatbots and Natural Language Processing technologies provide the ability for a network administrator to communicate with the network using a voice or chat interface while an orchestrator converts the user-intent to a policy understood by network orchestrator.

- Network troubleshooting and root cause analysis. Network troubleshooting and root cause analysis is another area where many vendors are trying to use AI concepts for faster resolution of problems. Most vendors today maintain a continuously evolving database of network issues that they encounter. Using this data source as learning samples, vendors can significantly improve root cause identification.

- Self-defending networks. Autonomous detection and mitigation of attacks. Enterprise networks are increasingly vulnerable to cyberattacks. In using the wealth of data that can be collected and analyzed using SDN, it is possible to use AI to automatically detect and mitigate attacks.

- Application performance. AI technology can be used to track multiple parameters and traffic characteristics as they relate to application performance and to dynamically insert additional services such as WAN acceleration on individual traffic flow basis.

- Dynamic bandwidth management. Bandwidth allocation in traditional networks is static, only changeable using manual service order processes. Using AI coupled with the real-time configuration possibilities introduced by SD-WAN, bandwidth can be dynamically adjusted based on real-time usage, network conditions, seasonality, time-of-day variation, market dynamics, and external events such as emergencies. This allows the network to operate more efficiently and customers to optimize their cost and performance.

- Self-healing networks. Combining network telemetry data with machine learning algorithms to determine the health of the network devices and associated probability of network outage due to failure, the network can implement measures to autonomously take corrective action, such as device reboot to avoid or repair network issues.

As apparent from the previous examples, AI technology can be embedded in many aspects of the enterprise WAN network. However, in general, there is a common theme to many of the use-cases described earlier that can help summarize the impact AI technology may have on WAN environment. It is basically the ability for machines or network platforms to understand and correlate many data-streams and parameters and facilitate activities that are costly, error-prone, or realize vision of self-learning, self-healing, and self-defending WAN network.

11.4.3 Artificial Intelligence Optimized Enterprise Wireless and Wired Local Area Network

The "enterprise LAN" is perhaps the most crucial section of an enterprise network. This is because a LAN network provides the connectivity to end-users and/or the devices where data is created and consumed. The rest of the enterprise network, including the WAN and datacenter, are built to serve these end-users, devices, and the data they originate.

In the last few decades, the enterprise LAN, comprising both wired and wireless networks, has evolved significantly in terms of performance, size, and complexity due to the expanding number of connected users, devices, and applications. To address the increased complexity and quickly respond to business requirements, some enterprises are also looking at "SDN" like solutions designed to manage the enterprise LAN environment. However, just like SD-WAN, existing solutions for the LAN currently focus on providing a "simplified" interfaces for user/device, capacity, and performance management using static policies.

As one imagines the future of the enterprise LAN with a new breed of IoT devices, smart devices associated with each user, and always-on and always-moving devices/users, the challenges for enterprise LAN increase significantly. For example,

- Increased number of devices and "connected things" will clamor for more network resources, such as wired LAN ports and wireless capacity.

- The explosion of applications used by new devices, each requiring the best possible response time, requires a newer scheme of network flow management.

- The dynamic nature of these devices that join the network only when needed will create challenges for network scaling.

- Wider surface area of attack from hundreds of devices type poses a significantly higher security risk that must be managed.

Existing LAN networking solutions in the market may only solve the earlier challenges by deploying higher port counts or denser wireless networks. We believe the use of AI and related technology can further improve large enterprise LAN environments. For example,

- It may be possible to avoid deployment of new access points, if AI technology can be used to increase the transmitter power of existing "nearby" access points depending on "user population" near a specific access point deployed to serve a defined area.

- New AI algorithms can be used to optimize the existing wired or wireless infrastructure by improving the accuracy of the oversubscription ratio by monitoring the bandwidth usage, application type, and priority.

- Security could be better managed by deploying new machine learning algorithms as part of device and user authentication.

Software-defined LANs are in the early stages of maturity, and the examples earlier are illustrative of the opportunities in a campus LAN environment. As the technology matures, we believe that just as in datacenter and WAN, AI and associated technologies will also be embedded into enterprise LAN products.

11.5 IMPACT OF ARTIFICIAL INTELLIGENCE ON NETWORK DEVICES AND ARCHITECTURE

In the previous section, we discussed how AI and related technologies can be used to solve some of the emerging challenges in enterprise networks. However, the impact of AI on networks is not limited to solving individual problems in existing enterprise environments. Artificial intelligence and related technologies have the potential to transform the enterprise network architecture as we know it today.

Current industry trends suggest that a next-generation enterprise environment will have many more devices embedded with AI capabilities. Due to the heavy reliance of these devices on streaming telemetry and associated policy engines, it is reasonable to expect that these devices will continue to require increased throughput, reliability, security, and analytical capability from the enterprise WAN network. These new network requirements could, in turn, drive a further evolution in WAN networks. However, the key architectural shift could come from the changes in datacenter/cloud environment. In the current generation architecture, an enterprise primarily leverages "centralized" public and private clouds for the application workload. In recent years, with the adoption of concepts, such as network function virtualization and open source cloud technology, workloads in localized branch environments can also achieve cloud benefits, such as ease of deployment, elasticity, and hardware agnostic infrastructure.

With the exponential increase in number of devices in the branch, the "centralized" cloud approach to store and analyze that data is becoming very costly. Some in the industry are exploring an architecture whereby machine-learning algorithms employed at centralized locations can control and instruct the WAN edge to gather additional data or filter away unnecessary data to reduce the storage and compute requirements in the centralized location [20]. In addition, as AI and related technology is embedded into many other things that we interact with on daily basis, the need for graphical processing unit (GPU) processing at branch locations will increase significantly. It is very likely that the future generation WAN edge devices (UCPEs) could be bundled with GPUs in addition to traditional CPUs to accelerate deep learning (see Chapter 2), analytics, and engineering applications. Some of the use-cases that facilitate "decentralization" of the cloud to the branch edge include:

- Executing latency sensitive workload or other types of workloads that are significant to local branch only, thus providing more control to local teams without opening additional touchpoints in workloads running private or public clouds

- Executing workloads to preprocess or summarize the data locally, thus enhancing the security posture and limiting the cost associated with data stored in public clouds or private clouds

- Moving multiple physical functions to the virtual environment, thus enabling better cost structure, more control in terms of high-availability design, operations etc.

- Creating the edge cloud on-demand temp basis events, pop-up stores, etc. while reducing the need for 24×7 high-speed WAN connectivity

To address these use-cases, enterprise architectures will need to evolve so that centralized cloud nodes are extended to the branch edge. This will shift application architectures to be distributed between the traditional centralized cloud nodes and UCPE nodes on customer premises. Artificial intelligence applications will take advantage of this power by performing compute-intensive applications in the core network, while running real-time or near real-time applications at the edge. The network will be able to make autonomous decisions to optimize which functions should be performed at the premises, edge and core. For example, security models could be trained in the core and executed at the edge or on the premises. Real-time security functions could be trained at the edge and executed at the customer premises. The trend toward edge computing will cause applications to be fundamentally rearchitected to take advantage of this power, optimizing network resource consumption, and enabling low latency. Artificial intelligence applications will be among the biggest beneficiaries of such transformation.

11.6 SUMMARY

In this chapter, we described AI opportunities for the enterprise. Driven by the digital transformation, the application of AI in the enterprise can be divided into two major areas: digital transformation of the enterprise business model and transformation of enterprise networks to meet the new business model. The transformation of the enterprise business model is heavily influenced by the IoT, and the ability to store, process, and integrate diverse data in the cloud. The transformation of the enterprise business model has, in turn, stimulated changes in the fundamental enterprise network architecture. The key drivers of network transformation are the datacenter transition to the cloud, the WAN transition to SD-WAN, including virtualization of the Premises network, and wired and wireless LAN transformation. The transformed enterprise network also requires AI to meet the flexibility, security, and dynamic adaptation needs of the new business models.

As the transformation continues, we expect continuing evolution, with increased functionality at the network edge to accommodate the rigorous demands of the emerging applications.

REFERENCES

1. IDC, Digital transformation (DX): An opportunity and an imperative, Adapted from IDC MaturityScape: Digital Transformation (DX), Document #254721, March 2015, https://www. idc.com/prodserv/decisionscapes/RESOURCES/ATTACHMENTS/IDC_254721_ExecBrief_ Digital_Transformation.pdf
2. Rashid, B., Digital transformation and innovation in today's business world, *Forbes*, June 13, 2017, https://www.forbes.com/sites/brianrashid/2017/06/13/digital-transformation-and-inno vation-in-todays-business-world/#6aff6a849052
3. DeNisco Rayome, A., Report: Digital transformation spending to hit $1.7T by 2019, TechRepublic, November 1, 2017, https://www.techrepublic.com/article/report-digital-transformation-spending-to-hit-1-7t-by-20
4. AT&T, AT&T Flexware, https://www.business.att.com/solutions/Service/network-services/ sdn-nfv/virtual-network-functions/, accessed January 18, 2018.
5. Verweij, G., A. Rao, and J. Woods, Sizing the prize: What's the real value of AI for your business and how can you capitalise? www.pwc.com/AI, June 21, 2017, PWC, https://www.pwc. com/gx/en/issues/analytics/assets/pwc-ai-analysis-sizing-the-prize-report.pdf
6. Bughin, J., E. Hazan, S. Ramaswamy et al., How artificial intelligence can deliver real value to companies, McKinsey Global Institute, June 2017, https://www.mckinsey.com/business-functions/ mckinsey-analytics/our-insights/how-artificial-intelligence-can-deliver-real-value-to-companies
7. Cisco, Reinventing retail: Cisco reveals how stores can surge ahead on the digital transformation journey, January 2017, https://www.cisco.com/c/dam/en_us/solutions/industries/retail/ retail-digital-transformation-readiness.pdf
8. National Federation of Independent Businesses (NFIB), Energy, http://www.nfib.com/ advocacy/energy/, accessed January 18, 2018.
9. Tracy, P., Internet of Things Blog, The top 5 industrial IoT use cases, April 19, 2017, IBM, https://www.ibm.com/blogs/internet-of-things/top-5-industrial-iot-use-cases/
10. Altexsoft software r&d engineering, Digital transformation stories: How Starbucks, Walmart and Sephora revolutionalize retail industry, March 21, 2017, https://www.altexsoft.com/blog/ business/digital-transformation-stories-how-starbucks-walmart-and-sephora-revolutionize-retail-industry/
11. Alton, L., How financial services use AI to serve customer needs, Forbes Brand Voice, September 8, 2017, https://www.forbes.com/sites/centurylink/2017/09/08/how-financial-services-use-ai-to-serve-customer-needs/#3016a8786e3b
12. Altexsoft software r&d engineering, Digital transformation stories: How Mastercard and Capital One have joined the Fintech wave, June 6, 2017, "https://www.altexsoft.com/blog/ business/digital-transformation-stories-how-mastercard-and-capital-one-have-joined-the-fintech-wave/
13. Donovan, J. and K. Prabhu, *Building the Network of the Future: Getting Smarter, Faster, and More Flexible with a Software Centric Approach*, Chapman and Hall/CRC, 2017.
14. Bodenski, D. Artificial intelligence uses in datacenters, Belden, May 11, 2017, http://www. belden.com/blog/data-centers/artificial-intelligence-uses-in-data-centers
15. Beyney, C.-A., Artificial intelligence and the evolution of datacenters, February 22, 2017, http://www.datacenterknowledge.com/archives/2017/02/22/ artificial-intelligence-evolution-data-centers

16. SDX Central, What is Software-Defined WAN (or SD-WAN)? https://www.sdxcentral.com/sd-wan/definitions/software-defined-sdn-wan/, accessed November 22, 2017.

17. Scarpati, J., SD-What? Understanding SD-WAN, September 2015, Tech Target, http://searchsdn.techtarget.com/feature/SD-What-Understanding-SD-WAN

18. Butler, B., SD-WAN: What it is and why you'll use it one day, June 12, 2017, NetworkWorld, https://www.networkworld.com/article/3031279/sd-wan/sd-wan-what-it-is-and-why-you-ll-use-it-one-day.html

19. Millman, R., What is intent-based networking, and what can it do for your business? ComputerWeekly.com, September 2017, http://www.computerweekly.com/feature/What-is-intent-based-networking-and-what-can-it-do-for-your-business

20. Wilson, C., SDN + AI: A powerful combo for better networks, LightReading, September 1, 2016, http://www.lightreading.com/analytics/analytics-systems/sdn--ai-a-powerful-combo-for-better-networks/d/d-id/725705

CHAPTER 12

Artificial Intelligence for 5G+, Edge Compute, and Internet of Things

Rittwik Jana, Mark Austin, and Wenjie Zhao

CONTENTS

12.1   INTRODUCTION

Artificial intelligence (AI) is not only an interesting technology for improving accuracy and prediction on a variety of problems, but it is ultimately required to be used to extract intelligence from the enormous amount of data produced on modern-day networks. Indeed, not only is today's data large, it is growing so fast, that 90% of the world's data has been produced in the last two years. Additionally, while the world has 7.9 Zettabytes of data today, by 2020 the total digital data universe is expected to grow to 44 Zettabytes, with each person generating 1.7 Megabytes every second [1]. Some of the motivation and enablers behind this explosion of data are described in this chapter along with the drivers and solutions behind 5G, edge compute and Internet of Things (IoT).

12.2   BACKGROUND MOTIVATIONS DRIVING TECHNOLOGY EVOLUTION

Data demand driven by video: Since the introduction of the iPhone in 2007 by AT&T and Apple, data usage has skyrocketed an amazing 250,000% [2] from 2007 to 2017 for AT&T and similarly for the industry. This data growth has certainly been driven by the introduction of faster data speeds on networks coupled with smartphones and apps, which ultimately enabled the ease of delivery of video. Indeed, AT&T [2] and Cisco [3] report that the majority (60%+) of the usage in modern wireless networks is now video, which is expected to proportionally grow to 78% by 2021 as shown in Figure 12.1.

Device growth driven by IoT: In addition to the migration of wireless usage from voice, text, and web-browsing to video, there is another change underway in regards to the mix of devices on the wireless network. In 2017, mobile phone penetration has virtually reached 1:1 for every person in the USA (at ~81% from [4]), and the growth of connected devices, other than phones, is accelerating. To this end, Ericsson [5] forecasts that IoT devices will be the largest category of growth over the next few years, growing from 5.6B connected devices in 2015 to ~17.6B devices in 2020, as shown in Figures 12.2 and 12.3.

Wireless network architecture evolution: Coupled with the massive data usage growth and change in device mix trends, there are a number of architecture trends underway as shown in Table 12.1.

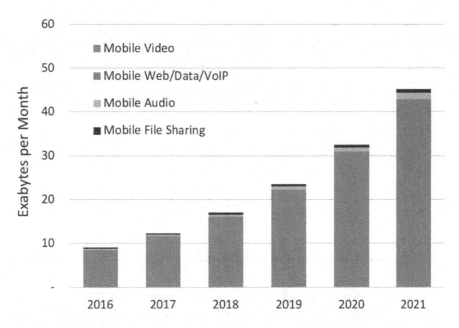

FIGURE 12.1   IoT and Connected Device Forecast. (From Internet of Things Outlook, Ericsson, https://www.ericsson.com/en/mobility-report/internet-of-things-outlook; https://www.ericsson.com/assets/local/publications/white-papers/wp-iot-security-february-2017.pdf.)

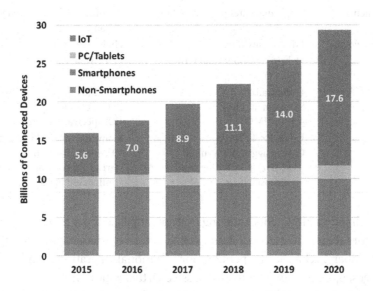

FIGURE 12.2   IoT and Connected Device Forecast. (From Internet of Things outlook, Ericsson, https://www.ericsson.com/en/mobility-report/internet-of-things-outlook, https://www.ericsson.com/assets/local/publications/white-papers/wp-iot-security-february-2017.pdf.)

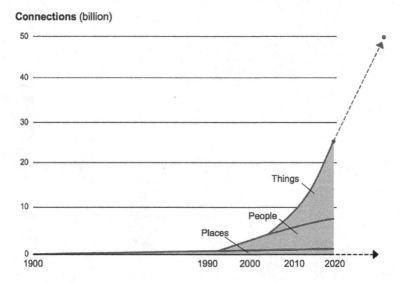

FIGURE 12.3 The growth of connected "things" will drive future growth. (From Internet of Things outlook, Ericsson, https://www.ericsson.com/en/mobility-report/internet-of-things-outlook, https://www.ericsson.com/assets/local/publications/white-papers/wp-iot-security-february-2017.pdf.)

TABLE 12.1 Wireless Network Architecture Evolution Trends

Network Characteristics	Today	2020+
Cell site deployments	Single digit sites per square km	10s of sites per macrocell per square kilometer
Backbone connectivity	Low-density fiber	High-density fiber
Core network	Hybrid traditional and virtual (NFVs)	Full virtualization
RAN network	Decentralized RAN Some small cells 4 × 4 MIMO	Cloud RAN EDGE computing 10X spectrum utilized
Device	Up to 4 × 4 MIMO Carrier aggregation (up to 50 MHz) + including some unlicensed band	Many antennas (Massive MIMO) 10X spectrum utilized Carrier aggregation (5 way bands) + unlicensed bands (e.g., 3.5 MHz band)

Denser cell-site deployments, utilizing multiple small cells per macrocell, are occurring as operators attempt to meet the skyrocketing data usage demand. In turn, this is driving a denser fiber backbone. In parallel, for additional operational and cost-efficiency advantages, operators are turning to massive virtualization[1] in the core network (CN). For example, in 2017 AT&T had more than 55% of its CN virtualized [6], and other operators are attempting to follow suit [7]. While software-defined radios have been the mainstay in some areas in the defense industry for years, virtualization of the radio access network (RAN) is expected to also materialize in the mainstream wireless industry in the near future. The virtual RAN will likely entail portions in the cloud while

---

[1] Virtualization denotes the migration of a network function from vendor proprietary hardware and software nodes to a software solution running on standard "off-the-shelf" hardware.

keeping some functions at the edge based on the application needs. The capabilities of devices are also evolving, which will enable much wider bandwidths of noncontiguous spectrum, both licensed and unlicensed, to be consumed using multiple air interface standards. While some of this architecture evolution, such as the virtualization, can be accomplished without standards changes, much of this can be further facilitated and driven via standards evolution towards 5G+, which is summarized in the next section.

12.2.1 5G+

While in second, third, and arguably some early versions of fourth-generation wireless standards there have been multiple competing standards, the industry has migrated to 4G with long-term evolution (LTE) as defined by the industry consortium 3GPP [8]. Typically, performance goals, such as data speeds, coverage, and capacity, from a user perspective for wireless capabilities, are set globally by a consortium of operators, vendors, and countries in the International Telecommunications Union (ITU). The ITU first started such user requirements in the late 1990s for the year 2000, in a specification called IMT-2000, after which the 3G standards were developed. The latest incarnation of ITU requirements are for the year 2020, called IMT-2020, which defines the user desired requirements for 5G, for which 3GPP is developing the technical specifications. Figure 12.4 summarizes these requirements, with low-cost targets to support the expected device growth with IoT (machine to machine low cost), extreme mobile broadband goals for the expected usage growth, and ultra-reliability to enable new low-latency applications and high bandwidth everywhere.

Specific targets are set in some cases relative to 4G (LTE), such as 10–100X more devices and 10,000X more traffic, while in other areas absolute targets such as <1 milliseconds latency, 10 Gbps peak, 100 Mbps everywhere, and at least 10 years' battery life for machine-to-machine (M2M) devices are defined.

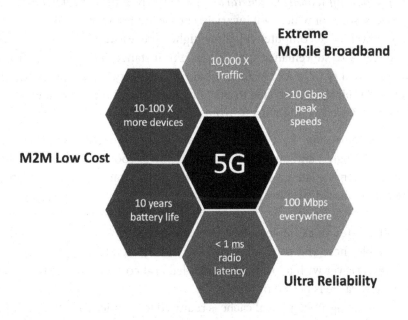

FIGURE 12.4   5G performance requirements as defined by IMT-2020.

Some of the new capabilities in the extreme mobile broadband area, such as 10 Gbps peak, 100 Mbps everywhere, and 10,000X more traffic, may actually open up new cost-effective fixed wireless in suburban and urban geographical areas, which has typically only been deployed in rural areas. Given these new capabilities, a new optimism is growing, as ABI research (https://www.abiresearch.com/) [9] recently wrote that 5G is expected to spur the growth of fixed wireless to 151M people covered by 2022, with AT&T and Verizon starting rollouts in 2017.

Needless to say, the increase of 10,000X traffic usage with 5G poses significant challenges in network optimization, routing, and potential data insights. To put this in perspective, for an operator the size of AT&T, which in 2016 carried 118 Petabytes of data per day, this would amount to processing 1.18 Zettabytes (10^{21} bytes) per day, while in comparison the entire world's data amounted to 7.5 Zettabytes in 2015 [10]. Network optimization and gleaning any sort of data insights off of data this size is virtually impossible to do centrally, and edge computing solutions will be imperative.

12.2.2 Mobile EDGE Compute

In addition to needing computation abilities at the edge of the network to process the sheer volume of network data for insights, moving compute to the edge is driven by a number of additional motivations. For instance, Ahmed [11] summarizes a few of these motivations as follows:

- *Dynamic content optimization*: Similar to the function of the Content Distribution Networks today, edge compute and local caching provide the ability to host content on the edge closer to the users, which provides reduced latency, transport, and cloud server costs. Depending on the content cached at the edge and the users' applications, AI can assist in traffic flow, and the savings in transport can be significant.

- *Computational off-loading in general and for IoT*: Given the expected tens of billions of IoT devices, some of which will invariably be wearables, with minimal on-device processing power, edge compute will allow higher processing applications, such as augmented reality or surveillance applications. For instance, if one was wearing a virtual/augmented reality (VR/AR) headset where VR/AR processing was in the cloud, and one moved their head from side to side, one would want the AR rendering to keep up and not be delayed as might occur from a traditional distant data center.

- *Smart transportation*: In a world of everything connected, smartphones, traffic meters, traffic lights, and other vehicles, the ability to coordinate and share information locally and with low latency can lend itself to new applications in smart transportation as the data is shared, and insights are provided for the local community.

Figure 12.5 illustrates an example of how edge compute is incorporated into the wireless network to enable these and other applications. In this architecture, a new Mobile Edge Compute (MEC) server with a local cache is added and co-located with the enode-b, and an additional CN cache is placed in the CN.

In some cases, using an edge local cache is required for applications such as VR/AR processing, where the latency needs to be very low, while in other applications, such as video

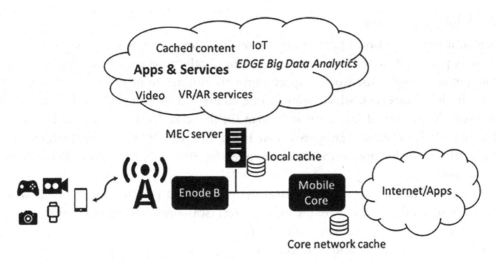

FIGURE 12.5   5G performance requirements as defined by IMT-2020.

content distribution, the frequency and demand of the content will likely drive the most appropriate staging area.

Understanding the trade-offs of different staging locations for content is an active research area, where a number of authors [12,13] have suggested methods to characterize and minimize the "normalized delivery time" of any content that is desired by the end mobile user. Needless to say, the permutations of placing content on the edge, core, or Internet cloud are enormous with significant performance and cost implications, since they also depend on the dynamic in nature of the users connected at any moment. Consequently, this is a research and application area that can likely only be solved by measuring the performance of different configurations and solving for the best configuration versus user needs and attributes.

In addition, to make the "AI edge compute optimization problem" even more challenging, consider Figure 12.6 where the "mobility variable implications to local caches" is illustrated.

This figure highlights that a mobile using App1 served by MEC server on enode-b1 needs to also have access to App1 on the MEC server on enode-b2; otherwise, either the connection will be dropped, or a delay will occur in reconnecting with App1.

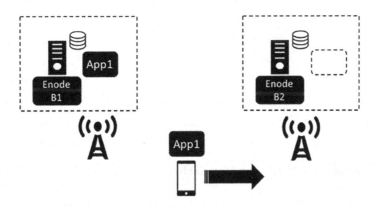

FIGURE 12.6   5G performance requirements as defined by IMT-2020.

12.2.3 Internet of Things

As mentioned in Section 12.2, the main growth of devices on wireless networks of the future is projected to be from "connected things," otherwise called the enabling of the "Internet of Things." One would expect a growth in usage to be coupled with a growth in public IoT awareness, which seems to be confirmed by Google Trends data, which captures the number of times a search term (in this case "IOT") is searched by a user (Figure 12.7). Here one sees an approximate 10X uptick in IoT Google search interest since 2012–2013, with the most search interest appearing from Southeast Asia (South Korea, China, Singapore).

Figure 12.8 further breaks the interest by region down per city, where one also sees that cities in Southeast Asia have the most interest (searches), albeit Santa Clara in Silicon Valley, California, area comes in at number four.

While the interest, demand, and technology appears to be coming in place for massive IoT, it will be the applications and analytics that will have the greatest need, growth, and monetary potential (60%), as described in a recent Boston Consulting Group [14] report as shown in Figure 12.9. Internet of Things applications are literally expected to be everywhere and in all industries [15].

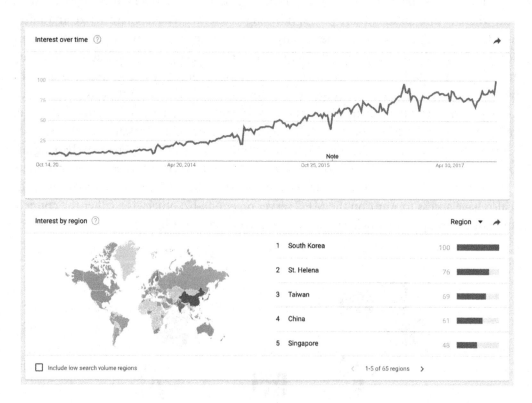

FIGURE 12.7   IoT Interest over time, and interest by region from Google Trends data (11/2017).

FIGURE 12.8   IoT city area of interest from Google Trends data (11/2017).

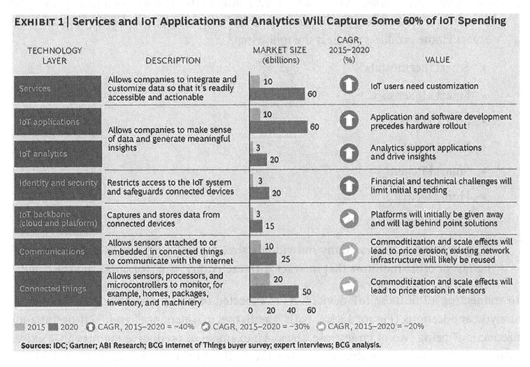

FIGURE 12.9   IoT analytics, applications and services growth, and potential. (From Winning in IoT: It's all about the business processes, Boston Consulting Group (BCG), https://www.bcgperspectives. com/content/articles/hardware-software-energy-environment-winning-in-iot-all-about-winning-processes/ [14].)

- *Airlines*: An often-touted example by GE is that current jet engines collect 500 Gb of data per flight, for over 5,000 parameters from various sensors measuring vast amounts of temperature, altitude, and performance data on the engines. As compared to older engines, which only had 1 Kb of data, they were able to improve the reliability 287 times.

- *Oil rigs*: Oil companies outfit costly drilling equipment with sensors to detect degradation and to provide visual recognition so as to recommend preventive maintenance to avoid costly downtimes, and to inspect equipment without needing to send a team.

- *Transportation and manufacturing*: It is already quite common today to drive in cars with multiple sensors, which some models such as Tesla and others use to assist in self-driving. In the future, it is expected that not only will sensors communicate within the vehicle but also potentially interact with surrounding sensors along the road and in other vehicles.

- *Smart buildings/homes*: AT&T has a M2X platform that allows millions of connected devices to connect data to the cloud [16,17]. For example, the AT&T "Digital Life" Smart Home products connect the following:

  - Smart thermostats

  - Smart air sensors

  - Smart HVAC

  - Smart water

  - Smart kitchens

  - Home security

  - Child monitoring

- *Body sensors/wearables*: Many individuals already wear connected watches, exercise bands, or other monitors that interact with each other, smartphones, and the cloud.

In connecting all of these IoT devices, AI is expected to be a key enabler of a number of analytic applications (Figure 12.10), with "predictive maintenance" and "self-optimizing production" being two of largest use cases. An example of predictive maintenance exists in the rail industry where they determine the health of the track and possibly lifetime left before maintenance, by monitoring track vibration through sensors as trains pass by. Self-optimizing production is the large category that can use a closed-loop machine learning (ML) system, which may be constantly evaluating an overall "objective function" and may optimize a variety of tools (e.g., settings, use, or adjustments) and processes to correct for any defects to further optimize yield or to reduce cost/energy.

It's really no wonder why the forecasters are predicting massive potential for AI on IoT, as the potential of large scale IoT would not be fully utilized unless the mountain of data produced can be processed in an automated and intelligent manner [18].

EXHIBIT 2 | Ten Use Cases Will Drive IoT Growth Through 2020

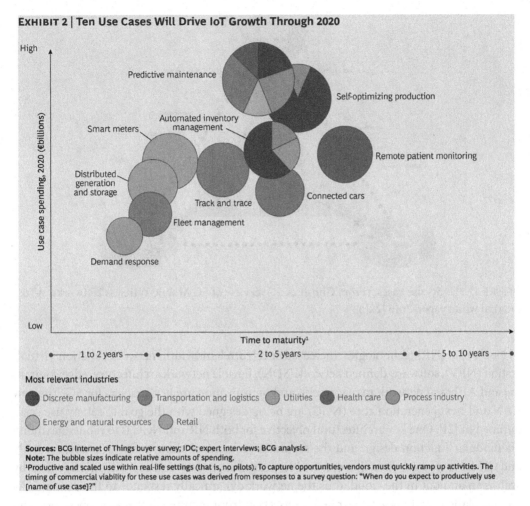

Sources: BCG Internet of Things buyer survey; IDC; expert interviews; BCG analysis.
Note: The bubble sizes indicate relative amounts of spending.
[1]Productive and scaled use within real-life settings (that is, no pilots). To capture opportunities, vendors must quickly ramp up activities. The timing of commercial viability for these use cases was derived from responses to a survey question: "When do you expect to productively use [name of use case]?"

FIGURE 12.10   IoT use cases. (From Winning in IoT: It's all about the business processes, Boston Consulting Group (BCG), https://www.bcgperspectives.com/content/articles/hardware-software-energy-environment-winning-in-iot-all-about-winning-processes/ [14].)

12.3 NETWORK AND ACCESS ARCHITECTURE

12.3.1 Key Drivers for a New Architecture

To fulfill the promise of providing connectivity anywhere, anytime to anyone and anything, the network of future (5G and beyond) needs to address key challenges related to capacity, data rate, end-to-end (E2E) latency, massive number of connections, cost, and quality of experience [19,20]. Furthermore, the network is required to simultaneously support applications with diverse characteristics. Use cases such as enhanced mobile broadband with speed over 1Gbps, smart city, smart home with a large number of sensors, and ultra-reliable, low-latency applications such as autonomous cars and mission critical IoTs represent scenarios that define extreme values along speed, connection density, latency, and reliability dimensions [21]. See Figure 12.11 for more details.

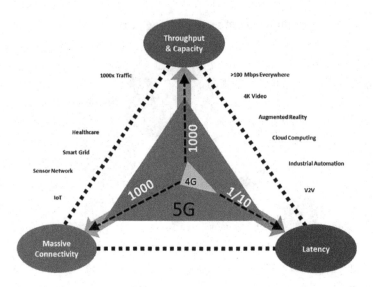

FIGURE 12.11 5G use cases. (From Ghosh, A., Overview of 5G Mobile Wireless Networks, AT&T internal white paper, 2016 [22].)

New radio (NR) technologies, increased spectrum bandwidth, network function virtualization (NFV), software-defined network (SDN), flexible network architecture, edge computing and AI-based network management, and optimization are key enablers for 5G. The new RAN and next generation core (NGC) are being designed with the goal to satisfy use cases outlined in [21]. One key architectural objective for both NR and NGC is to render flexibility via modular function design and the separation of control plane and user plane. As RAN and CN functions get virtualized, it enables real-time, end-to-end capacity management by scaling in and out in the cloud, thus the network dynamically responds to the demand. As control plane functions get separated, innovation from incumbent vendors, operators, and third parties alike can be introduced rapidly to control the behavior of the network in real time via SDN. 5G architecture supports network slicing, which gives operators the capability to partition network resources to cater the need of individual services. With the increased network flexibility, it comes with added complexity. The number of network functions and interfaces, the set of network slices, the number of connections, the throughput of measurement data, and the fine granularity of control at individual connection level drive the need for automation in 5G network management and optimization via AI.

Edge computing capability is required to support low-latency use cases, such as self-driving cars, e-Health, and immersive experiences. Content delivery applications can benefit significantly when they are hosted at the edge of the network to reduce transport cost and improve user quality of experience. The virtualized RAN (VRAN), core, and transport network functions deployed at MEC will collocate with other MEC applications, enabling real-time information exchange between network and applications. The access to real-time RAN measurements and location information with the ability to influence the behavior of RAN via open Application Program Interfaces (APIs) will power innovative solutions from third parties and operators to serve enterprise and consumers. The convergence of cloud computing, real-time network information, high bandwidth, proximity to end users, and devices is the unique characteristics of MEC. It is a key pillar of 5G-era network.

12.3.2 5G System Architecture and Core Network Functions

With the use case requirement and operator's deployment flexibility via NFV and SDN in mind, 3GPP has defined a service-based 5G system architecture. Figure 12.12 is the non-roaming reference architecture from 3GPP TS 23.501. There is a clear separation of user plane and control plane functions. User plane traffic traverses between User Equipment (UE) to the data network (DN) via RAN (or other access network) and the CN user plane function (UPF), as shown in the bottom part of the diagram. The rest of the diagram depicts various 5G CN control plane functions, such as access and mobility management function (AMF), session management (SMF), and authentication server function (AUSF). The communications among different control plane network functions are defined as service calls. Though a point-to-point interaction between two functions can still be viewed as going through a

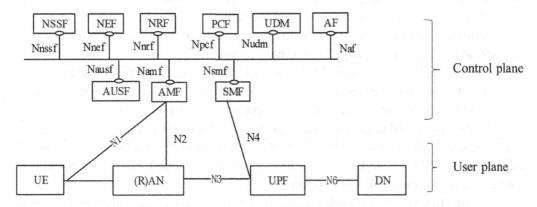

FIGURE 12.12   5G System Architecture. (From 3GPP TS 23.501, Technical specification group services and systems aspects; System architecture for the 5G system; Stage 2, Release 15, September 2017 [28]. Please refer to Table 12.2 for NGC function abbreviations.)

TABLE 12.2   NGC Abbreviations

AF	Application function
AMF	Access and mobility management function
AUSF	Authentication server function
DN	Data network
NEF	Network exposure function
NRF	Network repository function
NSSF	Network slice selection function
PCF	Policy control function
SMF	Session management function
UDM	Unified data management
UDR	Unified data repository
UDSF	Unstructured data storage function
UPF	User plane function

pair-wise interface, the service call concept to access a network function provides greater modularity and flexibility in deployment scenarios with the potential to source different network functions from different vendors.

User plane functions can be deployed separately from the control plane functions to reduce end-to-end latency and enable cost-efficient data transport. For example, ultra-reliable, low-latency communication (URLLC) services need to be supported by UPFs at MEC locations. Similarly, when application contents are positioned to the edge for performance and cost saving, local UPFs should be selected to route the traffic to realize the benefits. Intelligent decisions can be made at the individual session level for the optimal UPF selections using ML algorithms, considering operator's policies, UE location, application server address, application type, mobility, load, cost, and other network, UE, and application information.

The unified data management (UDM), unified data repository (UDR), and unstructured data storage function (UDSF) in the 5G system architecture provide the capability to store and retrieve both structured and unstructured data related to policy, UE subscription, UE authorization, UE preferences, UE historical, expected mobility pattern, etc. Such information can be accessed by network functions directly to complete access and mobility management, session management, and other procedures.

The network exposure function (NEF) makes UDM and UDR data available to applications and other external entities. Applications can use the exposed network information to understand UE level behaviors, recommend changes to influence policy control function (PCF) on routing decisions and improve overall application performance and UE quality of service. Operators can develop or procure from third parties ML algorithms that subscribe to the CN information via NEF (or via UDM, UDR directly) to propose adjustments to RAN and core configurations to optimize network performance.

5G architecture enables network slicing. Operators configure different slices to tailor to the unique requirements of enhanced mobile broadband (eMBB), massive IoT (MIoT), and URLLC services. The network slice selection function (NSSF) in the 5G system architecture determines the allowed network slices for a UE and makes the slice selection. A UE can be configured with multiple network slices, and there can be more than one defined slice for each slice/service type (Slice/Service Type [SST], such as eMBB, MIoT, URLLC). A network slice must be configured across core, RAN and transport network. End to end slicing is further described in Section 12.3.5.

The 5G core functions can be virtualized and deployed in operator's or third-party clouds as virtual network functions (VNF). When functional behaviors, interface protocol, and data model are standardized, VNFs can be sourced from multiple vendors and be able to interoperate via service calls. Virtual network functions can be further decomposed into or assembled from microservices to increase software reuse, reduce development cost, and accelerate time to market. In addition, with the use of a VNF orchestration and control platform such as ONAP (Open Network Automation Platform [23]), the life-cycle management of these VNFs can be greatly simplified. The benefits derived from a flexible 5G architecture can be realized to a higher potential via automated, insight-driven policies and UE-level controls. A more detailed description of ONAP-based control for 5G can be found in Section 12.3.7.

12.3.3 New Radio Access Network Architecture

In the last 25 years, we have experienced rapid evolution in wireless technology from 2G, 3G, to 4G with a thousandfold increase in theoretical peak downlink (DL) speed (from about 300Kbps to over 300Mbps). This advance has fueled the advent of smartphones and many thousands of mobile applications that we interact with daily. However, as noted in Section 12.3.1, emerging use case scenarios exert demands in speed, connection density, reliability, and latency that are to 10–1000 times higher than what can provided by the 4G network. RAN is the crucial part of the wireless network. New radio technologies and new RAN architecture are needed to meet the capacity and performance requirements.

12.3.3.1 New Radio Technologies

Antenna technology: To increase capacity by 100 times per unit area, 5G RAN will reply on large bandwidth over 50 MHz or more. In the US, available spectrum below 6 GHz is very limited. Centimeter wave (cmWave) and millimeter wave (mmWave) are being considered to provide 5G RAN capacity due to the large bandwidth. In the cmWave band, several hundred MHz spectrum can be potentially used. While the available spectrum for mmWave exceeds 1 GHz. The small wavelength presents many challenges for Radio Frequency (RF) signal propagation. mmWave interacts with air and water molecules, and it is affected by climate pattern, weather events, and vegetation. On the other hand, phased array antennas with many small elements can be utilized to transmit/receive mmWave signals. This technology not only helps to solve propagation challenges but also enables the use of massive Multiple Input and Multiple Output (MIMO).

Massive MIMO: Via spatial multiplexing and other techniques, massive MIMO has the potential to increase spectral efficiency and cell capacity and, in the meantime, reduce radiated energy and latency [24]. Spectral efficiency and capacity increase comes from the fact that a massive MIMO system can use large number of antennas to simultaneously serve 10 times more UEs than a traditional system. Directional, narrow beams used in the system concentrate energy in a small region to improve efficiency. Latency reduction by 10 times is one of the major requirements for 5G. The large number of antennas and beam-forming capability in a massive MIMO system can effectively reduce the occurrence of fading dip caused by the multipath issue, thus reduce the chance of waiting for channel quality to improve when fading dip happens.

Dense network: Given the propagation pattern, the coverage area of a mmWave radio is very limited. However, this seemingly disadvantageous characteristics makes mmWave small cells well suited to provide needed capacity in traffic hotspots. The capacity and coverage requirements for 5G RAN can be addressed separately. Deployment of NR in sub 6 GHz bands and the use of existing LTE carriers with advanced features can provide wide area coverage and required reliability to support high-mobility scenarios. A densified layer with mmWave small cells can increase the peak data rate up to 10 Gbps and cell edge throughput to more than 100 Mbps.

This mmWave layer is capable of satisfying the need of a wide range of eMBB and URLLC use cases that are stationary or with low mobility.

Interference management: Interference management is critical for a densified RAN. As the coverage radius shrinks by a factor of 3, the number of cells required to cover the same area will increase by a factor of 9. The co-channel interference needs to be effectively managed to maintain good signal to noise ratio. UE mobility behaviors, both historical and expected, device capability, application level details, 3D geo spatial environment conditions, and neighboring cell activities must all be considered to make the transmission scheduling decision jointly and holistically for a cluster of cells. Which UE to serve, how much radio resource to use, which subset of transmission points to use, and the down tilt of antenna ports should be all coordinated with neighboring cells to minimize interference and maximize the combined objective of network capacity, UE performance, and fairness. Given the highly dynamic nature of the RF environment, the complex interactions among UEs, applications and the radio network, and AI-based interference management approach holds the great potential to improve 5G RAN quality.

Multiconnectivity: 5G UEs should support multiple waveforms including Wi-Fi, LTE, and NR. Based on the use case scenario, one or more of these technologies can be used for performance and quality needs. This is particularly true in the early stage of NR deployment when NR is available in limited area. The wide area coverage from LTE and capacity off-load to Wi-Fi are still crucial for good quality of experience. This multiconnectivity requirement has implications on RAN and CN connectivity options. The distributed unit (DU) and central unit (CU) functional split in NR logical architecture is not determined by the multiconnectivity requirement though.

12.3.3.2 Radio Access Network and Core Network Connectivity Options

There are multiple options being considered to connect RAN to the CN. These options provide flexible migration paths that a carrier can take to deploy 5G on top of existing LTE network. On the RAN side, we have three types of nodes including LTE evolved Node B(eNB), eLTE eNB, and NR next Generation Node B (gNB). Choices for CN are LTE Evolved Packet Core (EPC) and NGC. The connection for control plane and user plane can be separate. Among the options being considered in 3GPP, option 3, and 3A (Figure 12.13) support dual connectivity for UEs that are LTE and NR capable. In both options, gNB is deployed as non-standalone and EPC is used as the core. In option 3A, gNB user plane is connected to EPC directly rather than going through LTE eNB.

In option 2 (Figure 12.14), gNB has direct connection to NGC for both control plane and user plane. This would enable LTE and NR capable UEs to send to and receive from user plane data to NGC via gNB.

In the early stage of 5G deployment where coverage is limited, the non-standalone options are advantageous since existing LTE EPC can be reused to support gNBs, thus reduce 5G deployment time and cost. However, as 5G is more widely deployed, gNBs need to have direct connection to NGC to support 5G low-latency use cases, which require UPF

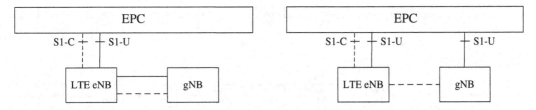

FIGURE 12.13 RAN and CN connectivity option 3 and 3A. (From 3GPP TR 38.801, Technical specification group radio access network; Study on new radio access technology: Radio access architecture and interfaces, Release 14, March 2017 [26].)

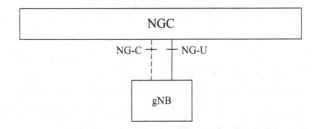

FIGURE 12.14 RAN and CN connectivity option 2. (From 3GPP TR 38.801, Technical specification group radio access network; Study on new radio access technology: Radio access architecture and interfaces, Release 14, March 2017 [26].)

to be closer to or co-located with the RAN. The modular and flexible NGC architecture with control plane and user plane separation enables such UPF deployment scenarios.

12.3.3.3 Radio Access Network Logical Split Architecture

Baseband units (BBUs) that perform layer 1 to layer 3 processing are traditionally provided by RAN vendors as proprietary, integrated hardware and software. Baseband units are typically hosted at cell sites for macrodeployment with space, power, and backhaul needs. As RAN gets densified, it makes economic sense to centralize BBUs at a hub location, to reduce the operation and maintenance cost. In addition, the performance of the RAN can be improved if the baseband processing can be coordinated across neighboring cells. Coordinated multipoint (CoMP) transmission and reception can increase cell coverage, cell-edge throughput, and overall system throughput. Reference [25] describes various Downlink (DL) and Uplink (UL) CoMP schemes and performance gains under different scenarios for LTE. In the meantime, with NFV and SDN, the industry has made great progress in virtualizing core and transport network functions. As MEC gets deployed, virtualized computing, storage, and networking resources become available at the network edge. It presents a unique opportunity to move part or all of BBU processing to the MEC.

There are multiple ways to split the baseband functions between a DU and a CU for NR where the DU stays at the cell site while the CU can be hosted at a MEC as virtualized functions. Figure 12.15 from [26] displays eight possible split options.

From option 1 to option 8, more functions get centralized in CU. It provides more opportunities to coordinate among neighboring sites and increase the potential network benefit

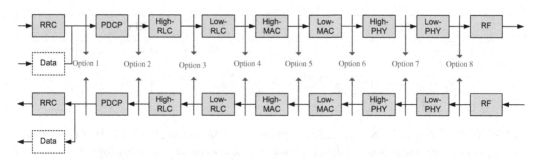

FIGURE 12.15 Function split between central and distributed unit. (From 3GPP TR 38.801, Technical specification group radio access network; Study on new radio access technology: Radio access architecture and interfaces, Release March 14, 2017 [26].)

in terms of capacity and performance. However, there are strict latency requirements for each option. Radio Resource Control (RRC), Packet Data Convergence Protocol (PDCP), and high Radio Link Control (RLC) processes can tolerate longer delays. The required one-way transport network latency for option 1–3 is on the order of a few to 10 milliseconds. For options 4–8, the requirement is much more stringent with one-way latency less than 250 microseconds. Another important factor to consider is the required transport network bandwidth. For a 100 MHz LTE system with 256 QAM, 8 MIMO layers and 32 antenna ports, the DL CU to DU connection bandwidth drastically increases from 4 Gbps in option 1 to a staggering 157 Gbps in option 8 [26].

For option 2, RRC and PDCP are in the CU while RLC, Medium Access Control (MAC), physical layer, and RF are in the DU. The CU can be further separated into control plane entity (RRC and PDCP Control Plane [CP]) and user plane entity (PDCP UP) (option 2-2). Since PDCP is centralized, it allows traffic aggregation and load balancing between NR and LTE. The control plane and user plane separation in CU supports the SDN concept and enables operators to evolve to a multivendor environment with greater degree of control on network operations and service quality management. The UP/CP separation at RLC, MAC, and physical layer requires further analysis and investigation, since the transport and scheduling of both signaling and user plane data are tightly integrated to optimize radio resources.

The split can be made at different granularities. Per UE, per bearer, and per slice split can provide greater ability to operators to configure central and distributed functions at a fine-grained level to improve RAN efficiency and performance. The split can also be dynamic over time. The complex decision on how, when, at what level to split can be made by AI-based algorithms, considering current and predicted analytics on UEs, applications, RAN quality, capacity, and performance.

12.3.4 5G Transport

As noted in Section 12.3.3, the CU/DU split option has major implications on transport bandwidth requirements. Figure 12.16 depicts a sample deployment scenario where split option 2 and 8 co-exist and NR gNBs have direct connection to both NGC UPF and control plane.

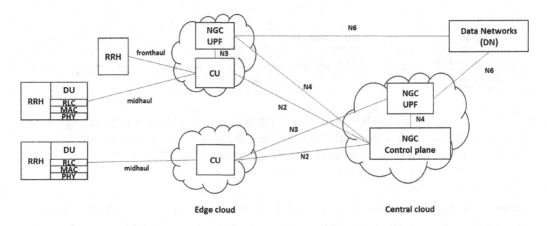

FIGURE 12.16 A NR deployment scenario with both split option 2 and 8. gNBs connect to NGC directly for both control plane and user plane.

The use of wide spectrum bandwidth, massive MIMO, coupled with an ultra-dense RAN creates key challenges to 5G transport network. To realize the benefit of CoMP, it is desirable to centralize as much baseband processing as possible. However, the DU to CU connection (referred as midhaul) must support very high peak rates. With option 8, all baseband functions are moved to CU. The connection between DU (Remote Radio Head [RRH] only) and CU becomes fronthaul. Fronthaul bandwidth requirement can easily exceed several hundred Gbps and even reach several Tbps [27]. Wavelength division multiplexing (WDM)-based fiber transport is necessary in such situations.

The backhaul connection (connectivity from DU to the CN) will also see dramatic increase in peak rate for 5G. To minimize the backhaul cost, NGC UPF can be deployed in the edge cloud (EC) to connect to the target DN locally when feasible.

The fronthaul link has stringent latency requirement. It confines the fronthaul distance from 10 to 20 kilometers. 5G URLLC use cases also set the strict end-to-end latency. Midhaul and backhaul must be designed to satisfy the overall delay needs. Mission critical applications demand high reliability. Dual or triple connectivity is required between CU and DU (fronthaul, midhaul) as well as CU and CN.

The 5G transport network needs to support multiple network slices simultaneously. As outlined in Section 12.3.1, diverse use cases stretch the limit of the network in different dimensions. Network slicing is an important 5G technology that shares the network resources based on operator's policies to address the distinct requirements for different classes of use cases. For the transport network, SDN-enabled programmability becomes critical to provide needed flexibility to manage the life cycle of network slices.

The topology design and ongoing operation of 5G transport network can benefit greatly from the use of AI algorithms. Problems related to optimal transport link upgrade, most-efficient routing, fail over scenarios, optimal capacity partition, and sharing all require continuous, data-driven insights. Deep learning (DL) algorithms can be applied to monitor network Key Performance Indicators (KPIs), predict future states, and recommend control actions.

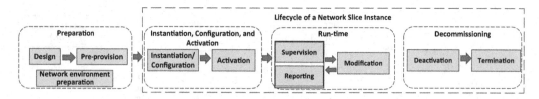

FIGURE 12.17   Life cycle of an NSI. (From 3GPP TR 28.801, Technical specification group services and system aspects; Telecommunication management; Study on management and orchestration of network slicing for next generation network, Release September 15, 2017 [29].)

12.3.5 Network Slicing

Network slicing is a key feature for 5G system architecture. It provides network operators the capability to create logical networks from underlining physical and virtual resources to serve customers with distinct service level agreements (SLA). A network slice may consist of components from CN, access network, or both. References [26] and [28] have identified initial requirements to support network slicing from CN and RAN, respectively. The life-cycle management of network slicing is studied in [29].

To support a communication service with defined SLA characteristics, network slice instance(s) (NSI) may be created. An NSI consists of network slice subnet instance(s) (NSSI). Each NSSI is composed of network functions (NF, physical, or virtual) and/or other NSSIs. NSIs are managed by network slice management function. The life cycle of an NSI is depicted in Figure 12.17 from [29].

Network slicing provides flexibility but also introduces complexity to the network. For the life-cycle management of an NSI, AI algorithms can be used to perform self-configuration, run-time optimization, and self-healing, much like Self-Organizing Network (SON) for LTE. Since one NSI can be shared by multiple services with different SLA requirements, conflicts may arise when diverging requests are being made to the underlining network functions, such as to change a NF parameter value in opposite directions. Resource contention among NSIs need to be managed as well. Policy-based conflict resolution, such as the capability provided by ONAP and automation via AI, will be critical to operate a slicing enabled 5G network successfully.

12.3.6 Edge Computing

URLLC use cases represent one of the major challenges and opportunities for 5G and next generation network. To reduce end-to-end network latency and improve reliability, network resources need to be deployed closer to the users and devices. The disaggregated system architecture provides the flexibility to deploy 5G CN and RAN functions at different locations to minimize latency. Edge computing capability is critical to realize the benefit of the 5G architectural flexibility to address the need of URLLC class of services.

Edge computing provides cost saving to network operators by reducing backhaul traffic and optimizing the use of central office assets. To the end users, the quality of experience will be enhanced due to fast response time and network reliability improvement. To the third-party developers, they will have access to real-time network information via open network APIs to innovate new applications. With proximity to the end users and near real

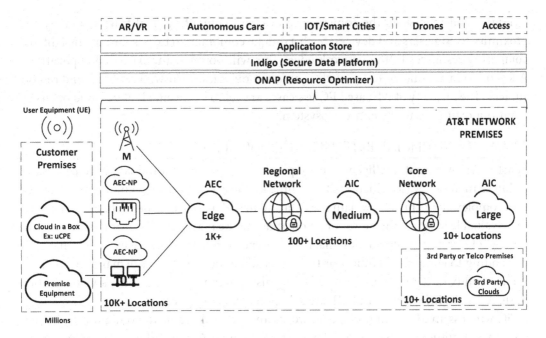

FIGURE 12.18 AT&T edge cloud (AEC) architecture. (From AT&T Labs & AT&T Foundry, AT&T edge cloud (AEC) – white paper, November 2017 [30].)

time, location aware services deployed in edge computing nodes have great potential to transform our daily experiences.

The architecture for edge computing has been studied by multiple open source and standard bodies [30]. Figure 12.18 is the architecture for the AT&T edge cloud (AEC).

Apart from AT&T specific recommendations, key features represented in this architecture reflect some of the discussions in the EC community. The EC is multiple access, explicitly supporting both wireline and wireless. This is also the view shared by The European Telecommunications Standards Institute (ETSI) [31]. Multiple access makes economic and technical sense. It enables better utilization of resources by supporting a wide range of services. The co-existence of EC and centralized cloud (CC) provides software developers the option to leverage the advantage on both ends. Edge cloud does not replace CC but addresses the compute needs that CC cannot fulfill effectively.

The orchestration and management capability is critical to automate the EC platform operation. Timely network data KPIs should be exposed to third-party developers via an Application Program Interface (API) layer. These functions are represented in ETSI MEC architecture as well [32]. AT&T edge cloud architecture achieves these via ONAP and Indigo, respectively. More details about ONAP orchestration and management capability can be found in Chapter 3, Section 3.5.

The number of EC nodes is an order of magnitude larger than the number of CC nodes. The placement of EC nodes is optimized based on demand, latency, cost, networking capability, and other factors. The processing latency for EC should be less than 10 milliseconds so that the end-to-end latency for EC served applications can be within 20 milliseconds [33].

Edge cloud represents the convergence of cloud computing, real-time analytics, and proximity to end users and devices. Such a unique combination brings the data insight and computing resources to the network edge. This will power many AI-based applications. A few of them are known today, such as autonomous cars, industrial robotics, and remote surgery. The majority of AI-based EC use cases are yet to be invented. Edge cloud opens up many opportunities to the entire ecosystem.

12.4 WHY ARTIFICIAL INTELLIGENCE FOR 5G+?

What is AI? Artificial intelligence encompasses ML, DL and natural language processing (NLP) to name a few (see Chapter 2). Machine learning relies on large amounts of data and uses complex algorithms to explain the data and to seek patterns or predict outcomes. With these valuable insights, the power of automation can be maximized. Natural language processing interprets key information that machines need from speech and texts. Automatically responding to equipment failures or tuning backhaul bandwidth on-demand to address a sudden influx of demand are some of the goals of automation and today's virtualization push. Artificial intelligence and ML are key ingredients for this effort.

5G wireless and IoT will reshape networks and network traffic in even more unpredictable ways in future compared to today's network. Tying AI and ML into the SDN control layer is critical to enable the network to respond faster than humans can to those unpredictable spikes. Analysts forecast that there will be 20 billion IoT connected devices by 2020. This will generate massive amounts of data and with access to this kind of information, there will be more opportunities that offer "value-added" services.

Intelligent decision-making for extreme traffic and managing complex topologies in real time will leverage AI and ML techniques. Humans will effectively "teach" the network how to respond in similar situations in the future. As networks get more and more sophisticated, so are the expectations of the regular consumers. They expect network services to be delivered faster, better, cheaper, and on-demand. In a resource-constrained environment, the ability to smartly and intelligently move 5G traffic from one point to another requires AI and ML to anticipate traffic and not just react after the event.

12.4.1 How Will Artificial Intelligence Help?

Artificial intelligence is rapidly becoming integrated into many aspects of communication, applications, content, and commerce to greatly enhance user experience, significantly improve productivity, as well as create new and profitable business opportunities. In Section 12.7 we touch upon some promising use cases. Just to name a few broad categories, AI will be used in the following areas.

- AI and ML-based design and optimization for wireless networks
- Self-learning and adaptive networks
- Root cause analysis, auto-detect, and auto-mitigate
- User experience-driven design for intelligent phones
- Personalized virtual assistants in the EC

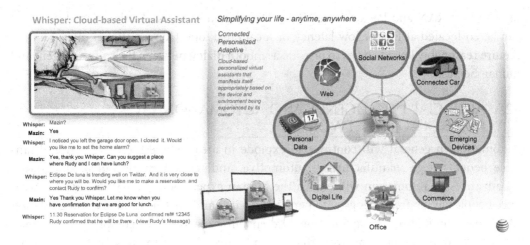

FIGURE 12.19   Cloud-based personalized agent and an example of an interactive dialogue.

One important industry solution is the use of AI in realizing a personalized virtual assistant. Autonomous agents are used to provide an intelligent conversational user experience. In contrast to "Question and Answer"-based sessions that are prevalent in the market today (e.g., Amazon Alexa, Google Home, Apple Siri [34–36]), a personalized virtual assistant will be able to participate in a conversational dialog with an objective to simplify our lives anytime, anywhere. Figure 12.19 provides an example of a cloud-based personalized agent and an example of a contextual ongoing dialog with an Intelligent Personalized Virtualized Assistant in the cloud.

12.4.2 Where Will Artificial Intelligence Elements Reside in the Next-Gen Architecture?

Components or microservices that use AI will be sprinkled throughout the network in various locations. The placement of such elements will depend on a use case by use basis. Figure 12.20 shows that the mobile infrastructure is becoming more disaggregated and virtualized with both distributed and centralized (pooled) elements. Edge computing will be

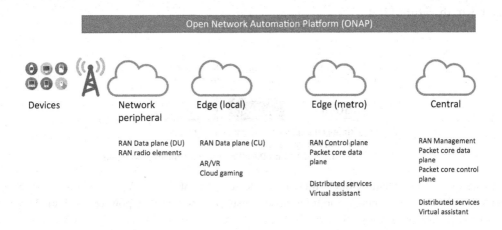

FIGURE 12.20   Virtual assistant deployment architecture.

used to host RAN and Packet Core VNFs. Distributed services like the Virtual Assistant can be co-located at EC for low latency or local break out. Conversational microservices require reasonably low latencies to provide a smooth dialog between the software agent and human beings.

12.5 ARTIFICIAL INTELLIGENCE AND AUTOMATION FOR NEXT-GEN NETWORKS

Automation in general will continue to explode in areas where there are real and tangible benefits (e.g., manufacturing, automotive, and telecommunications). Integrating AI advances to automation will enrich the human experience. We will begin to experience people having free dialogs with personal devices and obtaining advice and guidance. Much like automation, AI applications are enabling machines to complete real human tasks. Some of the application areas that AI is making progress in are speech recognition, decision-making, and visual perception [37].

12.5.1 Why Automation?

There are some key advantages to automation. First, there will be an overall improvement in efficiency, which may increase revenue or reduce operational and capital costs. Software agents/robots are good at doing repetitive tasks to streamline production output, reduce or eliminate human errors, and deliver high quality of assurance. Second, shifting to automation and AI will mean technicians are working fewer hours in dangerous conditions, which will lead to less workplace casualties. Third, this will also provide interesting opportunities for workers to focus on more complex and innovative tasks [37].

12.6 ARTIFICIAL INTELLIGENCE AND AUTOMATION FRAMEWORKS

When conducting an internal survey across AT&T's Big Data and Data Science Teams in regards to the amount of time they spent across the various aspects of producing data-powered products, it was found that approximately 50% of their time was spent on finding and exploring data, 20% on ML, and 30% of the time on enabling the data into production as shown in Figure 12.21.

FIGURE 12.21 Big data developer and data science time spent. (From Austin, M., Data powering AT&T and yourself: Benefits, methods and measurements for data powered, AT&T Internal Document, 2017 [39].)

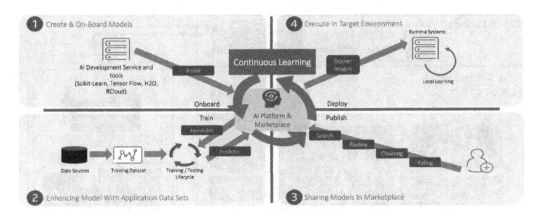

FIGURE 12.22   AI platform and marketplace lifecycle.

As this issue was studied in regards to process improvement, it was clear that efforts needed to be done to facilitate both the front-end data findability and exploration as well as to expedite deployment to production. The resulting solution consisted of developing an AI platform framework as shown in Figure 12.22 [38].

To address the "time spent finding data" area of concern, AT&T has developed a number of data discovery tools (data 360), and Data Visualization Tools that allow the data scientists to rapidly find, explore, and deploy data sets in the data lakes for analytics and ML.

The recently announced AI platform, Acumos, seeded by AT&T and Tech Mahindra, and open sourced by the Linux foundation [38], is one solution that satisfies the capabilities of Figure 12.22.

The first functional attribute of the AI platform is the ability to create and on-board models. Models can be created from many ML sources, R, Python, etc. and either uploaded as Predictive Model Markup Language or as appropriately documented sources with libraries, which can be translated to executables and deployed as microservices in docker images. The second attribute of the AI platform (Module 2 in Figure 12.22) is that it has the ability enhance the model with different training sets and subsequently update the coefficients of the models themselves. Nevertheless, once the models are developed, they need to be discoverable and buildable by others, for which a "marketplace" (Module 3 in Figure 12.22) has been developed, which allows sharing of both the models and the microservices created by them. Finally, an executable run-time ability to deploy said models is available thus allowing developers and data scientists to go virtually straight from development to production without needing to re-code ML algorithms.

Figure 12.23 illustrates generically how the AI platform is deployed both internally and what portion is deployed to the open source Acumos platform [38].

It is the hope and vision that algorithms that are developed in both the internal AI platform, which any company could also deploy their version within their own fire-walled data lakes, and those from the public domain marketplace, can be shared, when appropriate, to yield both better solutions and faster time to production.

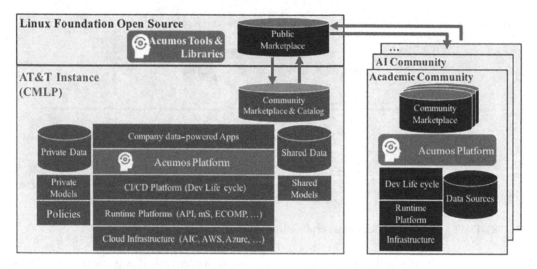

FIGURE 12.23   AI platform framework.

12.7 USE CASES

In this section, we provide a quick overview of some compelling data-powered 5G use cases that illustrate the intersection of 5G, AI, and automation.

12.7.1 Using the POWER Methodology to Evaluate Data-Powered Use Cases

Undoubtedly in any company with a lot of data (which will be nearly all companies in the future), there will be many potential uses cases that people will want to explore, and some sort of use case prioritization is usually needed. In fact, once the first few insights are produced on any use case by the data scientists, they will likely be overwhelmed with additional requests for projects or AI solutions. Unless prioritization is done, data scientists will be overwhelmed with requests, and perhaps one of the most important data-powered use case process methods enshrined after working through hundreds of data powered use cases is to make sure that the **five most important questions** are answered before any activity is started. We have seen so many data-powered projects fail, and many person-months are lost as a result of at least one of these questions not being addressed up-front.

To facilitate the ease of communicating the five most important questions that are essential for the actionability of any good data-powered project, we have constructed a framework using the acronyms DATA POWER, which define the goal (actionability of the analytics) and what is needed to achieve it:

- **Driving**
- **Analytics**
- **To**
- **Action**

requires a

- **P**roblem that is actionable
- **O**wner of the action
- **W**hat data (analytics) is needed for the action
- **E**TA expected to produce the action
- **R**OI expected of the action

It is amazing how many proposed data-powered projects, which can start as an interesting question, but one that is not actionable or one that is missing an "owner," that can take the action. Additionally, while something may be a good idea, if one doesn't have the data to do it, the problem cannot be solved (i.e., the What data is needed question…). Finally, understanding the ETA to produce the action and the potential ROI is of utmost importance when deciding which project or AI solution to invest in amongst the plethora of options that one will undoubtedly have.

Formulating the problem/AI solution in the POWER framework can usually be done quickly in order to do some simple cross-prioritization of multiple projects. Additionally, the POWER framework can also be done throughout the project to further define the "What," such as even defining the AI framework components of the AI platform as described in Section 12.6. For instance, Table 12.3 illustrates several AT&T internal use

TABLE 12.3   Use Case Examples Done in the POWER Framework

Business Driver for Use Cases	Use Cases		
	Incident Management	**SON Tool**	**Dispatch**
P: Problem that is actionable	By identifying the root cause in near real time of network incidents, analysts' time is optimized and unnecessary dispatches are avoided	By providing throughput guidance to video clients, improve the video QoE and reduce the network traffic	Analytics-driven approaches reduce the imbalances between loads and resources by time and geography
O: Owner of action	Tech Ops.	Tech Ops.	Dispatch Optimization Center
W: What is required (data, tools, …) for the action?	Data: Alarms, Tickets, KPIs Source: Pub-Sub msg bus	RAN KPIs Pub-Sub msg bus	Alarms, KPIs, Weather, etc. Pub-Sub msg bus, Data router
	Runtime container: Reddis, Neo4J, Drools for action rules	Runtime container: Kafka, 3rd party app	Runtime container: Kafka, 3rd party App
	Microservices: Topology, customer info., ML scoring	Microservices: ML Scoring, 3rd party microservices	Microservices: forecasting, recommendation engine
	Workflow: Jenkins	Workflow: Jenkins	Workflow: Jenkins
	Publishing: Pub-Sub, DMaaP	Publishing: Pub-Sub, DMaaP	Publishing: Pub-Sub, DMaaP
E: ETA of product solution	Medium time	Medium time	Medium time
R: ROI of product solution	Large	Medium	Medium

cases outlined in the POWER framework, where one can see not only the problem, owner, ETA, and ROI estimates but the AI platform components highlighted, including what microservices are needed to be built as well as the specific run-time container needed. The publishing mechanism is a publish-subscribe message bus called Data Movement as a Platform (DMaaP) [23].

12.7.2 End-to-End Incident Management for Existing and 5G Networks

Any network will ultimately need to be robust to element or connectivity failures, and root cause identification of the problem at any time will be of utmost importance, especially as the network gets more complex and distributed. Figure 12.24 illustrates an AI platform approach toward "Incident Management" (root cause detection), which uses both real-time components (e.g., alarm data), as correlated through the network topology, enriched by customer end-point data, and correlated and scored in real time against a historical ML model. The AI platform is deployed in modular fashion consisting of four chained microservices (MS-1 through MS-4), as well as the ML predictive scorer (MS-4a). To achieve AI learning, the tickets produced are "graded" by technicians working the problem, and the results are fed back into the learning system and the model is recalibrated.

The AI platform solution in Figure 12.24 was conceived and deployed on AT&T's AI platform in proof of concept mode within several months, thus illustrating the power of utilizing a microservice AI platform approach toward solving data-powered problems.

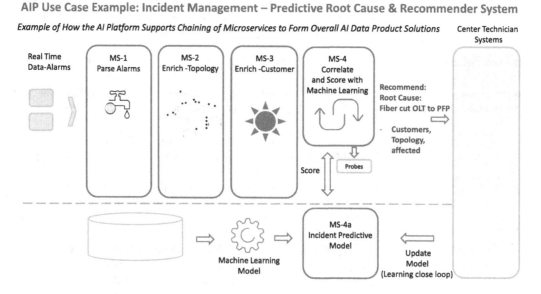

FIGURE 12.24 Use case examples done in the POWER framework.

12.7.3 5G Use Case Survey

5G increases the capability in data rate, capacity, and device density and reduces latency and energy consumption drastically. This powerful combination enables a wide range of use cases that will mark a significant transformation in our lives. From smart homes, smart cities, smart cars to AR/VR, 3D video, and e-health, 5G network will become a ubiquitous infrastructure that touches our daily living in many aspects. In the meantime, innovative industrial applications enabled by 5G are being utilized to monitor, alert, diagnose, and control activities across manufacturing, energy, utilities, transportation, smart grid, security, and public safety. The use of SDN, NFV, and edge compute in 5G brings greater flexibility to the use case applications by dynamically scaling resources, offering compute capability near to the devices and exposing real-time network measurements for AI-based decision-making.

Chapter 13 highlights some of the key 5G use cases in different industries and how AI can be utilized to support them. 5G-powered drone technology may revolutionize the last-mile transport/delivery services. The automotive industry will experience a fundamental change as assisted and automated driving becomes a reality with the deployment of ultra-reliable, low-latency 5G network, and V2X communication technology. Manufacturing processes will be further automated with the use of robotics and remote supervision. The energy and utility industries will deploy efficient devices to continuously monitor and control the transmission infrastructure to realize the smart grid benefits. The health-care industry will be transformed with remote monitoring, continuous care, and telemedicine.

REFERENCES

1. 'Big Data' is no longer enough: It's now all about 'Fast Data', May 2016, https://www. entrepreneur.com/article/273561
2. Kagan, J., Jeff Kagan: AT&T mobile data, 250,000 percent growth, https://www.equities.com/ news/jeff-kagan-at-t-mobile-data-250-000-percent-growth
3. Cisco visual networking index: Global mobile data traffic forecast update, 2015–2020, Cisco, https:// www.cisco.com/c/dam/m/en_in/innovation/enterprise/assets/mobile-white-paper-c11-520862.pdf
4. Mobile phone penetration as share of the population in the United States from 2014 to 2020, Statista, The Statistics Portal, https://www.statista.com/statistics/222307/forecast-of-mobile-phone-penetration-in-the-us/
5. Internet of Things outlook, Ericsson, https://www.ericsson.com/en/mobility-report/internet-of-things-outlook,https://www.ericsson.com/assets/local/publications/white-papers/wp-iot-security-february-2017.pdf
6. S. Marek, Update: AT&T's Stephens: More than 40% of network functions are virtualized, https:// www.sdxcentral.com/articles/news/atts-stephens-47-network-functions-virtualized/2017/07/
7. S. Buckley, Verizon says virtualization will enable it to reduce costs by $10B, https://www. fiercetelecom.com/telecom/verizon-says-virtualization-will-enable-it-to-reduce-10b-costs
8. 3rd generation partnership project, www.3gpp.org
9. M. Alleven, 5G to help drive fixed wireless to top 151M in 2022: ABI, http://www. fiercewireless.com/tech/5g-to-help-drive-fixed-wireless-to-top-151m-2022-abi
10. The 7 V's of Big Data, https://www.impactradius.com/blog/7-vs-big-data/
11. A. Ahmed, and E. Ahmed, A survey on mobile edge computing, *2016 10th International Conference on Intelligent Systems and Control (ISCO)*, January 7–8, 2016.
12. A. Sengupta et al., Fog-aided wireless networks for content delivery: Fundamental latency trade-offs, *IEEE Transactions on Information Theory*, 63(10), 2017.

13. R. Tandon, and O. Simeone, Cloud-aided wireless networks with edge caching: Fundamental latency trade-offs in fog Radio Access Networks, *2016 IEEE International Symposium on Information Theory (ISIT)*, July 10–15, 2016.

14. Winning in IoT: It's all about the business processes, Boston Consulting Group (BCG), https://www.bcgperspectives.com/content/articles/hardware-software-energy-environment-winning-in-iot-all-about-winning-processes/

15. Leveraging the upcoming disruptions from AI and IoT, https://www.pwc.com/gx/en/industries/communications/assets/pwc-ai-and-iot.pdf

16. AT&T Digital Life Home, https://my-digitallife.att.com/learn/home-security-and-automation

17 AT&T M2X, How smart is your home, https://m2x.att.com/iot//industry-solutions/iot-data/smart-homes/https://m2x.att.com/iot//industry-solutions/iot-data/smart-homes/

18. IoT platforms: Enabling the Internet of Things, March 2016, IHS Technology, https://cdn.ihs.com/www/pdf/enabling-IOT.pdf/

19. P. Agyapong, M. Iwamura, D. Staehle, W. Kiess, and A. Benjebbour, Design considerations for a 5G network Architecture, *IEEE Communications Magazine*, 52(11), 2014.

20. A. Gupta and R. Kumar Jha, A survey of 5G network: Architecture and emerging technologies, *IEEE Access, Special Section on Recent Advances in Software Defined Networking for 5G Networks*, 2015.

21. ITU, Recommendation ITU-R M.2083-0, IMT vision—Framework and overall objectives of the future development of IMT for 2020 and beyond, 2015.

22. Ghosh, A., Overview of 5G Mobile Wireless Networks, AT&T internal white paper, 2016.

23. ONAP, http://wiki.onap.org

24. E. G. Larsson, F. Tufvesson, O. Edfors, and T. L. Marzetta, Massive MIMO for next generation wireless systems, *IEEE Communications Magazine*, 52(2), 186–195, 2014.

25. 3GPP TR 36.741, Technical specification group radio access network; Study on further enhancements to Coordinated Multi-Point (CoMP) operation for LTE, Release March 14, 2017.

26. 3GPP TR 38.801, Technical specification group radio access network; Study on new radio access technology: Radio access architecture and interfaces, Release March 14, 2017.

27. P. Öhlén, B. Skubic, A. Rostami, Z. Ghebretensae, J. Mårtensson, K. Wang, M. Fiorani, P. Monti, and L. Wosinska, Data plane and control architectures for 5G transport networks, *Journal of Lightwave Technology*, 34(6), 2016.

28. 3GPP TS 23.501, Technical specification group services and systems aspects; System architecture for the 5G system; Stage 2, Release September 15, 2017.

29. 3GPP TR 28.801, Technical specification group services and system aspects; Telecommunication management; Study on management and orchestration of network slicing for next generation network, Release September 15, 2017.

30. AT&T Labs & AT&T Foundry, AT&T edge cloud (AEC)—white paper, November 2017.

31. ETSI white paper No. 20, Developing software for multi-access edge computing, September 2017.

32. ETSI GS MEC 003 V1.1.1, Mobile Edge Computing (MEC); Framework and reference architecture, March 2016.

33. A. Abella, keynote address at Fog World Congress, What's in it for us? A Carrier's perspective of edge computing, October 2017.

34. Amazon Alexa - https://en.wikipedia.org/wiki/Amazon_Alexa

35. Google Home - https://en.wikipedia.org/wiki/Google_Home

36. Apple Siri - https://en.wikipedia.org/wiki/Siri

37. From man to machine, Computer Science online, https://www.computerscienceonline.org/cutting-edge/automation-ai/

38. ACUMOS - https://www.acumos.org/

39. M. Austin, Data powering AT&T and yourself: Benefits, methods and measurements for data powered, AT&T Internal Document, 2017.

CHAPTER 13

Artificial Intelligence for Infrastructure Monitoring and Traffic Optimization

Laurie Bigler and Vijay Gopalakrishnan

CONTENTS

13.1 INTRODUCTION

As mobile networks and smartphones have become a critical component of everyday lives, there has been a constant tension between network speed and capacity on one hand, and network cost and resiliency on the other. Networks of tomorrow must find the right balance between these competing pressures and support emerging Internet of Things (IoT) use cases for new vertical industries, including autonomous vehicles, drones, and smart cities to name a few. This chapter introduces opportunities for applying artificial intelligence (AI) for both monitoring and optimizing the network. Artificial intelligence promises more efficient utilization of network capacity and spectrum, increasing network scale in terms of devices, as well as opportunities to improve user experience.

Section 13.2 gives an overview of the trends, gaps, and opportunities in current-day networks. Section 13.3 describes the technological evolutions that make the use AI for network monitoring and optimization possible. Section 13.4 describes traffic optimization and user experience scenarios where AI promises to help improve the network. Section 13.5 describes new emerging 5G use cases that will rely on AI for automation. Section 13.6 will summarize the chapter and describe the challenges and safeguards that must be addressed to realize the full potential of AI.

13.2 TREND, GAPS, AND OPPORTUNITIES

13.2.1 Usage Trend and Traffic Variety in Mobile Network

As highlighted in the previous chapter, mobile networks have experienced unprecedented wireless traffic growth since the advent of smartphones. The rapid traffic growth has exerted great demands on mobile networks. Operators have had to continuously densify their network, expand spectrum bandwidth, and improve spectral efficiency via new technologies and network optimization techniques in order to meet the growing demand. The use of smartphones has also drastically changed the traffic profile. The dominant cellular traffic has transformed from switched voice to streaming video. Network traffic also includes a great variety of data applications, including web browsing, social networking, gaming, and file download. Note that not all of the traffic can be easily classified by operators due to the use of encryption protocol such as HTTPS. The unknown traffic increases the difficulty of network monitoring and optimization.

The variety of devices and the applications running on them not only increases the network data volume, they also impose very different requirements on network resources. Network optimization would be much less challenging if all applications had similar requirements on network resources, but that is rarely the case. As an example, streaming video requires sustained high bandwidth but can tolerate high network latency, while web browsing is sensitive to network latency but doesn't require sustained high bandwidth. In the future, services like augmented reality and virtual reality (AR/VR) will require both high network bandwidth and low latency, whereas smart grid devices have much less stringent requirements [1]. The ability to optimize network resource allocation and utilization to simultaneously meet the demand of different applications has become the critical question to answer for all mobile operators.

The evolution of technology only adds more dimensions to the network optimization problem. Today's wireless network sees multiple coexisting technologies (3G, 4G, Wi-Fi), noncontiguous spectrum (5–20 MHz bands scattered from 700 MHz all the way up to 5 GHz), and various cell sizes (macrocell, microcell, picocell, etc.) [2]. The introduction of 5G technology will further increase the network complexity and introduce new service paradigms and use case scenarios.

13.2.2 Gaps of Current Network Analytics and Opportunities

Network analytics have different forms that vary in their level of sophistication and value to optimizing network performance. Descriptive analytics are the simplest form of analytics. They often involve aggregating network event data into key performance indicators (KPIs) to characterize a system or a service statistically, and then monitor, track, and trend the KPIs in dashboards, scorecards, or general web tools. There are many well-known network KPIs, such as traffic volume, application usage, spectral efficiency, and energy efficiency, and service quality KPIs, such as voice call drop rate, data download speed, and latency. For a complex system like a mobile network, there could be hundreds of KPIs from application layer all the way down to physical layer. They can be stratified into different layers based on correlation with end-user experience, geographical aggregation, or temporal aggregation.

Descriptive analytics are relatively simple, intuitive, and most widely used today, but they are only about the past network behavior and performance. Modern operators need diagnostic analytics to understand the network behavior, and predictive analytics to determine the probable future outcomes or the likelihood of a particular event to occur. Predictive analytics employs statistical techniques that include machine learning (ML), modeling, data mining, and game theory to assess current and historical facts to predict future events. A step further from predictive analytics is prescriptive analytics, which automatically synthesizes big data, business rules, and ML to suggest the decision/action options to take advantage of the predictions [3].

Artificial intelligence can assist in prescriptive actions by collecting and analyzing data for improving automation and extracting intelligence and information. The marriage between AI and software-defined network (SDN) will result in the fully autonomous network, which is resilient, self-healing, and self-learning. It can collect and analyze data and take actions to improve its state. Here are some of the prominent areas where we will see the potentials of AI and related technologies:

1. Automated and Closed-Loop Optimization. Today, network optimizations still largely rely on engineering's domain knowledge and a manual trial-and-error approach. Since network optimization is mathematically maximizing or minimizing a certain network KPI, the effective approach is often an iterative process similar to the gradient descent algorithm, which is widely used in ML/deep learning model training. Network engineers make small and incremental changes to configuration parameters to gradually improve network performance; if a change degrades network performance, they change the direction. This process can become increasingly time

consuming and labor intensive as networks scale and technology evolves. The rapid increase in traffic volume and application variety, coupled with the growing complexity of network technologies and ever-present cost-saving pressures, call for more automated and scalable network analytics and optimization. We need multivariant (radio, user/application, traffic) decision models for network optimization. Software-based networks and the application of AI have opened up new opportunities to achieve a fully automated and scalable solution.

2. Anomaly Detection and Root Cause Analysis. Today we rely on alarms for monitoring; however, static alarm thresholds often lead to either missed alarms or false alarms due to the dynamic nature of the cellular and wireline environments and application usage. For root cause analysis, we rely on knowledge-based troubleshooting guidelines, but engineers often propose one-size-fits-all rules, and they may be inaccurate or need to be adapted to a different networks and different applications. More importantly, the troubleshooting guidelines are limited by engineering knowledge and are useful only for detecting "known" issues. We often miss new or unexpected issues. By applying ML-based techniques for anomaly detection and pattern recognition, we may be able to proactively detect issues and/or speed up root cause analysis, and dynamically learn new traffic patterns over time.

3. User Experience-Driven Network Optimization. Traditionally, network KPIs have been about the performance of the *network* itself (including mobile devices), rather than that of services or user groups. It was not a critical issue when the dominant traffic was voice calls. However, with today's widespread applications this network-centric KPI design increasingly fails to meet the need of customers and services. We need customer-specific and service-specific KPIs so that we better characterize their needs and optimize the network to meet them. Even if service KPIs are available, engineers still face great challenges in optimizing the network for user experience. This is because the interaction between service/users and the network is extremely complicated and there are no good models that capture the relationship between service and network KPIs. If we can establish appropriate KPIs in various layers, then AI's sophisticated probability models will be able to discover and characterize the relationship across different layers of the networking stack.

13.3 TECHNOLOGY TRENDS THAT ENABLE INTELLIGENT NETWORKS

Network designers and operators have long attempted to control the behavior of the network in response to various conditions and application needs. However, traditional network optimization has remained network-centric due to many architectural challenges. First, most of the network elements have been closed, proprietary boxes that offer very little insight into their functioning and expose limited control mechanisms. These boxes also have limited support for Application Programming Interfaces (APIs). Second, due to the separation of network and compute, it has been very difficult to collect both network and application level data and process it in a timely manner to affect useful network level changes. The challenge has been, in part, the inability to process the data as it is collected; as a result, large volumes of data have to be transferred to locations with sufficient storage and compute. This has resulted in the inability to collect fine-grained data, in the times-cales that are needed for sophisticated network control. Finally, since it takes a long time for changes to be monitored (and rolled back if needed), operators have relied on long, and detailed, offline analysis to understand the impact of each change before they make it. When they make the changes, they tend to make small and incremental changes. This results in a long-drawn process before big changes are made within the network. The con-sequence of all this has been that the network has evolved very slowly and has tended to lag behind compared to the progress made with applications and computing in general.

The increasing application demands, the evolution of the network, and consequent need for fine-grained and (near) real-time network control is forcing a rethink of the traditional manual approach to network control. For example, the 5G network will sup-port billions of devices, highly heterogeneous traffic with a wide range of performance attributes, and a diverse set of demanding applications. Supporting all this requires a large network with thousands of cell sites and a heterogeneous set of wireless technolo-gies. There is no doubt that the traditional manual network management and control will not scale; maintenance will be prohibitively expensive and slow to react to conditions. Instead, there is a clear need for data-driven, intelligent, network monitoring and control that can detect and react to situations in real time. The challenge, of course, is the ability to collect and process the large volume of data needed for intelligent decision-making in real time, and the ability to enforce appropriate actions. There is also the cost associated with enabling all this; unless the benefits outweigh the costs, it will be hard to justify the adoption of such automation.

Fortunately, there are several developments that make intelligent network control possible. The first trend is the move toward software-based networks. Carriers are adopt-ing technologies like cloud computing and network function virtualization that bring network and compute capabilities to run on the same platform. This allows us to collect fine-grained data from the network elements and quickly process them on compute ele-ments as soon as they are generated. Further, the move toward edge computing makes it possible to run such computation in a very large and distributed setup; this eliminates the need to collect the data in a central location and as a consequence eliminates delays in accessing and processing the data or making network changes [4]. The second trend that is critical is the push toward disaggregated 5G core, radio access network (RAN), and white box versions of network elements [5,6]. This allows for the opening up of fine-grained APIs for both data collection and control and provides the flexibility to easily scale network capacity and deploy latency sensitive functions closer to the end-users and applications.

The adoption of network management platforms like Open Networking Automation Platform (ONAP) is another important factor in facilitating fast, fine-grained control (see Chapter 3). These platforms handle traditionally time-consuming tasks like data collection, analytics, policy specification, and support automatic closed-loop actions. The availability of mature ML frameworks within the network management platforms allow users to tackle use cases that were previously impossible to implement. For example, the use of edge clouds and network management platforms like ONAP will allow for correlating between fine-grained network and application level performance and make real-time network changes to effectively manage user quality of experience (QoE) while maximizing network efficiency.

5G will also provide key network technology changes that will enable AI use cases. 5G networks will provide an environment with high reliability, ultra-high data speeds, extremely low latency, very low packet loss, and flexible use of licensed and unlicensed spectrum. The increase in throughput and connection density coupled with drastic reduction in network latency ushers in many use cases where AI can be applied to automate industrial and personal applications. In addition, with 5G network slicing, a service provider can share one common network infrastructure to address the diverse needs from very different applications simultaneously.

The key 5G network architecture/technology changes are summarized as follows:

- Drastic increase in throughput and capacity

- Reduced latency

- Massive connection density

- Disaggregated and distributed 5G core network and RAN

- Edge cloud

- Network slicing

As a result of these technology trends and enhanced 5G network capabilities, operators are well positioned to take advantage of the rapid innovation in AI/ML for network control capabilities.

13.4 APPLYING ARTIFICIAL INTELLIGENCE IN NETWORK MONITORING AND OPTIMIZATION

Self-organizing networks (SON) is an example of automated network control in cellular networks today [7]. With SON, operators can change network configurations automatically through software, instead of relying on the traditional manual processes. The current SON functions defined in 3GPP for long-term evolution (LTE) focus on improving network efficiency as well as operational savings. Features such as Random Access Channel Optimization, Load Balancing, and Coverage and Capacity Optimization provide network optimization capabilities, while self-configuration features, such as Automatic Neighbor Relations, Physical Cell ID planning, energy savings, cell outage detection, and mitigation features offer operational savings. However, due to the volume of data, and the challenges to collect the data in real time, most SON algorithms still operate on rather long timescales (on the order of hours or days) to detect and react to conditions in the network. They also tend to make small, incremental changes over time to try to improve network performance.

With the move to 5G networks, and the consequent scale and diversity, there is a compelling need for further intelligent network control. The use of real-time monitoring and control via (AI) and (ML) techniques offer compelling opportunities for telecom operators to reduce both capital expenditure (CAPEX) and operational expenditure (OPEX), while improving the quality of service. Cellular providers have been embarking on a path to enable near real-time (5–10 seconds) network monitoring and control for centralized SON use cases and real-time control (<100 milliseconds) for real-time use cases with the 5G evolution to edge cloud.

Examples of using ML to improve performance and maximize network efficiency are given in the following sections. It is also important to point out that network optimization usually involves trade-offs. Machine learning (e.g., Section 2.3.5.2) serves as a promising tool to search for the best outcome based on the defined goals. For example, control actions aimed at optimal spectral efficiency would reduce the deployment of additional carriers that would be required otherwise, thus realizing CAPEX savings. On the other hand, control actions aimed at improving energy efficiency would attempt to reduce the energy cost while maintaining good spectral efficiency, thereby reducing the OPEX costs.

13.4.1 Applying Artificial Intelligence to Network Performance

Solving network performance problems can be broken into two phases, as shown in Figure 13.1. These include (1) diagnostics/root cause analysis and (2) mitigation/optimization.

The diagnostics phase uses machine analysis of multiple sets of KPIs. If the predicted performance is below service-level agreements (SLA), a classification algorithm with proper training will generate the root cause, such as interference, coverage, or load. The optimization phase requires a "what-if" scenario analysis in order to select the best action. This is a much more challenging phase, which requires accurate prediction. The difficulty is that KPIs can be impacted by so many factors in the wireless world. It is critical to use domain knowledge to identify a proper set of variables in order to achieve accuracy and speed in prediction. Figure 13.2 gives an example of using neural network for KPI modeling (see Chapter 2). Data preparation is a

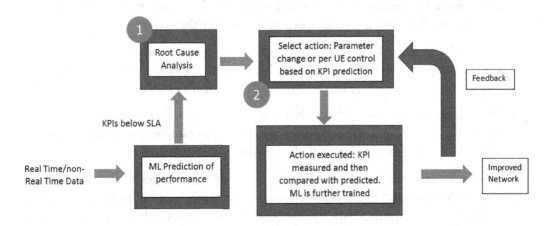

FIGURE 13.1　A two-step performance improvement approach using ML.

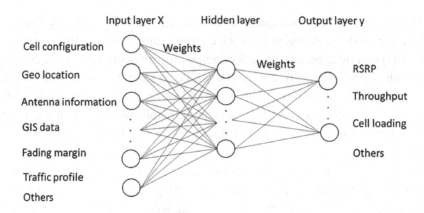

FIGURE 13.2   Neural network for KPI prediction in Phase 2 optimization.

critical step for modeling, including data selection, preprocessing, and transformation. It takes time, discipline, experience, and domain knowledge to achieve consistent and accurate results. At the initial training stage, we anticipate that a propagation tool "calibrated" by network measurements can provide a reasonable set of training data. Network event data, User Equipment (UE)-based measurements, and probe-based application data can all be useful in the calibration. Once the algorithm is running, the feedback loop will be used to fine tune the predictions.

A summary of the advantages and challenges of AI/ML for network optimization are given as follows:

- ML can deal with the complexity of handling multiple users and cells in near real time.

- ML will converge more efficiently than the current SON approach (trial and error search for optimal solutions due to multiple suboptimal minimums in the optimization surfaces) and also adapt appropriately.

- ML, in particular neural networks and deep learning, can extract/learn the complex nonlinear relationships between available inputs (measurement and counter data) and relevant KPIs and not require experts to identify them.

- The challenge with ML-based network optimization is the volume and timeliness of data required for real-time optimization. In many cases, collecting the data in time and processing it would take far longer than the time budget available for the optimization.

- The quality of outcome with ML-based optimization is also heavily dependent on the quality of data and its availability. While ML can handle missing data, building models that can robustly deal with data quality issues is not trivial.

- Finally, for ML to deal with minute cross-layer impacts requires building representative models that accurately capture these interactions. This not only requires large volumes of fine-grained data (which is often hard to come by), but also requires periodic and frequent updates to models as the network usage patterns, applications, and as a result the interactions change.

13.4.2 Improving Spectral Efficiency

For a wireless service provider, the single most critical resource from a capital investment perspective is spectrum; optimum spectrum utilization is, therefore, of paramount importance. While fundamental advances in the underlying radio technology aim at higher and higher spectral efficiency over a specific geographic area (expressed in bps/Hz/Sq. Area), even for a given deployment (4G, 5G) there exists significant potential for optimization of resources at the system level.

In wireless networks, the system spectral efficiency is defined as the overall transferred bit rate (in bits/second), normalized by the utilized bandwidth. Distinct from the point-to-point spectral efficiency whose upper bound is defined by the well-known Shannon-Hartley theorem [8] as a function of signal-to-interference-and-noise ratio (SINR), the system spectral efficiency depends on the SINR *distribution* of all users in the system. Further, the system spectral efficiency is also impacted by various factors like radio access technologies, network topology, transmission configurations, and traffic distribution as shown in Figure 13.3.

1. *Technology*: New generations of radio access technologies employ different access techniques, each of which strive to improve spectral efficiency. For example, Wideband Code Division Multiple Access (WCDMA) technology employed in 3G systems uses spread-spectrum techniques. 4G LTE replaced WCDMA with Orthogonal Frequency Division Multiplexing (OFDM) techniques; an OFDM is superior in combating intersymbol interference caused by multipath propagation. 5G will further evolve classical multicarrier waveform OFDM to support an integrated filtering component to improve spectral containment properties of the transmit signals.

2. *Topology*: Network topology impacts spectral efficiency in the sense that the co-channel interference among neighboring cell sites largely depends on the inter-site distance (ISD). Interference tends to be higher in dense urban areas, where the average ISD is in the range of several hundred meters. Interference plays the most

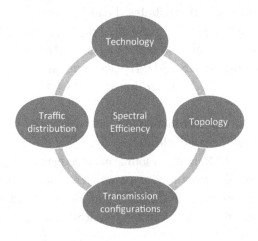

FIGURE 13.3 Spectral efficiency system impacts.

crucial role in determining spectral efficiency as it directly impacts the SINR. In 5G cellular networks, a large number of low-power small cells would be deployed along with macrocells in the so-called heterogeneous networks (HetNets), which provide flexible coverage areas. By enabling a reduction in the average radii of cells, HetNets promote improved spectral efficiencies due to the increased spectrum reuse, given that the co-channel interference is well managed [9]. AI/ML techniques are applicable to network topology (e.g., densification planning) as discussed in Section 13.4.4.

3. *Transmission configuration*: Configuration of transmission parameters, such as transmit power, Multiple Input Multiple Output (MIMO)/beamforming techniques, and link adaptation with different modulation and coding schemes, can directly influence spectral efficiency as well. In high SINR regions, using higher rank MIMO spatial multiplexing or higher modulation schemes such as 256QAM (quadrature amplitude modulation) would significantly increase transmission efficiency. However, increasing transmission power may not always lead to better efficiency, as it can also increase the interference level in the neighboring cells. There has been considerable research interest in the area of power control toward finding the optimal equilibrium of transmit power settings [10–13]. AI/ML techniques are applicable to the area of power control as described in Sections 13.4.3 and 13.4.4.

4. *Traffic distribution*: Traffic distribution plays an important role in determining spectral efficiency, which depends on the SINR distribution. If traffic originates predominantly at cell edges, then the overall spectral efficiency would be low due to the poor average SINR. Traffic distribution thus depends on the locations of cell towers relative to the user communities, as well as on the radio propagation characteristics. Optimal choices of the physical locations, antenna heights, tilts, gains, and choice of carrier frequencies would all critically impact the radio propagation attributes and coverage of individual cells. In a HetNet environment, the power settings of HetNet nodes relative to those of macrocells would determine whether a particular user should be associated with a macrocell or a small cell to achieve the best spectral attributes. Load balancing is a fundamental control function and research area to improve spectral efficiency and user performance by redistributing traffic among different cells, either through antenna tilt optimization, or through traffic steering. AI/ML techniques are applicable to load-balancing techniques and is addressed further in Section 13.4.3.

Artificial intelligence-based control functions for optimization of spectral efficiency in a multiuser and multicell environment fall within the purview of the radio resource management (RRM) modules within the RAN. Radio resource management is a system-level management function within the eNodeB for optimizing parameters, such as transmit power, modulation and coding schemes, resource allocation, beamforming, and handovers [14]. In today's mobility networks, operators typically can only statically configure parameters to manage the RRM functions, which is suboptimal and largely dependent on manual optimization and tuning. Superior performance can be achieved through a dynamic RRM, by continual modification of parameters to adapt to the changes in traffic volume, application mix, user distribution, and quality of service targets. In this context, AI algorithms can add significant value, given their ability to learn from the changes in the environment and make adjustments to the control parameters in a smarter way.

Among the major categories of learning algorithms, i.e., *supervised learning, unsupervised learning, reinforcement learning,* and *deep learning through neural networks,* reinforcement learning and deep learning have been demonstrated to be the most appropriate tools for RRM optimization [15]. Extensive research has been conducted in the application of these techniques in enhancing the functionality as well as performance of the RRM. From the discussion earlier, achieving higher spectral efficiencies depends on achieving a higher SINR, which in turn depends on the management of the overall interference profile as a key capability. In the following section we survey some important developments relative to interference management based on AI techniques.

13.4.3 Interference Management with Artificial Intelligence

Power control is one of the major strategies for interference management. In [16], a reinforcement learning (RL) approach has been proposed to adjust the transmit power of cells in the network to achieve maximum average user throughput. The cellular network serves as the environment of the RL algorithm, and the state is represented by a set of features based on local measurements in each cell. A Q-Learning algorithm with its Q-function represented by a neural network is utilized to maximize the reward, which is defined as the user throughput.

Reinforcement learning algorithms have also been adopted in other RRM functions for interference management, especially for the HetNet scenario. Of special interest is the joint optimization of antenna tilts and transmit powers and other handover parameters among groups of cells in a cluster. The focus is in attaining the right balance of coverage, interference, and power settings among a group of cells via antenna tilt, power, and other parameters (e.g., handover) adjustment, so as to optimize the overall performance in the area. In general, this question is challenging because there is a risk of creating coverage holes that are difficult to detect. However, the problem can be simplified when we relax the coverage constraint by maintaining a static coverage layer as shown in the Figure 13.4.

The configuration of the coverage layer (generally in low frequency bands, like 700 MHz or 850 MHz) remains unchanged, which significantly reduces the risk of coverage hole creation due to tilt/power changes. Artificial intelligence algorithms can, therefore, focus on adjusting the configuration of those capacity layer cells to manage interference and improve the overall performance. Various AI algorithms can be used to achieve the goal. Figure 13.5 illustrates the use of deep reinforcement learning to change the system configuration of a cluster of cells based on policies pushed to SON platform for network optimization.

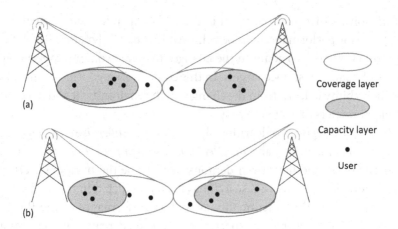

FIGURE 13.4 Joint optimization of traffic and coverage. (a) Traffic and coverage in time n and (b) Time and coverage in time n+1.

The cluster of cell sites is the environment for the RL algorithm. The selective KPIs of each cell would be collected as input to an artificial neural network. These KPIs serve as the state of the RL algorithm. Domain knowledge can be utilized here to reduce the size of the state space such that the algorithm can be trained much faster. As shown Figure 13.5, the proposed KPIs for the inputs to the neural network are all cell level metrics, including traffic load, resource utilization, average Channel Quality Indicator (CQI) values, average reference signal strength, and other distance metrics like timing advance. The reward is the aggregated cluster-level performance, such as overall user throughput and so on, the change of which will back propagate to adjust the weights of the neural network hidden layers. The output of the neural network is the policy mapping the input state to the actions, which would be performed by the SON platform to automatically change the configuration of the cells in the cluster.

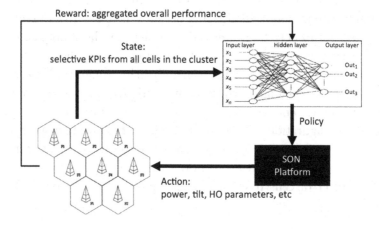

FIGURE 13.5 Deep reinforcement learning for optimizing system configuration.

The AI neural network will learn as the environment changes, such as traffic pattern change, and adaptively change the configuration to optimize the network. This can be a powerful tool for reducing the resource utilization and improving network efficiency.

13.4.4 Improving Energy Efficiency

Energy efficiency is generally defined as the amount of information reliably transferred per Joule of consumed energy, i.e., in the unit of bit-per-Joule [17]. The definition itself infers that there is a trade-off between energy efficiency and spectral efficiency. In general, substantial energy efficiency gains can be achieved at the price of moderate throughput reduction [18]. Apart from its environmental benefits, the goal of energy efficiency is also toward the reduction of operational expenses for mobile network operators. Current networks are designed with the aim of maximizing performance metrics, such as spectral efficiency, throughput, and latency. However, a paradigm shift to energy-efficiency-optimized communications has begun in the 5G era due to the unprecedented number of low-cost devices for massive IoT.

Approaches relevant to increasing the energy efficiency are summarized in the survey paper [19], where the techniques are grouped into four major categories: resource allocation, network deployment, energy harvesting, and hardware solutions. The objective in such cases no longer aims at maximizing the amount of information to be transmitted but rather focuses on maximizing the amount of information transmitted per Joule of consumed energy. Various algorithms have been proposed to achieve this goal, and the details can be found in the survey paper and the references therein. The common challenges for these techniques, however, are that the complexity of solutions is prohibitively high, especially when considering the practical interference-limited networks with high density of heterogeneous nodes [19]. A promising direction toward effectively addressing such challenges would be based on the use of AI techniques, which can naturally handle problems of such large-scale complex systems with learning intelligence and automation capabilities.

For example, one way of increasing energy efficiency is to allocate resources (e.g., power settings) with the objective of maximizing energy efficiency under power constraints. This problem is conceptually similar to the question related to allocating resources for maximizing spectral efficiency. Artificial intelligence techniques, such as reinforcement learning, can be applied in a manner analogous to their application in the spectral efficiency context as described in previous sections, with the reward function now modified to energy efficiency related metrics. As a special use case, if we allow the power of certain cells to be completely turned off, the algorithm can be used to switch cells on/off to adapt to the traffic conditions to achieve frugality in energy consumption. Off-loading techniques specifically for 5G are also considered for energy efficiency, such as the device-to-device (D2D) communications, where devices can communicate directly with each other on a peer-to-peer basis using a cellular frequency under the supervision of the base station (thus taking advantage of mutual proximity and averting the higher energy costs of a base-station hosted communication).

One of the early approaches toward energy efficiency, applicable even in the current 4G networks, is network densification (as in HetNets). Densification refers to the paradigm where capacity and coverage growth is achieved by larger numbers of low powered micro- and picocells deployed across smaller intercellular distances, as opposed to the traditional model with few macrocells providing coverage over larger territories. By strategically placing small cells in proximity of population centers, such as offices, malls, and cafeterias (particularly those that offer readily available backhaul infrastructures), fewer users get to share the capacity of each cell, under lower path loss and interference, thus leading to superior spectral efficiencies as well as UE throughput. As the small cells off-load significant proportions of user traffic, the macrocells continue to offer coverage across open areas, albeit at lower power settings. This scenario highlights the correlation among higher energy efficiency, improved spectrum utilization, and user experience. Advantages of densification would be particularly marked with small cell deployment in confined areas such as buildings, the outer structures of which offer interference isolation.

There are many opportunities to apply AI technologies during the densification planning cycle. At the initial design phase, it is crucial to identify qualified facilities at candidate locations for radio equipment deployment, such as utility poles, lighting poles, and other types of low-clutter street furniture. We need to capture not only the location of the facility but also all the relevant attributes, such as height, shape, materials, and availability. Artificial intelligence technology based on deep learning/image recognition has been applied on open data (satellite images, street view images, etc.) to capture these attributes accurately at large scale [20]. And in many cases, the city has specific ordinance/rules regarding attachment of telecom equipment to the utility poles. Artificial intelligence technology, such as natural language processing, can be utilized to automatically extract such ordinance from relevant government website. AI technologies, including supervised and unsupervised learning, have also been applied to surgically identify "hot zones," which are suitable for future densification deployment. These hot zones allow multiple planning teams to gain advance visibility and pre-plan in parallel in early phase of the planning cycle.

Densification becomes one of the key design pillars in 5G wireless systems [21]. Millimeter wave cellular deployment would employ phase-array-based beamforming in combination with interference-aware baseband-level beamforming [3]. Such highly directional beams would improve the link budget and enable very dense spatial reuse through spatial/angular isolation. This in turn would enable very dense deployment of very low power millimeter-wave base stations, with significant overlap in coverage areas yet unburdened by intercell interference—in effect, achieving a high user experience at low energy.

Millimeter wave has very different propagation characteristics than the traditional sub 6 GHz cellular bands. Due to the small wavelength, the absorption by water vapor and oxygen becomes important [22]. Furthermore, diffraction, reflection, and scattering exhibit unique behaviors at millimeter wave frequencies. Objects such as buildings, trees, and street furniture all impact propagation. Even the presence of humans has pronounced effects. Though a ray-tracing capability can be used to achieve good accuracy in a static setting, lack of high-resolution 3D geo-model, human mobility, and other moving objects create difficult challenges to propagation prediction. Machine learning algorithms can be developed and trained to recognize objects in a 3D Radio Frequency (RF) environment with a high degree of accuracy. Operators typically spend significant time and resources to calibrate propagation models via extensive drive test. A deep neural network can be used to determine the optimal values of the tunable parameters for a RF prediction model, ray-tracing or otherwise, by assimilating UE-level measurements on a continuous basis for a targeted design area. This approach will yield highly localized models with self-learned parameter settings, along with dynamic, self-adjustment capability.

13.4.5 Improving User Experience

Improving user experience is always the ultimate goal of network design and optimization. User experience is tightly tied to specific applications, which may have very different QoE requirements. Video accounts for the bulk of the network traffic today (more than 50% of cellular network traffic), but users' QoE over the cellular network may leave a lot to be desired. The QoE requirements of video are dependent on high video quality bit rate, quick start-up time, and low (or zero) video freeze. In this section, we use video as an example to illustrate how AI is used in operators' network to improve user experience. The examples on video can be extended to other Internet applications.

Artificial intelligence's first use case is for traffic classification, which is needed to identify the Internet video traffic on mobility networks. In the past, packet inspection has typically been used to classify traffic. However, as more Internet traffic is encrypted (with HTTPS or QUIC), it is challenging to apply packet inspection to classify video traffic, since network signature (like HTTP header) is no longer available. Instead, traffic pattern, that is, numbers of packets/bytes transmitted in a series of time slots, is considered a more fundamental traffic feature. Artificial intelligence provides a powerful tool set to perform classification, which naturally fits the problem of classifying video and non-video traffic based on traffic pattern. Indeed, AI algorithms are being developed to classify traffic from encrypted Internet traffic [23,24].

In addition to traffic classification, AI can be used to identify and isolate network issues impacting video QoE. Various network issues can adversely impact video application performance. Policies on mobility gateway servers could be configured incorrectly. The video encoding rate for quality tracks could be poorly optimized for mobility networks, which may result in video stalls during handover. To pinpoint the root cause of these issues requires correlating video application layer UE logs and network performance statistics data from network probes and call trace data. Today, the data collected from various subsystems of the video delivery ecosystem must be manually correlated and analyzed, which is time consuming and tedious.

Artificial intelligence-based solutions that automatically measures video QoE and correlates all the network performance data are the most promising way to resolve network problems in timely manner. The AI-based solution should include a video performance model (supervised or unsupervised). This model can be used to detect networkwide video QoE anomalies in real time. The performance model should be able to separate isolated poor performance instances, for example, those due to poor coverages, from systematic problems such as those caused by gateways misconfigurations or wrong

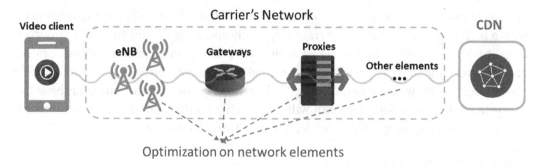

FIGURE 13.6   Video optimization (e.g., with traffic shaping) on network elements.

video encoding rate design. The AI-based solution is expected to increase accuracy and reliability of its model by continuously learning and fine-tuning the calibration while monitoring the network. The AI-based solution should also include drill down capabilities that can work from the application layer to lower network layers, such as Transmission Control Protocol (TCP) or RAN, in order isolate the problem.

Artificial intelligence can also be used for traffic shaping to improve the video user experience. The basic idea of traffic shaping is to change traffic patterns of video and non-video traffic to improve video experience, see Figure 13.6 for elements affecting video performance. Since video traffic is more time stringent, it is desirable to shape video traffic to a less bursty pattern with a relative constant throughput. The ability to improve video performance while not sacrificing performance of other applications and to balance video performance across multiple video sessions remains challenging. Moreover, a static traffic-shaping policy is not able to adapt to very dynamic network conditions. Fortunately, these again can be formulated to AI problems. Reinforcement learning can be a good candidate to learn dynamic traffic scenarios and adapt to the best strategy on traffic shaping. In this way, an operator does not need to provide specific traffic shaping policies. Instead, it only needs to provide video experience criteria and user experience criteria of other services and let the learning algorithm determine the best traffic shaping policies.

The example of applying AI on traffic shaping can be generalized to other network optimization schemes. In a generic network optimization scheme, the network element attempts to select the best action (e.g., by selecting the best network configuration, resource allocation, operating point) from a set of actions. Short-term and long-term rewards with a selection are evaluated based on the provided user experience criteria. The learning process keeps updating its knowledge to converge to the series of best selections, thus achieving the optimal user experiences across video and other services.

Another design approach to improving the video user experience is to expose network information (e.g., throughput, delay, packet loss rate) to Over-the-top (OTT) video content service providers so that they can optimize their own video applications, as shown in Figure 13.7. One

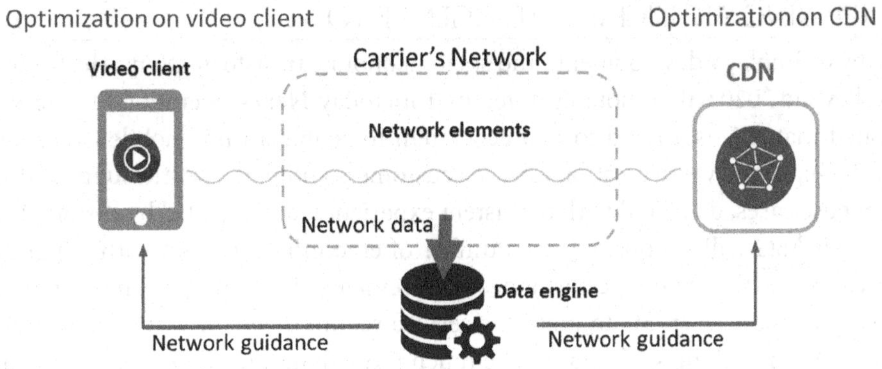

FIGURE 13.7   Video optimization with network guidance.

on-going effort with this approach is to publish so-called throughput guidance by operators to help video applications to optimize video adaptation algorithms used in HTTP Live Streaming (HLS) and Dynamic Adaptive Streaming over HTTP (DASH). HLS/DASH are the dominating protocols for Internet streaming adopted by most Internet video services (e.g., YouTube and Netflix). With such a capability, a video client in the mobile device selects the best video rate based on its predicted throughput. A typical video client has a limited view of network condition, which can lead to wrong decision on video rate selection, resulting in lower resolution video or video freeze. A network operator has a much more complete view of its network and can employ advanced AI algorithms to provide a more accurate throughput prediction based on real-time network data. The video client obtains the predicted throughput via publisher's API, in order to make an informed decision on video rate selection. Indeed, preliminary testing shows that significant video performance gain is achieved with throughput guidance [25]. Artificial intelligence has a powerful set of tools, like recurrent neural network, to build throughput prediction models (see Chapter 2).

Finally, ML and AI can be applied to the video adaptation algorithms to help the client decide which video quality to request and render on the device. The algorithms try to balance network bandwidth, amount of video already buffered, the likelihood of a stall, etc. to determine the right video quality. Machine learning has recently been applied to determine the right video rate to pick with very promising results. Experiments show that a cloud-based ML algorithm can help the video player choose qualities that balance different QoE metrics to match if not beat the state-of-the-art video adaptation algorithms.

All of the previous examples show that AI plays a critical role to improve user experience. While there is significant activity (and promising results) in this area, we are still far away from having realized its full potential.

13.5 APPLYING ARTIFICIAL INTELLIGENCE TO 5G

Driven by technology developments and socio-economic transformations, the 5G business context beyond 2020 will be notably different from today. Next Generation Mobile Network envisioned that "5G is an end-to-end ecosystem to enable a fully mobile and connected society. It empowers value creation towards customers and partners, through existing and emerging use cases, delivered with consistent experience, and enabled by sustainable business models." 5G will support a large number of emerging use cases with a high variety of applications with varying performance requirements. The concept of network slicing is thus being introduced in 5G to meet the service requirements of vertical industries and processes. As the volumes of data will be much more dynamic and beyond what humans can handle at scale, cognitive learning will become the foundation to manage and optimize service performance. This will also be the key, as the cloud and service orchestration will be service-model driven, and edge computing will emerge to enable local data collection, processing and action.

As discussed in Chapter 12 and as shown in Figure 13.8, a software platform for edge computing will be a key enabler for the 5G "real-time" services. Edge node site placement can minimize cost while maintaining QoE. Size, location, and configuration will vary depending on storage and performance requirements for the node. Once such systems are widely deployed, they could have significant impact on mobile networks. For example, devices could off-load work to the edge and save battery life. An AR/VR device can run without tethering to a computer but using mobile-edge compute. The combination of edge and centralized cloud will provide service verticals with a cost effective and seamless experience. As shown in Figure 13.8, edge cloud is designed to meet applications whose experience require latency in 10–30 milliseconds.

Currently operators are actively engaged in a number of proof-of-concept "real-time" service trials with industry partners and service alliance, in the areas of AR/VR, autonomous cars, eHealth, etc. These will drive the need for real-time computing via enhanced networking, built-in AI, and big data analytics at the edge location. In the following sections,

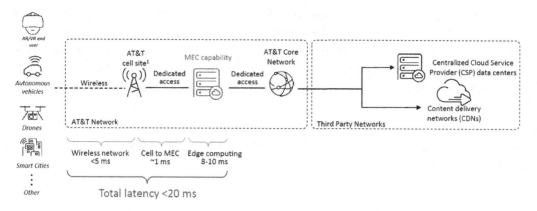

FIGURE 13.8   Edge compute architecture. (From AT&T Keynote Alicia Abella, What's in it for us? A Carrier's perspective of edge computing, *Fog World Congress*, 2017 [26].)

we will look at how the autonomous network is going to manage a world of enhanced Mobile Broadband with low latency and high bandwidth, and create foundations that will revolutionize industries such as automotive, manufacturing, energy, and health care.

13.5.1 Artificial Intelligence Application to Virtual Reality, 360 Video, Augmented Reality

Analysts have projected that the global VR, 360 video, and AR market will reach upwards of $50 billion by 2021 [27]. While a lot of the hype today is focused on AR/VR headset gear and gaming software, significant network advancements are required to deliver these technologies. Each of these modes of video requires high bandwidth and very low latencies to support an immersive experience. Machine learning and AI will play a key role in efficient delivery of content, in off-loading computation to the cloud, in identifying potential opportunities to reuse computation across users, and in data security.

In this section, we use 360 video as an example to demonstrate the use of AI for efficient delivery of content. 360 degree videos, also known as immersive or spherical videos, play a critical role in the VR ecosystem. They provide users with panoramic views and create a unique viewing experience when used in combination with 3D video technology. When watching a 360 video, a viewer at the spherical center can freely control the viewing direction, so each playback creates a unique experience. As shown in Figure 13.9, a user wearing a VR headset can adjust the orientation by changing the pitch, yaw, and roll, which correspond to rotating along the X, Y, and Z axes, respectively. 360 video players compute and display the viewing area based on the orientation and the field of view (FoV), which defines the extent of the observable area. It is usually a fixed parameter of a VR headset (e.g., 110 degree horizontally and 90 degree vertically).

Measurements on two commercial 360 video platforms show that 360 video largely inherits the delivery scheme from traditional videos. While this simplifies the deployment, it makes 360 video streaming bandwidth intensive; this is because video players have to fetch both visible and invisible portions of the video, in high quality. This leads to tremendous resource inefficiency on networks and high device radio energy consumption.

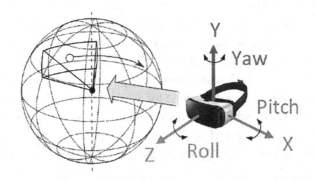

FIGURE 13.9   Adjusting 360 video viewing directions.

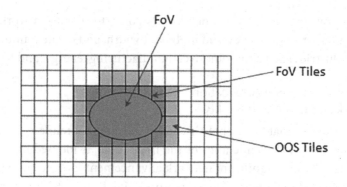

FIGURE 13.10   Spatial segmentation of a video chunk into tiles.

One possible approach to reducing the bandwidth requirement is to use FoV-based methods for delivery of 360 videos. At a high level, the idea is to get the player to predict the FoV of a viewer and fetch only the content in the FoV in order to reduce the bandwidth consumed. To accommodate FoV adaptive 360 video streaming, each 360 video chunk is pre-segmented into multiple smaller chunks, which are called tiles. The client only requests the tiles overlapping with the FoV as shown in Figure 13.10.

The player would have to combine multiple data sources, such as head movement patterns of viewers, video content analysis, and user profile, in order to accurately predict the FoV. Artificial intelligence and ML can be used to predict the FoV that a user will observe for a given video at any instance in time as well as predict the head movements of users. Different classes of videos and types of users can be used to collect the typical head movement of users for each video and train the ML models. Other signals such as audio and factors that capture a viewer's attention can also be incorporated into the model. Since the data and the compute needed for such predictions will not be available on the end device, such head movement predictions can run on edge clouds. Running on edge clouds will also allow for the predictions to adapt and optimize quickly to changes, as well as allow for the application to get the predictions quickly.

There are similar applications of AI for other emerging video technologies like AR. The key constraint with AR is that a video feed of what the user is observing has to be processed and augmented with virtual information quickly and seamlessly. Since the data needed for augmentation cannot always be stored on the display device, the cloud will play a crucial role in processing and augmenting the video streams. AI can help dynamically determine what aspects of the processing pipeline can be off-loaded to the cloud versus executed on the device locally. Further, given the close tie-in to the real world, there are opportunities for reusing computation done for augmenting one user with that of another. AI can be used to determine what classes of users can reuse computed augmentations and when. Such reuse has the potential to significantly impact how certain classes of users (e.g., first responders responding to an emergency) share information with each other.

13.5.2 Drones

The cost of drone technology is falling so quickly it will soon be cost effective to perform many modern society everyday tasks by drones. The transport industry may be the first to be revolutionized by drones. They have already started to utilize drones to provide "last mile services" in many countries, where for example postal carriers are usingdrones for deliveries in tough-to-reach mountain regions [28]. Sophisticated drones could soon be performing tasks like fertilizing crop fields on an automated basis (precision agriculture), monitoring traffic incidents, surveying hard-to-reach places, or even delivering pizzas to name a few.

Most drone services will be realized through a system architecture shown in Figure 13.11 comprising the drone itself, the cloud, and a centralized traffic management entity along with ML analytics located at an edge cloud location.

The traffic management entity provides automated and adaptive flight routes to/from the drone wirelessly at the mission start and during navigation. Trajectories should be compliant to regulations (fly only within permitted regions) and optimized in a way that wireless network performance is not impacted. Artificial intelligence capabilities are projected to be part of the drone traffic management system architecture to improve operability and efficiency. AI algorithms could be employed and trained to adapt the assigned flight routes according to unpredictable and dynamically changing constraints including weather (e.g., rain, wind), and human conditions (e.g., accidents, traffic). In these specific cases, the decision-making algorithms needs to reside at a higher centralized layer and cannot

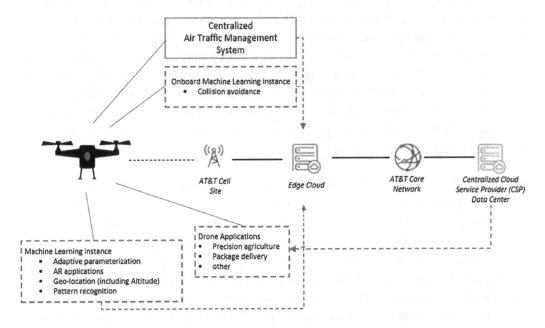

FIGURE 13.11   Drone system architecture.

be distributed at the drone level. However, the demand for instant analysis of datasets and decision-making will push on board ML capabilities to the drone. Applications where the drones are tasked to fly among obstacles and above people will require an instant detection of unpredictable changes of the surrounding environment and the making of critical safety decisions in real time. Some of these decisions will have to be made autonomously through the onboard embedded "thinking" capabilities.

Swarming technology is a very exciting drone application where AI is used to enable drones to act in groups of several coordinated units to accomplish a complex task. Within the swarm there will be a single or a few leading (or pilot) units that are directly connected via radio to the cloud and/or the centralized traffic management entity. The pilots will in turn dispatch commands via D2D wireless links to the rest of the swarm units for tasks execution in dynamic environments. The level of autonomy of each swarm component will be modulated depending on the onboard hardware sophistication of the simple non-pilot units. Promising utilization of the swarming technologies for commercial purposes are in the construction business and AR. The opening ceremony at the 2018 Winter Olympics in Pyeongchang, South Korea, featured a record setting 1,218 drones flying in sync in celebration of the Olympic games [29].

There will be inherent challenges for network operators to support the radio connectivity between the drones and the traffic management entity. Historically, cellular networks were designed and optimized to serve users at ground vicinity. The introduction of radio-connected drones communicating at high altitudes creates some new challenges in terms of interference management, especially on the uplink direction (drone to cell site base station). Moreover, the very stringent latency requirement imposed by the real-time drones' applications represent an additional challenge that network operators must deal with. With the introduction of new 5G network solutions, some of these problems will be resolved due to the ultra-low latency characteristics of the radio links and the advanced low interference antenna system features. *Beam steering* should minimize the level of disturbance a drone can introduce onto the network when in connected mode since the spurious emissions will be reduced by the adaptive beamforming. Finally, AI algorithms could be implemented at the network level to identify drone-generated interference on cluster of cells and mitigate it in real time using adaptive parametrization.

13.5.3 Automotive (High-Speed Collision Avoidance, Assisted/Automated Driving)

Back in the 1990s, in San Diego, a stretch of a freeway became a new experiment for a smart highway system [30]. Since then, researchers and scientists across the world, along with car manufacturers and telecom operators, have been testing new ways to enable this revolutionary technology with the goal of fully automated driving. In Europe, the smart highway system, or the Cooperative ITS Corridor, is being built with sensors and high-speed mobile technologies [31]. In 2016, in a BMW race track in South Korea, two cars using 5G technology were capable of sharing information with the driver, and in the future, the goal is to use 5G vehicle-to-vehicle communications so that the cars can directly communicate [32].

Machine learning and AI will be key enablers in the future car industry with the help of low latency and highly reliable 5G edge cloud network technologies. Using ML techniques

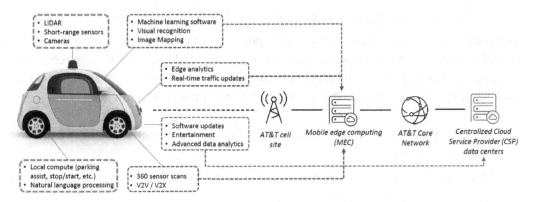

FIGURE 13.12   In-car and low-latency edge compute for real-time decision-making for autonomous cars. (From AT&T Keynote Alicia Abella, What's in it for us? A Carrier's perspective of edge computing, *Fog World Congress*, 2017 [26].)

at the edge, regular and irregular patterns and incidences can be analyzed via pattern recognition and computational learning to make better and safer decisions for future driving. Using real-time cameras, sensors, weather radar, and other vehicles' data, ML techniques on the vehicle itself will enable future cars to become a safer solution for humans. Cellular-based V2X or C-V2X technology (such as 5G) makes the real-time communication among cars, devices, infrastructures, pedestrians, etc. a reality [33].

As shown in Figure 13.12, the autonomous car must be able to instantaneously respond to irregular incidents, such as a pothole in the road or a tree that just fell in the middle of roadway. During an irregular incident, the car's sensor would detect an anomaly on the road and the local ML algorithm on the car would immediately instruct it to slow down and move away from the obstacle(s) without harming other cars or road barriers. Immediately and within milliseconds, after the car sensors identify the issue, it reports it via a C-V2X real-time message to all surrounding cars and road infrastructures up to a certain defined radius. That communication will go through high-speed and low-latency cellular cell sites and to an edge cloud server, where ML software will make decisions on the next communication steps in real time. The edge analytics will also send alerts to the appropriate first responders, such as police, firefighters, and road worker teams, to dispatch their personnel to the location of the incidence and alert and notify other cars in the area (within a specified radius distance from the incidence) to change their speed and driving algorithm. The road infrastructure sensors (light poles, fences, traffic light, etc.) and the online mapping system will be also alerted by the edge computing algorithm to change their schedules. The notified cars will reduce speed to avoid any major congestions and will be veered to the right to keep an open lane for emergency responders.

This is one of many examples that can be implemented using AI/ML and 5G technology network with connected and autonomous car solutions to improve our lives and make us safer.

13.5.4 Manufacturing (Process Automation, Remote Supervision, Cloud Robotics)

With advancing technology, robots and process automation have taken over the manufacturing world at a staggering pace. Between 2011 and 2016, the average robot sales increase was at 12% per year and is expected to increase by at least 15% on average per year till 2020 [34]. The same report cites several challenging prospects in this area, including:

- Use of collaborative robots, IoT, and ML/AI to further enhance efficiency and drive new opportunities

- Allow robots to acquire and adapt new skills and respond to unexpected problems in the manufacturing process

While great strides have already been made with the deployment of Robotic Process Automation in the industry, combination of 5G and ML/AI technologies will lead to the next revolution in this space by addressing the earlier key challenges [35]. The World Economic Forum has termed this as the 4th Industrial Revolution, that will be driven by the afore-mentioned technologies [36].

5G connectivity can help provide the high-throughput and low-latency communications across multiple domains and locations. Combined with cloud and edge computing, this will enable massive data collection and analysis from a variety of devices on the edge itself (e.g., sensor data, images, and video), thereby enabling real-time automated collaboration between the robots. Advanced ML/AI techniques such as deep learning can help drive proactive identification of problems by combing this data, generating models to predict trends and patterns, building accurate anomaly signatures, and even recommending remedial actions.

Following are three key areas in the manufacturing space that can greatly benefit from these technologies and help drive new business opportunities:

1. **Automated diagnostics and recovery:** Robots and machines come equipped with variety of sensors and collect data related to the manufacturing process, the immediate environment, and the health of the machines themselves. By using 5G connectivity, edge computing, and big data techniques, enterprises can easily gather and analyze critical data from thousands to millions of these sensors in real time, even across distributed segments. By utilizing advanced ML/AI algorithms, models can be developed to identify anomalies and enable self-diagnostics and recovery for the machines. Further, these technologies can enable D2D communication between the machines to enable them to act in a coordinated manner to monitor various processes and respond to any issues in a timely manner. Lastly, it is not a stretch to use enhanced self-learning and neural-net-driven algorithms to identify issues proactively in the manufacturing process and take corrective actions such as diverting the workflow to a new set of machines.

2. **Smart lean manufacturing and workflow/supply chain management:** 5G and ML/AI can help drive efficiencies in the increasingly complex landscape of manufacturing workflow and supply chain/inventory management, especially when it comes to

large-scale operations that span multiple locations and domains. These processes are impacted by both internal and external factors, and significant cost improvements can be achieved by making them more efficient. One potential application is to collect data points along the manufacturing process, such as origin and transit, and use advanced algorithms and models to proactively assess the implications of delays in any one point in the manufacturing workflow on the overall deadline via advanced algorithms. Missed deadlines can be assessed even before they occur, and remedial actions can be taken. Another possible application is to drive efficiencies in the supply chain process by moving toward smarter lean manufacturing. By combining data from a variety of sources, accurate models can be generated to predict the exact demand based on a multitude of factors. Automated techniques, enabled by 5G technologies such as D2D communications and tactile Internet, can be used to proactively increase or decrease the production rate to match the demand.

3. **Remote infrastructure monitoring and diagnostics:** Various industries today involve monitoring key infrastructure, such as power lines, cell towers, water or gas distribution systems pipes, dams, industrial boilers, and nuclear power plants. Various factors prohibit comprehensive inspection and monitoring of such infrastructure, including excessive cost and dangerous or inaccessible domains of operations. Robots or drones can be used to monitor such equipment or facilities, relying on 5G connectivity for video/image collection or sensor data collection. Data-driven models and edge computing can be leveraged to quickly identify remedial actions and drive these robots or drones to perform actual repair work. Or advanced models can help guide the drones or robots to focus further on specific parts or areas and collect more data, which can help human engineers to further diagnose the issue. This can help in driving down the cost of inspection and monitoring, as well as help avoid putting human operators in dangerous situations.

In the areas of process automation and cloud robotics, both 5G and AI have a critical role to play, and offer major benefits to business. Constant and reliable connectivity will be imperative for future industries, and the wireless nature will provide flexibility and help drive down costs in terms of maintain connectivity with changing landscape. Coupled with edge computing and cloud technologies, 5G will help realize the benefits of real-time tactile response times for manufacturing. Advances in ML/AI will help to drive further automation, collaboration, and proactive mode of operation, bringing further gains and opportunities for manufacturing industry. Universal customer premises equipment—white boxes that serve as small clouds hosting virtual routers, firewall, IoT gateways, and limited AI functions—will be a key enabler for supporting enterprise services and applications (see Chapter 11).

13.5.5 Energy, Utilities, and Smart Grid

Current energy systems are evolving to meet the unprecedented challenges of global population growth and climate change, which drive greater demand for affordable, secure, and sustainable energy. Across the globe, the traditional electric grid is being replaced by the "smart grid," which uses the latest information and telecommunication technology to transform the energy industry into a new era of efficiency in production and distribution of electricity. 5G and AI will play central roles in smart grid evolution.

The main challenge in managing power grids is to align supply and demand and prevent blackouts. Traditional power systems maintain alignment almost entirely by controlling the supply-side with the ability to ramp up power production quickly to meet new demands. With the increasing use of renewable energy resources in the grid, however, the systems do not have the same supply-side control as with the fossil-fuel-based power stations. Renewable energy sources, such as solar panel and wind turbines, are heavily impacted by weather conditions and seasonality. As the variations in energy resources grow to levels far beyond what is seen today, the smart grid must be able to flexibly manage resources to maintain system reliability and availability.

The smart grid can address the challenges of increased variability in energy resources by employing ML/AI technology to make optimal system level decisions. On the supply-side, historical and real-time data can be gathered from wind turbine sensors and used to learn the correlations between the weather conditions and the supply capacity of the wind turbines. The pattern can be utilized to accurately predict the wind turbine's supply capacity based on near real-time weather conditions, so that the smart grid can dynamically adjust capacity from other energy sources to meet the overall demand. The smart grid also provides demand-side flexibility that take advantage of various energy sources stored in different equipment and processes, such as warehouse air conditioning units and supermarket refrigerators, whose electricity consumption is not necessarily time-critical. On windy days, if the wind turbines push high electricity volume to the grid, the smart grid will control supermarket fridges to use more energy, pushing the temperature to its lowest allowed. And when electricity demand outstrips supply, those fridges can defer their consumption temporarily, as long as their temperature stays below its highest limits. Demand-side flexibility options in the smart grid depend heavily on control and communication capabilities provided by modern telecommunication infrastructure, such as 5G.

Blackouts in electric grids over the course of history have caused billions of dollars in damages to the economy and great inconvenience to the general public. Blackouts are usually caused by unexpected incidents, such as lightning strikes or energy equipment failures, and typically happen when the system is running at its highest capacity. The traditional electric grid enforces strict standards on power generation equipment and processes from power stations to prevent blackouts. However, more and more ordinary energy consumers are becoming energy suppliers through, for example, the solar panels on their rooftops, and pumping electricity back to the grid. With the large number of suppliers and the variation of their equipment, it is very difficult to impose the same level of equipment standards as traditional power stations. The lack of strict equipment guidelines will significantly increase the chances of equipment failures and system blackouts, and make blackout prevention much more challenging. The smart grid must implement sophisticated network monitoring system and use proactive methodologies to address the potential blackout issues. 5G and AI will play an important role in tackling blackouts by minimizing the outage risk, controlling the affected scale of the blackouts, and reducing the recovery time by quickly localizing the fault. Based on the historical data and instantaneous usage reported by sensors through 5G network, ML techniques can be used to accurately estimate the affected customer demand. If the demand exceeds the spare capacity of other parts (plants, transmission towers) of the grid, AI could make intelligent decision to isolate the affected region and prevent the outage from spreading. Meanwhile, with the help of AI-based fault isolation, the technician can speed up the diagnosis and repair process and recover the failure quickly.

5G telecommunication networks will provide the monitoring, data collection, and data/control transmission infrastructure that ensures the benefits we envision from the smart grid become a reality. Software-defined network using AI technology can be applied to many areas in smart grid, such as accurate supply and demand forecasting, demand-side flexibility, consumer controls, and blackout prevention, for providing reliable, affordable, renewable energy.

13.5.6 eHealth Monitoring and Continuous Care

Health monitoring is more ubiquitous today than it has even been. LTE-M technology improves network coverage in hospitals and other medical facilities with signal penetration issue. 5G is poised to further expand the relevance of mobile networks into the healthcare industry. Precision medicine that uses ML and AI methods to address proactive prevention (health monitoring), medical equipment connectivity, continuous care, and decentralization and virtualization of health services (telemedicine), are the next new advances.

Accessories like wrist sensors will evolve in 5G to support patient tracking and retrieval of other health-related information, which will make identifying health issues much easier. By introducing connected medical devices, patients' vital parameters can be transmitted in real time to doctors. With ML, an accurate prediction of a patient's health status could reduce the number of clinic visits for patient in good condition while send alarms to patients in need of immediate treatment. Continuous care is needed for people with chronic disease, such as asthma, diabetes, stroke, and heart disease. To deal with chronic diseases, people usually need to regularly visit a clinic to keep track of their health profile and adjust treatment plans (e.g., medicine type and dosage), but these regular visits may become unnecessary with real-time health monitoring. An accurate and effective treatment plan can be designed based on full records of patient's daily measurement. Precision medicine becomes possible with accurate measurement of personal reaction to medicines, resulting in more effective treatment in terms of targeting a patient's specific disease and ailments.

Telemedicine will also benefit from 5G features. High data rates with extremely low latency and low packet loss, could make remote surgery and real-time analytics related to diagnostics a more practical and reliable implementation than with current 4G mobility networks. With 5G network and remote operations, the distance between patient and doctor/hospital is no longer the obstacle. Surgery could be performed remotely on patients, who cannot be transported to hospital due to physical reasons (transportation, wound severity, underdeveloped region, etc.), by surgeons or local robotics.

Machine learning has the potential to change the way health care is provided, not by replacing medical doctors, but by improving diagnostics and predicting outcomes using deep learning and AI methods. In the future, during a doctor appointment where you are reporting certain symptoms, the physician will be able to enter them into a ML platform that almost immediately presents the latest research that might be useful for diagnosis and successful treatment while pulling medical records and analysing MRI and X-ray imaging. With all that information, the ML framework then can suggest a specifically tailored diagnosis and treatment. In terms of diagnosis, ML applied to medical imaging is a promising field, one where deep-learning algorithms on computers can help recognize patterns. There are other related fields where AI is supporting research on early prediction of cancer using ad-hoc blood tests, using AI with AR to help surgeons interpret an X-ray image, or with predictive analytics trying to categorize outcomes related to symptoms, diagnoses, procedures, and medications for individual patients or patient groups. And this is just the beginning.

Real-time monitoring requires low latency and continuous coverage (mobility) anywhere any time. Large amounts of data collected from various devices has to be synchronized and uploaded to the network. Reliability is critical for telemedicine and remote surgery applications, and security is another challenge to guarantee privacy protection of personal data. 5G networks will provide such an environment with high reliability, ultra-high data speeds, extremely low latency, very low packet loss, and flexible use of licensed and unlicensed spectrum, functionalities that are well-suited for connecting medical equipment (i.e., transmission of MRI or X-rays) where reliable mission-critical operation is key and high bandwidth is a must-have. Since 5G will support multiple network topologies, even with the limitations of very-high transmit frequencies, it would be possible to equip medical facilities with internal mesh, D2D, and other architectures that would provide the required services.

13.6 SUMMARY

This chapter introduced multiple different applications of ML and AI to support automated and closed-loop network optimization, as well as user experience-driven network optimization. While many of the network capabilities have existed for some time now, there were numerous technical limitations that restricted the ability of mobile operators to fully realize the potential of fully autonomous networks. Network traffic patterns change rapidly over time with new applications and network characteristics. Not all network data is available at the same granularity or on the same timescales, and real-time data that is important to make optimal network decisions is not always available. In addition, there is not a clear model between network and service-specific KPIs; relationships between cause and effect are not always known or understood across the protocol stack.

The advancements in networking technology—fast, scalable, low-latency 5G wireless networks supporting a large class of devices, open interfaces, and disaggregated network elements, and the ability to process data in real time at the edge—are critical enablers that will allow us to gather large volumes of rich data and process the data in real time. Also crucial are advancements including software packages supporting the state-of-the-art AI techniques, network management platforms like ONAP, and real-time access to large volumes of data and data processing across the various layers of the networking stack. These advancements will enable operators to easily build and deploy intelligent network optimization applications without requiring experts to extract complex nonlinear relationships between network and service KPIs. We are already starting to see the adoption of ML/AI to influence network protocols (e.g., TCP congestion control), and application behavior (e.g., video bit rate selection). However, we believe that this is just the beginning; as discussed in this chapter, there are numerous opportunities where AI can influence the monitoring and optimization of the network. We are only limited by our imagination and the availability of data. In the following chapter, we will discuss the opportunities to apply AI to improve customer experience and care.

ACKNOWLEDGMENTS

The authors wish to acknowledge Weihua Ye, Jin Wang, Mario Kosseifi, Huahui Wang, Zhengye Liu, Ernest Tsui, Dhruv Gupta, Enrique Ulffe Whu, and Giuseppe De Rosa for their contributions to this chapter.

REFERENCES

1. P. Kansal, and A. Bose, Bandwidth and latency requirements for smart transmission grid applications, *IEEE Transactions on Smart Grid*, 3(3), 1344–1352, 2012.
2. A. Osseiran, J. F. Monserrat, P. Marsch, *5G Mobile and Wireless Communications Technology*, Chapter 6, Cambridge University Press, 2016.
3. Gartner, Predicts 2013: Information innovation, Retrieved from https://www.gartner.com/doc/2278715/predicts--information-innovation
4. AT&T, AT&T edge cloud (AEC) – White paper, Retrieved from http://about.att.com/content/dam/innovationdocs/Edge_Compute_White_Paper%20FINAL2.pdf
5. AT&T, AT&T is deploying white box hardware in cell towers to power mobile 5G era, Retrieved from http://about.att.com/story/att_deploying_white_box_hardware_in_cell_towers.html
6. AT&T, Towards an open, disaggregated network operating system, Retrieved from http://about.att.com/content/dam/innovationblogdocs/att-routing-nos-open-architecture_FINAL%20whitepaper.pdf
7. M. Nohrborg, Self-organizing networks, Retrieved from http://www.3gpp.org/technologies/keywords-acronyms/105-son
8. H. Taub, D. L. Schilling, *Principles of Communication Systems*. McGraw-Hill, 1986.
9. E. Hossain, M. Rasti, H. Tabassum, and A. Abdelnasser, Evolution towards 5G multi-tier cellular wireless networks: An interference management perspective, *IEEE Wireless Communications*, 21(3), 118–127, 2014.
10. J. Zander, Performance of optimum transmitter power control in cellular radio systems, *IEEE Transactions on Vehicular Technology*, 41(1), 57–62, 1992.
11. G. J. Foschini and Z. Miljanic, A simple distributed autonomous power control algorithm and its convergence, *IEEE Transactions on Vehicular Technology*, 42, 641–646, 1993.
12. C. Sung and K. Leung, A generalized framework for distributed power control in wireless networks, *IEEE Transactions on Information Theory*, 51(7), 2625–2635, 2005.
13. H. Boche and M. Schubert, A unifying approach to interference modeling for wireless networks, *IEEE Transactions on Signal Processing*, 58(6), 3282–3297, 2010.
14. T. O. Olwal, K. Djouani, and A. M. Kurien, A survey of resource management towards 5G radio access networks, in *IEEE Communications Surveys & Tutorials*, 2016, pp. 1656–1686.
15. F. D. Calabrese, L. Wang, E. Ghadimi, G. Peters, and P. Soldati, Learning radio resource management in 5G networks: Framework, opportunities and challenges, arXiv: 2017.
16. E. Ghadimi, F. D. Calabrese, G. Peters, and P. Soldati, A reinforcement learning approach to power control and rate adaptation in cellular networks, *IEEE International Conference in Communications (ICC)*, 2017.

17. C. U. Saraydar, N. B. Mandayam, and D. J. Goodman, Pricing and power control in a multicell wireless data network, *IEEE Journal on Selected Areas in Communications*, 11(3–4), 185–396, 2015.

18. A. Zappone and E. Jorswieck, Energy efficiency in wireless networks via fractional programming theory, *Foundations and Trends in Communications and Information Theory*, (ICC), 2017.

19. S. Buzzi, I. Chih-Lin, T. E. Klein, H. V. Poor, C. Yang, and A. Zappone, Survey of energy-efficient techniques for 5G networks and challenges ahead, *IEEE Journal on Selected Areas in Communications*, 34(4), 697–709, 2016.

20. Audebert, N. et al., Beyond RGB: Very high resolution urban remote sensing with multimodal deep networks, *ISPRS Journal of Photogrammetry and Remote Sensing*, 2017.

21. Bhushan, N. et al., Network densification: The dominant theme for wireless evolution into 5G, *IEEE Communications Magazine*, 52(2), 2014.

22. T. S. Rappaport, R. W. Heath Jr., R. C. Daniels, and J. N. Murdock, *Millimeter Wave Wireless Communications*, 1st ed., Chapter 3, Prentice Hall, Upper Saddle River, NJ, 2014.

23. R. Bar-Yanai, M. Langberg, D. Peleg, and L. Roditty, Realtime classification for encrypted traffic. In: Festa P. (Eds.) Experimental Algorithms. SEA 2010. Lecture Notes in Computer Science, Vol. 6049. Springer, Berlin, Germany, 2010.

24. T. T. Nguyen and G. Armitage, A survey of techniques for internet traffic classification using machine learning, *IEEE Communications Surveys & Tutorials*, 10(4), 56–76, 2008.

25. X. K. Zou, J. Erman, V. Gopalakrishnan, E. Halepovic, R. Jana, X. Jin, J. Rexford, and R. K. Sinha, Can accurate predictions improve video streaming in cellular networks? *Proceedings of the 16th International Workshop on Mobile Computing Systems and Applications*, February 12–13, Santa Fe, NM, 2015.

26. AT&T Keynote Alicia Abella, What's in it for us? A Carrier's perspective of edge computing, *Fog World Congress*, 2017.

27. Statista Digital Capital Augmented/Virtual Reality Report. Retrieved from https://www.statista.com/topics/3286/augmented-reality-ar/.

28. A. Glaser, Retrieved from https://www.recode.net/2016/12/19/14009398/france-mail-drones-delivery-dpdgroup-postal-service, 2016.

29. https://www.intel.com/content/www/us/en/sports/olympic-games/drones.html

30. K. Ellingwood, Project begins to test 'Driver-less' freeway system. *Los Angeles Times*. Retrieved from http://articles.latimes.com/1996-06-28/news/mn-19436_1_highway-system, 1996.

31. P. Ross, Europe's smart highway will shepherd cars from Rotterdam to Vienna. *IEEE Spectrum*. Retrieved from https://spectrum.ieee.org/transportation/advanced-cars/europes-smart-highway-will-shepherd-cars-from-rotterdam-to-vienna, 2014.

32. P. Ross, World's first 5G-connected cars Demo'd in Korea. *IEEE Spectrum*. Retrieved from https://spectrum.ieee.org/cars-that-think/transportation/infrastructure/korea-demos-5gconnected-cars, 2016.

33. S. Lucero, C-V2X offers a cellular alternative to IEEE 802.11p/DSRC. Retrieved from https://technology.ihs.com/579612/c-v2x-offers-a-cellular-alternative-to-ieee-80211pdsrc9, 2016.

34. IFR World Robotics 2017 report, https://ifr.org/ifr-press-releases/news/ifr-forecast-1.7-million-new-robots-to-transform-the-worlds-factories-by-20

35. T. Torone et al., https://www.pwc.com/us/en/outsourcing-shared-services-centers/assets/robotics-process-automation.pdf, 2016.

36. K. Schwab, The fourth industrial revolution: What it means, how to respond, https://www.weforum.org/agenda/2016/01/the-fourth-industrial-revolution-what-it-means-and-how-to-respond/, https://genesisnanotech.wordpress.com/2016/01/15/the-fourth-industrial-revolution-what-it-means-how-to-respond-will-you-be-ready/, 2016.

CHAPTER **14**

Artificial Intelligence for Customer Experience and Care

Jason Hunt and Sunil Dube

CONTENTS

14.1 INTRODUCTION

In the cognitive era, exceptional customer experience is a necessity, not a need, and is vital as services shift to an autonomous network. Artificial intelligence (AI) plays critical roles in the front-end digital experience when interacting with the user, and in the back-end data processing for extracting intelligence that aid a human or a virtual agent. In successful enterprises, AI guides the end customer in finding answers, reaching the right resource, empowering the associates and executives with informed and better decision-making, creating products and services that meet individual needs, and scaling the customer support with assistance from AI systems that have been trained by the best resources in an enterprise.

This chapter reviews the role of AI in augmented decision-making for transforming the customer experience and care.

14.2 HOW THE AUTONOMOUS NETWORK IMPACTS THE CUSTOMER EXPERIENCE

14.2.1 History of Customer Care for Networks

The early days of telephone networks had very little automation, and many roles from telephone switching to customer care were handled 100% with telephone company employees. A 1950s Bell System training film [1] for customer service representatives depicted this "golden era" of customer service by explaining the five key steps in customer interaction:

1. Be a good listener

2. Get the facts

3. Do something about it

4. Follow up on the results

5. Above all, show your sympathetic interest

How has this customer care approach changed over the years?

14.2.1.1 Rule Based

As economic reality weighed on the service providers, they were pressured to automate as many support functions as possible, including customer service. As most customer care inquiries came via phone, this automation initially took the form of interactive voice response (IVR) systems. "Press 1 for billing issues, Press 2 for network issues" were very static methods for reducing the time spent by representatives routing calls, instead using an IVR to send calls to the most appropriate customer care department.

More recently, IVR systems have become more sophisticated through the introduction of business rules management systems [2]. These IVRs can be programmed by a set of business rules that can capture a variety of conditions and the corresponding action. With this type of system, a customer call about a network issue could trigger an automated network test and, based on the results, initiate a corrective action or creation of a trouble ticket—all without a support agent fielding the call.

14.2.2 Customer Care in the Cognitive Era

As capable as these rules-based systems are, they can still fall short in achieving the goal of satisfying the customer in an efficient manner. The interface to these IVRs is often still touch-tone based or, if voice based, require a specific list of words to be spoken, which can frustrate users. Whole websites are built around helping people find their way out of "IVR hell" to reach a live customer service agent.

Furthermore, rules-based systems are not well suited to solving problems outside of a known set of issues. Such systems may require thousands of rules, and all rules must be written and maintained by subject matter experts.

If there is to be any hope of a second "golden era" of customer care, it will require advancements beyond rules-based systems.

14.2.2.1 Natural Language

The first step in that 1950s customer service video was to "be a good listener," an area in which most customer care systems fall well short. Instead of punching numbers or speaking in short, precise phrases, what if a customer could simply explain their problem in natural language and be understood by a cognitive customer care system? Even if that could happen, dare we imagine a system that can not only reply in natural language but also "show sympathetic interest?"

14.2.2.2 Learning

Of course, a "friendly" agent isn't much help if it can't solve the customer's problem. So, to "do something about it," like the film implored, will require a system that can learn the best resolution to a customer's problem, not based on a fixed set of rules defined by a few experts, but on the collective experience across customer interactions. It would be a system that could "read" thousands of problem tickets and product manuals written in natural language and learn what is most likely to work for this customer.

Bringing these visions together leads us to what we call the transformed digital experience.

14.3 THE TRANSFORMED DIGITAL EXPERIENCE

In the transformed digital experience, the customer can engage with an enterprise using a variety of engagement mechanisms, including voice, chatbots, and a number of engagement channels like the mobile, web, phone, or kiosks. There is a great improvement in the understanding of natural language. Artificial intelligence technologies can now understand sentiments, context, tone, speech, keywords, concepts, intent, and entities. This enhanced understanding of the language opens the world of possibilities in enhancing customer experience.

14.3.1 Engaging the Customer with Chatbots

Traditionally, customers have picked up the phone and called the customer care number to get responses to issues related to their problems. The customer care rep, in turn, has used the systems of record to respond to customer issues. Chatbots, as the name suggests, are automated systems or bots that are trained through crowdsourcing by experts to come up with very specific responses to customer complaints and issues. Chatbots are not searches but are a trained system that provide responses based on natural language questions. For example, an AI conversation system like the IBM Watson Assistant is location independent and can be embedded in a car, a hotel room, an airport, or in a banking or Telco chatbot, and can converse in a natural language and perform tasks like check-in at a hotel, the closing of a window in a car, provide information about an airport, and give details about a telecom service plan [3]. These systems establish relationships between the intent of the user's questions, the entities in the questions, and the context with corresponding trained intents, entities, and context to come up with a response.

Chatbots are not meant as replacements of the human intelligence and human resources but as systems that augment human intelligence and decision-making. These bots can be embedded in a Facebook messenger, mobile phone chats, website chats, or other form factors that are part of the customer's own digital experience. There are two main types of chatbots:

14.3.1.1 Agent Assist

In this scenario, the call center representatives can make use of an AI system as assistants in decision-making. These chatbots improve the quality of customer care and augment the knowledge of the representative, reducing training times as well as assisting in scaling up during holiday seasons.

14.3.1.2 Virtual Agent

Virtual agents are automated systems that are trained to respond to specific customer questions; these systems learn with experience. When these systems do not know the response to customer's questions for which they have not been trained, they can then delegate the customer queries to a live agent. IBM Watson Assistant for automotive and hospitality are good examples of a virtual agent. As stated in this article, "Watson Assistant for Automotive—A solution to connect your vehicles and your drivers through a virtual assistant that also connects them to the world around them." And "Watson Assistant for

Hospitality—A solution to transform your hotel room with a virtual assistant that engages your guests in a new way [4]." Also, the iconic Staples Easy button is another example of a virtual assistant that has transformed the Staples Easy button into a virtual ordering and support system [3].

14.3.2 Voice Interfaces

With the introduction of touchtone dialing in the 1960s, the stage was set for more automated customer support systems. For decades, we have been used to either pressing multiple number options on the phone or responding via voice to reach the right customer care agent. The trained AI systems can understand the user via a combination of speech recognition (to translate speech to words) and natural language recognition. With that combination, the system can comprehend the intent behind the question on a voice interface and can route the request to right customer care agent through the usage of AI algorithms. Verizon uses such a system to transcribe incoming calls, identify the intent of that call, and use that call categorization in real time to adapt their call center operations [5].

An AI system can go a step further, providing specific responses to user issues and questions similar to what the chatbots do, but this time using text-to-speech or speech synthesis technologies to speak to the user. The AI system that responds to user queries is the same system that powers chatbots or any other system or end user that needs assistance in decision-making. An early example of such a system was built by AT&T Research, "AT&T, how may I help you? [6]"

Similar to chatbots, the voice interfaces can also act in an agent-assist mode. In this case, the end user call from the telephony system is forked in two calls, one that the customer service rep responds to and the other to the AI system. The call center rep can gain insights from the way the AI system is trained by the best call center resources to respond to a particular situation during the call.

14.3.3 Personalized Interactions, Including Personality

Customers' expectations can range from exceeded to not met. These two extreme ends of customer expectations might generate emotions that reflect sadness, happiness, and anger. The AI-trained systems can use the tone and sentiment analysis from user responses to understand the tone and sentiment of the customer. One such service is the Watson Tone Analyzer service, which is a pretrained service that can detect the tone in a spoken and written language. The tone can be positive, analytical, anger, confident, fear, or tentative. Another service like the IBM Watson Natural Language Understanding can detect the sentiment in a written text or a spoken language to be either positive, negative, or neutral. The combination of the sentiment and the tone can be augmented in a machine learning model to understand the customer's mood and personality. As explained in the article on tone analyzer [7] "The Tone Analyzer was developed with a machine learning algorithm that trained on customer support conversations on Twitter. It also detects how tones progress throughout conversations, and offers suggestions on when agents should be more sympathetic, polite, or excited during an interaction." Watson Tone analyzer assists the chatbot to take better informed decision.

The knowledge of personalized interactions and personality insights can be used to train the AI system to come up with personalized responses for exceptional customer experience.

14.3.4 Next-Best Action

We have all heard of smarter systems or smarter processes. These systems and processes leverage or embed analytics inside the systems or processes for better decision-making. Predictive systems or machine learning-based systems can predict the next-best action that should be taken based on customer insights and other factors for favorable business outcomes like retaining the customer. The AI systems add to these existing predictive systems' natural language understanding (see Chapter 2) and analysis that can assist in the identification of next-best action. In the customer care scenario, past historical records of the call center interactions either in a voice form or in a transcribed form is made available to the AI system. The first step, if it is a voice form, is to transcribe the call from voice to text. Once we have a transcribed call, care has to be taken that personally identifiable information like credit card is redacted. This cleansed copy without the personal information is now analyzed by the AI system to understand the tone, sentiment, context, keywords, entities, etc., and a machine learning model is created. Now this model can be used to identify similar situations in a real customer care scenario, and the trained AI system using the model can prescribe the next-best action to be taken by the call center rep.

For example, in a real scenario, a customer purchased two phones using the buy one phone get one phone free promotion. The customer paid for one phone by cash and the other phone on a monthly payment plan. He was supposed to get a Visa card equal in value of the price of a phone upon submission of the receipt to the telecommunications provider. After couple of weeks, the customer called to check the status of the claim. He was notified by the AI system that his claim was denied. The customer was upset and requested information on why his claim was denied. The trained AI system identified the tone of the customer to be upset and used the next-best action, which was to get an expert to assist the customer. The customer service expert immediately got on the line and explained to the customer that the reason the claim was denied was because both phones had to be purchased on a monthly payment plan. The customer service rep reversed the transaction, placed both phones on a payment plan, and processed the customer's claim.

14.3.5 Preventing Customer Churn

According to a research conducted at the NY EDU [8], $65M is lost every year by telecommunications companies because of customer churn. Twenty percent of the subscribers in the top Telcos change service providers every year. Artificial intelligence can prevent customer churn. As explained in the previous section, past historical records of call-center transcripts can be analyzed to identify parameters for churn. These parameters along with customer information, customer behaviors, and customer orders and usage can be used to create machine learning models that can predict customer churn. Once the trained machine learning model is deployed, a customer churn score and next-best action based on the churn score and available parameters can be suggested by the AI system. So, when the customer engages with the Telco, the customer's intent, tone, and sentiments can be identified. Based on this information and the customer information, the engagement system or the call-center rep can get a churn score and the next-best action from the AI machine learning model. Some of the recommendations can be transparency, more discount, competitive pricing, or finding the right representative.

Artificial intelligence systems have the potential to predict customer churn and reduce the losses associated with customer churn.

14.3.6 Recommender Systems for Proactive Care

While customer churn is resolved using the AI system in the context of the customer contacting the call center or engaging with customer care, a recommender system can be proactive (see Chapter 2). Using various parameters, past historical information, trends, competitive information, and past customer interactions with the telecom providers, predictive models can be created by the data science experts. These predictive models can be deployed in an AI/machine learning system, sometimes also called a recommender system. Periodically, based on changes in a customer's personal situation, market changes, and business events like introduction of a new phone, or by competitive changes, these recommender systems can detect and identify actions that can be taken proactively to improve customer service. These actions could be any of the following: providing a discount because of competitor actions, offering the newly released phone to the existing customer as a priority, leasing towers for improving network coverage, providing network boosters in areas where there is poor coverage or, proactively calling the customer if there is an outage in service.

14.4 BUILDING AN AI SYSTEM FOR CUSTOMER CARE

With an understanding of how a service provider can transform the experience of the customer, let's discuss the components that would comprise a complete AI-based customer care system, along with the techniques used to implement those systems.

Figure 14.1, adapted from IBM's publicly available Cognitive Conversation Reference Architecture [9], outlines many of the concepts covered in the denoted sections.

- Conversation System (14.4.1): The conversation system, in the top center of the diagram, is in many ways the heart of an AI-based customer care system. It ingests the input from the customer, identifies their intent, and replies, either directly or via assistance to a care representative.

- Predictive Models (14.4.2): Predictive analytics provide input to the system and care representative to customize the response to the client.

- Optimization Models (14.4.3): The execution of the customer care organization (and network operations organization) can benefit from optimization techniques.

- Enterprise Systems (14.4.4): Represented by several blocks on the right side of the diagram, the enterprise systems provide valuable context and data about the customer and the network, which enhance the AI and conversational systems.

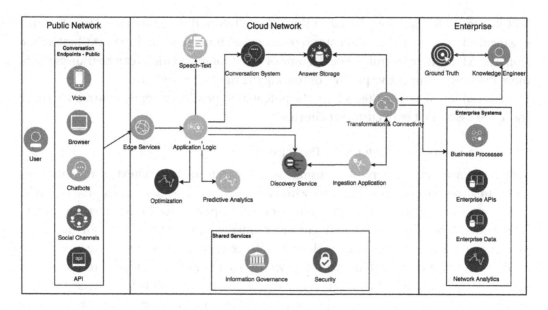

FIGURE 14.1   Reference architecture for customer care.

- Omni- and social channels (14.4.5 and 14.4.6): A well-designed system can support various forms of client input, whether traditional telephony (done via the speech-to-text and corresponding text-to-speech systems), mobile, proprietary chatbots, or social media integration, as represented on the left side of the diagram.

- Training (14.5.1 and 14.5.2): The AI-based customer care system will require training by a knowledge engineer using a combination of "ground truth" data from enterprise sources, as well as crowd-sourced data. Likewise, the training should be continuous, incorporating feedback from the running system.

- Discovery (14.5.2): Addressing all customers' inquiries may reach beyond the preprogrammed dialogs in the conversation system. A long-tail search capability, labeled Discovery in the diagram, allows the system to address broader, unanticipated queries.

14.4.1   Training and Modeling Conversations

The examples of chatbots, agent assist, and virtual agent mentioned previously are all variations on conversation-based systems: a back-and-forth interaction in natural language between, in this case, the customer and an AI system or an agent assisted by AI. Whether these conversation systems are voice or text-based, they all make use of several common concepts: intents, entities, context, dialogs, and tone.

14.4.1.1 Intents

At the core of any conversation system is the need to understand what the customer is talking about. This is called "intent," that is, what is the question, topic, or purpose of the customer's communications. If the customer says, "My phone's signal dropped at home an hour ago," that might indicate a network issue that needs investigation. Determining intent, though, can be difficult. One approach might be to iterate every possible customer utterance for each intent, but that will quickly prove to be infeasible because of the wide variations that customers might use in their queries. The opposite approach would be to specify keywords or phrases for the limited number of options available. This approach has been seen in the aforementioned voice-based IVR systems that require the customer to say "account update" or "billing" to be routed down the appropriate path. However, this approach does not provide an exceptional customer experience, because it requires the customer to essentially be trained by the system to say the right keywords. Customers can quickly become frustrated if their queries are not properly understood.

Rather than either of those approaches, conversational systems implement a variety of natural language machine learning models to determine intent. The training of these systems requires a list of customer utterances mapped to their corresponding intent. Given a new utterance, the system can provide the likely intent or intents that match that utterance, with a corresponding confidence score for each intent. Using our previous example, a conversational system may recognize that a customer has a network issue if she says, "I don't have any bars when I drive to work," even if that exact phrase was not used in the training data.

As with many of the machine learning models discussed in this book, identification accuracy increases as more training data is provided. Later in this chapter, we'll discuss techniques for building a good utterance data set.

14.4.1.2 Entities

While intents give us a starting point in creating a useful conversation with a customer, it is often helpful to understand more specifics about the customer's query. For example, if a customer says, "I'd like a TV package with CNN" and another customer says "I want to watch ESPN," both of those requests might map to a single intent for requesting a video package. But to make an informed recommendation on a video package (such as "news" vs. "sports"), you need to know which TV channel the customer requested. Creating separate intents for each channel will likely not work, as the utterances would be too similar to provide accurate differentiation between intents.

Alternatively, we can have a general-purpose intent for requesting a video package and then identify within the utterance channel they prefer. This concept of looking at objects within an utterance is called "entities." Entities can be thought of like parameters on a function and are useful when you want to take a similar action for a customer's query.

Entities in conversation systems are typically defined more declaratively than intent training. A list of possible entities is given to the system, along with synonyms or iterated values for those entities. In some systems, you can identify in the utterance training set which portion of the utterance would contain an entity, such as "I want to watch [channel]," where [channel] is defined by a finite list of possible channels or genres, like "CNN, ESPN, local news, comedies." Multiple entities could even be present in a single sentence.

14.4.1.3 Tone and Emotion

Properly trained intents and entities may be sufficient to "get the job done" in a conversational system implementation, but to deliver an exceptional experience for the customer requires a bit more refinement. One technique that can be used is to identify tone or emotion in the customer's communications. Many pretrained models for tone and emotion classification exist and can be used to understand the sentiment of an utterance. Given an utterance (a textual representation of the customer's communication, whether coming from a chat experience or transcribed from a voice channel), these models will return one or more identified tones with corresponding confidence scores. To understand how these models are built, see this example from the aforementioned IBM Watson Tone Analyzer:

> Given a set of customer support conversations and associated tones, we trained a machine learning model to predict tones for new customer support conversations. For the machine learning model, we leverage several categories of features, including n-gram features, lexical features from various dictionaries, punctuation, and existence of second-person reference in the turn. We use a Support Vector Machine as our machine learning model. In our data, we have observed that about 30% of the samples have more than one associated tone, so we decided to solve a multilabel classification task then multiclass classification. For each of our tones, we trained the model independently using One-Vs-Rest paradigm. During prediction, we identify the tones that are predicted with at least 0.5 probability as the final tones. For several tones, our training data is heavily imbalanced, and to address this issue, we find the optimal weight value of the cost function for each of these tones during training [10].

Tone and emotion can also be detected via the audio analysis of the voice directly, using techniques, such as pitch, timbre, loudness, rate of speech, and vocal tone [11].

In customer care, understanding tone might alter how to handle a customer inquiry. A customer that is becoming more frustrated may require a different approach or escalation to make her satisfied. Tone can also be used to understand how good a customer agent is at conveying sympathy or politeness. In an automated system, tone analysis could be used to choose the response that best addresses the customer's emotional state. For example, saying to a frustrated customer, "Thank you for your patience" or a satisfied customer "Glad that you are pleased with our service!" MetLife uses a set of animated icons to provide real-time feedback to call center agents on customer's tone—an approach that MetLife claims is improving customer satisfaction and reducing call duration [12].

14.4.1.4 Context

In addition to tone, bringing in other context about the customer situation can help guide the system to a better customer resolution. Context can take many forms. For example, given a history of call center interactions by that customer, the system could identify if this query relates to a previous or recurring problem. Other examples of context might include weather conditions, which could adversely impact satellite dish reception. Having a rich set of contexts is key to improving the accuracy of many machine learning models.

Obtaining context usually requires calls to systems external from the conversation system. Because these external calls may take time, a balance may need to be reached between multiple calls for context and ensuring a timely response to user. Caching certain context may be prudent.

14.4.1.5 Dialog

The means by which the conversation flows with the customer from one prompt to the next is called the dialog [13]. Using all of the other parts of a conversation system (intents, entities, tone, and context) will drive what response the system gives and what to expect back from the customer. Dialogs may be defined differently depending on the conversation system. There will typically be a set of conditions to match (most importantly intent), and then dialog logic will use the entities, tone, and context to determine a response to be sent to the user. Some conversational systems may use a graphical flow model that links conversation parts in dependent or independent sections. Others might use a state-machine model [14]. Yet others may simply define appropriate Application Programming Interfaces (APIs) and leave the dialog construction to custom code of the operator's choosing.

In any case, designing the dialog flow benefits greatly from user experience experts. A system should have a "personality" that is appropriate for the customer support scenario, striking the right tone with the customer. For example, having a variety of responses in a dialog for the same condition will prevent the perception that the system is "canned" or "stilted" in its responses. Likewise, too strict of a dialog flow might not much better than the IVR "trees" of touch-tone days past. A more flexible system might use additional machine learning models to determine the next step in a dialog flow.

14.4.2 Creating Predictive Models

With an interaction system in place via conversation, let's now discuss what other types of AI can be applied to a customer care scenario. Predictive modeling is a mainstay of AI for customer care. As mentioned earlier in this chapter, this type of machine learning can be used for cases such as predicting customer churn or recommending a next-best action for a customer care scenario. Generally, predictive models can generate a binary answer (yes/no, like churn), a categorization answer (like which product to recommend), or a numerical answer (like monthly data consumption, also called regression analysis).

Developing a predictive model is not too dissimilar from the process to train intents in the conversation system, in that both are supervised training models. The training data set includes all of the parameters that might influence the outcome, as well as the outcome for that scenario. In a customer churn case, each row of the training data might be characteristics about one particular customer (current plan, time as customer, average spend, zip code, etc.) and whether or not that customer churned. This training data is provided to the predictive modeling tool, which may choose the appropriate model algorithms for the data or may let the model developer choose the model.

A key aspect in training predictive models is evaluation. A set of historical data should be reserved for evaluation and not used in the training. After the model is created, the evaluation data set is applied to the model to check how accurate the model is at predicting the outcome. If the accuracy of the model against the evaluation set is low, then the developer needs to reexamine how the model was created.

Once the model is created and evaluated with a high enough accuracy, a best practice for deployment of the model would be to bundle it as a microservice. This microservice will take in all the required inputs for the model and return a confidence score on likelihood of the predicted outcome. This will allow the predictive model microservice to be called from other systems, such as the conversational system. For example, if a customer chat begins, and a call from the conversation system to the predictive model indicates a high confidence score for churn, the conversation system's dialog might take a different path to prevent that churn. The conversation system will use its state and context to continually adjust the dialog through the customer interaction.

14.4.3 Creating Optimization Models

Another class of AI that can be leveraged in customer care is optimization. Optimization problems look to maximize or minimize a certain outcome (max profit, max customer care, minimal cost, etc.) while operating under a set of constraints (resource availability, costs, etc.). Optimization can be leveraged throughout the network, whether it's for determining best antennae placement to network capacity planning to technician dispatch to Virtualized Network Function (VNF) allocation across regions. Specific for customer care, optimization solutions could be used to determine the best scheduling and allocation of customer care agents to optimize customer satisfaction. For example, the most experienced customer care agents can't answer every call, so an optimization solution could recommend the preferred customer profiles (perhaps based on churn likelihood, social network score, or projected customer lifetime value) that should be dispatched by the most experience agents.

Solving an optimization problem follows a modeling and execution flow. Modeling can vary by tool but requires expressing the constraints, preferences, and desired outcome in a mathematical or modeling language understood by the optimization tool. Then the optimization engine runs against that model to determine an outcome. There is a balance between problem execution runtime and how optimal the solution is.

14.4.4 Integration with Existing Systems

While it should not be a surprise, customer care systems for operators do not standalone. Integration with existing Business Support Systems (BSS)/Operational Support Systems (OSS) systems will be necessary. Whether it is as a data source for building your AI models, for real-time queries from a conversation system, or for transactions like orders and account updates, a careful integration architecture will be required to deliver an optimal customer experience. Best practices in this area include exposing appropriate microservices from the BSS/OSS with appropriate caching to insulate the customer care systems from any outages, particularly in legacy systems with scheduled downtime.

14.4.5 Omni-Channel Usage of the Trained Customer Service

A well-architected customer service system—that includes a conversational system, as well as predictive and optimization analytics—can be leveraged across customer channels. In the areas of text-based chat, the same core conversation system can drive interactions on a variety of social media channels, as well as Short Message Service (SMS) and operator-specific chat systems. Typically, this will require an adapter layer for each channel to map the channel's API calls into the conversation system's calls.

Conversational systems need not be limited to just text-based interfaces. With a voice gateway that leverages speech-to-text and text-to-speech engines, a conversation-based system can also drive voice systems in both virtual agent and agent-assist models. Keep in mind, though, that your user experience may dictate different dialogs and responses for text versus voice interfaces. Chat conversations, for example, tend to use more abbreviations and be more terse, particularly if the customer is on a mobile device. Likewise, some chat systems could support images (either photos sent by the customer or instructional images sent by the care representative), which would not be available in a voice-only system.

14.4.6 Integration of Customer Service with the Social Platform

Not only can your conversation system be used to drive customer care via social channels, but the social channel can be a valuable source of insights for customer care decisions. Analytics can be done against a customer's social media history to determine personality or sentiment. By linking with marketing systems, social history can drive product recommendations that could be leveraged for cross-sell or up-sell opportunities during a customer interaction. For example, if you have access and authorization to use data from social platforms, you can understand that customers have negative sentiments about international data service. This information can be used to come up with a reliable and cost-effective international data plan by partnering with other global providers. By leveraging the historical records, this new international plan can then be marketed to the likely international travelers.

14.5 SCALING EXCEPTIONAL CUSTOMER CARE FOR CARRIER NEEDS

In any carrier, there are resources who are best in handling customer conversations, and there are reps who are extremely knowledgeable about the products and services they provide. These experts are small in number. Sometimes these customer center reps are either referred as level 2 or level 3 support reps. In addition to the level 2 and level 3 reps, there are also a large number of reps (level 1) who provide generalized customer support. Artificial intelligence systems that are trained by these experts can now provide guidance to the level 1 support, thereby reducing the work load on the expert representatives. Also, these AI-trained systems can be used to train the new reps that come on board as well as the existing reps on new changes. These AI systems, thus, can scale the exceptional customer care by providing expert knowledge to the level 1 call center reps.

14.5.1 Crowd-Sourcing for Training of Artificial Intelligence Services

Customer care requires knowledge about customers, customer interactions, ways of responding to customer situations, product knowledge, marketing and sales, etc. So, who trains the AI system becomes extremely important in the confidence level of the end customer.

Who trained the AI systems is also sometimes referred to as transparency in the AI world. Borrowing the analogy from the open source software development process where we use crowdsource to develop the system or software, the best AI system training also has to be crowdsourced. So we have to leverage the best customer care center reps, product experts, and marketing and sales resources to train the AI system. The reason crowdsourcing is important is because one person may not know all aspects of the customer service to train the AI system. Knowledge from multiple experts from different areas are required to train the AI system for better results and accuracy. As published in the Forbes article, "Just as when we seek advice from a doctor or a lawyer because we are interested in their qualifications, we must be clear on the genealogy of training a cognitive system, which will determine its purpose [15]," it is important to get best knowledgeable resources in the business to train the AI system. Crowdsourcing is a way to get the best knowledgeable resources from various departments for training the AI system. This ensures better results and confidence in the usage of the system. Artificial intelligence systems that are trained by the best experts produce better results. As explained in the earlier section, these AI systems assist in the scaling of exceptional customer service, that is, that the same expert information and the way an expert will handle the customer service scenario is now available to all reps.

14.5.2 Continuous Training—Closed Loop for Customer Care

The first trained AI system would have limited knowledge. This knowledge is based on past historical customer call center records and notes. The AI system as described in Section 14.5.1 is trained by experts. Once the system is deployed, the trained AI system—in addition to crowdsourcing and past historical records—should be able to continuously learn. This is sometimes also referred to as the closed-loop system in which the feedback enhances the systems behavior or performance on a continuous basis, based on new information from current customer interaction and the creation and modification of personalized customer knowledge, competition situation, introduction of new products, launching of new marketing initiative, etc. The continuous learning can be unsupervised or supervised, as the system can learn from more test data and usage on its own or it can be trained by using new data. The continuous learning or the closed-loop control of the AI system increases the accuracy of the response and the confidence level of the response, thereby improving customer service.

14.5.3 Expanding the Knowledge Base

The AI system discussed so far is a trained system and can answer specific questions with a very high level of confidence. However, this trained AI system might not have answers to all the questions. This is the short tail scenario where there is a limited set of known customer situations and responses to customer situations. Knowledge expansion is a long tail scenario in which unstructured content is annotated and the content is augmented to find an answer in a series of documents. So, in this case, if the trained AI system does not have an answer to a specific problem, question, or situation, it delegates or consults the corpus, which is also trained to narrow the search using Natural Language Understanding to a few responses with a high level of confidence [16].

14.5.3.1 Building the Corpus

How do you build the corpus? A knowledgeable business Subject Matter Expert (SME) identifies the content sources and a few (three to six) representative content documents are used to train and to augment the content with metadata around sentiments, entities, concepts, keywords, etc. Custom models can also be built for creating the ontology. These documents should contain most of the information that the system needs to search for content based on search or research question. Once we have the foundation established, we now need to establish the relevance of the test results. Once the corpus is established, we then continue to use multiple queries and the results of those queries to improve the accuracy of the results. The corpus continues to grow in accuracy with the continuous usage and training. As we get precise in response in the research question or search query, the query and response can be moved to the short tail scenario or to the completely trained AI system we discussed before. According to IBM Watson services documentation, a leading AI vendor service, "You must train a minimum of 49 queries, and possibly more. Watson will give you feedback if it needs more queries in order to train [17]."

14.5.3.2 Establishing the Model Foundation

While the prebuilt content metadata in natural language understanding cover a broad array of content understanding, there are metadata and relationship specific to different industry solutions areas. This requires custom model creation with custom relationship for the training and creation of corpus. This model foundation can be used to train industry-specific content for knowledge expansion scenarios.

14.6 SUMMARY

Artificial intelligence systems require training. The training has to be provided by experts from multiple specialties. These trained AI systems have to continuously learn in order to improve accuracy of the customer response. A continuous learning AI system is a system that scales the exceptional service by providing access to the way the best experts would handle a particular customer situation. Also, the AI systems can identify actions that can be taken proactively to improve product or customer service performance. These AI systems assists in decision-making that transform a good customer service to exceptional customer service.

In the next chapter, we'll take a look at how AI techniques described here and previously can be used to envision a network of the future.

REFERENCES

1. https://www.youtube.com/watch?v=nL0TDHfvTSU
2. https://patents.google.com/patent/US8090086
3. https://www.ibm.com/watson/services/conversation/
4. https://www.ibm.com/blogs/watson/2018/03/the-future-of-watson-conversation-watson-assistant/
5. https://www.youtube.com/watch?v=Zg-_BJt6jdc&feature=youtu.be
6. Gorin, A.L., Parker, B.A., Sachs, R.M., and Wilpon, J.G. How may I help you? *Interactive Voice Technology for Telecommunications Applications 1996. Proceedings, Third IEEE Workshop on*, Basking Ridge, NJ, 1996.

7. https://www.zdnet.com/article/ibm-intros-watson-tone-analyzer-to-make-chatbots-emotionally-astute/

8. https://wp.nyu.edu/adityakapoor/2017/02/17/churn-in-the-telecom-industry-identifying-customers-likely-to-churn-and-how-to-retain-them/

9. https://www.ibm.com/cloud/garage/content/architecture/cognitiveConversationDomain/discoveryDomain

10. https://www.ibm.com/blogs/bluemix/2017/04/tone-analyzer-customer-engagement-7-new-tones-help-understand-customers-feeling/

11. Dasgupta, P.B. Detection and Analysis of Human Emotions through Voice and Speech Pattern Processing, *International Journal of Computer Trends and Technology (IJCTT)* – Volume 52 Number 1 October 2017.

12. https://www.wired.com/story/this-call-may-be-monitored-for-tone-and-emotion/

13. https://console.bluemix.net/docs/services/conversation/dialog-overview.html#dialog-overview

14. https://github.com/itsabot/itsabot

15. https://www.forbes.com/sites/ibm/2017/03/13/three-ways-to-foster-trust-and-transparency-in-the-cognitive-era/#5fb9250d7c4f

16. https://developer.ibm.com/dwblog/2017/chatbot-long-tail-questions-watson-conversation-discovery/

17. https://console.bluemix.net/docs/services/discovery/train-tooling.html#improving-result-relevance-with-the-toolin

CHAPTER 15

New Artificial Intelligence Frontiers for Autonomous Networks

Anit Lohtia and Chris Rice

CONTENTS

15.1 INTRODUCTION

The networks have gone through major transformations from a simple voice-wired network to hyperconnected mobile wireless networks. The next frontier is artificial intelligence (AI)-driven autonomous networks. A number of technologies will be seamlessly integrated to deliver value to the network users. The evolution to autonomous network will require evolution of processes and people as well. Many of challenges in this transition will not only be technical but also social.

An autonomous network will be built using a number of technologies of which many will be created in open-source communities. The machine learning (ML) and AI algorithms and models are becoming increasingly more advanced. This, combined with advances in the computing technologies, especially Graphical Processing Unit or application hardware, such as Tensor Processing Unit, as well as much faster and cheaper data storage, creates excellent opportunities to apply AI in a number of areas in networks, including network planning, operation, and security. These will structurally impact both carrier and enterprise networks. As with any technology advance, there are bad actors looking for leveraging the latest tools for unethical or illegal purposes. It is critical to carefully evaluate the new security risks introduced by these advances.

The software-defined network (SDN) enables program optimization of the network. The SDN networks will be designed with a strong focus on the detailed network data collection plans. These data sets will not only allow the reactive root cause analysis but also proactive predictive optimization of resources and performance. The Open Network Automation Platform (ONAP) allows the operator and even end-users to create new services using a portal. There are open application programming interfaces (APIs) to chain various virtual network functions (VNFs) to create new services optimally on the fly.

The block chain technologies will bring significant efficiencies with their distributed system of records. This potential to fundamentally change asset tracking, contracting, billing, and compensating entities efficiently even for small value adds.

A lot of these advances are coming from rapid innovation of open source projects such as OpenStack, ONAP, Kubernetes, Acumos, and many other. The de facto standards will be created where the contributions will continuous evolve solutions rather unlike debate of detailed standards specification a priori in the past. The organizations leveraging open source technologies efficiently will have a competitive advantage. Microservices allows each service to be implemented optimally and independently to deliver its focused functionality. It minimizes duplication of development of the same functionality.

The cloud technologies primarily were deployed in big data center. The next frontier enabled with SDN/network function virtualization (NFV) technologies is the edge computing. The compute and data storage move closer to the end-user for highly latency sensitive applications. The 5G networks will have much higher bandwidth and much lower latency, which will be critical for use-cases such as the autonomous vehicle.

Lastly, these technological advances will require folks in the industry to continuously learn new skills and keep up with paradigm shift in the network planning, design, operations, and security. The regulations will have also to evolve keep up these changes.

Section 15.2 recaps how the networks have transitioned over the last few decades. Section 15.3 describes how various components are evolving to enable autonomous networks. The next sections cover the evolution of processes and skills needed as the networks transform with technological advances. Section 15.7 has a couple of use-cases of AI-enabled autonomous network services to illustrate how it all is coming together. We end the book with opportunities for community to enable the transformation.

15.2 BASIC FUNCTIONS OF A NETWORK

A network is defined as a group of interconnected people, places, or devices. It is typically depicted graphically as a set of nodes interconnected by links. The more links between the nodes, the richer the interconnection is within the network and the higher the value of the network is to its participants.

Networks are both naturally occurring and man-made. Figure 15.1 shows how the rivers of the world interconnect through the seas and oceans, allowing people to navigate the waters. It was this "network" that interconnected remote regions gave rise to world trade. This rich network allowed goods and services to be freely traded, and it improved lives throughout the world. Its rich interconnectedness made it extremely valuable to early visionaries who saw what it could do, though it could take months to move simple goods from one part of the globe to another.

An example here for "richly connected" is the Panama Canal. The Panama Canal is a man-made waterway in Panama, about 50 miles long, that connects the Atlantic Ocean

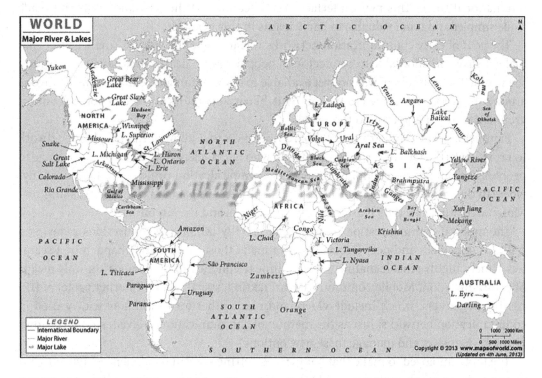

FIGURE 15.1   Rivers of the world Map. (From http://www.starsatnight.org/blog/educational-blog/one-tiny-drop/ [1].)

FIGURE 15.2   International Telephone Switching Center from 1940s and 1950s. (From http://www. snipview.com/q/switchboard_operator [2].)

with the Pacific Ocean. The canal, completed in the early 1900s, is a key connection for international trade. This new "interface" richly connected the East and West and made trade simpler and more valuable to participants in this network.

The goal of early communication networks was to make the world a smaller place and make it easy and affordable to connect with people, first in nearby areas and then around the world. The technology was not yet available to allow automated connections to anyone around the world, so people did the job. Switchboard operators allowed people to connect around the corner and around the world.

Figure 15.2 shows an early switchboard operation that allowed the telephone network to provide worldwide connection for anyone who had a telephone. Its impact was huge to people's lives and to the economy. Immediate communication could occur to almost anywhere in the world. The telephone network had political impact too, with the Washington–Moscow "Hotline" in 1963 between the White House and the Kremlin.

The modern communication network has literally billions of connections a day, and millions of devices and network elements to make those connections happen in a seamless, timely, highly reliable manner. The landline telephone call is no longer the only means of communication. Mobile communications, texting, social media, Internet protocol (IP) routing of packets, which include video, and many other forms are now widely used in communication networks. Just as the method of communication evolved, so did the tools to track, maintain, and manage these new options.

The tools employed to make that happen are cutting edge in data science. Figure 15.3 is an example of a tool used within AT&T and available in open source called Nanocubes. It lets billions of data points be viewed and manipulated within a standard web browser.

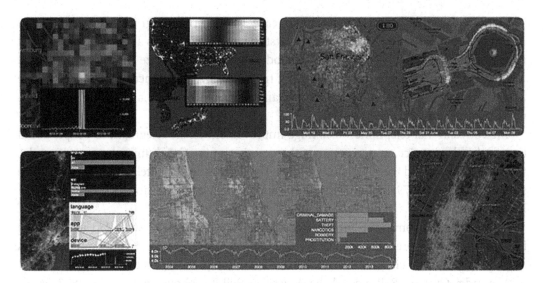

FIGURE 15.3 Visualization examples of connected people, places, and devices. (From https://venturebeat.com/2017/04/09/how-companies-and-consumers-benefit-from-ai-powered-networks/ [3].)

The example graphs show geography heat maps, device connections, and device-type concentrations within the network, but its use is very general.

At their core, networks are about connections. The types of connections, whether waters of the world, telephones, social media, mobile phones, dating sites, or professional relationships, define the type of network, but all have some things in common. The more richly they are connected and the more participants in the network, the more valuable they are, both to producers (network owners) and to consumers (subscribers).

Another attribute each has in common is that the more complex these networks become, the more difficult they are to manage. New tools are required. As the tools of data science have allowed the complexity of modern networks to grow reliably and affordably, the next phase of growth will require more. It is this next phase where AI and ML will play a role.

15.2.1 Communication Networks Evolution

Communication can be one way (from sender to recipient), which can be time bound (like a radio signal) or unbounded (like paintings on a wall in a cave); it can be two way, like conversations or signals between two people standing next to one another, or more distant like early smoke signals, flag colors, and drums used to call attention to important matters affecting the community.

Human communication started hundreds of thousands of years ago, with speech that was little more than grunts. Symbols followed as a way to deliver richer information that was difficult to convey in speech (a picture is worth a thousand words, or grunts). As these methods of communication evolved, so did the need to transmit those words and symbols over greater distance. The term *telecommunication* means communication over distance by some access means, whether cable, air, or even smoke.

Modern telecommunications began in early 1800s. The telegraph was invented in England in the 1830s by Sir Charles Wheatstone and Sir William Fothergill Cooke, but it was Samuel Morse who developed the code used to standardize the signaling on the telegraph, allowing wider-scale deployment, training, and acceptance of the medium. The first transatlantic telegraph cable was sent and delivered in 1866, allowing transatlantic telecommunication for the first time.

The conventional telephone was a huge improvement to the telegraph, as people could hear each other's voice, and experience the emotion of another human being. Alexander Graham Bell invented the telephone in 1876. The first commercial telephone services were set up in 1878 and 1879, in the United States and in England in the cities of New Haven and London, respectively.

Local telephone companies proliferated throughout the United States. As the telephone became more and more popular, this soon got out of hand. Figure 15.4 shows how the wires quickly took over the city's landscape as the various companies tried to serve every home.

Alexander Graham Bell created the American Bell Telephone company in 1877, which later became the American Telephone and Telegraph (AT&T) company in 1899. The goal was to provide local, long-distance services (regional bells and AT&T long distance) and manufacture the equipment to do so (Western Electric), and create any new technology needed (Bell Labs) all in one place, one company. This structure essentially existed until 1984, when AT&T was split up, divested, into a long-distance company and the "baby" bells were split off on their own as separate companies. Until 1984, aside from touchtone phones, and new features for business, the telecommunication landscape remained relatively unchanged.

At the time of the divesture, there was work going on within Bell Labs on a new mode of communication called cellular telephony. Cellular was the term used because there was a realization that the frequencies could be reused if they were separated by enough distance

FIGURE 15.4 Telephone wires over New York City 1880s. (From https://io9.gizmodo.com/photos-from-the-days-when-thousands-of-cables-crowded-t-1629961917 [4].)

and put on a hexagonal grid (tessellated); hence, mobile telephony was birthed. The only issue was that the early "handsets" filled a trunk of a car. When asked how many could be sold, a famous consulting company offered "10,000, at best." This was not the scale for AT&T; so, early pioneers adopted the work from the Labs to start mobile telephony, and AT&T bought their way back into the business for about $13 billion in 1994 with the purchase of McCaw Cellular.

In roughly this same time frame, other important technologies were starting to scale. The personal computer, coincidentally also brought to market in 1984, was starting to get widespread adoption in homes; these were multipurpose, data devices that were being interconnected through modems. Personal computer networks and electronic bulletin boards allowed the first versions of the Internet to be envisioned. Internet protocol communications were also scaling at that time, allowing there to be a standard protocol to connect all of these personal computers in people's homes. The last missing piece was the IP application equivalent of the telephone: a simple device or capability to provide seamless connectivity to web content. The web browser provided this ability. Hence, the perfect storm of technology alignment that created the dot.com web boom was in place. All of these technologies were required to make that happen, and in the span of five years or less, they all came together to deliver the Internet to the world. This new Internet put stress on a communication network built to deliver primarily voice. Many people got a second line but still more was needed. Fundamental limits of bit rate that a telephone modem could deliver were reached. It was clear; the way to build communication networks would have to change to handle these technology transitions.

15.2.2 Network Transitions—Voice to Data, Circuit to Packet, Landline to Mobile

There have been many fundamental pivots in wide area communication network design and deployment. Since its inception, the Public Switched Telephone Network was designed to deliver voice, circuit-switched voice to be precise; that was THE application for that network. Everything else was secondary. As the Internet grew, data traffic became more and more important as an application that needed first-rate status.

Around the year 2000, depending on the country, data traffic surpassed voice traffic. This rate of growth was so rapid, by 2007, voice traffic represented only 10% of the traffic on the public network [5,6]. This data growth necessitated fundamental changes in the way networks were designed. The IP took over for circuit switched Plain Old Telephone Service (POTS) networks; routers replaced switches; and figuring out how to do quality of service and voice over IP (VoIP) became necessary, as voice was just ONE application on this new IP data network. All of this conversion had to be done in a way that left customer reliability unaffected, allowed legacy and new applications to coexist, and provided cost-effective services to support the growing demand for data speeds. While this may have seemed simple and straightforward to many who were not involved in the details, it actually required a tremendous amount of engineering and operational skill to pull it off. New technology and tooling for the IP network were needed to make its reliability match that of the voice network (5–9s, or 99.999% reliable, about five minutes a year downtime). Early versions of routers were nowhere near this reliable, and it took substantial co-engineering and hardening of early versions to make them "network ready."

To keep up with the new data exhaust that the IP network gave off, even more scalable data science tools were necessary. As traffic increased tenfold and more over previous levels, the tooling had to reach new scale limits. Big data has its roots in telecom. For example, as of this writing (May 2018), there are over 200 Petabytes that flow over AT&T's network on a given day. If just 0.1% of that data is sampled for network management and quality reasons, that is still over 200 Terabytes that need to be processed each and every day; that is almost 2 billion transactions being processed per second, and it is growing at 30%–40% per year. The more that can be handled automatically or from which can be learned while processing, the more inexpensive the network becomes to manage. It is here where AI/ML will play a role in network management.

The switch from landline to mobile traffic was another fundamental switch. Mobile traffic surpassed landline traffic in 2009 [7a]. The type of traffic had a similar profile, whether landline or mobile, but the access mechanism and investment profile were substantially different. Again, the mobile network was originally primarily built for voice, and it had to be rearchitected for data, like in the landline case. This was another engineering feat that required operational excellence and technical acumen, as traffic shifts dictated different investment needs. New and better tooling and technology was required in mobility, which allowed items like airlink quality and capacity, cell site usage, cell site handoffs, and device/handset metrics to be monitored.

As we enter into a new era where more "things" will be on the network, whether mobile or landline, than people, technology will have to take another leap. The Internet of Things (IoT) must be served just as reliably, but at lower cost points and greater scale, maybe up to 10X scale [7b]. This type of cost-effectiveness and scale requires the use of AI/ML where metrics can be captured, processed, and acted upon automatically. More importantly, those metrics need to be agile and learned from, so that the tooling needs to get smarter after each action. This is another place where AI/ML will play a role to meet this new need for the IoT. As the number and different types of machines connected to the Internet grows, the need for more IP addresses grows. Fortunately, IoT is greenfield enough to be native IPv6, allowing over 10^{38} unique connected devices. Some have expressed concern over IPv6 addressing as being too unique, not allowing enough privacy. Gateways, NATing, firewalls, and other technology help to alleviate some of those concerns.

15.2.3 New Transitions to Internet of Everything

As we move into an era where more things may be on the network than people, we need to determine if the IP that gave rise to the Internet is still the best option. It has proven very durable over its 40 years of existence and over 20+ years of wide area network field use, but is it still the best option, or has its time come to an end?

Endpoints with people connected to the Internet and embedded devices connected to the Internet have very different needs. People connect to applications, email, web services, web pages, e-retailing, videos, etc. "Things" collect, aggregate, process, and relay information, data, and system metrics used to monitor them. While TCP/IP protocols are the *de facto* protocols used in today's data networks, there are important distinctions required for processing data for the things connected to the Internet.

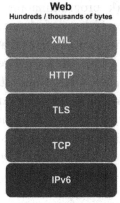

FIGURE 15.5   Web versus IoT for Network Stack. (https://www.wired.com/insights/2014/11/iot-wont-work-without-artificial-intelligence/ [8].)

Internet of Things devices are low power, usually wireless devices, with limited range. An IoT gateway is usually necessary for connection to the broader Internet. An IoT device uses HTTP/HTTPS to deliver eXtensible Mark-up Language (XML) or JavaScript Object Notation data information to an IoT hub/gateway, which forwards it to web servers. HTTP/HTTPS are the primary client-server model used for the web [9]. Security functions are performed at the server and the IoT gateway, as the security tax for the client is too high in terms of processing power at the IoT device.

Extensible Messaging and Presence Protocol (XMPP) is another example of a protocol that could be used effectively for IoT data delivery [9]. XMPP started as an instant messaging and presence information protocol but grew into VoIP, telepresence, and delivery of XML data.

Other options exist, like Constrained Application Protocol (CoAP) and Message Queuing Telemetry Transport (MQTT), but have limited scale or extensibility into wide area deployments. Figure 15.5 shows the differences in the network stack for an Internet based on people versus one based on things. While at the current time, people outnumber things on the Internet, and there is not a driving need for a new network stack, based on the previous transitions discussed previously, this is a technology transition likely to manifest itself in the next few years [9].

15.3 BRINGING IT ALL TOGETHER

15.3.1 Seamless Integration of Various Technologies to Create Autonomous Network

Just as the personal computer, the web browser, IP networking, web content, modems, and the search engines all came together to provide the necessary and sufficient ingredients for the Internet to happen, a similar technology perfect storm is happening in the networking domain. This new technology storm is giving rise to a new software-defined, AI-based network.

Software-defined networking is taking network programmability, flexibility, and speed of deployment to new heights (see Chapter 3). Network function virtualization is allowing common off-the-self hardware to provide network elements that were previously only available in integrated, speciality boxes; NFV allows the hardware to be separated from the software application. OpenStack, Kubernetes, ONAP, and other technologies allow communication service providers to create a true network cloud [10], capable of the throughput, latency, jitter, and quality-of-service requirements needed to deliver carrier-grade network performance from these virtual functions. Open source efforts like ONAP within the Linux Foundation are providing a community, a code development environment, for a system-level network operating platform.

Many people have demonstrated closed-loop DevOps capability in SDN; for example in ONAP, there is a project, known as Closed Loop Automation Management Platform, which can take the closed-loop DevOps capability to the next level, and this is where AI/ML comes into play; it can create a system allowing the use of that closed loop to inform ML models offline and add instances of the models in-line, making them part of the decisions within the closed loop, while still learning offline. Now, this provides a closed-loop learning system that can alter its decision based on the ML model. Instead of always making the same decision within the closed loop, it can alter its decision based on present information about the model parameters, like time of day, proximity to a maintenance window, or time since last software update.

This type of ML-based DevOps is close to being in production now; it will scale soon. This capability will be transformational for how networks are run. It will drive new levels of reliability at better cost-effectiveness. It will allow service providers to embed their best lessons learned into these models and have a systemic way of deploying those learnings to the field. This is a unique time in networking, seeing all of these technologies coming together, transforming the industry and the way networks will be built going forward. It also sets the entry bar higher, as the service providers with the best technical skills will distinguish themselves and distance themselves from others that do not possess such skills.

15.3.2 Modularity, Abstraction, Software-Defined Network, Microservices, Continuous Integration/Continuous Delivery Allow Rapid Innovation

Artificial intelligence/machine learning technologies in themselves will not allow the rapid innovation that is required for this next transition in networking. Just as the last section briefly described the other required technologies in the perfect storm for AI/ML to disrupt the networking industry, this section will go one level deeper, detailing the proper framework that needs to be in place for AI/ML to be effective.

The first technology that is a part of this new framework is making the interfaces to the network functions/elements open. Arguably, this is the most important attribute required for this transition. Without the interfaces being open, data cannot be collected, no data—no insights, nothing to drive the parameters in the ML model. Without open interfaces, it all breaks down. The move by the web scale companies to make their own switches and routers really comes down to needing open interfaces to drive the automation required to keep up with their scale. The same principle holds here—principle of openness.

With openness being the first necessary step, basing the SDN on models is the next step. Each unique service and network element cannot be a special coding effort. Every network function and each service must be abstracted as a model so that reuse can be applied for the next service or application. This "Lego Block" building approach ensures rapid delivery of services and applications, however a common framework for this abstraction needs to be in place. Models like Yet Another Next Generation (YANG) for network services, Topology and Orchestration Specification for Cloud Applications (TOSCA) for service abstraction, and HEAT for OpenStack cloud templates provide those modeling abstractions (see Chapter 3).

None of these technologies is deployed in a greenfield, meaning that new SDN applications and services must be connected to existing operational support systems (OSSs) and business support systems (BSSs). If the OSSs/BSSs are not taken care of, the existing OSSs/BSSs can become the limiting factor in realizing the benefits of SDN and the network cloud. Microservices are a technology to use that liberates the existing OSSs/BSSs, allowing them to be more modular and more agile in adapting to SDN. Microservices allow an application to be built in a modular fashion from existing smaller (think kernel-like) software modules. Each module supports a specific functionality and uses a well-defined API to communicate with other modular services. A microservice architecture is a variant of the service-oriented architecture, creating a new application that is made up of a collection of loosely coupled services. The benefits of decomposing bigger applications into smaller, kernel-like modules are as follows:

1. It improves modularity.

2. It makes the application easier to understand, develop, and test.

3. It improves later reuse.

4. It allows different teams on the same project to work more independently.

5. It enables continuous delivery and deployment.

Any software delivery system that is looking to optimize speed of innovations must be based on continuous integration and continuous delivery (CI/CD). Continuous integration is a software development technique where small updates to a code tree are added often, making detection and remediation of errors easier to correct. The purpose of a CI environment is to get fast understanding of working code and simplify the debugging process, especially between different development teams. Continuous integration software tools automate the software documentation process and continually test code in a similar fashion. "Continuous" can mean daily for some teams, or hourly, depending on the code and the teams involved. Continuous integration also allows project managers to have a better idea of code completion progress, since commits and testing occurs so rapidly.

Continuous delivery is an extension of CI. Whereas CI deals with the create/build/test part of the software development cycle, CD focuses on validating commits as good working code candidates for a particular release. An important goal of CD is to make the time between different deployments as short as possible. Short feedback loops allow tests to find bugs faster and makes pinpointing those issues simpler for the developer. If CD is ongoing and testing occurs early and often—a concept referred to as "shift left"—developers can work on fixes before they have moved on to another aspect of the development project. This can help increase productivity and speed delivery, as the code and changes are fresh in developers' minds, and they have not fully moved on to other sections of the code.

15.3.3 How Artificial Intelligence Makes Network Transition Different

With the technology framework described in the previous section in place, the question becomes how can AI/ML facilitate the network transition for SDN and cost-effectively deliver that technology in a DevOps manner, leading the way for the reliable, cost-effective transition to the IoT.

As the IoT becomes more and more real with early deployments, the question becomes "how to make it scale?" Internet of Things devices produce a lot of data, varied data, from a variety of devices: cameras, sensors, cars, medical devices, industrial devices, etc. This data can be used to better serve people (e.g., better roads with less traffic, safer homes), to better serve one person (e.g., optimal, automated insulin dispensing), or to better serve businesses (e.g., predictive maintenance on machines). The data provided from these IoT devices provide insight into operational performance and outages; each of these provides opportunities for learning and making better future decisions [11].

The engineering challenge to solve is how to analyze and react to all of this data with a goal of improving performance, providing better service, being more informed about situations, and doing this in a way that can scale cost-effectively. There are not enough people to throw at these problems, even if that was cost-effective, which it is not. Instead, systems that can learn from the data itself, while collecting, analyzing, and reacting to it in real time are required; these are AI/ML systems.

As data and devices grow in scale, without AI/ML systems, there is a risk that the potential to make roads safer, managing health better, and improve business efficiency is not achieved due to poor analysis and bad decisions. This is something that needs to be done correctly; the stakes are too high [12].

Machine learning can look at literally trillions of data points from billions of devices and only react to the ones that require attention. Determining what is "meaningful" will depend on the device, the environment, the situation, the time of day, etc. This is where proper ML models matter, and where the engineering attention needs to be focused. Whether the application is retail, health care, manufacturing, or network automation, the ability to analyze real-time data from billions of sources and only react to the "important" ones is what is required; models help determine what's within range and what's outside of normal operating levels. Similarities, correlations, and abnormalities must be identified and reacted to based on real-time streaming data. The realization here is that IoT's promise lies in its ability to gain the insights within the large, flowing stream of data it exhausts.

Artificial intelligence/machine learning has an ability to mitigate a trend in current networks—growth of complexity. This increasing level of network complexity gives rise to an increase in operating expenses. As the number of wireless technologies grows (4G, 5G, mmWave, LAA, Wi-Fi, etc.) and the number of frequency bands in use grows, the complexity to operate and maintain these networks and meet target performance levels gets increasingly difficult. Operating expenses need to drop as revenue growth slows. AI/ML has the potential to help operators provide service at the expected levels, of reliability, but at much lower cost points.

Within AT&T and AT&T Labs, researchers are using AI/ML to tackle even more complex tasks, such as optimizing the rollout of their 5G network. Traditional cell towers are usually placed near urban centers and form an imperfect grid, leading to gaps in coverage. They're also expensive to put up and maintain and incur challenges with real estate and property ownership. Small cells are less expensive and more compact and can be installed on inner city buildings on a much finer grid. Their role is to repeat the signal from the main cell towers to bring it closer to end-users. By analyzing mobile subscriber data, well-calibrated AI/ML systems assist in finding more ideal spots to build small cells and ensure maximum 5G signal strength for customers. Infrastructure is an enormous investment, even with small cells, so accurately modeling trends and usage growth is key to success. Demographic trends can cause previously underutilized areas to suddenly become hot traffic generators. While statistical models are useful for identifying trends in customer movement and throughout, AI and ML techniques create future projections from current data.

As Assistant Vice-President (AVP) of Big Data Research, Chris Volinsky in AT&T Labs puts it, "video is more than half of our mobile traffic. Video traffic grew over 75% and smartphones drove almost 75% of our data traffic in 2016 alone. We expect video traffic growth to outpace overall data growth in 2020. We need to visualize billions of data points in a spatiotemporal fashion." No tool existed to perform this task, so people on Volinsky's team built and open-sourced visualization tools, such as Nanocubes, a data visualization tool that can map out millions of connections of individual mobile phones and connected devices to cell phone towers. The generality of this tool is exemplified by its use outside the company to characterize sports fans in real time and to analyze crime rates and history [3].

Volinsky, who led the winning team for the Netflix Recommendation prize back in 2009, further states "algorithms and tools are not the bottleneck in terms of solving problems. The challenge is in the data and the data pipeline. Modern data-hungry AI approaches require a centralized data source, but gathering one across myriad networks with idiosyncratic standards is no trivial task. There is no world expert in data munging [collecting, sorting, verifying quality, etc.]. To succeed, you have to figure out organizationally how to access data in different silos, technically how to integrate with it, and ensure the formats are in line. This is not the stuff people learn in grad school."

15.4 PILLARS OF NETWORK TRANSFORMATION—TECHNOLOGY, PROCESS, AND PEOPLE

The advances in the computing and networking technologies have enabled a worldwide connected society. The global population is benefiting from the connectivity provided by the wireless networks.

In many of underdeveloped and poor nations across the world, connectivity has provided economic opportunities to hundreds of millions of people that wasn't even imaginable just a few years back. There are various mobile banking solutions enabling new businesses and microloans where the traditional banking is not available. The Internet provides access to educational material from academic institutions and private companies enabling world-class educational opportunities for populations in remote parts of the world.

In the advanced economic, the Internet and the social media combined with the digitization of the business processes are disrupting many industries with new business models, for example, Uber transportation, Airbnb hospitality, and many others. The processes in various aspects of the organizations and businesses will need to evolve to benefit from the technological advances and not be left behind by competitors that do adopt and adapt to new technologies.

15.5 HOW WILL PROCESSES EVOLVE IN THE TELECOM INDUSTRY?

The telecommunication industry has been a pillar of the economy growth over a century. The industry developed a robust set of processes to provide highly reliable services. The telecom industry has done an excellent job building processes to manage complexities. Generally, the telecom products were designed to meet the goal of a max service outage time of less than five minutes in a year, or five nines, (99.999%) reliability requirement. This approach delivered a very reliable network over the years; however, it has also created a very risk averse culture in the telecom industry.

The industry was dominated by a few major players; the future of the industry was controlled or at least managed by these few dominating players to a large extent. A typical product development cycle started with a well-defined set of requirements that predicted the state of technology and customer requirements three to five years out with a sense of high confidence level. The requirements definition process was months long. Once the requirements were locked, there was a product development cycle of many months that was followed by months of functional and regression testing. From a concept to the product introduction took 20–36 months or even more in some cases. There was limited flexibility to change the requirements or processes during the cycle. The risk-averse culture was built around "don't fail."

The IT world took the advantage of the converging on a few standard sets of the hardware and the operating systems. It enables concepts of CI/CD. The IT industry developed a set of processes to increase productivity leveraging these. There are a number of repetitive tasks and processes eliminated or automated to increase efficiency and pace of the product life-cycle management, for example, in large data centers, there is only one system administration for thousands of servers as compared to one system administrator for tens of servers in a traditional IT environment; a web company's ability to introduce new features or services multiple times a day.

In today's fast moving and dynamic world, a fundamental change to a culture of "fast fail" is needed to implement and adapt networking solutions in near real time. The SDN/NFV enables disaggregation of the integrated products, which allows faster changes to the network functions and services. It also provides the service providers the ability to introduce new products and services that can be managed by the end customer. For example, AT&T introduced the Network on Demand service where the end-users can configure the bandwidth they want by themselves in the real time. This service leverages the SDN/NFV and automation of the business processes.

The network transformation will have an impact on the processes from the product and service planning and design to network design, build, and operation. The product design team will have access to a broad customer data. This data augmented with the other sets of data will allow the product managers to personalize the services and pricing for the individuals. The industry will move from being a few sizes fit all plans to personalized telecom services, which will have a basic connectivity service integrated with many other value-added services, such as security, home monitoring, smart home, industrial IoT, and many more personalized services for an individual customer.

To deliver personalized services that can be optimized and configured by the end-users in near real time requires an agile BSS with northbound APIs to allow seamless integration with the end customer's system. The SDN/NFV-enabled networks will programmatically configure the network to deliver these services. For the end customers, the network will be seamlessly there.

In the past, a network service order was a split into multiple work orders distributed among many work groups. There were a number of manual steps and data entries to complete a service order. It would take days or weeks to complete an order. The processes that cause friction to reduce efficiency and speed will be automated in the SDN/NFV networks. The order completion duration will be reduced from days to minutes or better. The service delivery will become a frictionless highly automated process.

The networks have seen automation from the mechanical switching to the electro-mechanical switching to the digital switching, self-healing optical networks, and self-optimized networks. However, most of these automation solutions were achieved using predefined static rules. With the advent of SDN/NFV and associated automated monitoring and data analytics capability, along with ML and AI techniques, the network operators will have ability to autonomously dig deep into network nodes to monitor and optimize the network performance and service assurance.

15.6 WHAT WILL BE THE IMPACT ON PEOPLE IN THE INDUSTRY?

The impact of the technological evolution on the society has always been bittersweet. The technological advances create exciting new opportunities and open new frontiers for mankind. The combustible engine and automobiles enabled people to travel much farther comfortably at a much faster speed than horse carriages. Though it created a number of new economic opportunities and enabled new industries, it was disruptive to the transport businesses built around the horse carriage industry—the horse carriage drivers, producers, and folks in all other ancillary economic activities in the industry.

The technical evolution in the field of AI is no difference. It will create new economic opportunities in many areas, and it will eliminate jobs in certain areas just like any other technical evolution. The pace of change may be much faster and the magnitude of the change may be much bigger, but this evolution is no different fundamentally.

The advances in telecom networks have been nothing short of a miracle over the last few decades. There were phone booths in almost every corner in every city. A cellular phone

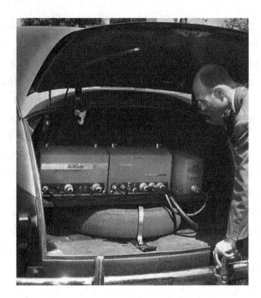

FIGURE 15.6   1946 Bell System introduced the first commercial mobile telephone service, called the Mobile Telephone System (MTS). (From https://smartphones.gadgethacks.com/news/from-backpack-transceiver-smartphone-visual-history-mobile-phone-0127134/ [13].)

was a luxury that only senior corporate executives and wealthy people could afford. The first mobile handheld phones were the size of a brick. Prior to that the cell phone had to be installed in a trunk of a car (Figure 15.6). The first-generation cell phone was based on the analog technology.

Within a few years, the cell phone became small and light enough that one could carry in a pocket. The second generation (2G) cell phone based on Global System for Mobile and Code Division Multiple Access technologies were introduced. These new standards made the first-generation mobile network skills less valuable. This was followed by third generation (3G) and fourth generation (4G) technologies with each new generation of technology introduction cycle duration being shorter. There were significant changes in the air interface technologies, and evolution from circuit switching to packet switching for cellular data. The stakeholders had to keep up with the advancements in technology to be relevant in the industry. The continuous learning has always been required in technology and has become even more important in the last few years.

As new advances are introduced in the telecom industry, the skills required will no doubt change. People will need to acquire new skills. It is a challenge to get out of one's comfort zone. However, it will not be prudent to wait for the change to happen before taking actions. The continuous learning to diversify the skillset is a must. One will need to have a broader understanding of the business and technology rather than a narrow focus in one area. Many organizations have started programs to reskill their workforce. Irrespective of one's role and position in an organization one should make efforts to continuously acquire new skills.

The telecom industry has had well-defined standardization processes that were led by a few standardization organizations such as 3GPP (Third Generation Partnership Project).

Though it served the industry well in the past, the open source collaboration has been able to drive innovation faster in the industry. The ability to participate to leverage open source solutions and to contribute to open source communities will become a valuable skill for the people in technology and telecom industries. Open solutions will continue to grow at a rapid pace. To efficiently leverage and build up on the open solutions will be a competitive advantage.

As AI becomes more integrated across the industry, the skills around ML, data analysis, and business insights will become increasingly valuable. There will be a lot of tools, algorithms, and data available; the ability to effectively and efficiently build solutions to create economic value will determine the winners.

To get on this exciting journey of lifelong learning:

1. Embrace the change

2. Understand implementation of the technology

3. Evaluate your current skills

4. Identify what you want to do

5. Take actions to upskill

15.6.1 Key Regulatory and Privacy Challenges

A number of technologies, computing, connectivity, sensor, and data analytics have simultaneously seen significant improvement in performance and cost reduction over the last few years. These technological improvements have enabled new business models in various industries. The data generated by social networks and sensors in various industries have created valuable troves of information. A large set of quality data is fundamental to the success of AI. Many of the AI algorithms have been around for a long time. The practical use of AI algorithms was limited due to access to the data because of high cost of producing, storing, and processing data. Both technology and regulations had been impediments to availability of the data in the past.

Social networks, sensor-generated data, and digitization of various personal records and literature have created an unprecedented amount of data. This combined with computing power and high density low-cost data storage solutions with high-speed connectivity can provide access to the data across the organizations and countries. The pieces of technology needed to provide universal access to data exist today. The bigger challenges are compliance with security, regulatory, and legal requirements. For example, medical records are being digitized in the U.S. To have broad access to medical records is valuable in the discovery of new drugs and optimizing cures for many diseases. However, there are strict privacy regulations in place to restrict the access to individual medical records. As more and more data becomes available, hard decisions have to be made to balance benefits and risks for data sharing to deliver maximum benefit to the society.

Many regulations and laws are static and slow to adapt to rapid technological advances. The AI will create a new set of issues that will have to be addressed, for example, if an autonomous car causes an accident due to an algorithmic failure, then who will have that responsibility?—owner, auto manufacturer, software developer. Another example, if an automated bot autonomously starts recording conversations, which may be illegal under a country's law, how does society address it?

In addition, there will be continuous evolution of the autonomous network and industry that will require the regulations and laws to be dynamic. The boundaries between the industries will become increasingly vague. Is Apple a technology or a mobile phone or a media or a financial company? Is Amazon a retailer, a media, or a technology company? The regulations that govern various services and industries have to evolve to this new world with not-so-clear delineation of the industries.

15.7 AUTONOMOUS NETWORK USE-CASES

15.7.1 Autonomous Network Operations

This section illustrates how automation is transferring the network operations. It touches the complete life-cycle management of the network services design, planning, deployment, and assurance. The Linux Foundation's ONAP project has developed a network operating system for network automation (Figure 15.7).

A network service product manager uses service design and creation (SD&C) model to design a new network product using service modules catalogued in the SD&C. A product manager can put together various network services, which are contained in the catalog, to create a product. He/she can validate the product in a sandbox. Once the product is validated, it can be automatically deployed in the production network through the Master Service Orchestrator (MSO). The MSO autonomously orchestrates the infrastructure, networking, and various network functions to deploy the service.

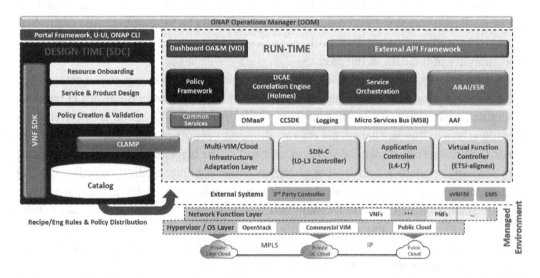

FIGURE 15.7 ONAP architecture. (From https://www.onap.org/wp-content/uploads/sites/20/2017/12/ONAP_CaseSolution_Architecture_120817_FNL.pdf [14].)

The Data Collection Analytics and Event (DCAE) module collects the data from network nodes. The DCAE runs the analytics on the data collected and identifies if there is any anomaly in the network performance. An anomaly is determined using policies from a policy manager.

If DCAE identifies an anomaly, the system can autonomously launch virtual probes to collect additional data from the nodes and interfaces to identify the root cause of the problem. This additional data is analyzed to automatically take actions to resolve the issue. For example, if the system identifies that the node (the VNF) is running at a higher capacity than its permitted high-capacity watermark, the system can automatically provision additional VNF instantiations to bring the usage within the limits. In case the system isn't able to resolve the issue, it is integrated with the fault management system to generate an alarm and notify technical personnel.

Data from the DCAE is stored in a data lake for training ML algorithms to predict the future network issues and recommended performance optimizations. There will be open source ML solutions available (e.g., the Linux Foundation project Acumos allows users to access, modify, and add various ML algorithms). The power of community combined with the access to continuous flow of quality data will be a powerful enabler for the network operations. One example of such solution is that DCAE data from the network node is used to predict the probability of failure of virtual machines running a VNF. It is not only able to predict the failure but also identify the cause of failure. This enables continuous improvement to avoid future failure.

On the business side, product managers will be able to correlate the customer experience with the network performance metric. This can be combined with other data sets, such as data from the sensors for industrial customers or social media for consumers, to provide better personalized user experience. This will also enable product managers to create new value-added features to offer new revenue-generating services.

15.7.2 Natural Language Processing to Reduce Service-Level Agreement Penalties

Many of a telecom operator's enterprise services come with the contractual agreement to meet a certain level of quality of service. There are financial liabilities associated with these agreements. If the service-level agreement (SLA) is not met, a service provider has to pay a penalty, which can have material impact on the bottom line.

Typically, a service outage duration time starts from the time a customer reports the problem, and it ends when the issue is resolved. There may be multiple interactions between the customer and the service provider to resolve the issue. Sometimes a customer's unresponsiveness can cause unnecessary delay in resolution of the problem. This can incur a larger penalty paid out by the service provider not for their fault.

A natural language processing (NLP)-based solution can help an operator expedite the resolution of a trouble ticket and identify the customer liability portion of penalty. Once a customer ticket is entered in the system, it is automatically classified and routed to the appropriate resolution team. The resolution team and the customer responses, as well as the logs from various systems, are processed automatically using NLP to generate a fact-based report from the start of an issue to the complete resolution. A detailed timeline supported by the immutable evidence generated autonomously helped one of our clients to save more than $15 million in a single year.

An even more important aspect of NLP of manual tickets is that it generates valuable data to provide a complete picture of an issue from the end customer to the network nodes. This generates data that can be used to train ML algorithms to predict future issues and take care of corrective actions in advance. After all, the best kind of insurance policy is the one that is not used.

15.7.3 Autonomous Car

According to the Society of Automotive Engineering (SAE), there are six levels to reach fully autonomous cars [15].

- **Level 0—No Automation**: The full-time performance by the human driver of all aspects of the dynamic driving task, even when enhanced by warning or intervention systems

- **Level 1—Driver Assistance**: The driving mode-specific execution by a driver assistance system of either steering or acceleration/deceleration using information about the driving environment and with the expectation that the human driver performs all remaining aspects of the dynamic driving task

- **Level 2—Partial Automation**: The driving mode-specific execution by one or more driver-assistance systems of both steering and acceleration/deceleration using information about the driving environment and with the expectation that the human driver performs all remaining aspects of the dynamic driving task

- **Level 3—Conditional Automation**: The driving mode-specific performance by an Automated Driving System of all aspects of the dynamic driving task with the expectation that the human driver will respond appropriately to a request to intervene

- **Level 4—High Automation**: The driving mode-specific performance by an Automated Driving System of all aspects of the dynamic driving task, even if a human driver does not respond appropriately to a request to intervene

- **Level 5—Full Automation**: The full-time performance by an Automated Driving System of all aspects of the dynamic driving task under all roadway and environmental conditions that can be managed by a human driver

For the cars to reach Level 4 (actually the fifth level, since it starts at Level 0), as defined previously, several transitions must occur. According to Michael Ronen, head of Goldman Sachs Investment Banking Auto 2.0 Team, these include the following [16]:

1. Engine technology switches → The internal combustion engine is displaced in favor of electric vehicles (simpler, lighter, fewer parts).

2. Car becomes a connected supercomputer → To keep up with all of the sensors, radar, analytics, ML/AI, internal (IP/Ethernet), and external (V2X) vehicle communications and mobile and sustained Internet connectivity, vehicles must become miniature roaming data centers.

3. Business model changes → Cars move from something you own, care for, and dispose of (an asset) to something that you call and use on demand (a service). Driverless cars enable this to be cost-effective.

4. Ecosystem adjusts → The effect on supporting industries (insurance, finance, housing, parking, Internet Service Providers (ISPs), real estate, content providers, etc.) is significant.

While the fully autonomous car (Level 5) is many years away, the timing of the semi-autonomous car is very near term, perhaps only a few years away. This new IoT (cars, in this case) demonstrates how connecting everyday devices to a network transforms what we can do with them. "Connected cars, communicating with each other and with the larger world, will not only reduce accidents and ease traffic. They will have powerful effects beyond the auto industry. Insurers, for example, will have new ways to monitor driver behavior, reward good drivers and distribute costs to bad ones. Ride-sharing companies can better connect idle cars with the customers that need them [16]."

In May of 2017, New York State opened up licensing and opportunities for car companies that wanted to test autonomous vehicles in their state. Audi applied for and received a license for testing their model A7, SAE Level 3 autonomous car, as shown in Figure 15.8. According to Audi, "to reach Level 4 autonomy by 2020, Audi will be relying on NVIDIA to assist with artificial intelligence and the processing power required to make autonomous driving safe while piloting a 4,000-pound vehicle at 70 mph [17]."

Dr. Raj Rajkumar, a George Westinghouse professor in the Department of Electrical and Computer Engineering at Carnegie Mellon University, has created a SAE Level 4 prototype

FIGURE 15.8   Audi A7 SAE Level 3 autonomous car. (From https://techcrunch.com/2017/06/06/audi-is-the-first-to-test-autonomous-vehicles-in-new-york/ [17].)

vehicle, an autonomous Cadillac SRX [18]. This SRX prototype demonstrates advances in technology and the practicality of autonomous driving. The vehicle has been used to demonstrate the technology to policymakers on Capitol Hill in Washington DC, driving itself around Capitol Hill and along the I-395 highway to/from Washington DC [19]. The car is an advanced prototype filled with sensors, radar, compute processing, and AI software, all concealed from view, trying to represent what a future SAE Level 4 autonomous car might look and perform like.

Artificial intelligence/machine learning plays a critical role in the autonomous car evolution and in making it a practicality for the use on the roads. There will be a number of AI applications in an autonomous car: voice and face recognition for the opening and starting a vehicle, route optimization, perception and object classification, and converting algorithm outputs to drive control signals to actuators for maneuvering a vehicle. There will be compute hierarchy with local, edge, and cloud computing for performance and cost optimization. The response latency, data bandwidth, and reliability of the networks will drive the optimum placement for various functions to enable autonomous vehicles.

Like any transition, this will take time. Early autonomous cars, at various levels, will be on the road at the same time; all levels from Level 0 to Level 5 are likely to be represented at any given time. This means that the AI/ML software will have to take into account human drivers with whom there is little or no interaction/communication; semi-autonomous cars with which there is no interaction/communication; and semi-autonomous cars with which there is sharing of information. The need to collect data at regular intervals, update maps, update software, change ML models, etc. make automation of the operational model critical, especially when autonomous cars scale to tens of millions of cars. This "compatibility" matrix of autonomous cars makes the transition happen more slowly, as this will be a brownfield, meaning that all cars on the road will not switch overnight. It also makes AI/ML even more important, as the behavior of the other cars on the road are more difficult to predict, meaning more parameters are required in the ML models, meaning more calculations are required to make intelligent decisions, meaning that the AI algorithms need to be more complex.

Venture funding to make autonomous cars a reality has been dramatic. One example is Intel's purchase of Mobileye for $15 billion. Mobileye produces sensors, devices, and AI software for autonomous cars. Intel created a fleet of 100 self-driving cars (SAE Level 4) and announced them at CES 2018 [20]. According to Intel, the vehicles will combine Mobileye's "computer vision, sensing, fusion, mapping, and driving policy" with Intel's "open compute platforms and expertise in data centers. The autonomous car **platform** will include 5G communication technologies from Intel to deliver a complete 'car-to-cloud' system." The fleet will consist of a variety of car brands and vehicle types to demonstrate its versatility and adaptability. This connection to the mobile network is differential compared to earlier systems but provides the much-needed high-bandwidth connection to data systems and up-to-date information in the cloud, about the car itself, software updates, road conditions, weather, work areas, etc. [21].

According to Intel, the biggest factor in consumer adoption of autonomous cars is **Trust**. Trust in the technology. Intel's Automotive Solutions are designed to deliver field systems more quickly; they include in-vehicle computing, software development tools, 5G-ready connectivity, a robust data center platform, and the latest advances in AI [22].

A wireless network will be an integral part of the autonomous car solutions. There are four types of V2X communications defined in 3GPP [23]: vehicle to vehicle (V2V), vehicle to infrastructure (V2I), vehicle to network (V2N), and vehicle to pedestrian (V2P). V2V and V2P transmissions are generally broadcast between vehicles and people to provide information about a vehicle speed, direction, and location.

V2I and V2N support bidirectional information exchange between a vehicle and a wireless network. There are widespread deployments of cellular base-stations that can be extended as the radio side units (RSU). An RSU can host autonomous vehicle applications and perform local processing to minimize network delay. This will be augmented with the backend cloud-based applications. This hybrid configuration with near real-time processing at the edge and the extensive back-end processing for continuous learning will meet stringent latency performance requirements for the autonomous vehicle applications and leverage massive data continuously generated by vehicles to optimize the autonomous vehicle operations.

One of the key advantage of V2I communications is that collective learning of vehicles can be leveraged. Learnings from any vehicle can be distributed autonomously and continuously to all the other vehicles that may benefit from the updates. The USDOT study [24] estimates that the technology can address close 80% of all vehicle target crashes.

Many analysts say that the car is the next smart platform, and if that is true, then just like for the smartphone, connectivity, specifically 5G mobile connectivity, will be critical to the success and usefulness of the smart autonomous car. This 5G connectivity will also play a critical role in informing the AI algorithms that provide the intelligence of these vehicles. 5G networks will provide very high data link with low latency, which are two stringent, but critical, requirements for autonomous vehicles. In addition, 5G deployments are going to be even denser than the 3G/4G base-station deployments. These 5G base-stations will provide mobile edge computing capabilities to processing with minimal network delay for the time-sensitive applications.

15.8 WHAT'S NEXT

Artificial intelligence and ML are already being used in many consumer and industrial applications. As we continue to make progress in the core underlying technologies of computing, storage, networks, and sensors, the ML will be applied to more and more use-cases in various industries. The next-generation networks will be enablers and beneficiaries of these.

Though the rate of change in networking may have changed over last 100 years, the change has been a constant fact in this industry. The industry is on the cusp of another exciting evolution with the pieces of the autonomous network starting to come together in SDN/NFV environment. The opportunities to innovate is unbounded for those willing to step up to learn and think innovatively.

REFERENCES

1. http://www.starsatnight.org/blog/educational-blog/one-tiny-drop/
2. http://www.snipview.com/q/switchboard_operator
3. https://venturebeat.com/2017/04/09/how-companies-and-consumers-benefit-from-ai-powered-networks/
4. https://io9.gizmodo.com/photos-from-the-days-when-thousands-of-cables-crowded-t-1629961917
5. Tennenhouse, David. (1998). Modeling the Communication Network's Transition to a Data-Centric Model.
6. Coffman, Kerry & M. Odlyzko, Andrew. (1998). The Size and Growth Rate of the Internet.
7. a. https://www.ericsson.com/en/press-releases/2010/3/mobile-data-traffic-surpasses-voice
   b. https://www.statista.com/statistics/471264/iot-number-of-connected-devices-worldwide/
8. https://www.slideshare.net/zdshelby/standards-drive-the-internet-of-things (From Zach Shelby's presentation, Slide 3, "Standards Drive the Internet of Things.")
9. https://blogs.cisco.com/digital/beyond-mqtt-a-cisco-view-on-iot-protocols
10. https://www.openstack.org/;https://www.cncf.io/;https://www.onap.org/
11. https://www.wired.com/insights/2014/11/iot-wont-work-without-artificial-intelligence/
12. https://venturebeat.com/2017/04/09/how-companies-and-consumers-benefit-from-ai-powered-networks/
13. https://smartphones.gadgethacks.com/news/from-backpack-transceiver-smartphone-visual-history-mobile-phone-0127134/
14. https://www.onap.org/wp-content/uploads/sites/20/2017/12/ONAP_CaseSolution_Architecture_120817_FNL.pdf
15. https://www.sae.org/news/3544/
16. http://www.goldmansachs.com/our-thinking/technology-driving-innovation/cars-2025/index.html
17. https://techcrunch.com/2017/06/06/audi-is-the-first-to-test-autonomous-vehicles-in-newyork/
18. https://users.ece.cmu.edu/~raj/
19. https://users.ece.cmu.edu/~raj/Capitol-Hill-DC/index.html
20. http://www.thedrive.com/sheetmetal/17514/intel-reveals-first-of-100-self-driving-test-cars-and-more-at-ces-2018
21. http://fortune.com/2017/08/10/intel-mobileye-autonmous-car-deal-100-vehcile-fleet/
22. https://www.intel.com/content/www/us/en/automotive/autonomous-vehicles.html
23. https://www.regulations.gov/contentStreamer?documentId=NHTSA-2014-0022-0001&attachmentNumber=1&disposition=attachment&contentType=pdf
24. http://www.5gamericas.org/files/2914/7769/1296/5GA_V2X_Report_FINAL_for_upload.pdf

Index

Note: Page numbers in italic and bold refer to figures and tables, respectively.

Printed in the United States
by Baker & Taylor Publisher Services